CRASH OF THE HEAVENS

THE REMARKABLE STORY OF HANNAH SENESH AND THE ONLY MILITARY MISSION TO RESCUE EUROPE'S JEWS DURING WORLD WAR II

DOUGLAS CENTURY

AVID READER PRESS

NEW YORK AMSTERDAM/ANTWERP LONDON
TORONTO SYDNEY/MELBOURNE NEW DELHI

Avid Reader Press
An Imprint of Simon & Schuster, LLC
1230 Avenue of the Americas
New York, NY 10020

First Avid Reader Press hardcover edition November 2025

Interior design by Ruth Lee-Mui
Maps by Paul J. Pugliese

Manufactured in the United States of America

1 3 5 7 9 10 8 6 4 2

Library of Congress Control Number: 2025945129

ISBN 978-1-6680-3527-6
ISBN 978-1-6680-3529-0 (ebook)

Mediterranean and European Theater of World War II, 1943–45
Warsaw
POLAND
hwitz-Birkenau
LOVAKIA
ská
rica
NGARY
apest
Arad
ROMANIA
Ploești
Bucharest
Constanța
SOVIET UNION
Black Sea
SLAVIA
Serbia
ljak
BULGARIA
Sofia
LBANIA
Istanbul
TURKEY
GREECE
Aegean Sea
Athens
French Mandatory SYRIA
LEBANON
British Mandatory PALESTINE
Tel Aviv
Jerusalem
Mediterranean Sea
Benghazi
Tobruk
El Alamein
EGYPT
Cairo

AVID
READER
PRESS

ALSO BY DOUGLAS CENTURY

Street Kingdom: Five Years Inside the Franklin Avenue Posse

Barney Ross: The Life of a Jewish Fighter

The Last Boss of Brighton: Boris "Biba" Nayfeld and the Rise of the Russian Mob in America

DEDICATED TO

The seven who fell:
זיכרונם לברכה

AND FOR

Marcia and Lena—and all
the brave, brilliant women
shining in every generation

Blessed is the match consumed
in kindling flame
Blessed is the flame that burns
in the secret fastness of the heart
Blessed is the heart with strength to stop
its beating for honor's sake
Blessed is the match consumed
in kindling flame

—Hannah Senesh

We must parachute into Europe—like a mother breaking into a burning house to rescue her children.

—Haviva Reik

If we want to live, we must be ready to die, to go towards the looming dangers. . . . Even in death, there are signs of life.

—Enzo Sereni

CONTENTS

AUTHOR'S NOTE

Crash of the Heavens is a work of nonfiction. All the characters are real; the events depicted true. Any conversations I've placed in quotation marks come from primary-source documents and interviews. References to gestures and physical actions are based on accounts by someone either participating or witnessing the events. Since most primary sources about the Yishuv parachutists' mission are Hebrew memoirs, I've occasionally retranslated from the original when the previously published dialogue seemed a bit stilted or unnatural in contemporary English.

When rendering Hebrew words and names, I've used the English transliteration style set forth by the *Encyclopedia Judaica*. Anglicizing gets particularly complex with the letters khet (ח) and khaf (כ) that can appear as *kh*, *ch*, or *h*. I've generally opted for *ch*—spelling, for example, the Haganah's elite strike force companies as Palmach instead of Palmah.

Hannah Senesh's most famous poem, "A Walk to Caesarea" (or "Eli, Eli"), is transliterated as "Halicha L'Kesariya," but readers may find it published in many other English variations. The ancient Roman capital of the province of Judea is spelled in Hebrew with the letter kof (ק)—a hard *k* sound—and Hannah's original handwritten manuscript is titled:

הליכה לקיסריה

Nonetheless, most English speakers refer to the city as *seez-ah-REE-ah* (sɛzəˈriːə), and in Israel today both pronunciations of Caesarea are accepted as correct.

Whenever an individual chose to spell his or her first name in English differently than the conventional manner—Arye as opposed to Ari; Haim as opposed to Chaim—I've opted for the form preferred by that person.

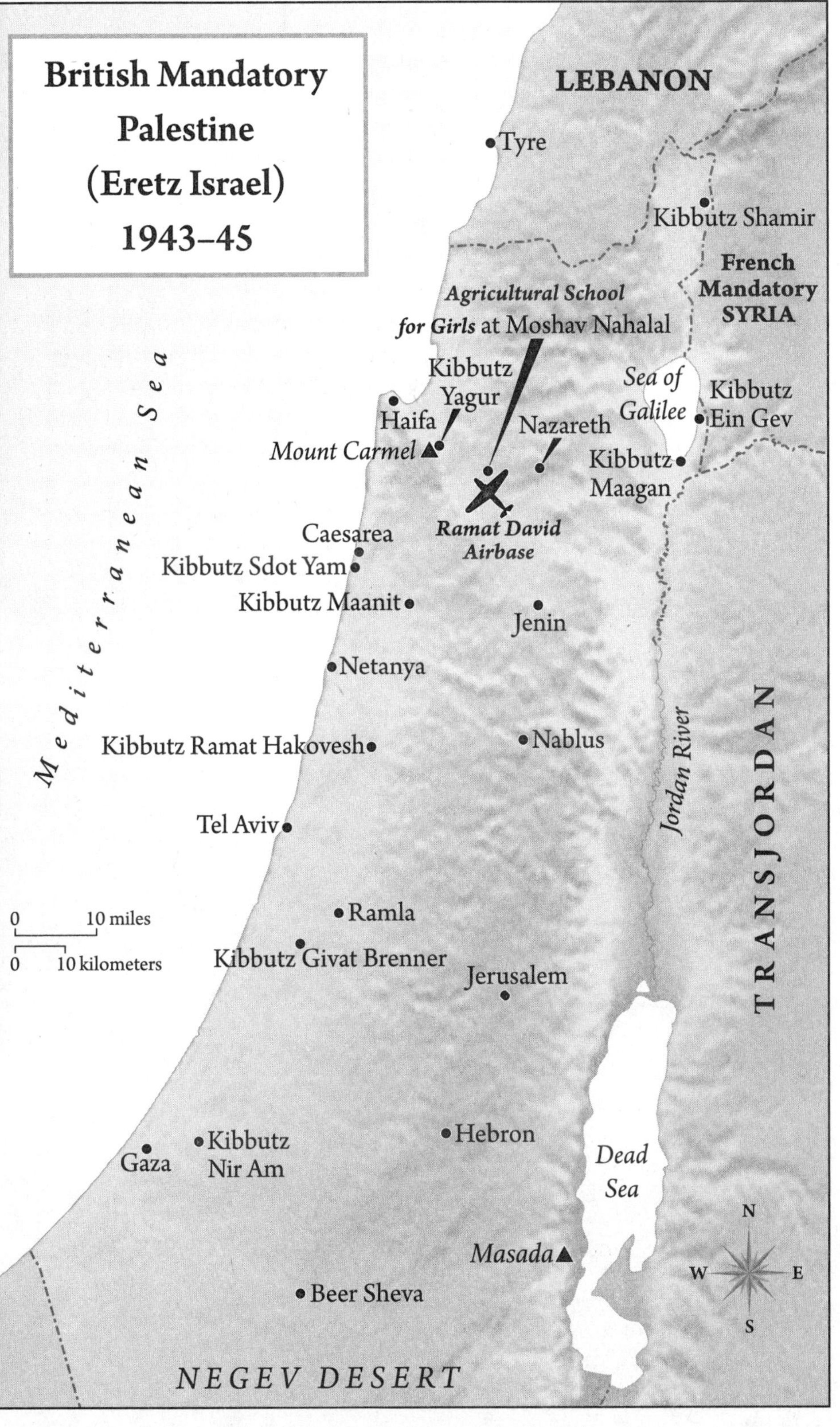

British Mandatory Palestine (Eretz Israel) 1943–45
LEBANON
Tyre
Kibbutz Shamir
French Mandatory SYRIA
Agricultural School for Girls at Moshav Nahalal
Kibbutz Yagur
Haifa
Mount Carmel
Nazareth
Sea of Galilee
Kibbutz Ein Gev
Kibbutz Maagan
Ramat David Airbase
Caesarea
Kibbutz Sdot Yam
Kibbutz Maanit
Jenin
Netanya
Mediterranean Sea
Kibbutz Ramat Hakovesh
Nablus
Jordan River
TRANSJORDAN
Tel Aviv
0 10 miles
0 10 kilometers
Ramla
Kibbutz Givat Brenner
Jerusalem
Hebron
Gaza
Kibbutz Nir Am
Dead Sea
Masada
Beer Sheva
N
W
E
S
NEGEV DESERT

Prologue

Spring 1943
Tel Aviv, Mandatory Palestine

They gathered late in the heart of the White City under the darkening ink blue Mediterranean sky. They strolled down the wide, tree-lined street: alone, sometimes in pairs, careful not to attract the attention of any British authorities or their informants.

The British had no inkling that the home at 23 Rothschild Boulevard, a whitewashed gem of Tel Aviv's Eclectic architectural style, had become the nerve center of an underground paramilitary organization. The Haganah—Hebrew for "defense"—had been established in 1920 from an earlier loose network of armed patrols protecting Jewish settlements, but by the 1930s its ranks had swelled to include nearly all the men and women of the kibbutzim as well as thousands of volunteer fighters from the cities. The British had since outlawed it; any use of armaments, even defensively, was deemed illegal, for they feared that it was only a matter of time until the Jews of Mandatory Palestine rebelled against the Crown and fought for an independent Jewish state.

Arriving at the three-story house belonging to the founder and commander of the Haganah, Eliyahu Golomb, the visitors slipped inconspicuously inside. They represented the leadership of the Yishuv, the Hebrew name for the 600,000-strong Jewish community in Mandatory Palestine. The Mandate allowed the Jews to have an executive body to represent their political interests and promote immigration for a future Jewish state. Although the Yishuv was governed by Great Britain's Colonial Office in London, the Jewish Agency Executive, based in Jerusalem, served as the de facto internal government.*

David Ben-Gurion, the head of the Jewish Agency Executive since 1935, was indisputably the most powerful political leader in the Yishuv. His closest friend, the intellectual pillar of Labor Zionism, Berl Katznelson, worked as the editor of *Davar*, the highest-circulation Hebrew-language daily paper in Mandatory Palestine. Reuven Zaslani led the Yishuv's Intelligence Division. Eliyahu Golomb's brother-in-law Moshe Sharett oversaw the Jewish Agency's foreign policy and led negotiations with senior government figures in London. The lone woman in this inner circle, Goldie Meyerson—born in Kiev, Russian Empire (now Ukraine), raised in Milwaukee, Wisconsin—served as the Yishuv's indefatigable fundraiser.

In the years ahead, all would make history as iconic figures in the fledgling Jewish state. Ben-Gurion would declare Israel's independence in 1948 and serve as its first prime minister. Zaslani would be appointed the first director of the Mossad in 1949. And Meyerson would become the first female head of government in the Middle East in 1969 as Prime Minister Golda Meir.

Bypassing the building's columned portico with its street-front double doors, dipping through the canopy of royal poinciana and ficus trees into a narrow side alley, they entered through a kitchen door, where Eliyahu Golomb's mother-in-law, Fanny, whom they all called Mamochka, often stood at her ironing board, pressing shirts, skirts, and trousers. Ada Golomb, Eliyahu's wife, offered every guest a steaming hot glass of tea.

Since the outbreak of the war in September 1939, the lights had never gone off inside 23 Rothschild Boulevard, nor did the buzz of political and military strategizing ever quiet.

The guests may have arrived with breezy expressions, making small talk in Hebrew, Yiddish, and Russian, but once the group convened in Golomb's office, the mood turned grim. The news that had brought them together was unprecedented in the three-thousand-year history of the Jewish people.

Yishuv is the Hebrew word for "settlement." Historians often make a distinction between the "Old Yishuv," dating back to the Jewish-Roman Wars, including small communities in Jerusalem, Hebron, Tiberias, and Safed, and the "New Yishuv," the influx of Jewish immigrants into Palestine after the advent of modern Zionism.

The Jews of Europe were being annihilated at an unimaginable pace. Throughout the early years of the war, reports of atrocities had shocked the Yishuv, but the arrival of the first seventy-eight civilians from Germany, the Netherlands, Belgium, and Poland in mid-November 1942 had been a turning point. The refugees, mostly women and children released from Nazi ghettos and concentration camps, were taken to the port of Haifa in a series of prisoner swaps for German citizens, members of a fundamentalist Christian sect known as the Templars, who'd been living in colonies in Jaffa, Haifa, and Jerusalem and interned by the British as enemy nationals. When the first group of newly arrived Jewish refugees was debriefed in Haifa, they provided grisly never-before-heard details of the worsening situation in Europe.

They gave the first eyewitness accounts of the *Aktionen* ("actions"), as the Nazis euphemistically referred to the liquidations of the eastern European ghettos. Though the geographical details varied, the pattern was always the same: Jews were required to wear yellow stars on their clothing and were crammed into disease-filled ghettos from which any attempt at escape meant death. Roaming German soldiers, often drunk, shot mothers with babies in their arms for sport. Early-morning roundups of screaming women, children, and the elderly were clubbed or whipped into train boxcars meant for livestock. The Jews were always told that they were being resettled "in the East," where they'd be productive workers for the Reich, when their true destinations were killing centers in eastern Poland named Chełmno, Sobibor, Treblinka, Majdanek, and Auschwitz.

Ben-Gurion had traveled to Haifa to meet with one of the refugees, Halinka Goldblum, a seventeen-year-old from the ghetto of Sosnowiec, Poland. For three hours, she told him stories of "horrors and misery," he later wrote, "which no Dante or Poe could have ever invented." After she finished speaking, Ben-Gurion sat and wept.

Those seventy-eight refugees, from diverse locations and backgrounds, had experienced near-identical brutality. The testimonies they gave left no doubt: A crime beyond comprehension—a crime without a name—was being perpetrated.

Virtually every member of the Yishuv had family trapped in Europe. Kibbutzniks and capitalists, socialists and Communists, atheists and the ultraorthodox—no segment of society was untouched. There'd already been official days of mourning and fasting, massive rallies in the streets of New York and London, Tel Aviv and Jerusalem.

International outrage reached its peak on December 17, 1942, when British Foreign Secretary Anthony Eden read a Joint Declaration by Members of the United Nations Against Extermination of the Jews to the House of Commons. Speaking on behalf of Great Britain, the United States, the Soviet Union, and eleven other nations, he described the "appalling horror and brutality" with which the Nazis were implementing "Hitler's oft repeated intention to exterminate the Jewish people in Europe."

No British or American denunciation to date had resounded with such fury or urgency. In "the principal Nazi slaughterhouse" of Poland, he said, "ghettoes established by the German invaders are being systematically emptied of all Jews except a few highly skilled workers required for war industries. None of those taken away are ever heard of again. The able-bodied are slowly worked to death in labour camps. The infirm are left to die of exposure and starvation or are deliberately massacred in mass executions. The number of victims of these bloody cruelties is reckoned in many hundreds of thousands of entirely innocent men, women and children."

Eden warned that the perpetrators responsible for planning and executing that "bestial policy of cold-blooded extermination" would not escape retribution once the Allies were successful in overthrowing "the barbarous Hitlerite tyranny." All Members of Parliament stood and observed a spontaneous moment of silence. The speech was reprinted on the front pages of major newspapers such as *The New York Times*.

The Joint Declaration did not, however, propose any military steps to rescue Jews trapped in Nazi-occupied Europe. Nor did it offer any new hope of asylum. No Jew who managed to escape Europe would be welcomed as a war refugee in the United States, nor in any corner of the British Empire—including Mandatory Palestine.

The Yishuv leadership knew that with each passing day, another thousand-year-old Jewish community vanished. More than two million Jews in Poland had already been slaughtered. In September 1942, between eighteen thousand and twenty-three thousand Jews were being gassed daily in three death camps—Treblinka, Belzec, and Sobibor—while thousands died of disease and starvation in the largest ghettos—Warsaw, Łódź, Vilna, and Białystok.

Behind the closed door of his book-lined office, Eliyahu Golomb was adamant: The surviving Jews of Europe needed to be reached and warned. They needed to be urged to rise in defiance, wield whatever weapons they could find or make—old military rifles and pistols, Molotov cocktails, hatchets, and butcher's knives—in order to avoid boarding those eastbound trains. Those who couldn't fight—those too young, too old, too weak—needed trained Jewish rescuers to guide them to safety, to the resistance-held territories in the mountains and forests.

"We knew that if we could only penetrate enemy territory and send our boys into the heart of Europe, they would form concentrations of Jewish youth, especially of young Zionists, and organize them into fighting units," he later wrote. "We were certain we could create cadres of Jews who would resist the Nazis, and upon whom, whatever their ultimate fate, would be bestowed the privilege of dying in combat."

For over a year, the Haganah had strategized ideas for infiltrating Nazi-occupied Europe on a rescue operation. Some were outrageous in their ambition—such as sending a thousand commandos into Poland who'd smuggle weapons to the resistance fighters in the ghettos.

After months of planning and debate, only one viable approach emerged. The Haganah had already trained over two thousand young, elite volunteers to fight as guerrillas if the Nazis conquered British Palestine. Those fighters were known as the Palmach, an acronym from the Hebrew *Plugot Machatz* (Strike Companies). Why not use their passion to rescue Jews, their eagerness to exact revenge, by creating small commando units to conduct covert missions behind enemy lines?

On paper, the idea was daring and brilliant. But there was a hitch: The Jews of Mandatory Palestine did not own planes, ships, or submarines. For military assistance and transport, they were wholly dependent on His Majesty's government in London. But would the British authorities—Englishmen who, with a few notable exceptions, had shown little empathy for Jewish causes—agree to help?

The answer, for over a year, had been no. Great Britain's political and military leaders reiterated that the Allies' tactical objectives didn't include saving Jewish civilians. But in the early spring of 1943, in a series of late-night meetings in the stately home on Rothschild Boulevard, the Yishuv leadership began hearing of a breakthrough. After much bureaucratic wrangling, the Jewish Agency and the British authorities were on the verge of reaching an agreement.

Moshe Sharett, the Jewish Agency's chief diplomat—erudite, polished, with impeccable London School of Economics credentials—had been pressing his political contacts in London to approve Jewish combat units. Reuven Zaslani, meanwhile, a veteran of numerous covert Zionist missions, had been negotiating behind the scenes with the few high-ranking officers in British Intelligence who were sympathetic to the Jewish cause.

The proposal was unwritten and remained top secret: Volunteers in the Palmach—though it was technically an outlawed militia—would be carefully screened, given ranks in the Royal Air Force, and granted permission to work with three branches of British Intelligence: the Special Operations Executive (SOE), Secret Intelligence Service (MI6), and British Directorate of Military Intelligence Section 9 (MI9).

The British would acquire a cadre of passionate young paratroopers who had unique skills to assist thousands of Allied pilots and aircrew shot down in Nazi-occupied Europe—valuable airmen lost behind the lines, unable to speak the local languages—to return to flying combat missions. The Palmach would in turn receive British intelligence training and access to Royal Air Force planes.

Whether the British understood it or not, however, the focus of Ben-Gurion's Jewish Agency and Eliyahu Golomb's Haganah remained *solely* rescuing Jews. They would need to find volunteers for the most daring mission of their lives: the only military operation of the Second World War designed for the preservation and salvation of the Jewish communities of Europe. Millions of civilians trapped in ghettos, refugees hiding in forests, were waiting, on the verge of being consumed by the flames.

But who would be willing to jump back into the inferno?

PART ONE

A VOICE CALLED

1

Winter 1943
Kibbutz Sdot Yam, Mandatory Palestine

She was a *chalutza*, one of a bold new breed: members of left-wing Zionist youth movements, pioneers, revered to this day for their idealism and sacrifice in building up the Land—Eretz Israel.

"In the days of the *chalutzim*." It's an expression you often hear today in Israel, used almost as Americans refer to the Greatest Generation. The word *chalutzim* summons up images of tanned agricultural workers in khaki shorts draining swamps, planting orange groves, dancing horas, and singing around campfires after long hours of fieldwork. They were the young pioneers who built Israel out of a wasteland, who famously "made the desert bloom."

But for Hannah Senesh, the quotidian reality of Kibbutz Sdot Yam was a rude awakening. In 1939, when she'd made *aliyah*, she'd been wide-eyed and idealistic, set to study the science of agriculture for two years, imagining herself toiling in groves of olives and grapes as she did so, or filling straw baskets with ripe pomegranates and date palms.* Instead, she found herself doing nine-hour mindless shifts in the communal laundry, hand-washing, as she'd recall in her diary, one hundred fifty pairs of socks daily.

She couldn't mask her frustration and disappointment. She had been raised a privileged bourgeois girl in cosmopolitan Budapest, and now she was

*"Making *aliyah*," from the Hebrew word for "ascent," refers to Jews returning from the Diaspora to the Land of Israel.

a self-described "proletarian" woman, building Kibbutz Sdot Yam from scratch alongside her fellow *chalutzim*. They'd been on the site only since 1940 and were still living in tents and a few rickety shacks by the stormy Mediterranean coast, barely protected from the elements. At night, with hands nearly too chapped and frozen to hold a pen, she would record her thoughts by the light of her kerosene lamp.

Nothing in Hannah's early years could have prefigured this transformation.

She was born Anna Szenes in Budapest on July 17, 1921, into an assimilated Hungarian Jewish family. Her father, Béla Szenes, was an acclaimed playwright, author, and journalist who'd changed his surname from the Jewish-sounding Schlesinger at the start of his career. Her mother, Katalina "Katherine" Salzberger, was from a middle-class, assimilated, cultured Jewish family in the village of Bősárkány, northeast of Budapest.

From childhood, Hannah had watched as her father wrote with the furious intensity of an artist who knows his days are numbered. Rheumatic fever had left him with a damaged heart from a young age, and even the best cardiologists in Budapest couldn't give him any hope of longevity.

In 1921, he began writing a weekly humor column under the pen name "The Coalman"—Szenes means "coal" in Magyar—for *Pesti Hírlap*, one of Hungary's most widely circulated newspapers and, under his own name, became celebrated as an author and playwright. His 1924 young-adult novel, *Csibi*, about a street urchin turned football star, was one of the bestselling books in the Kingdom of Hungary and was translated as *Der Schandfleck der Klasse* in Weimar Germany. He found his greatest success, however, on the stage. Beginning in 1921, he penned eight hit plays—including *I'll Never Marry*, *Houseguest*, *Rich Girl*, and *The Sleeping Husband*—all of which premiered at the Vígszínház, the Comedy Theatre of Budapest—making him the talk of the city's café society.

Often rehearsals at the Comedy Theatre ran until nearly dawn, and he kept a Bohemian schedule, writing late at night and staying in bed all morning. Before school and on weekends, Anna and her older brother, Gyuri,* would jump

*Guryi is a popular diminutive for György, the Hungarian version of George. Many accounts of Hannah's life refer to him by that English name. For purposes of consistency

onto the pillows next to their father, and he'd summon up whatever stories popped into his imagination—adventures about pirates, medieval knights, or cowboys in the American Wild West. Those spontaneous yarns, never written down, were told for his pleasure as much as theirs. Béla loved to watch Anna and Gyuri smile, giggle, or laugh so hard they'd tumble off the bed.

In May 1927, when Anna was six, Béla Szenes died of heart failure in his sleep. He was thirty-three. Though she was scarred by the premature loss, she nonetheless continued to thrive with an outwardly happy childhood: She had piano and tennis lessons, learned amateur photography, took ski vacations to the Alps and summer trips to Italy. She documented it all eloquently in her journals, which she began keeping at age thirteen.

As she was coming of age, Europe was descending into turmoil. For a sensitive girl who followed world affairs closely, the headlines were terrifying. Anna wrote in her diary almost daily about Adolf Hitler's rise to power and his increasing territorial demands; she was especially anxious when Germany's bloodless conquest of Austria brought Nazi troops to the border of Hungary.

Anti-Semitism had always been present in Budapest, but by the mid-1930s, it was exploding as never before. A homegrown Hungarian fascist militia, the Nyilaskeresztes Párt—Hungarista Mozgalom (Arrow Cross Party), wore uniforms that mimicked those of the Nazis and adopted the pseudoscience of "racial" anti-Semitism, categorizing Jews as *Untermenschen* (subhumans), foreign, and a parasite on the "true Hungarian" nation. Anna's brother, Gyuri, had planned to attend university in Vienna, but once the city was absorbed into Hitler's Greater Reich, that was no longer an option. Instead, on July 10, 1938, he left to study textile design in Lyons, France.

Only at that point did Anna begin to think of herself as a *Jewish* Hungarian. Watching Hitler's influence spread across western Europe had brought a new perspective to the fifteen-year-old's sense of faith and identity and had significantly impacted her understanding of her place in the world.

At age nine, she had been accepted by the Baár-Madas Református Gimnázium, a prestigious Calvinist girls' boarding school that had opened new quarters in an Art Nouveau building on the western slope of affluent Rózsadomb (Rose

---

and clarity, I use "Gyuri" or "Gyura" rather than "George" throughout.

Hill), a short walk from home. Its students had previously been exclusively Protestant, but Roman Catholic girls could attend if they paid double the tuition fees; the very few Jewish pupils paid triple. The school made a rare exception in Anna's case in light of her outstanding grades (straight A pluses in every subject) and the fame of her father. (Baár-Madas told Katherine Szenes that it would, magnanimously, charge only double fees, treating her daughter as if she were Roman Catholic.)

Anna was taught Hungarian literature by the school's principal, the distinguished poet Lajos Jékely, who wrote under the pen name Lajos Áprily. He'd known Béla Szenes well and was impressed enough by Anna's early poems that he encouraged her to pursue a future as a writer.

Anna enjoyed being part of the school's Literary Society and was nominated by the girls in the senior classes to be its secretary, a high honor. There was only one problem. "A lot of things happened today, among them one that is very unpleasant," she wrote in her diary on September 16, 1937. "At the statutory meeting of the Literary Society I was nominated for office, along with several of my classmates. I was elected. The Literary Society generally accepts officers elected by the class, but in this case, they called for a new election and nominated two other girls to stand with me as candidates. This clearly indicated that they did not want a *Jew*—me, that is—to become an officer, which hurts me very much." She added, "Had I not been elected I would not have said a word, but this way it was a decided insult. Now I don't want to take part in, or have anything to do with, the work of the Society, and don't care about it anymore."

She began to see in her rejection a crucial lesson: As a Jew, she could not be an officer of the school's Literary Society; as a Jew, she would never be accepted by Hungarian society. It was a difficult realization, but she masked her hurt well, finding refuge in books by Fyodor Dostoevsky, Somerset Maugham, and Aldous Huxley. She read omnivorously, from *War and Peace* to *Gone with the Wind*. Then she found a unique way to reconnect with the father she'd lost at six. "I'm just finishing Daddy's book *The Eleventh Commandment* and am completely captivated by it," she recorded in another diary entry. "Thanks to this book, Daddy seems so close, even closer than before. . . . I want to read Daddy's other books now. It's really about time!"

Soon Anna's personal humiliation at the Literary Society was globalized—

codified through a series of anti-Semitic laws passed by the Hungarian Parliament. The idyllic world she'd known in Jewish Budapest began to rapidly vanish.

In the prewar years, the population of the majestic capital, known as the Queen of the Danube, had been one-quarter Jewish. Unlike many other cities in Europe, Hungary's Jews had assimilated thoroughly; they lived among their non-Jewish neighbors, socialized with them, and didn't just speak Hungarian but *felt* Hungarian. Many of them—such as Béla Schlesinger—changed their names to sound more like Magyar ones.

By the early 1900s, Jews formed the backbone of Budapest's middle class; before the First World War, 59 percent of the city's doctors and 61 percent of its lawyers were Jewish. The city's economy was reliant on Jewish merchants—over 60 percent—and the powerful industrialists Manfréd Weiss, Sándor Hatvany-Deutsch, and Leó Goldberger were Hungary's Rockefellers, Vanderbilts, and Morgans. Jews also made up a majority of Hungary's cultural exports: Joseph Pulitzer; Arthur Koestler; Robert Capa; Adolph Zukor; László Bíró, journalist and the inventor of the ballpoint pen; Erik Weisz, better known by his stage name, Harry Houdini—all were assimilated Hungarian Jews. (So dominant a role did Jews play in Budapest's economic, cultural, and sporting life that Karl Lueger, a mayor of Vienna under the Austro-Hungarian Empire, regularly referred to the city as "Judapest.")

But on May 29, 1938, the Hungarian Parliament passed the Law for the More Effective Protection of Social and Economic Life, placing a quota of 20 percent on Jews in various professions. Overnight, thousands of Jewish doctors, lawyers, journalists, and engineers found themselves out of work. The restrictions extended to the cultural realm: As Béla Szenes was a comedy writer, his plays could no longer be performed at the Comedy Theatre; his novels could no longer be sold in bookstores. After his death, Hollywood had released two hit comedies adapted from his plays: *Don't Marry* (1928) and *Last Stop* (1935), the latter produced by the Hungarian Jewish mogul William Fox—born Wilhelm Fuchs—the founder of Fox Film Corporation.

Without the royalties from her father's books and plays and their American film adaptations, Anna's family lost its primary source of income. Like hundreds of thousands of other Jews in Budapest, Anna suddenly felt like a stranger in her own land.

Anna witnessed hatred of Jews being expressed more and more openly; many Hungarians now boasted of their anti-Semitic bona fides. "I have been an anti-Semite throughout my life," wrote Admiral Miklós Horthy, the country's ruler since 1920, in a letter to one of his ministers. "I have considered it intolerable that here in Hungary everything, every factory, bank, large fortune, business, theater, press, commerce . . . should be in Jewish hands, and . . . the Jew should be the image reflected of Hungary, especially abroad."

"To my way of thinking, you have to be someone exceptional to fight anti-Semitism, which is the most difficult kind of fight," Anna wrote in her diary on May 15, 1937. "Only now am I beginning to see what it really means to be a Jew in a Christian society. But I don't mind at all. It is because we have to struggle, because it is more difficult for us to reach our goal, that we develop outstanding qualities."

If Hungary was not her home, Anna would have to find one elsewhere. In the year following her rejection by the Literary Society, five months after the passage of the First Jewish Law, she made an announcement in her journal, almost offhandedly: "I don't know whether I've already mentioned that I've become a Zionist," she wrote on October 27, 1938. "This word stands for a tremendous number of things. To me it means, in short, that I now consciously and strongly feel I am a Jew—and am proud of it. My primary aim is to go to Palestine, to work for it."

In truth, she'd been exploring an interest in Zionism for three years. Though she was fluent in German, French, and English, and was studying Italian, she had never learned Hebrew—synagogue had never held much interest for her—and like most assimilated Hungarian Jews, she couldn't even read or write the Hebrew alphabet. She now dedicated herself to learning the language, working with a private tutor to make up for lost time. She joined Hashomer Hatzair—Hebrew for "The Young Guard"—the first and largest of the Socialist Zionist youth movements, with seventy thousand members worldwide.

That newfound passion excited and empowered her. "One needs something to believe in, something for which one can have whole-hearted enthusiasm," she wrote. "One needs to feel that one's life has meaning, that one is needed in this world. Zionism fulfills all this for me."

The father of political Zionism was a man not unlike her own father. Theodor Herzl was born into a secular, acculturated Jewish family in Budapest and became a successful journalist, lawyer, playwright, and novelist in Vienna. Galvanized by the rampant anti-Semitism sweeping through western Europe, he had published his short manifesto, *Der Judenstaat* (The Jewish State), in 1896, which argued that the only solution to persecution in the Diaspora was Jewish self-determination in its ancestral homeland. "The Maccabees will rise again," he wrote. "We shall live at last as free men on our own soil and die peacefully in our own homes."

In April 1939, when Anna was seventeen, she stood up at a meeting of her Bible Society and read aloud an essay she'd written called "The Fundamentals of Zionism." "When anyone in Hungary spoke of Zionism five or even two years ago, Jewish public opinion condemned him as a traitor to Hungary, laughed at him, considered him a mad visionary, and under no circumstances heard him out," she said. "Today, due perhaps in large measure to the recent blows suffered, Hungarian Jews are beginning to concern themselves with Zionism. But the question least frequently voiced is, 'What is the purpose of Zionism, its basic aim?' If we had to define Zionism briefly, perhaps we could best do so in the words of Nahum Sokolow: 'Zionism is the movement of the Jewish people for its revival.'"*

She succinctly spelled out her remedy for the centuries of Jewish persecution in the Diaspora: "One of the fundamentals of Zionism is the realization that anti-Semitism is an illness that can neither be fought against with words nor cured with superficial treatment. On the contrary, it must be treated and healed at its very roots. We don't want charity. We want only our lawful property and rights, and our freedom, for which we have struggled with our own labors. It is our human and national duty to demand these rights. We want to

*Sokolow was a Polish-born Zionist leader, author, translator, and pioneer of Hebrew-language journalism. He translated Herzl's 1902 novel *Altneuland* (Old New Land) into Hebrew, rendering its German title as *Tel Aviv*—literally, "Ancient Hill of Spring." He had adopted the name of a Mesopotamian site mentioned in Ezekiel 3:15. *Aviv* in Hebrew means "the season of spring," symbolizing renewal, and *Tel* is a mound or hill created over centuries through the accumulation of successive layers of civilization's debris. So inspired was Sokolow's choice that in 1909, Tel Aviv was adopted as the name of the first modern Hebrew-speaking metropolis.

create a Homeland for the Jewish spirit and the Jewish people. The solution seems so very clear: we need a Jewish state."

Zionism was by no means Anna's only political interest. Since childhood, trying to carry the journalistic mantle of her late father, she'd privately been documenting geopolitical events. Her diary entries in the late 1930s, with Europe on the brink of war, capture the anxiety of a young Jewish girl in Budapest during that tumultuous time, detailing day-to-day developments, much like William L. Shirer's accounts from prewar Berlin.

On March 13, 1938, Anna had written about the *Anschluss,* the Nazis' bloodless invasion of Austria, as Hitler and his troops entered Vienna's streets, lined with adoring crowds giving the Nazi salute and throwing flowers. Fear and angst swept through Hungary, a relatively young nation that had, after all, been part of the Austro-Hungarian Empire just three years before Anna's birth. All of the discussions at Hannah's school and social gatherings centered on geopolitics and the threat of war. "What will happen to us in the shadow of an eastward-expanding nation of seventy million?" she wrote.

In September 1938, as Hitler set his sights on Czechoslovakia, claiming that the German minority in the Sudetenland was being persecuted, Anna wrote in frustration, "The devil take the Sudeten Germans and all the other Germans, along with their führer! Why ruin the world and turn it topsy-turvy when everything could be pleasant? Or is that impossible? Is it contrary to the nature of man?"

She was glued to the radio, scribbling diary entries that read like journalistic dispatches, as Hitler made more ultimatums and the entire world's attention focused on Munich. "Today, at the last moment, Chamberlain, Hitler, Daladier, and Mussolini are making a final attempt to save the peace," she wrote, fully realizing that the strategy of appeasement would prove futile. Her school classes were constantly interrupted by air raid drills.

In May 1939, with the world on the brink of war, the Hungarian Parliament enacted the Second Jewish Law, which prohibited Jews from holding government positions, drastically reduced the quotas permitted in numerous professions, and for the first time—clearly influenced by the Nazis' Nuremberg Laws—defined Hungarians according to the spurious concept of race. Anyone with more than one Jewish grandparent, it decreed, was legally a Jew and therefore susceptible to systematic oppression. Jews could not be editors or journalists at newspapers—and the quota of Jews among actors, physicians, lawyers, and engineers was whittled down to just 6 percent.

The passage of the Third and Fourth Laws followed soon after, banning Jews from purchasing or owning land and stripping away their right to vote. Intermarriage with non-Jews became illegal, and for the crime of "race defilement," any Jewish man caught having sexual intercourse with an "honorable" Christian faced five years' imprisonment.

Anna could see that her future was sealed. Since childhood she'd aspired to be a writer—a poet, playwright, novelist, and perhaps even a "great soul"—as well as a schoolteacher. But pursuing either career—or *any* career—amid the climate of anti-Semitism in Hungary was now out of the question. She needed another option, a place where she would not be targeted or limited and where her pride in being Jewish would be accepted, not outlawed.

"The only thing I'm committed to, in which I believe, is Zionism," she wrote on March 10, 1939. "Everything connected with it, no matter how remotely, interests me. I can barely think of anything else. . . . Until now I have had to cast my sights in many directions. Now I have the right to look only in one direction—the direction of Jewry, Palestine, and our future."

On the eve of war in 1939, making *aliyah* was by no means an easy feat. Since 1923, the British had imposed strict quotas on the number of Jews allowed to enter Mandatory Palestine; an applicant needed to have an entry visa, a character certificate, a health certificate, and proof of financial means and was classified as capitalist, artisan, laborer, pupil, or refugee. Anna required an immigration visa from the British authorities and a certificate proving a reason for her entry—in her case, to study the science of agriculture and become a productive worker.

In March 1939, she applied to attend the Canadian Hadassah Agricultural School for Girls located on Moshav Nahalal in the Emek Valley. She received an acceptance letter from Hanna Meisel, the school's principal, in April, offering admission under the condition that she show sufficient knowledge of Modern Hebrew. Anna was proud that she'd been able to complete the application entirely in Hebrew. But now she needed to wait for the certificate of immigration from the British Colonial Office.

Much of the Middle East had been under British rule since 1917. After the First World War, the League of Nations had established various territorial "mandates," and Great Britain had defined the borders of what it now called Mandatory Palestine—an area encompassing modern-day Israel, the West Bank, Gaza, and Jordan.

Anna's timing was remarkable. In the wake of the 1936–1939 Arab Revolt, Prime Minister Neville Chamberlain's government recognized that the British Empire couldn't risk fighting a war in Europe while also dealing with an uprising by Arab militias threatening control of the Suez Canal. In May, Great Britain abruptly and drastically changed its existing policy on immigration to Mandatory Palestine. The White Paper of 1939 dictated that over the next five years, only ten thousand Jews could immigrate annually, with an additional twenty-five thousand granted temporary refugee visas. That decision crushed the hopes of millions of European Jews, leaving them vulnerable to Nazi terror without a legal means to emigrate to Mandatory Palestine. Had Anna applied for an immigration visa even a few months later, her chances of gaining entry would have been remote.

"I've got it; I've got it—the certificate!" she wrote in her diary on July 21, 1939. Indeed, she was one of the lucky few. With the certificate from the Agricultural School for Girls and her immigration visa in hand, she needed to make plans to be in Nahal by September.

Katherine Szenes was far from thrilled. Her only daughter had just graduated summa cum laude from Baár-Madas, the most prestigious girls' school in Budapest, and now she was going to become a *farmworker*? If Anna insisted on going to the undeveloped Mandate of Palestine, why not attend the Hebrew University of Jerusalem, where she could earn a degree in education and become a teacher, as she'd always wanted to do? Why not follow her passion, enroll in a literary program, and continue to write poetry and plays? Why choose to study something so foreign to her life's experiences as *agricultural* work? "Mother, there are already far too many Jewish intellectuals in Palestine," Anna told her. "The great need is for workers who can help build up the country. Who can do the work if not us—the youth?"

But the rapid pace of geopolitical events nearly prevented Anna's departure. What they'd most feared had finally begun, she wrote in her diary on September 8, 1939, seven days after the Nazis launched their blitzkrieg into

Poland. "There is now war between Germany and Poland. . . . and France and England, Poland's allies, have entered the war." How would all this affect her immediate plans? She wasn't sure. "I received the certificate, and yesterday I also received the visa. I long to leave already, even though a sea journey now is not particularly safe."

After a tearful farewell to her mother on the platform of the Budapest Déli train station, Anna set out on a seven-day journey: two by train from Budapest to Bucharest and then to the port of Constanța on the Black Sea. She spent five more days aboard the *Bessarabia,* a Romanian passenger ship, which set sail on September 13, 1939.

On September 19, the *Bessarabia* docked in Haifa. Slim and radiant, elegantly dressed in a simple black dress and black patent leather shoes, Anna stopped to pose for a photograph. It was the last image of her "before." Within days, she was immersed in the Agricultural School for Girls at Nahalal.

"I have chosen to work on the soil," she explained in her journal. "I want to be a part of the working class in Palestine. This is not theoretical, because it permeates all my actions."

2

Fall 1940
Agricultural School for Girls, Nahalal

A life of hard physical labor was only the beginning. Anna wanted to make a total transformation. Instead of her given name—or her family nickname, Anikó—she decided soon after her arrival at school that, moving forward, she would use only her Hebrew name: Chana (or "Hannah" in English), and she rendered the Hungarian spelling Szenes as "Senesh." In Hebrew characters the names, each three letters long, have a minimalist symmetry: חנה סנש.

Though it was a period of great self-actualization, Hannah's transition to the agricultural school wasn't easy. The girls woke up at 5:30 a.m. for classes in agronomy, botany, horticulture, and animal husbandry and then put in eight-hour workdays picking olives, milking cows, and tending to chickens. There was a strict curfew, with the girls locked in their rooms at 8:00 p.m. (though many, Hannah included, learned to sneak out the window to take clandestine walks with boyfriends or "prospective suitors").

Hannah specialized in the poultry industry, and she wanted to combine her expertise with her passion for education. "One of my most beautiful plans is to be a poultry farming instructor," she wrote on November 2, 1940, "to travel from one farm to another, to visit settlements, to advise and to assist, to organize, to introduce record-keeping, to develop this branch of the economy." She could visualize herself roaming up and down the Land, and in the evenings, she would conduct seminars for kibbutz members, "teaching them the important facets of the trade." Her second plan had been legally blocked in Budapest—"it seems I only want to teach children"—but perhaps here, in the Land, she could find "a position in a regional agricultural school. . . . The old dream," she wrote, "is to combine agricultural work with child guidance and teaching."

She graduated with top grades and was chosen to give the farewell address in the name of her class on September 1, 1941. She thanked the school's director, Hanna Meisel, a pioneering feminist agronomist and Zionist leader, as well as the teachers, counselors, "and the entire region for unconsciously teaching us by the example of their daily lives and the Hebrew atmosphere" it had provided.

"Our road was not an easy one," she wrote. "It was filled with obstacles, contradictions, misunderstandings. There were also differences of opinion. And we still don't know how well we'll stand the rigors of a life of work, a life which will demand our best possible efforts, and all the knowledge and preparation we acquired here. . . . We'll prove to the school and to ourselves that we really benefited from our two years here. One thing we know already: We're going out to do a peaceful kind of battle. To work. We're armed with a valuable weapon: a knowledge of agriculture."

In her diary the next morning, she recounted that after her speech she "could barely shake hands with all those who wanted to congratulate me because they thought my farewell address was very beautiful. There were some who actually wept when they heard it, and that certainly was not my purpose. In short, the day is over. And we are free. I'm starting to pack. . . . I'm leaving for a kibbutz, filled with energy and excitement."

The only question now: On which kibbutz should she choose to work? Before graduation, she'd been touring the north, researching the various kibbutzim, each of which had its own distinct character and culture. The most logical choice would have been Kibbutz Maagan on Lake Kinneret—the Sea of Galilee—founded by a group of intellectual Hungarian Jews, many of whom Hannah already knew. But at Maagan she'd be tempted to speak in Hungarian every day—not immersing herself fully in Hebrew, a language in which she was now conversationally skilled but still struggling to find her literary voice.

She also didn't want to live on one of the established settlements—such as Degania Alef, founded in 1910, or Degania Bet, founded in 1920—because they had fixed traditions and a distinct communal culture. That was quite typical of Hannah's ambition: She wanted to blaze her own trail, to build something from scratch. In the end, she decided to join a group of young, idealistic *chalutzim* who had just founded a kibbutz on a barren stretch of the Mediterranean within walking distance from the ancient Roman ruins of Caesarea Maritima. They'd chosen a poetic-sounding name: Kibbutz Sdot Yam. Fields of the Sea.

In 1941, the Zionist movement sparked by Theodor Herzl and Max Nordau was still young, but its spiritual roots stretched back more than two millennia. Jewish liturgy has been filled with a longing to return to Mount Zion—the hill of Jerusalem—since the Babylonian captivity under King Nebuchadnezzar II in the sixth century BC.

"By the rivers of Babylon, we sat down, yea, we wept as we remembered Zion," begins the lament of Psalm 137. After Emperor Hadrian crushed the Bar Kokhba revolt in AD 135, the Romans renamed the perpetually rebellious province of Judea "Syria Palaestina" in an attempt to erase the name from which the very word *Jew* (Yehuda) is derived. For the enslaved Jews scattered throughout the Roman Empire, the bond to Eretz Israel—the Land of Israel—was further woven into Jewish prayer, ritual, literature, and culture; the two thousand years of exile were perhaps most clearly expressed in the closing words said every year in the Passover Seder: "Next year in Jerusalem."*

That sense of return, of prophecy fulfilled, drew travelers to the ruins of Caesarea, built by Herod the Great circa 10 BC—the Roman seat of power, the capital of Judea, where Pontius Pilate and previous governors had lived. The city had gained notoriety after the Bar Kokhba revolt, when (at least as Jewish tradition holds) the Romans tortured and executed ten martyrs, the greatest scholars of the era, including Rabbi Haninah ben Teradion, who was wrapped in a sacred Torah scroll and burned alive. The Talmudic account says that Roman soldiers put wet sponges on his chest to make sure he didn't have a quick and easy death. His students gathered around and asked, "Our rabbi,

*Before Nathan Birnbaum coined the word *Zionism* in 1890, a more religious-based movement throughout Europe had called itself Hovevei Zion (Lovers of Zion), seeking a return to the ancestral Judean homeland in response to the pogroms decimating the Jewish communities of eastern Europe.

what do you see?" Ben Teradion replied, smiling, with his last breath, "I see the parchment burning, but its letters are flying up to the heavens."

Hannah found the seascape of Caesarea "beautiful and magnetic," but the wind howling off the Mediterranean in February was bone-chilling. The majority of the kibbutz members—roughly eighty young men and women—were living in temporary quarters farther up the coast on the outskirts of Haifa, in a few wooden huts, but mostly in canvas tents. The coastal site the young pioneers had chosen was nothing but arid wilderness and jagged rocks, with soil unsuitable for growing any kind of crop. The only flora surviving in the salty ground of those "future fields" was Phoenician desert junipers, Palestine buckthorns, golden samphire shrubs, and, in the summertime, flowering Syrian broomrape and sea marigolds. Having arrived in midwinter, she found the conditions at the settlement harsher than she could have imagined. How could a band of inexperienced pioneers convert a few acres of rocky wilderness into a fertile, productive farm?

On February 4, she visited Caesarea and during the morning chill walked among the ancient stone ruins, while in the afternoon she gazed out at the fields—or to be more precise, the expanse of wilderness where the *future* fields would supposedly be planted. When she watched the waves storming the coast "with foaming fury," then saw how silent and placid they became when they broke on the beach, she thought that perhaps the "enthusiasms and fumings" of the *chalutzim* were no different. When the white crests of the waves pounded against the rocks, they were full of "virility and vigor," but when they reached the shore, they were "broken and tamed, and played in the golden sand like good little children."

As she walked through the ruins of the concrete aqueducts, the remnants of the hippodrome, and the once great seaport, she thought of the Ten Martyrs. As a girl, she'd heard "Eleh Ezkerah," the penitential poem about the ten royal martyrs, sung in synagogue every year on Yom Kippur. Those proud rabbis had never cowered, never broken under torture, never renounced their faith. Instead, they had chosen to die *al Kiddush Hashem*.*

*To die *al Kiddush Hashem*: Sanctifying the Holy Name, a phrase that appears throughout rabbinic literature, referring to a sacred kind of martyrdom—giving up one's life in the name of the Lord.

In her mind she saw the meticulously inked letters of the Torah scroll turning from shimmering black to luminous gold—one by one, ascending to the heavens. Such Talmudic legends, fanciful or not, moved her. She thought about Emperor Titus's destruction of the Second Temple and the tens of thousands of Jewish captives sold into slavery and scattered throughout the empire. Later, by kerosene light, she wrote:

To Caesarea

Hush, cease all sound.
Across the sea is the sand
The shore known and near
The shore golden, dear
Home—the Homeland.

With step twisting and light
Among strangers we move
Word and song hushed
Towards the future-past
Caesarea . . .

But reaching the city of ruins
Soft a few words we intone.
We return. We are here.
Soft answers the silence of stone
We awaited you two thousand years.

3

"Everyone is discussing politics; everyone is positive that the front is getting closer," Hannah wrote in her diary on April 23, 1941. "But no one dares ask: What will happen if the Germans come here? The words are meaningless—on paper. But if we close our eyes and listen only to our hearts, we hear the pounding of fear." She continued:

> I'm not afraid for my life. It's dear to me, but there are things I hold dearer. Whether I want to or not, I must imagine what the fate of the Land will be if it has to confront Germany. I'm afraid to look into the depth of the abyss, but I'm convinced that despite our lack of weapons and preparedness, we won't surrender without resisting strongly. Half a million people can face up to a force, no matter how greatly it is armed . . .
>
> But will there still *be* an Eretz? Will it be able to survive? It's dreadful to contemplate the possibility of its end at close hand. And though everyone wants to be hopeful, to reassure himself, deep within is submerged the thought . . . perhaps . . .

She didn't finish the sentence. Three weeks later, she described the first terror bombings of the war in Mandatory Palestine, as the Port of Haifa and the heart of Tel Aviv—completely undefended targets—were attacked by Benito Mussolini's Regia Aeronautica.

"Greece has fallen and so has Crete," she wrote on May 5, 1941. "The war is now raging in Egypt and Syria. The British Army marched into Syria three days ago, so the war is now virtually on our doorstep. Haifa was bombed for two nights. We went outside and listened to the bombs exploding and the firing. Today we heard that Tel Aviv was bombed last night, too, leaving many dead and wounded. The city is defenseless—an easy prey. It looks now as if the war is starting here."

As she composed her poem titled "Lamut?" (To Die?), Hannah felt trapped in a nightmare in which she wanted to scream, "but no voice comes from my throat; I'd like to run, but my legs lack the strength. I can't come to terms with the thought that everything might be lost, destroyed. . . . I want to believe that the catastrophe won't come to pass. But if it does, I hope we'll face it with honor. And if we can't hold out, that we'll fall honorably."

But then, she wondered, what could possibly make a death honorable? To die *al Kiddush Hashem*—to consecrate God's name as the ten martyred rabbis of Talmudic myth had done? "Is it possible to consecrate God's name in a manner divorced from life?" she wrote. "Is there anything more *holy* than life itself?"

To Die?

To die . . . so young to die . . . no, no, not I . . .
I love the warm sunny skies,
Light, songs, shining eyes,
I want no war, no battle cry—
No, no . . . not I.

But if it must be that I live today
With blood and death on every hand
Praised be He for the grace, I'll say
To live, if I should die this day . . .
Upon your soil, my country, my Homeland.

For the Yishuv in Mandatory Palestine, the seven-month period from March through November 1942 would come to be known in Hebrew as *matayim yamei kharada*: the Two Hundred Days of Dread. Field Marshal Erwin Rommel's Afrika Korps was sweeping east in the Desert Campaign, toward the Suez Canal and Mandatory Palestine. A newly formed SS extermination unit, Einsatzgruppe Ägypten (Task Force Egypt), was prepared to follow in Rommel's wake and take "executive measures" on the Jews of Palestine.

SS Standartenführer Walther Rauff, a Nazi executioner with extensive experience in killing Jews in Poland and the Baltic states, arrived in Egypt in 1942 to make logistical plans for the extermination of the Jews of North Africa and British Mandatory Palestine.

During the Two Hundred Days of Dread, when it seemed inevitable that Rommel's Afrika Korps would conquer Palestine, the leadership of the Haganah had no illusions about what lay in store for the six hundred thousand Jews of the Yishuv should Einsatzgruppe Ägypten cross the desert sands.

An ambitious plan was laid out by Yitzhak Sadeh, a veteran Haganah commander, who, in May 1941, on orders from Eliyahu Golomb, had created the Palmach. Born Izaak Landoberg in Lublin, then in the Russian Empire, Sadeh had once been a wrestling champion in St. Petersburg. When the First World War broke out, he'd fought in the czar's army and then, in 1920, had made *aliyah* to Eretz Israel. Like most *chalutzim*, he had Hebraized his name—Landoberg morphing into Sadeh (Field). But to the public, he was always Ha-Zaken (the Old Man), the seasoned commander who schooled an entire generation of Israeli military officers including Moshe Dayan, Yigal Allon, and Yitzhak Rabin.

Sadeh prepared for a scenario in which the British Army pulled out and abandoned the six hundred thousand Jews of the Yishuv to fend for themselves. He chose the plateau of Mount Carmel; its fertile land and natural defenses could shield the community without totally isolating it. Rising 1,700 feet above the Mediterranean coast, it favored defenders; even if Mount Carmel was surrounded, its eastern side was open to supply from the sea. Should the German Army capture Palestine, it might be possible to move the *entire* Yishuv population up to fortifications on Mount Carmel, deserting Tel Aviv, Jerusalem, Haifa, and all the kibbutzim and moshavim.

The idea was officially called the North Plan, though the Palmachniks referred to it as "Masada on the Carmel." Protected by the Haganah, the Yishuv could hunker down, resist, and wage guerrilla warfare in nighttime raids against the Nazi occupiers. If the SS sent in its Einsatzgruppen to wipe out the

Jews of Yishuv, Sadeh was determined to fight to death—holding out to the last man and woman. It would be a grim end, to be sure, but at least it meant dying with dignity. He estimated that it could hold out for many months—even years.

The logistical planning for Masada on the Carmel was short-lived: In early November 1942, radios throughout Mandatory Palestine broadcast news bulletins about a titanic battle occurring over three hundred miles southwest of Mount Carmel on the Egyptian coast, at a previously unheard-of railway station called El Alamein.

In the fourth stage of the battle, code-named Operation Supercharge, Lieutenant General Bernard Law Montgomery's Eighth Army routed Field Marshal Rommel, destroying or capturing much of his Afrika Korps, chasing the Desert Fox out of Egypt and into Libya. After more than two years of war, El Alamein was the first British victory. Montgomery had stopped Rommel from taking the Suez Canal, thus keeping Great Britain's shipping lines open, securing vital oil supplies, and preventing the Mediterranean Sea from falling under Nazi control.

For the Yishuv, the Two Hundred Days of Dread were over. As Montgomery continued to drive Rommel westward, out of Libya and into Algeria, capturing vital airfields and ports, North Africa provided the springboard for the Allied invasion of Sicily and Italy. But the significance of the Battle of El Alamein extended far beyond strategic aims; the battle symbolized a shift in both military momentum and British morale.

Prime Minister Winston Churchill instantly seized upon El Alamein as a turning point in the war. "We have victory—a remarkable and definite victory," he proclaimed on November 10, 1942, in one of his most well crafted and widely quoted pieces of wartime oratory, addressing the Lord Mayor's Day Luncheon at Mansion House in London. "A bright gleam has caught the helmets of our soldiers and warmed and cheered all our hearts. . . . The Germans have received back again that measure of fire and steel which they have so often meted out to others." He then added, "Now, this is not the end. It is not even the beginning of the end. But it is, perhaps, the end of the beginning."

So, too, was it for the Palmach. With no imminent threat of a Nazi occupation, the British authorities ordered the dismantling of the Palmach, which caused Sadeh and his troops to go underground. The Palmach became a fully mobilized voluntary force consisting of young men and women organized into six platoons, hidden on numerous kibbutzim. There, Sadeh's companies continued to train as rigorously as ever, but the Old Man ordered a switch from defensive to offensive tactics, from protecting Eretz Israel to aiding the Allies in defeating Nazi Germany.

What the Palmach lacked in numbers—it had at most two thousand volunteers—it made up for in passion, high-quality training, and tactical nous. Palmachniks specialized in guerrilla warfare, demolition and sabotage, and intelligence gathering. As members of an illegal paramilitary force in the eyes of British authorities, Sadeh's men and women had to camouflage their activities on the kibbutzim. Throughout 1942 and 1943, the Palestine Police conducted raids of various kibbutzim in order to seize Palmach weapons, though the strict British military censorship prevented the public from reading about them in the press.

Yigal Allon, a protégé of Sadeh who would become one of Israel's most decorated generals, later wrote that "just as other underground armies like the French Maquis or Yugoslav Partisans needed to take cover in the dense woods of Europe, the Palmach—in order to deceive their British rulers—used the kibbutz movement as its forest." On various kibbutzim, a Palmach member divided each month into eight days of military training, fourteen days of working in the orchards and milking cows, and seven days off. Those Jewish commandos, Allon wrote, "looked, dressed, and for half of their military service, functioned as fully-fledged members of kibbutzim. Stables, milking sheds, and orchards partly replaced the barracks of more conventional armies."

With the Battle of El Alamein the Two Hundred Days of Dread had come to an end, but now the attention of the Yishuv shifted to the fate of European Jewry. Hannah, of course, was consuming whatever news she could about the fate of Jewish civilians trapped in Nazi-occupied lands, facing what the historian Lucy Dawidowicz would later define as a distinct war within a war: "The War Against the Jews." Hannah well remembered the infamous "prophecy" Hitler had made in the Reichstag in January 1939—his threat that should another world war break out, *one* people would pay the ultimate consequence.

"If international finance Jewry inside and outside Europe should succeed in plunging the nations once more into a world war," he had declaimed, "the result will be not the Bolshevization of the earth and thereby the victory of Jewry, but the *annihilation* of the Jewish race in Europe."

On August 24, 1941, Winston Churchill gave a radio broadcast on the BBC in which the first reports were delivered of German troops systematically murdering civilians during Operation Barbarossa, the code name for Nazi Germany's invasion of the USSR in June 1941. In Hitler's "war of annihilation" against the Soviets, the specialized task forces—or Einsatzgruppen—followed the frontline troops, carrying out mass executions. Under the pretext of military necessity, they orchestrated the killing of over half a million people—mostly Jews—in just nine months. "Here is a devil who, in a mere spasm of his pride and lust for domination, can condemn two or three millions . . . of human beings to speedy and violent death," Churchill said. "Since the Mongol invasions of Europe in the sixteenth century there has never been methodical, merciless butchery on such a scale or approaching such a scale. . . . We are in the presence of a crime without a name."

Yet in inner Nazi circles, there was, indeed, a name—or at least a chilling euphemism. In July 1941, Hermann Göring had ordered SS Obergruppenführer Reinhard Heydrich to commence planning for *die Endlösung der Judenfrage*: the Final Solution to the Jewish Question.*

On January 20, 1942, Heydrich gathered key German state and Nazi Party officials at an elegant villa near Berlin for the Wannsee Conference. Next to him sat the meeting's recording secretary, Obersturmbannführer Adolf Eichmann, the head of the Gestapo's Referat IV B4, the office responsible for all "Jewish affairs and evacuation."

Although hundreds of thousands of Jews had already been killed by the Einsatzgruppen—in the so-called Holocaust by Bullets—at Wannsee,

*The phrase *Final Solution* would not appear in English until long after the end of the war. Neither would *Holocaust* or *Shoah*, the ancient Hebrew word meaning "catastrophe." When Churchill spoke of a "crime without a name," he was being literal: The word *genocide* would not be coined until 1944. A Polish Jewish lawyer, Raphael Lemkin, a survivor of the Holocaust, describing the Nazi policies of systematic murder of European Jews, created the word *genocide* by combining the ancient Greek *genos* (race) and the Latin *cide* (killer). The word first appeared in Lemkin's book *Axis Rule in Occupied Europe*, published in 1944 by the Carnegie Endowment for International Peace in Washington, DC.

Heydrich outlined plans for a coordinated Europe-wide *Endlösung* using a more efficient method than shooting hordes of naked civilians in massive pits. From now on, he explained, Jews would arrive by trains at a string of six camps in eastern Poland that were far different from the hundreds of concentration camps already dotting the Third Reich. Constant deception was crucial. The Jews would be deceived until the very last seconds of their lives—facades of train stations with realistic-looking timetables would greet them, giving the illusion that they'd actually come to places of work—and then, after undressing for mandatory showering and delousing, they would be gassed to death with carbon monoxide or the insecticide Zyklon B.

Those efficient, mechanized, modern killing centers were something new in the long history of human civilization and barbarity. The Nazis coined the words *Vernichtungslager* (extermination camps) and *Todeslager* (death camps), used interchangeably when referring to camps whose sole function was genocide.

Aktion Reinhard, named for Heydrich and commencing in March 1942, marked the most intensive and concentrated murder campaign of the entire Holocaust. Between January and December 1942, some three million Jews were murdered, the peak occurring from March to December 1942 by lethal gassing at Chełmno, Belzec, Sobibor, Treblinka, Majdanek, and Auschwitz-Birkenau.

On November 22, 1942, the Jewish Agency Executive released an official report detailing Nazi Germany's systematic annihilation of European Jews. When the news spread among the Yishuv population, denial was replaced with what the leading Israeli historian Yehuda Bauer described as "stupefaction" and "helpless rage."

The Jewish Agency proclaimed three days of "alarm, protest, and outcry" from November 30 to December 2, 1942. Hebrew- and English-language newspapers in Palestine ran with black borders. Signs in cities announced:

DECEMBER 2
INTERNATIONAL DAY OF MOURNING

Most of the Yishuv observed twenty-four hours of fasting and prayer, public transport was halted, and all workers not essential to the war effort went on strike. One hundred thousand people, nearly one-fifth of the Jewish population of Mandatory Palestine, took part in processions to mourn the murdered, the condemned, and the vanishing of a once rich civilization.

In an editorial for *Davar*, Berl Katznelson asked, "Why has there been no way to rescue the oppressed people from their murderers? Anyone who has the strength—take up arms!"

The collective rage accelerated the Yishuv's efforts to aid the Jewish civilians in Europe militarily. Jewish leaders lobbied US President Franklin D. Roosevelt and Churchill to do something to save the Jews of Europe. Yet the Allied leadership steadfastly stuck to the policy position that the fight against Hitler could not be perceived as a *Jewish* war. The only way to save the Jews of Europe, the reasoning went, was to save the free world from Nazism. Allied war aims remained unchanged: to crush Hitler and his Axis militarily, to beat Nazism and fascism into unconditional surrender.

After the International Day of Mourning, walking once again through the ruins of Caesarea, Hannah wrote a two-verse poem she called "At the Crossroads":

A voice called. I went.
I went, for it called.
I went, lest I fall.

At the crossroads
I blocked both ears with white frost
And cried
For what I had lost.

4

January 1943
Kibbutz Sdot Yam, Mandatory Palestine

Hannah lit her kerosene lamp and picked up her Biro ballpoint pen. Flipping the page in her notebook, she inked the date in the European fashion—1943.1.8—then boxed the date with a rounded rectangle. In neat, flowing Hebrew script, she began to take stock of what she had lost.

The world was entering the fourth calendar year of that cataclysmic war. She hadn't seen her mother since September 1939 or her brother since July 1938. In fact, she had no idea if either of them was safe—or even alive. "I can think of nothing now but my mother and brother," she wrote. "I'm sometimes overwhelmed by dreadful fears. Will we ever meet again? And one question keeps torturing and tormenting me: Was what I did intolerable? Was it unmitigated selfishness?"

She'd lost her family forever—or at least it *felt* that way. She'd lost her sense of joy, of purpose—she'd even lost her sense of *self*. A few days earlier, while she had been working at the Haifa shipyard harbor, one of the other kibbutzniks had playfully asked her whether she considered herself to be a "good" person. She later pondered the question. "Perhaps I'm not good. I'm cruel to those who are dear to me, who love me. I only appear to be good. The truth is, I'm hard-hearted with those I love, perhaps even with myself."

She'd also lost her initial idealism about what a life of self-sacrifice and physical toil in the Land would entail. In fact, she'd go *mad* soon if she didn't escape from the monotony of the kibbutz. Her high expectations had come crashing down into reality, like huge whitecaps against Caesarea's rocks. She was isolated and lonely; the tedium of laundry duty and her latest position—kibbutz store clerk—was soul numbing.

"I hate my work. It's a pity to waste more years of energy and strength on something I so dislike doing, and which will hinder my development in other directions," she wrote. She then chastised herself for complaining—that was not in the socialist kibbutznik ethic of selfless sacrifice—but still couldn't rid herself of the belief that some of the most precious years of her life were being wasted. She had so much more to contribute to the "upbuilding of Zion" than hand-washing socks and stocking shelves in the communal storeroom. "I feel like an empty vessel," she wrote. "Or more precisely—like a vessel with holes in it, so that everything poured into it spills out."

The robotic days of work often left her feeling so drained that she strained even to write in her diary. Writing—the one thing she felt she could not live without—escaped her. Some nights the ink in her ballpoint pen went dry; other nights her little lamp ran out of kerosene—and in the flickering darkness she found she could no longer even organize her thoughts. "I often recall Scarlett in *Gone with the Wind*. At difficult moments she would stall until 'some other time.' I'm that way: I'll consider what life is about, the value of society, the purpose of man, the future—at some other time."

Finally a letter arrived from her mother. Hannah recorded her thoughts in her diary on January 22, 1943:

> "I'm well, only my hair has turned a bit gray," Mother writes. It's obvious, reading between the lines, why her hair has turned gray. How long will all this go on? The comedic mask she wears, and those dear to her so far away? Sometimes I feel a need to recite the Yom Kippur confession: I have sinned, I have robbed, I have lied, I have offended—all these sins combined, and all against one person. I've never longed for her the way I long for her now. I'm so overwhelmed with this need for her at times, and with the constant fear that I'll never see her again. I wonder, can I bear it?

Her mother was safe, at least for the time being. Hungary's Jewish community was the last haven in Central Europe and the Balkans, home to the largest Jewish community still untouched by the Nazis, having swelled to a million with the arrival of fugitives from Poland, Yugoslavia, and Slovakia. But what about the Jews who couldn't go there, the ones trapped in those countries and possibly doomed to die there?

As if a thick gray sea mist had lifted over the ruins of Caesarea, revealing a brilliant blue sky, Hannah had an epiphany: She needed to return to Budapest. "I feel I must be there during these days in order to help organize the youth *aliyah,* and also to get Mother out," she wrote. "Although I'm quite aware how absurd the idea is, it still seems both feasible and necessary to me."

To return—yes, that was certain. But *how*?

Hannah found a few men on the kibbutz who'd already enlisted in the Palmach and a few others who'd served in the British infantry and fought in the Desert Campaign. They could see her passion but raised the obvious questions: Did she really think the British Army would accept a young Jewish woman with no military experience and then train her for some kind of special operations unit? Even if she did enlist—yes, it was true, many Jewish women in Palestine, if they were unmarried and childless, had volunteered for service—what British officer in his right mind would authorize sending her on a rescue mission back into the heart of occupied Europe in the middle of the chaotic world war?

A few weeks later, in February 1943, a twenty-three-year-old kibbutznik visited Hannah at Sdot Yam. After months of depression and isolation, Hannah was so thrilled to see Yonah Rosen that she rushed to hug him like a close family member, even though they'd only briefly met two years earlier when she had been touring the north, looking at various kibbutzim. Yonah belonged to the group of young intellectual Hungarians who'd made *aliyah* in the late 1930s and were building Kibbutz Maagan on the southern shore of the Sea of Galilee.

Two and a half years older than Hannah, born Gyula Rosenfeld in 1919 in the small city of Cluj in the Transylvania region, Yonah was a small, sinewy man with fine features and a winsome smile. He looked almost boyish, Hannah thought, but for the way his thick black hair was already receding high at the crown. Married and the father of a young son, he had enlisted in the Palmach two years earlier and was already a senior commander. Now he confided in Hannah that he was helping to organize a top secret military mission, to rescue the Jews of Hungary, Central Europe, and the Balkans.

Hannah's eyes opened wide at the mention of Hungary—at the very *possibility* of return. Yonah explained that he was recruiting volunteers who could speak Hungarian and were familiar with Hungary's diverse terrain—should the mission be approved, there would ultimately be a designated Hungarian infiltration team. Meanwhile, other Palmach commanders were looking for volunteers fluent in Romanian, Bulgarian, Slovakian, and Croatian. The plan was still hazy and highly confidential, but nine months earlier, the secretariat of Kibbutz Sdot Yam had put forth Hannah's name as a possible recruit for the elite underground.

She was in peak physical shape. Naturally athletic, an avid tennis player and swimmer back in Budapest, she had grown even leaner and stronger over her years at Nahalal and Sdot Yam. Most important, Yonah said, she had the passion that would make her a perfect candidate for the mission.

"How strangely things work out!" Hannah wrote on February 22, describing her encounter with Yonah but prudently not naming him in her diary. "A few days ago, a man from Kibbutz Maagan, a member of the Palmach, visited the kibbutz. . . . He told me that a Palmach unit was being organized to do exactly what I felt that I wanted to do. I was truly astounded. The *identical* idea!"

Hannah told Yonah that of course she was ready—*absolutely* ready. He cautioned her that the mission was still in the planning stages, but he considered her "admirably suited" for it. "I see the hand of destiny in this just as I did at the time of my *aliyah*," she wrote. "I wasn't master of my fate then, either. I was enthralled by one idea, and it gave me no rest."

In 1938, while only seventeen, finishing high school in Budapest, Hannah had resolved that she would leave fascist Hungary. She was single-minded and driven, dedicating herself to learning Hebrew, studying Zionism, intent on making *aliyah* regardless of whatever obstacles stood in her way. Now she again sensed "the excitement of something important and vital ahead . . . the feeling of inevitability connected with a decisive and urgent step." There was a chance, of course, that the whole idea would "miscarry," that she'd receive a message informing her that the mission was being postponed or, worse, that Palmach officers more senior than Yonah had judged her not qualified. "But I think I have the capabilities necessary for just this assignment, and I'll fight for it with all my might."

In her freezing canvas tent that night, she couldn't sleep as she visualized returning to wartime Hungary, not as the delicate, demure, bookish schoolgirl Anna Szenes but as a tough, trained Palmach fighter. Yet how would she notify her mother of her arrival? How would she organize the Socialist Zionist youths to either resist or escape, as she had done, to the Land of Israel?

For the next few weeks, she continued preparing herself mentally and physically to become a soldier. Yonah would update her regularly, but he kept saying that progress on the mission was slow. Hannah had little idea that the various branches of British Intelligence, military agencies, civil servants, and politicians were clashing, tying up the mission in bureaucratic gridlock.

The British Middle East Command in Cairo and Churchill's war cabinet in London were locked in a wide-ranging dispute over the wisdom of arming, training, and thereby *legitimizing* the Haganah. When war had broken out, with the hated White Paper having dramatically capped Jewish immigration, David Ben-Gurion had fired off his famous epigram: "We must support the British Army as though there were no White Paper; and fight the White Paper as though there were no war."

It was "a good play on words," wrote the historian Yehuda Bauer. "In reality, however, the double course was impossible. The line taken by the Jewish Agency—echoed by the Haganah—was that cooperation might prove to the British that the Jews were loyal allies, potentially influencing the many British statesmen uneasy about the White Paper. British military headquarters in the Middle East, on the other hand, regarded the Jews with marked skepticism."

Yonah also hadn't had the heart to tell Hannah that the Palmach had encountered stiff resistance from British military authorities about allowing women volunteers to enlist. For the Haganah, gender was never an issue: On the kibbutzim a woman was expected to do everything a man could do, even pick up arms and fight in the defense of the Homeland.

That attitude was not shared by senior military officers or policymakers in 1943. Although Great Britain had 640,000 women in uniform during the Second World War, none was officially allowed in combat. The US armed forces similarly boasted 350,000 women in the services but kept them from the front lines. Among the Allies, only the USSR made full use of approximately 1 million female troops; Soviet women were frontline infantry, combat pilots, aircraft gunners, and, in several notable cases, such as the legendary Lieutenant Lyudmila Pavlichenko, among the most decorated snipers in the Red Army.

The notion of allowing a woman—Jewish or otherwise—to parachute behind enemy lines in uniform seemed ludicrous to the British officials who heard about the Palmach's proposed rescue mission. If captured by the Germans, they argued, any female in uniform would almost certainly be tortured by the Gestapo and shot as a spy.

Sending women paratroopers into combat wasn't the only issue the British and the Palmach disagreed about. They clashed on many other matters, both political and ideological in nature, as would soon become readily apparent.

After interviewing more than thirty candidates as potential paratroopers, the Special Operations Executive selected fourteen Jewish volunteers and, in March 1943, sent them to Cairo for signals and intelligence training. Several of the volunteers excelled as Morse code radio operators, and before long, they were instructing the students at the Signals School in Cairo. British Army Corporal Peretz Rosenberg—born in Hungary in 1919, raised in Jerusalem and Tel Aviv—had become an expert radio operator for the Haganah while still a teenager and would soon be selected as the first parachutist from the Yishuv to operate behind enemy lines.

SOE instructors informed the volunteers in Cairo that completing British assignments was their primary operational goal after jumping behind the lines. Tensions mounted, and soon trainees began to disobey orders. Most of the fourteen Palmach volunteers were infuriated at the idea that British Intelligence objectives should trump their main mission. They insisted that their *only* reason for volunteering was to rescue Jewish civilians, and that was what they intended do.

Several volunteers refused to enlist in the British armed forces or accept military pay, declaring their intention to remain entirely independent and fight for the Palmach under the Star of David flag, not the Union Jack. Others complained about the poor quality of the training in Cairo, saying that the British instructors "knew nothing" about the target countries into which the volunteers were going to parachute. Reacting to that near mutiny, the British threatened to halt their training and send the entire lot back to Palestine.

Eventually, that was what occurred. Most of the initial group returned one by one to their kibbutzim, frustrated and disillusioned. The mission stalled in uncertainty.

5

Spring 1943
Rehavia, Jerusalem

By late spring 1943, with the air war intensifying, the priority of British Intelligence switched from infiltrating occupied Europe with small teams of espionage agents and saboteurs—SOE's specialty—to aiding in the rescue and escape of Allied airmen who'd been forced to bail out during their missions.

MI9, the British Directorate of Military Intelligence Section 9, had begun its work in the Mediterranean theater of operations in 1941. Unlike SOE, MI9 had but two objectives: assisting in the escape of Allied POWs and helping Allied airmen evade capture after being shot down or trapped behind enemy lines in Axis-occupied territories. In military shorthand, it was known as "E&E"—for "escape and evasion." Under the command of Lieutenant Colonel Dudley Clarke, based in Cairo, Advanced Headquarters (or A Force) was established to launch E&E missions in the Mediterranean theater.

For the Jewish volunteers of the Yishuv, cooperation with MI9 proved to be much easier than their thorny relations with SOE. This progress was largely due to the unique personality of one man: Lieutenant Colonel Anthony Simonds. He'd been recruited to create and command the N Section of A Force and was in charge of E&E for downed Allied airmen and POWs across occupied Central Europe and the Balkans. "I required skilled agents who would infiltrate all parts of occupied Europe," he later wrote, noting that his attempts to do so with British-born agents had been less than promising. "It is hard to find an Englishman who can successfully pose as a Bulgarian, Greek, Romanian, or Hungarian."

Almost alone among British officers, Simonds recognized the Yishuv's unique resource: its people. The young Jews of Mandatory Palestine could prove to be a secret weapon in the intelligence war. "There's practically not a country in the world that does not have a Jewish minority familiar with the local way of life and language," he wrote. "As a consequence of the Nazi horrors, Palestine served as a refuge for Jews who escaped to it from Nazi-conquered lands, and they comprised a natural pool of potential agents."

To the young volunteers who would soon meet him, Tony Simonds looked like the prototype of the career British officer: tall, burly, with a well-groomed mustache and immaculately pressed uniform, walking with a leather swagger stick under his arm—an imposing man who, as one Jewish parachutist joked, "was always *hopelessly* punctual."

Simonds came from a well-known family in Reading, Berkshire. The brewers H&G Simonds—a company founded in 1785 and one of the earliest brewers of India pale ale—were his cousins. Throughout his time in the Middle East, he was fond of saying "There's no such thing as bad beer."

Simonds's father, grandfather, and great-grandfather had all served in the British Army. Educated at the Wellington School in Somerset, Tony was commissioned as a second lieutenant in the Royal Berkshire Regiment in August 1931. By 1936, he was serving on the intelligence staff in Palestine, the immediate subordinate of the legendary Captain Orde Wingate.

Wingate was either a visionary or a madman, depending on whom you asked, but his tactical methods and combat philosophy in Mandatory Palestine were profoundly influential. A zealous Christian turned Zionist, raised in the strict Plymouth Brethren church, he carried a Bible with him everywhere he went in Palestine, quoting long passages of scripture and citing prophetic visions of Christian redemption through the Jews' return to their ancestral homeland where, he was confident, they would soon establish the first autonomous Jewish state since the Hasmonean Kingdom of Judea.

During the Arab Uprising of 1936–1939, when the kibbutzim and other Jewish settlements were under constant attack by Arab militias, Wingate worked with Haganah leaders such as Yitzhak Sadeh, Eliyahu Golomb, Moshe Dayan, and Yigal Allon to create the Special Night Squads, a counterinsurgency unit that, beginning in 1938, successfully defended the Iraq Petroleum Company pipeline against frequent Arab sabotage attacks. The Special Night Squads also launched many nighttime operations against the Arab militias, at times executing noncombatant Arabs en masse, due to Wingate's tactical belief in collective punishment as a deterrent.

In 1936, Tony Simonds joined Wingate as an intelligence officer, helping to train and refine the Special Night Squads and quickly picking up some of the Zionist zeal, though, unlike Wingate, he never learned to speak a word of Hebrew.

Later, in 1940, Wingate and Simonds were transferred to Sudan, where they created Gideon Force, a Special Operations Executive commando unit that fought the Royal Italian Army in occupied Ethiopia. From Khartoum, Wingate and Simonds carried the exiled emperor, Haile Selassie, through the desert on camelback and managed to reinstate him on his throne in Addis Ababa. By early 1943, Wingate had been transferred to Burma to lead guerrilla units fighting the Japanese, while Simonds was sent to serve in the Desert Campaign against Rommel.

While Wingate was a zealot, his Zionism driven by deep-seated fundamentalist Christian beliefs, Simonds came to champion the Jewish cause from a position of humanistic empathy. Unlike many British officers, he was driven by an intellectual curiosity about the lands and people wherever he happened to be stationed in the empire upon which the sun never set. Before being posted to the Middle East, he had admittedly known nothing about the history of the Jews and Arabs and their competing claims in the Holy Land, so he embarked on an educational tour, visiting Bedouin camps in the Negev Desert, the Arab towns of Nablus and Jenin, and the kibbutzim in the Jordan Valley and Galilee.

One evening, he attended a party in a beachfront Tel Aviv hotel, where he met a well-dressed young man speaking English with a German accent. He was taken aback when he glanced down at the man's hands; they were mutilated, each finger crudely lopped off at the top knuckle. "I was a successful pianist in Germany," the man explained; but when the Nazis came to power and began their persecution of the Jews, he said, "they cut off all my fingers." Simonds stood mute, stunned by the casual resignation in the pianist's voice. "How horror-struck I was," he later wrote. "How angry I felt. I began to understand the meaning of the Jewish tragedy and the motives of the Yishuv leaders who wanted to set up a national home here."

6

Spring 1943
Jerusalem

As an intelligence officer, Simonds was allowed to wear civilian clothes and to live off base. In May 1943, he rented an apartment in the upscale Jerusalem neighborhood of Rehavia, west of the Old City, where his neighbors included two men with whom he'd worked closely while posted in Palestine in the mid-1930s.

Moshe Shertok—later known as Moshe Sharett—had been tirelessly driving from Tel Aviv to Cairo and flying to London, trying to persuade the British to allow Jewish volunteers to enter the war. Born in Kherson in the Russian Empire (now in Ukraine), Shertok emigrated to Ottoman-controlled Palestine as a child with his parents and served as an officer in the Ottoman Army from 1916 to 1918. Sophisticated and multilingual, with a degree from the London School of Economics, he was handpicked by Ben-Gurion to be the interlocutor in all negotiations with British officials.

In Cairo, Shertok met with Brigadier Iltyd Clayton, the head of the General Staff of the Middle East Command, and proposed parachuting Jewish commandos and radio operators into Bulgaria, Hungary, Romania, and Slovakia. Those small advance units, linking up with local underground fighters, would then radio for more Palmach soldiers—up to fifty Jewish paratroopers per country. "Nowhere outside Nazi-dominated Europe have young Jews smarted more bitterly under the humiliation of their brethren being slaughtered like sheep than they have done in Palestine," he said. "Nowhere has their desire for revenge been more intense."

Clayton was unmoved, dismissing the rescue plan as "disingenuous," merely a "front" for illegal Jewish immigration into Palestine. Shertok met with Winston Churchill's son, Randolph, who by mid-1943 was living at Shepheard's Hotel in Cairo while serving as an officer with British Intelligence. Shertok presented his parachutists' plan to Randolph, hoping he would relay it to the prime minister. Randolph said he very much liked the proposal and promised to tell his father about it.

While Shertok presented arguments to disinterested British politicians and civil servants, Reuven Zaslani's brief was somewhat more shadowy. Born in Jerusalem and an expert on Arab affairs, he went by the Haganah code name Shiloah—from the ancient Israelite city—and in the years ahead, after the establishment of the State of Israel, as first commander of the Mossad, he would change his name to Reuven Shiloah.

As early as January 1943, Zaslani visited British officials in Cairo and informed General Richard Loudon McCreery, the chief of staff at Headquarters, Middle East Command, that the Yishuv could provide a thousand men and women knowledgeable about various European countries. His offer was flatly rejected.

Simonds confided in his friends that he, too, was experiencing a great deal of pushback from both the Foreign Office in London and military paper pushers in the Middle East. "I explained the extent to which the Jews could assist the Allied war effort by providing agents who would infiltrate the occupied countries," he later said.

The Palestinian police officials and administrators headquartered at the King David Hotel in Jerusalem and Citrus House in Tel Aviv vehemently opposed Simonds's proposal. "I dare say they were not only pro-Arab but also anti-Semitic," Simonds wrote. When he met with General Sir Evelyn Hugh Barker, the commander of all British forces in Palestine, he was shown the door.

John Bennett, a career diplomat who was the head of SOE's Yugoslav Section in Cairo, wrote in a scathing memorandum, "I have little doubt that this is only an ostensible purpose, and that—with more than usually bare-faced effrontery—the Jewish Agency wants to get the British Army to train these

Palmach units in tactics which will subsequently be turned to good account against us."

Another British officer warned that integrating Jews with British troops would threaten Allied operations in countries such as Yugoslavia due, he claimed, to the virulent anti-Semitism among local Balkan populations. For his part, Simonds realized that he was battling virulent anti-Semitism among his own countrymen. During the deliberations, one British official casually said, "The Jews have been found to turn traitor, and have on other occasions lost their nerve at the critical moment."

The most cynical opinion came from Lord Moyne—Dublin-born Walter Edward Guinness, the Colonial Office secretary. Moyne saw an upside in approving the Yishuv parachute mission, reasoning that if the Palmach volunteers were among the best and the brightest young Jews in Mandatory Palestine, why not allow them to jump back into Nazi-occupied Europe on what sounded like a suicide mission? "The scheme would remove from Palestine a number of active and resourceful Jews," he wrote in an official memorandum. "The chances of many of them returning in the future to give trouble in Palestine seems slight."

"My activities to enlist Jewish agents did not find favor with the British Army commanders in Palestine," Simonds wrote, with considerable understatement, "so I was not surprised when I was arrested one day on Ben Yehudah Street in Tel Aviv by the Palestine military police and sent packing back to Cairo on the excuse that I lacked an overnight pass for Palestine."

That only fueled Simonds's determination; enlisting Palmach volunteers in his E&E operations was now beyond theoretical. He needed units of covert E&E parachutists *now*. Both Great Britain and the United States faced an acute pilot shortage. Throughout the fourth year of the war, thousands of Allied airmen bailed out over Romania, Hungary, Yugoslavia, Bulgaria—countries in which they were lost and couldn't speak a word of the local language. Meanwhile, factories in Great Britain, the United States, and Canada were producing bombers and fighters in record numbers. But the RAF required much more time to train a pilot than it did to build the Hawker Hurricane, Supermarine Spitfire, or Avro Lancaster he'd be piloting.

Simonds calculated that training an RAF pilot took a minimum of fourteen months at a cost of £5,000—nearly $400,000 in today's currency. If even *one* experienced pilot could be rescued by Jewish parachutists and returned to his squadron, he argued, the entire mission would be justified.

Having been unceremoniously booted out of Tel Aviv by the British Military Police, he found a sympathetic listener in his commanding officer, Dudley Clarke, who was now a full colonel. Clarke was no conventional military man. Known today as the Second World War's "Master of Deception," the South African–born Clarke was a visionary—instrumental in creating modern warfare's first special forces units.

In 1940, following the British Expeditionary Force's evacuation from Dunkirk and the Fall of France, Churchill had demanded "specially trained troops of the hunter class [to] develop a reign of terror down the enemy coast." Clarke had been tasked with its creation, and he had proposed forming a small, aggressive unit to conduct rapid hit-and-run nighttime raids in occupied France.

Clarke's name for his special forces was an inspired choice—taken from the Afrikaner units of the Second Boer War called Kommandos, guerrillas known for highly unorthodox and, to the British, unchivalrous and unmanly tactics: "Hit sharp and quick—then run to fight another day." Anglicizing the Boer spelling, Clarke both coined the word *commando* and brought it into the English vernacular. Churchill, having served in the Boer War as a young man, was impressed by Clarke's creative thinking, and on June 24, 1940, the first successful raid by the British commandos was launched at Pas-de-Calais.

Clarke had chosen to keep his MI9 A Force headquarters not in the upscale Garden City neighborhood of Cairo, on the Nile's east bank, where most British military officers, diplomats, and colonial officials were based, but several blocks north at 6 Kasr-el-Nil, in a small, rented office discreetly located on the ground floor beneath a not-so-discreet brothel.

Simonds sat with Clarke, explaining his lack of success with hidebound British operatives who simply couldn't master the languages or learn the terrain. By contrast, many of the young Jews of Palestine, now living on kibbutzim, had only recently emigrated from countries in Europe and needed no linguistic training: Their first languages were Hungarian, Romanian,

Bulgarian, and Serbo-Croatian. All were young, physically fit, motivated, and well educated. Moreover, Simonds said, the Yishuv's intelligence operatives based in Istanbul had established contacts with Zionist resistance cells operating in the Balkans and Central Europe. Jewish parachutists could embed themselves in the target countries better than any British MI9 operative could.

As expected, Clarke asked for more logistical details—he needed hard numbers. Simonds had come prepared with a detailed proposal from Reuven Zaslani. The Jewish Agency "would provide, select, and coordinate as many agents as MI9 required to penetrate German and Italian occupied Europe, all volunteers, and at no cost in pay, to rescue Allied service personnel, POWs, escapers, and evaders—provided that all such agents were allowed to help in rescue efforts to save Jews."

The Yishuv would even train its own people, Simonds told Clarke, a tidy benefit that seemed to seal the deal. The Palmach's basic training course, focusing on guerrilla tactics, was far more intensive and specialized than anything the British could offer. As for parachute school, the Jewish volunteers would need access for a few weeks to Dakota cargo planes already on the runways of the RAF air base at Ramat David in the Emek Valley.

The only training MI9 would provide was in operating MK III wireless transmitters, Morse code, cryptology, and the standard infiltration techniques: forging identity papers and travel passes, rapidly switching up undercover disguises. All those skills were already being taught—in great secrecy, of course—by British Intelligence experts in Cairo.

Clarke instantly understood what Simonds was offering: a unit of "ready-made" Jewish commandos at virtually no cost to the British. He also grasped an all-important intangible—that these were young volunteers with expertise and passion, highly motivated to rescue their fellow Jews and exact retribution against the Nazis. That kind of passion and motivation could never be instilled by training alone.

But Clarke could also see that by following the official channels, as Simonds had thus far been doing, working through the labyrinthine British chain of command in the Middle East and the inflexible politicians of the Foreign Office, his novel E&E proposal could be tied up in paperwork indefinitely. It could be in limbo until the end of the war.

The simplest solution? Cutting the Gordian knot.

"Together," Simonds later recalled, "we bypassed the Foreign Office and the British military commands in Cairo and Palestine completely and sent a cable directly to Churchill." Within twenty-four hours, the prime minister had cabled his friend Clarke back an answer: MISSION APPROVED.

7

May 1943
Kibbutz Sdot Yam, Mandatory Palestine

"Such a long silence," Hannah wrote in her diary on May 5, 1943. "I wonder why. Hasn't anything happened?"

Of course, even Yonah Rosen didn't know how much had been happening behind the scenes, nor would he have been at liberty to tell Hannah if he had. She continued with her quotidian duties on the kibbutz, feeling utterly miserable and, in myriad ways, unfulfilled:

> After work—a bit of reading, a great void. I miss some good company, or, specifically, a companion. I know—just one bold step and I would find a companion. But not *the* companion. Or perhaps yes. The whole thing is so strange. The boys . . . they're all right; yet, the same inner voice says, "Not this one." But does the one I'm looking for really *exist*? Or is he someone my heart and imagination have invented?

Throughout her diaries, going back to her girlhood in Budapest, Hannah had been grappling with what she drolly called "the boy question." From ages seventeen to twenty-two, she never grew less mystified by her attitude toward men or their attitude toward her. "I'll soon be twenty-two, and who would believe I've *never* kissed a boy? It's silly, especially the way it bothers me. I joke with all of them, but I think I'm cold, heartless. Joking, joking—but something must be missing within me, or perhaps it's buried very deep."

As she was preparing for her Palmach call-up, a brand-new member of Kibbutz Sdot Yam named Eli instantly grew infatuated with her. "Today he openly stated he loves me even though he has known me just two weeks. If he could be just another member for half a year, without talking about love, and if we would eventually discover we have things in common, I *could* learn to love him. But when love is the primary topic, as of the first moment—I have no way of establishing rapport with him." She added, "Are *all* men like this? And is this their attitude toward all girls? Or is this blitzkrieg my special problem?"

While studying at Nahalal, she'd "swatted away" several prospective boyfriends. "Hannah had expressive light blue eyes, an athletic, proportional, and beautiful body," her best friend, Miryam Pergament, later wrote. And once she'd ditched the high-necked conservative-looking dresses she'd brought from Budapest and started wearing the typical Sabra's khaki shorts, "every guy was running after her." Intelligent men were drawn to her elegance, charm, and conversational wit. "She wanted so much to say *yes* to someone but since the ideal loved one didn't come, she wouldn't compromise."

During Hannah's first years in the Land, her most ardent suitors were two very different Hungarian men, both living in Jerusalem. One was a brilliant intellectual named Joseph Weiss. They'd met previously in Hungary. Born in 1918, he'd graduated from the University of Budapest, then earned a degree from the city's Jewish Theological Seminary. After the passage of Hungary's anti-Jewish laws, he had made *aliyah* and was completing a doctorate at the Hebrew University of Jerusalem, where he was a favored protégé of the German-born philosopher Gershom Scholem, the world's foremost expert on the Kabbalah and Jewish mysticism. Hannah often sent Weiss her latest poems to critique. He dutifully did so. He also wrote several long romantic letters to her, expressing his desire that she be his wife.

Her other serious admirer was Ayush Friedman, whom Hannah called "Alex," a young businessman from a bourgeois Hungarian family. Hannah had known Friedman about a year; he drove his new car up to Nahalal many Saturdays, always bringing her a box of fine chocolates. In May 1941, he told Hannah that he loved her and asked her to marry him. In her diary, she laid out the pros and cons: Alex was serious in his intentions. He was an honest, decent, good man—and, yes, he truly loved her. But although she *did* like and respect him, she was certain that they weren't compatible. Their educational backgrounds and interests were too different. She could probably live a pleasant, simple life with Alex Friedman—but it would be an unfulfilling life.

Hannah didn't want a Hungarian-speaking man, whether he was a member of the Jerusalem intelligentsia, like Weiss, or the bourgeoisie, like Friedman. Her mind was set on a Sabra, a native Hebrew speaker, a man who shared her ideological beliefs and humanistic values. And she was determined that any man she married would *have* to be a socialist.

It was a hard line but one she was satisfied with. When she became a Zionist, observed Peter Háy, a Budapest-born author and perhaps the best of her biographers, Hannah began to "define her goals in political and social terms, not by the pursuit of personal happiness. These were goals she would have to achieve by herself or with comrades, not with a husband—although she longed to share them with the undefined 'right one.'"

Almost nothing seemed to frighten Hannah—she showed boundless courage, both physical and moral—except the prospect of giving up her sense of independence, the pursuit of her dreams, settling for conformity, and being trapped in a conventional marriage with someone like Ayush Friedman. Joseph Weiss once teased her in a letter, "You prefer ideas over people."

The flesh-and-blood Hannah was a deeply romantic, lonely woman who longed to find a life "companion." But she couldn't compromise, couldn't give herself over to romance, or desire, unless it was with the *ideal*—or, perhaps, unrealistically *idealized*—one.*

By mid-May 1943, as Hannah distracted herself by grappling on the page with her "boy question," Yonah Rosen learned, to his relief, that Colonel Simonds was willing to overlook the official British stance on accepting female volunteers, though Simonds presumed that the young women would parachute behind the lines as radio operators rather than gun-carrying combatants. The fact that the original fourteen Palmach members who'd gone to train in Cairo

*The intensity of the romance between Joseph Weiss and Hannah Senesh was not fully known until decades later, when a trove of previously unseen love letters was discovered and published in Hebrew in 1996 as מפליג חלום (Sailing a Dream), subtitled *Love Letters to Hannah Senesh*. Weiss, who became one of the world's leading scholars of Jewish mysticism and Hasidism, committed suicide in London, England, on August 25, 1969.

with SOE had dropped out meant that there were now spaces for many more volunteers. Yonah hoped that with those developments, he'd soon have some solid news to report back to Hannah.

Though the differences between British Intelligence and the Palmach were never fully resolved to the satisfaction of either side, pragmatism, in the end, prevailed. Training for the Yishuv parachutists' mission would now proceed rapidly for the members of the Palmach who were willing to enlist in the British military and don Royal Air Force uniforms. Rosen addressed the misgivings of some of the volunteers. "We've found a haven here in the Land of Israel," he said. "We're returning to Europe to lend a hand to our brothers, albeit in British uniforms, but without denying our Jewish identity. Even now, in the middle of this war, Jews *remain* Jews."

Another important reason for the Palmach's productive relationship with MI9 as compared to SOE was the fact that Simonds had brought on board a squadron leader from the Royal Air Force named Ben Lawson. A middle-aged veteran of the First World War, straight-backed and broad-shouldered, with thinning hair he carefully swept back to cover his bald spot, Lawson had been transferred to MI9's A Force in Cairo to act as a liaison with the RAF and assist Simonds with recruiting and screening volunteers. The Yishuv parachutists found him surprisingly sympathetic for a stereotypically stiff, formal, by-the-book British officer—until months later, when they learned that he was, in fact, a Jew. He came from an assimilated, nonobservant Jewish family in London. The horrors of Hitler's war had awakened in him a profound reconnection with his coreligionists.

"My entire being is preoccupied with one thing: departure," Hannah wrote in her diary on May 27, 1943. "It's imminent—*real.* It's possible they'll call me any day now. I imagine various situations and sometimes think about leaving the Land . . . leaving freedom. . . . I would like to inhale enough fresh air so as to be able to breathe it even in the Diaspora's stifling atmosphere, and to spread it all around me for those who do not know what real freedom is." She added, "There is absolutely no question but that I must go. The hardships and hazards entailed are quite clear to me. I feel I'll be able to fulfill the assignment. I see everything that has happened to me so far as preparation and training for the mission ahead."

8

May 27, 1943
Montenegro, Yugoslavia

On the very day that Hannah was writing about departure, the first young Jewish volunteer from the Yishuv was deployed as a paratrooper. Peretz Rosenberg, the signals and coding whiz in the original fourteen volunteers sent to Cairo, was a participant in one of the most strategically important intelligence missions of the entire war. A corporal in the Royal Corps of Signals, Rosenberg was selected as the radio operator for Operation Typical, led by Captain William Deakin of the SOE.

In early 1943, a sense of confusion reigned in the mountains of Yugoslavia. Two rival guerrilla armies clamored for Allied backing: the pro-monarchy Serbian Chetniks, commanded by General Draža Mihailović, and the Communist Party–backed National Liberation Army and Partisan Detachments of Yugoslavia under Josip Broz, the Croatian Communist officer who went by the nom de guerre Marshal Tito. The two rebel forces seemed to spend as much time fighting each other as they did the Nazis. Prime Minister Churchill demanded answers: Which guerrilla army should Great Britain support with men and materiel? Which side was committed to the unconditional surrender of Nazi Germany?

Churchill dispatched Captain William Deakin (later Sir William Deakin), his close friend and long-standing "literary assistant," to gather on-the-ground intel. Deakin's brief was simple: Report directly back to Churchill about whether the British should support Mihailović or Tito.*

Operation Typical was the first British mission directly assigned to rendezvous with the National Liberation Army. And for the first time, a member of the Palmach would parachute as part of an Allied intelligence mission.

The six SOE operatives, including Rosenberg—whose code name was Corporal Rose—left Derna airfield in Libya on May 27, 1943, and were successfully dropped near Žabljak in Montenegro. Within days of their rendezvous with Marshal Tito, the Axis launched a massive counterinsurgency offensive code-named Operation Schwarz, aiming to clear the Partisans from the Adriatic coast of Yugoslavia and wipe them out altogether. The operation involved 120,000 troops of the Wehrmacht, Royal Italian Army, as well as Croatian and Bulgarian volunteers and three hundred aircraft. In the ensuing shelling and bombing, two British SOE operatives were killed, and Tito was wounded.

Escaping from Operation Schwarz to a secure Partisan redoubt in the mountains, Rosenberg sent his expert eyewitness assessment via radio messages to London. Marshal Tito's forces were well trained, well disciplined, and loyal—excellent both as frontline soldiers and as saboteurs. General Mihailović and the Chetniks, on the other hand, were highly unpredictable, switching sides with alarming frequency and collaborating directly with the Nazis and the Ustaše fascists in Croatia whenever it served their own interests.

Despite his lifelong, ardent anti-communism, Churchill ordered that all British military support would henceforth go to Tito—none to the Chetniks. The decision was strategically vital to both the Yishuv's parachute mission and the final years of the war. Tito's Partisans—numbering 650,000 fighters, both men and women, organized into fifty-two divisions—would prove to be Europe's most effective anti-Nazi resistance movement.

For six months behind the lines, Rosenberg's skills as a radio operator made him the only contact the British forces in the Balkans had with the

*Deakin, a talented historian in his own right, played a crucial role in the writing of Churchill's four-volume *Life of Marlborough, A History of the English-Speaking Peoples,* and the six-volume *The Second World War,* for which Deakin was later called, by *The Guardian,* "the drafter-in-chief."

outside world. Though Deakin was unaware of it, before leaving Palestine, Moshe Shertok and Reuven Zaslani had instructed Rosenberg to get information about the fate of Jews in Yugoslavia. What Rosenberg learned was grim: Yugoslavia's once sixty thousand–strong Jewish community had been decimated by 1943, either deported by the Nazis to death camps in Poland or killed by Croatian fascists in the notorious Jasenovac concentration camp.

Though his work as a radio operator technically preceded its official launch, Rosenberg is still counted as a key member of what we now call the Yishuv Parachutists' Mission. During his six months in Yugoslavia, he put the lie to the British claim that the Jews of Palestine couldn't be trusted. On the contrary, he showed that the Yishuv's volunteers could successfully integrate with British special forces in fierce guerrilla warfare and intelligence gathering.

"I do my daily work as usual but sometimes feel as if I'm seeing things from a distance," Hannah wrote in her diary on May 29, 1943. "I look at everything from one point of view only: Is it or is it not necessary for my mission? I don't want to meet people. It'll be easier to leave if I don't. . . . I pray for only one thing: that the period of waiting will not be too long, and that I can see action soon. As for the rest, I'm afraid of nothing. I'm totally self-confident, ready for anything."

As she waited to receive word from the Palmach, Hannah had ample time to prepare for departure. The first order of business was to compile her literary work. In addition to many poems, she'd written a short play in Hebrew, *The Violin*, a semiautobiographical rendering of her journey from Hungary to life on a kibbutz. In a suitcase under her bed, kept secret from everyone else on the kibbutz, she had five exercise books. Four were filled with her diaries and poetry; the fifth was solely for practicing and improving her Hebrew vocabulary.

She reflected on the version of herself as rendered on the page—developing, evolving, maturing, throughout those four notebooks. The journey had begun with a short and poignant entry on September 7, 1934, when she was thirteen, after a visit she'd taken with her mother and brother to Kerepesi, the oldest Jewish burial ground in Budapest. "This morning, we visited Daddy's grave. How sad that we had to become acquainted with the cemetery so early in life."

Finally, in June 1943, Hannah received word from Yonah Rosen that she was now officially enlisted in the Palmach. She would, of course, need to pass the Palmach's physical, mental, and emotional assessment. And before that, she would need permission to take leave from Kibbutz Sdot Yam.

At a meeting of the kibbutz secretariat on June 12, 1943, Hannah faced rigorous questioning, explained as much as she was at liberty to divulge about the top secret mission, and asked for the right to enlist in the Palmach and begin training. She then left the room and waited anxiously for ten minutes before being summoned back inside.

By unanimous vote of the secretariat, her request was granted.

9

June 1943
Tel Aviv

Hannah arrived early at Citrus House on King George V Road in Tel Aviv and glanced up at the smooth, curved whitewashed lines of the office, built in the International Style in 1936. The uniformed guards at the entrance, thoroughly checking her identification, left no doubt that she was in the right place: British Military Headquarters. Once inside, she was led by a stone-faced, silent sergeant upstairs to a conference room. She took a seat at the foot of a long table, where she knew she would soon face a grilling from a panel of British military officials and Jewish Agency representatives.

The British were represented by Lieutenant Colonel Henry Hunloke, the defense security officer in Palestine; RAF Squadron Leader Robert Taylor; and Lieutenant Colonel Tony Simonds of MI9. The Jewish Agency, meanwhile, had sent David Ben-Gurion and Shaul Avigur, the founder of the Haganah's Intelligence Department and commander of the Mossad L'Aliyah Bet (Institute for Immigration B), the code name of the Haganah's unit organizing clandestine immigration of Jews into Mandatory Palestine.*

*Mossad L'Aliyah Bet is not to be confused with the better-known Mossad, an abbreviation for the State of Israel's national intelligence service. *Mossad* in Hebrew means "institute." The full name of the national intelligence agency, founded in 1949 by Prime Minister Ben-Gurion and Reuven Zaslani, is Ha-Mossad le-Modiin ule-Tafkidim Meyuhadim (The Central Institute for Intelligence and Special Operations).

Lieutenant Colonel Hunloke, an upper-crust British Intelligence officer not known to be sympathetic to Jewish causes, led the interview. "You're a very young woman who's never been in military service," he began. "You've asked to volunteer for a potentially dangerous operation. What do you know about it?"

Hannah glanced quickly at the faces of the five men at the table, knowing she needed to parse her English precisely. A mission was planned—or, rather, was in the planning *stages*—to send a unit of Jewish volunteers from Palestine behind enemy lines in Europe, she said.

And what was the nature of the mission? Hunloke asked.

The mission's priority, Hannah replied, was to establish contact with the local underground leadership and resistance fighters and, together with them, help downed Allied airmen and escaped prisoners of war get back to Allied lines. After the completion of those British Intelligence assignments, she continued, the volunteers could contact local Jewish communities, set up similar escape routes for Jewish refugees, and assist them in fomenting armed resistance against the Nazis and their fascist collaborators.

Colonel Simonds took a much softer tone than Hunloke, asking Hannah how, provided her application was successful, she proposed to return to Europe.

Hannah could imagine only two possible methods: by submarine or by airplane. And since the RAF was represented by Squadron Leader Taylor and no officer from the British Navy was at the table, it wasn't difficult to deduce the means of transport.

Simonds was impressed by the spirited, clever, and beautiful young woman.

Hunloke, displeased, asked Hannah a trickier question, a Solomonic dilemma designed to trip up any candidate: "Miss Senesh, it's my understanding that your mother still lives in Budapest."

"She does."

"What would you do if given the choice between saving your mother's life or the lives of twenty downed British airmen?"

Hannah met Colonel Hunloke's penetrating gaze. "Sir, I believe my mother would forgive me for the difficult choice I would have to make."

• • •

As Hannah left Citrus House, she strolled confidently in the bright sunshine of King George V Road. But in truth she was anything but confident; she was simply doing her best to mask her anxiety, not having a clue how she'd done inside Citrus House. Had she come across as overeager? Flippant? Too cocksure?

It was several days before she got word from Yonah Rosen: She'd acquitted herself perfectly at the screening, cleared the first hurdle, and now needed to await further instructions. Her training would begin with the Palmach, first an ideological phase and then the rigorous basic training. If she made the cut, she would proceed to parachuting school at the RAF's air base at Ramat David in the Emek Valley.

10

September 1943
Beit Rutenberg, Haifa

Hannah couldn't help but feel in awe when she first saw him: Ha-Zaken, the Old Man. In mid-1943, Yitzhak Sadeh, the founder and commander of the Palmach, was an almost mythical figure in the Yishuv. At Beit Rutenberg, a stunning mansion on Hanassi Avenue in Haifa, where Hannah had begun her Palmach training, she would occasionally catch a glimpse of him overseeing their progress, wearing khaki shorts, a rumpled wool sweater, wire-rimmed glasses, and a red beret cocked to one side.

The Old Man tried to meet each Palmach candidate personally. Hannah took to him immediately: barrel-chested, avuncular, brimming with energy. Besides being a brilliant military strategist, he was a fine writer. After he retired as a general from the Israeli military, he launched a second career, publishing essays, stories, plays, and memoirs under the pen name "Y. Noded," short for "Yitzhak the Wanderer."*

After the loneliness and the bleak life of Kibbutz Sdot Yam, Hannah enjoyed the luxurious respite at Beit Rutenberg, where, as part of her Palmach training, she attended a monthlong seminar organized by Hanoar Haoved Ve-Halomed, the left-wing Working Youth organization.

*Sadeh's most widely read book is *Misaviv Lamedura* (Around the Bonfire), a collection of essays he published in 1946 under the name of Y. Noded. Since 1972, the Yitzhak Sadeh Prize has been awarded annually in Israel for the finest book on a military topic.

The Old Man wanted his prospective Palmachniks to first study Jewish ideals and values, the history of persecution in Europe, and the root causes of anti-Semitism, which, in the end, provided the ideological rationale for Zionism. Hannah had experienced much of that discrimination firsthand only five or six years earlier, so she found the lectures rather rudimentary. The classes were better suited to the Sabras, born and raised in the Land, who'd spent their teenage years working on the kibbutzim, learning more about the science of horticulture than about political theory. Many had never heard of—let alone read—Max Nordau's *Zionistische Schriften,* Nahum Sokolow's two-volume *History of Zionism, 1600–1918,* or even Theodor Herzl's 1902 utopian novel, *Altneuland* (Old New Land).

Hannah had been devouring those books in her spare time and had been speaking and writing about them, with maturity and eloquence, since joining the Hashomer Hatzair youth organization in Budapest.

On September 19, 1943, Hannah marked the fourth anniversary of her arrival in Mandatory Palestine—fittingly enough in Haifa—but she was not in a celebratory mood. Instead, she wrote long, melancholy entries in her diary. The quiet nights alone in her room in Beit Rutenberg, away from the constant activity and lack of privacy on the kibbutz, gave her ample time to reflect on the choices she'd made along that strange journey. "I arrived in The Land four years ago. Immigrant House, Haifa. Everything was new; everything beautiful; everything a world of the future. Only one figure takes me back to the past: my mother at the railway station. Four years. I never would have believed the distance between us could ever be so great, so deep. Had I known—or perhaps I *knew* but didn't dare admit it."

As she often did in her diaries, she made cogent, logical, and often scathingly critical assessments of her decisions. She wasn't afraid of the military mission ahead. She wasn't afraid of parachuting behind enemy lines. "But there *is* something that terrifies me," she wrote. "I'm twenty-two years old and I have no joy in life. I can't remember the last time I was really happy, looking forward, or joyous, if only for a few minutes. I feel a certain indifference. Sometimes I catch myself asking: 'What *is* this? Is my whole life going to pass like this?'" She'd forgotten how to laugh, or at least "how to *really* laugh, heartily, as I once could with Gyuri while wrestling on the couch until we rolled off onto the floor, laughing about nothing but the joy of living, of being young and alive."

She wondered if the years of isolation in Eretz Israel, at Nahalal and Sdot Yam, were the reason for her anhedonia. Or was she afflicted with a kind of unique sorrow that came with the sudden death of a parent in childhood? She had been so young, after all, just seven years old, when she had stood beside her father's grave in Budapest's Jewish Cemetery and begun to compose her "first poems about the hardships in life." Her present mood, she decided, was perhaps "the same sort of tristesse I suffered when I was sixteen. . . . I hope it's really that, and nothing more, and that it will soon pass."

Despite her doubts about some of her choices, she was crystal clear about one: volunteering for the Palmach's rescue mission. "Would I enlist? Of course. In my life's chain of events nothing was accidental. Everything happened according to an inner need."

11

August 1, 1943
Ploeşti, Romania

As Hannah continued her Palmach preparations, Colonel Tony Simonds kept shuttling between Jerusalem, Tel Aviv, and Cairo, trying to get the first of his MI9 infiltration teams airborne and dropped behind enemy lines. Then came the news of Operation Tidal Wave, which changed everything for both Simonds and the parachutists of the Yishuv.

Operation Tidal Wave was the code name for the epic air raid of August 1, 1943—the biggest the United States Army Air Forces (USAAF) had staged to date. Their target? The Ploeşti oil fields in Romania, which were crucial to Hitler's ability to continue waging war since Nazi Germany relied almost entirely on imported petroleum. By 1943, at peak production, the Ploeşti refinery complex supplied about 60 percent of the Third Reich's crude oil. Dubbed "Hitler's Gas Station," it held such strategic importance that some Allied leaders believed that its complete destruction could shorten the war by an estimated six months—or perhaps even deliver a knockout blow to the entire German war effort. Ploeşti was nothing less than "the taproot of German might," in the words of Prime Minister Churchill.

On August 1, five USAAF bomber groups launched 178 B-24 Liberators flying from Benghazi, Libya, in a low-altitude raid targeting nine refineries at Ploeşti. The bombers took no fighter escorts—the flying distance to Ploeşti and back was still too great for even the best American fighters, the P-38 Lightning and P-47 Thunderbolt. The P-51 Mustang long-range fighter had yet to become operational and make its impact on the European air war. But the aircrews of the Liberator bombers were assured that they didn't need fighter escorts since the latest intelligence reports said that they'd meet little resistance in the skies north of Bucharest.

Those intelligence reports proved to be horrifically wrong.

In the summer of 1943, the Ploeşti oil complex was arguably more highly defended than Berlin. As soon as the American bombers reached Ploeşti, they were met by ferocious 88mm anti-aircraft fire and swarms of Messerschmitt Bf 109s. The Allies lost fifty-two aircraft. Three hundred ten American airmen were killed during the raid, 130 wounded, and over a hundred were taken prisoner of war. An astonishing *five* USAAF flyers on the operation received the Congressional Medal of Honor, three of them posthumously.*

Despite such heroism, Operation Tidal Wave stands as one of the great Allied air losses of the war, a strategic failure that came at an almost immeasurable cost. "Hitler's Gas Station," though badly damaged, was not put out of commission. On the contrary, its oil refineries were back to full production within mere weeks.

Allied bombers didn't dare to attack Ploeşti again until April 1944.

If the tremendous number of Allied airman lost during Operation Tidal Wave created a sense of desperation and urgency for MI9's A Force, the news was shortly followed by another major development in the European theater—code-named Operation Baytown, which offered cause for optimism.

On September 3, the British Eighth Army, led by Field Marshal Montgomery, fresh from its victorious campaign in Sicily, began fighting its way up the Italian boot. Operation Baytown precipitated the Fascist government's unexpected surrender to the Allies, with an armistice signed on September 8. Despite German forces preparing to defend the country without Italian support, only a couple of German divisions faced off against the Eighth Army, while one remained at Salerno, disarming the Royal Italian Army. The Allies

*The five American airmen awarded the Congressional Medal of Honor for their heroism during Operation Tidal Wave were Lieutenant Colonel Addison Baker (posthumous), Major John Jerstad (posthumous), Second Lieutenant Lloyd Hughes (posthumous), Colonel Leon Johnson, and Colonel John "Killer" Kane.

launched a series of rapid advances up the Italian peninsula, with the British Eighth Army making the capture of ports and airfields its main objective.

On September 27, 1943, British forces overran the Regia Aeronautica airfield at Bari, Puglia. Overnight, the Allied air forces had a crucial logistical hub for further advances up the Italian peninsula. The US Army's Fifteenth Air Force made Bari its forward base for bombing missions, expanding the reach of its best heavy bombers, the B-17 Flying Fortress and B-24 Liberator.

Since the Yishuv parachutists were dependent on RAF and USAAF aircraft, the seizing of the Bari airfield now made it much easier to launch covert parachute operations into the Balkans and Central Europe. Bari became a hub of activity for all Allied intelligence agencies: the US Office of Strategic Services (OSS), the British SOE, and MI9. Colonel Simonds made Bari the forward base for all his A Force units conducting nighttime E&E operations into Nazi-occupied Europe.

It had taken Corporal Peretz Rosenberg in Operation Typical eight hours to fly in a Halifax from Libya to the drop zone in Montenegro. From Bari airfield, on the other hand, a Halifax could make a relatively short hop across the Adriatic to drop zones in Yugoslavia. Simonds calculated the distance at three hundred miles, roughly two to two and a half hours' flying time. In the ferocious air war, such small margins often meant the difference between success and disaster.

"It's been about a month since I finished the seminar and I'm home now, in Caesarea," Hannah wrote in her diary on October 2, 1943. "I've worked in the kitchen, the garden, the laundry, scrubbing floors, and now I'm on guard duty. It makes little difference to me what work I'm doing. I'm happy to be home—to see people."

She found respite from her gnawing anxiety about the mission's departure date in the place to which she'd so often escaped and been inspired to write poetry: the vast city of ruins, the Roman Empire's Judean capital, Caesarea Maritima. "I bathe in the sea, swim out far, climb up on a rock, and enjoy the sea, air, sand, new and ancient Caesarea," she wrote. "Afterwards I dive back into the sea and feel fine—just *fine*!"

12

October 1943
Bucharest, Romania

While Hannah was swimming in the frigid Mediterranean waves out to Caesarea's ancient Roman concrete breakwater, then getting back to shouldering her Enfield rifle and counting out the paces on overnight guard duty at the kibbutz, the first mission of the Yishuv parachutists, Operation Mantilla, was launched from the Bari airfield. MI9 had decided to prioritize the parachutists from the Romanian infiltration team, largely in response to the devastating Ploeşti oil field raid that summer.

On October 1, 1943, Lyova Gukowsky from Kibbutz Yagur and Arie Fichman of Kibbutz Beit Oren boarded a Halifax bomber at Bari. It was a cold, moonless night, and they were about to make a "blind jump," the riskiest form of airborne infiltration—meaning a jump without a ground "reception committee" lighting flares, waving flashlights, or forming bonfires in the designated landing zone.

Lyova Gukowsky was unlike most of the other volunteer parachutists—he wasn't an intellectual, idealistic dreamer like Hannah Senesh, nor was he an enlisted British Army soldier like several of the other volunteers. He liked to think of himself as a "simple shepherd." He was a gentle, blue-eyed, broad-shouldered man who spent his days tending to his flocks of sheep at Kibbutz Yagur on the northeastern slopes of Mount Carmel.

Nonetheless, the Palmach had recruited him back in 1942: Gukowsky was strong and fit, and Romanian was his mother tongue. Before departure he wrote succinctly in his diary, "We have to come to them—to the exiled." It was an ambitious mission—planned carefully, down to the smallest detail. That it failed was no fault of Gukowsky and Fichman.

The Jewish Agency in Istanbul had informed the Zionist underground in Romania that it should expect the arrival of two parachutists; a large sum of American cash had been sent to Bucharest earmarked for Gukowsky and Fichman's efforts to rescue Jews.

Gukowsky, wearing a flight suit over his uniform of a second lieutenant in the RAF, watched Fichman jump first from the Halifax; he later captured the moment in his diary:

> Your heart pounds, thick sweat floods your body, the opening to the depths below darkens before your eyes, and suddenly, after all the stress of expectation, you see the signal. The shades of light playing on the airplane give the command: *Jump.* When I jumped, the parachute opened, and I felt enfolded in its secure arms. *Sh'ma Yisrael** flashed like lightning in the darkness of my soul—a sort of feeling of the sanctification of God's name that passed—cut off. And along with this came a sense of death. My ears perceived the bullets buzzing around me.

The two parachutists' descent was met with bursts of machine-gun fire. The brilliant white curves of their silk parachutes against the jet black sky made them perfect targets. The pilot of the Halifax had made a massive navigational error: He'd signaled for the green jump light to flash several miles from the designated drop zone, a broad field located five miles south of the city of Timişoara. With machine-gun fire whizzing past them during the descent, Gukowsky realized that they'd been betrayed. "We knew that an alarm had been sounded all over the country and that the plane was being watched," he later wrote.

Fichman had the abysmal luck to descend right into the courtyard of the town police station. Gukowsky landed on a roof, then slid down onto a wagon,

**Sh'ma Yisrael, Adonai Eloheinu, Adonai Echad!* From Deuteronomy 6:4: "Hear O Israel, the Lord is our God, the Lord is One." This is the central affirmation of Judaism and is often considered to be its most important prayer.

breaking his leg. Patrols came by quickly and caught both parachutists. The broken leg proved to be a blessing in disguise for Gukowsky; he was taken to a hospital for POWs and given medical treatment. Fichman, meanwhile, was handed over to the Gestapo, who took him to Germany, where he underwent interrogation and torture.

Neither parachutist gave any information about the mission, nor did they really need to. As a cover story, the British had dropped propaganda leaflets from the Halifax moments before the men had jumped. The next day, an official Romanian communiqué read: "Enemy planes that dropped leaflets were shot down. Two British pilots parachuted. Their names were: Lieutenant Colonel Yosef Kahana and Lieutenant Colonel Gadayev Yaakovson."

The first sentence was obviously Romanian propaganda: No planes had been shot down. Nor were the parachutists "British pilots." Kahana was Gukowsky's cover name, and Yaakovson was Fichman's. The news made all the Palestinian papers, in both English and Hebrew. The Romanian authorities were said to be investigating whether the "two RAF pilots" from British Mandatory Palestine were engaging in espionage.

Fichman was lucky to be released by the Gestapo alive; they returned him to Romania; he and Gukowsky were sent to Lagărul de Prizonieri 14 (POW Camp 14) about three hours north of Budapest. In contrast to the brutal conditions for Soviet soldiers who surrendered on the eastern front, the Romanians handled British and American airmen with kid gloves—in fact, POWs sometimes called Camp 14 "the gilded cage" because the conditions were surprisingly decent. Gukowsky and Fichman established themselves as leaders within the camp's underground, making contact with recently shot down Allied flyers. They were soon able to get messages smuggled to the outside world.

From MI9's perspective, even in that failure there were valuable lessons to be learned. Blind jumps such as Operation Mantilla were far too risky. Going forward, they would make "guided jumps," drops in which Partisans or underground members signaled with flares or bonfires on the ground. Blind jumps would be authorized only in cases of extreme necessity.

Beyond the pilot's navigational error, the fact that Gukowsky and Fichman had come under fire the moment they jumped meant, as Gukowsky correctly deduced, that they'd been betrayed. The Romanian military must have received advance warning and been waiting for the solo Halifax bomber, machine guns pointed at the sky. But who had betrayed them? Could SOE or MI9 agents in Cairo or Bari have been compromised?

The most likely source of the leak was Istanbul. Turkey remained neutral for most of the Second World War, and its capital was an open city, rife with gangsters, black marketeers, and hundreds of spies. Istanbul was a city of "scoundrels" hanging around hotel bars, as one of the Jewish Agency's operatives later remembered, where for the right amount of money any piece of information could be bought. American greenbacks and French napoleons traded hands everywhere.

In wartime Istanbul, even the savviest intelligence handlers had difficulty distinguishing allies from imposters. A trusted asset might simultaneously be on the payroll of the Jewish Agency, SOE or MI9, the OSS, Romanian or Hungarian military intelligence, the Gestapo, the Sicherheitsdienst, or Nazi Germany's military intelligence and counterintelligence agency, the Abwehr.

All the details of Operation Mantilla were known by the Mossad L'Aliyah Bet office in Istanbul, run by Teddy Kollek, who would later become a renowned, colorful, long-serving mayor of Jerusalem. David Ben-Gurion had stationed Kollek in Turkey throughout the war because it was the most crucial nation for the Yishuv's efforts to rescue Jews, close enough to Europe that escaping refugees could be smuggled by ship across the Black Sea into Turkish waters, then overland by train and on foot into Palestine. Unlike Nazi-occupied countries, Turkey's neutrality made it relatively easy for the Mossad L'Aliyah Bet to operate openly. Wartime Istanbul had also become the hub of a wide collection of anti-Nazi refugees.

One such refugee, working for both the OSS and SOE, was code-named Agent Dogwood, and by early 1943, he'd been introduced to Teddy Kollek. The Dogwood Chain, as it became known, was a major network of espionage agents, couriers, and smugglers.

But who was the mysterious Agent Dogwood?

He turned out to be a thirty-nine-year-old Czech-born Jew named Alfred Schwarz who'd studied psychology and philosophy in Prague and Vienna before becoming a successful—if shady—businessman in Istanbul. The OSS had been paying him handsomely to be its chief intelligence expert on Central Europe. Agent Dogwood claimed to have connections with anti-Nazi members of the Abwehr, but according to the Israeli historian Tuvia Friling, he'd been feeding his OSS handlers "reams of intelligence, most of it planted by the Germans. He never revealed his sources"; in communications, Agent Dogwood always referred to them as his "flowers"—"merely assigning them codenames, making the intelligence he provided impossible to verify."

Through the Dogwood Chain, the OSS and SOE received false reports about German troop movements, industrial resources, and strategic targets. The bogus information planted by Nazi counterintelligence misdirected many Allied operations, most crucially bombing raids and parachute drops flown by both the RAF and USAAF. Through Agent Dogwood, one of the most prolific and damaging double agents of the Second World War, the Nazis could lead the Allies to attack virtually any target of their choosing and be lying in wait. An advance tip from the Dogwood Chain was precisely the reason that Lyova Gukowsky and Arie Fichman came under machine-gun fire as they parachuted into Romania.

It would be over a year before the OSS, SOE, MI9, and Mossad L'Aliyah Bet would learn the truth about Agent Dogwood. But by then the damage had been done.

13

December 1943
Kibbutz Ramat Hakovesh, Mandatory Palestine

In the first week of December, Hannah hopped on a public bus going from Caesarea to Tel Aviv, arriving at the bustling Central Bus Station in the Levinsky Market neighborhood in the south of the city. There, she transferred to another bus that would take her to Kibbutz Ramat Hakovesh. It was a seemingly routine, if rather bumpy, forty-minute ride to the kibbutz northeast of Tel Aviv, but it was her first journey into the dangerous underground world of covert training centers with caches of illegal weapons.

At that time in Mandatory Palestine, there was an almost farcical disconnect between the various branches of British military authority. Throughout 1943 and 1944, in terms of policy, the left hand didn't have a clue what the right hand was doing. Even as Colonel Simonds and his MI9 team were actively recruiting Palmach volunteers to enlist in the RAF and help rescue downed Allied airmen, the British Army and Palestine Police Force were conducting raids, almost all of which went unreported in the press, looking to crush the Palmach and seize its weaponry.

Only three weeks earlier, on November 16, 1943, Ramat Hakovesh had been the scene of a massive and violent confrontation between the British military and members of the Palmach. It had begun on November 14 when, during a random inspection of a bus, British soldiers had discovered three submachine guns hidden in a sack fastened to the roof. The soldiers had begun to question two young men, Uri Ariav and Elkana Gali, who claimed to be kibbutzniks from Ramat Hakovesh but were in fact commanders of the Palmach, secretly training underground fighters on the kibbutz. After arresting both men, two days later, the British conducted a dawn raid of the kibbutz on the pretext of searching for "deserters from Anders' Army"—the Polish armed forces in the east, then under the British Middle East Command and stationed in Palestine.

The British burst through the kibbutz gates with a battalion of soldiers and hundreds of policemen. An RAF surveillance plane circled overhead. The kibbutz members initially resisted—young women, men, and even children pelting the British with stones—while the Palmach commanders wisely chose not to shoot it out when faced with the overwhelming firepower of the hundreds of British troops.

During the daylong search, the British could find no cache of guns and managed to confiscate only three of the Palmach's hand grenades. In a wild melee, one kibbutznik named Shmuel Wolynetz was struck viciously in the head. After lying unconscious for five days, he died in the British government hospital in Nablus. Fourteen other kibbutz members were wounded, and thirty-five were taken into custody.

On November 18, *Davar* boldly broke British press censorship laws by running a front-page story headlined "Police Brutality at Kibbutz!" The British responded by shutting down *Davar,* and in solidarity all other Jewish newspapers stopped publication for eleven days. On November 19, hundreds of Jews, including David Ben-Gurion, Moshe Shertok, and Golda Meir, streamed into Ramat Hakovesh to show their support.

The embers of the November 16 firestorm were still smoldering when Hannah arrived at Ramat Hakovesh in early December. For the Palmach, covert training was continuing at full throttle, just as it had before the raid. Like the other Palmach volunteers, Hannah began her military career by "hiding in plain sight"—playing the role of an eager agricultural worker on the kibbutz before embarking on thirty-seven days and twenty nights of rigorous basic training. During that time, she learned the Palmach's ambush and infiltration techniques, such as how to secure a perimeter, and the hit-and-run tactics of guerrilla warfare. In bruising unarmed combat drills, she was taught judo throws, jujitsu choke holds, boxing hooks and crosses, and karate kicks and sweeps. The Palmach instructors trained her in the lethal use of various knives and in a homegrown stick-fighting technique known as *kapap*—an abbreviation of *krav panim el panim* (fighting face-to-face.)

Hannah's only experience with a gun had been carrying the standard Lee-Enfield bolt-action rifle during guard duty at Sdot Yam while patrolling the kibbutz perimeter. But she'd never had occasion to fire it, nor had she been properly trained in firearms. The Palmach couldn't afford to be choosy about their guns, most of which were smuggled, pilfered, or bought on the black market. Many were relics from the First World War—or earlier. The large armory at Ramat Hakovesh—which the British raid had been unable to discover—was a motley assortment of Sten guns, Thompson submachine guns, Lee-Enfield rifles, and an assortment of sidearms, ranging from Colt .45 and Webley .38 revolvers to 9mm Beretta pistols.

Hannah learned through repetition how to reload firearms rapidly under time pressure and the paramount importance of cleaning her gun, especially in the wintry, muddy field conditions in which she would soon find herself.

As training progressed, she was glad to learn that she wasn't the only young woman who'd volunteered for the mission. Many potential candidates didn't survive the grueling tryouts, but in the end, two female Palmachniks made the cut: Surika Braverman from Kibbutz Shamir and Haviva Reik from Kibbutz Maanit.

Both women, who were slightly older than Hannah, had been members of the Palmach for over a year and were now squad commanders. Born in Botoşani, Romania, in 1918, Surika Braverman had made *aliyah* in 1938 and, like Hannah, had first enrolled in a girls' agricultural school specializing in dairy farming. She'd been recruited by the Palmach in 1942, joining Platoon B, and by 1943 had completed the commanders' course. As a volunteer for the rescue mission, MI9 assigned her to the Romanian infiltration team. In her khaki drill uniform, Surika was a petite, soft-spoken, striking soldier; Colonel Tony Simonds teasingly referred to her as "The Blonde Bombshell."

Haviva Reik, from Kibbutz Maanit, was neither a blonde nor a bombshell. She considered herself plain looking—neither pretty nor ugly but something in between. Her physique was strong and stocky, but her bright eyes and warm laugh seemed to charm every young man she met. Back in Banská Bystrica, a small city in central Czechoslovakia, everyone knew young Marta Reik—her given name—simply as "the girl on the motorcycle." She was an adventurous, seemingly fearless young woman—she wore her dark hair in a bob and was considered a free-spirited tomboy. In the 1930s, people rarely saw young women riding motorcycles in major cities such as Prague, Paris, or Budapest, let alone a small Czechoslovakian town such as Banská Bystrica. Passersby would stand and gawk as Haviva roared through town on her prized Jawa 175, a popular lightweight Czech-made motorcycle.

Haviva didn't come from a privileged, well-educated family as Hannah did. Her parents were lower middle class, and money was always tight. She needed to contribute by working after-school jobs. She enrolled in a vocational school and studied bookkeeping, shorthand, typing, and accounting, neither harboring literary ambitions nor planning to attend university. At a meeting of Hashomer Hatzair, she met a tall, blond, lantern-jawed Czechoslovakian Jew named Aharon Martinović. They fell in love and were married in a civil ceremony in April 1938.

Haviva and Aharon made *aliyah* in December 1939 and became members of Kibbutz Maanit, a new settlement about twenty kilometers east of Kibbutz Sdot Yam. But their marriage was rocky, and upon arriving at Kibbutz Maanit, they decided to separate, though they never officially divorced.

After Aharon left the kibbutz, Haviva had several serious romantic and sexual relationships. There was nothing scandalous about it; the secular left-wing kibbutz culture wholly embraced the idea of "free love," or at least equal standards of sexual freedom for both men and women, long before they were the norm in much of Europe and North America.

As far as the kibbutz was concerned, as long as Haviva was being a good socialist and Zionist, contributing to the collective good of the settlement, she could have as many lovers as she chose. What *did* become a problem for Haviva was her passionate affair with Zvi Arison, a young man from one of the Yishuv's wealthiest families. The Arisons were Romanian Jews, cofounders of Zikhron Yaakov, a prosperous town just south of Haifa. They owned expansive fruit orchards, as well as a number of very successful businesses in Jerusalem and Tel Aviv.

Zvi Arison lived in the luxurious home of his older brother in Tel Aviv near Rothschild Boulevard. In the winter, he could afford to travel to Switzerland for skiing vacations and in the summer fly to the French Riviera for a week of yachting. He asked Haviva to leave the kibbutz and join him on his worldwide adventures.

"They were very much in love," said Surika Braverman. In early 1942, after Haviva had separated from her husband, Zvi asked Haviva to marry him. That created quite a scandal within the Kibbutz Maanit community. "Haviva was ostracized by her kibbutz," Surika recalled. "She was told that she would need to choose between the Movement and her capitalist boyfriend."*

For Haviva, it was not a difficult decision: She flatly turned down Zvi's proposal, broke off with him, and chose the kibbutznik life. In 1942—personally recruited by Yitzhak Sadeh—she became one of the first women to enlist in the Palmach.

Hannah Senesh, Haviva Reik, and Surika Braverman were all products of Sadeh's philosophy of gender equality in the military, his insistence on frontline combat service for women, a concept many decades ahead of its time. Sadeh prioritized fighting spirit and intelligence over physical strength. He insisted on equal training for male and female recruits—with no exceptions. That philosophy shaped the culture of the Palmach and later the Israel Defense Forces. Women served as platoon commanders, intelligence officers, and frontline infantry.

The Old Man insisted that the women of the Palmach be given all the necessary tools and training they needed to enter combat; he was confident that they'd prove themselves under fire, much like the women soldiers of the Red Army and the female Partisans fighting against the Nazis in the forests of eastern Europe and the mountains of Yugoslavia.

At its peak, more than 30 percent of the Palmach's fighters were women. But Sadeh's philosophy was more nuanced than mere gender equality; he argued that women often possessed unique skills and qualities that many men lacked—some excelled as sharpshooters or demolitions experts, others

*The Arison family would later become one of the most prominent families of billionaires in Israel. Shari Arison, born in 1957 in New York City, is a financier and philanthropist, and in 2007, *Forbes* ranked her the "richest woman in the Middle East." Her older brother, Micky Arison, is today the owner of the NBA's Miami Heat and chairman of Carnival Corporation, the world's largest cruise operator.

as radio operators, cryptographers, and cryptologists—and therefore each woman in a Palmach unit should be directed to a military specialization according to her individual physical and mental abilities.

On a wet and windy December morning at the RAF air base at Ramat David, less than three kilometers from the Agricultural School for Girls at Nahalal, Hannah met her fellow paratrooper trainees. Built by the British in 1942, Ramat David Airbase was run by RAF staff, though the Palmach volunteer parachutists were given relatively free rein to learn their jump skills.

Hannah was issued a jumpsuit and a steel helmet lined with thick rubber. The typical twenty-one-day jump course was compressed into ten days. In order to graduate, she needed to complete five daylight jumps from a Douglas DC-3 Dakota transport plane and one nighttime jump from a Vickers Wellington bomber. The first day began with a six-kilometer run in boots and full parachute gear. The instructors were Nepalese—members of the Brigade of Gurkhas—overseen by a stern RAF major. For several days, the Gurkha drill sergeant, wielding a thin stick, put Hannah through obstacle courses, somersaults, and jumps from the roofs of one-story and three-story buildings in a parachute harness. Before every practice jump the sergeant shouted at them, "Feet together! *Never* open your knees!"

On the morning of her first jump, Hannah strapped herself into the harness, the instructor double-checking to see that she'd done it properly. The DC-3 began its taxi and ascent. In moments she could see the Jezreel Valley, a magnificent patchwork—almost like a rolling quilt—with brown squares of plowed fields, light green squares of orange groves, dark green splotches of pine woods. She gazed at the unique circular design of Moshav Nahalal, something of a geometric marvel from the air, and the campus of the Agricultural School for Girls, each familiar building looking to her like a tiny toy house.

The aircraft circled over the Jezreel Valley, and suddenly the instructor's voice cut through the roar of the engines: "Attention!"

The red light turned green. Hannah needed to jump the moment the instructor shouted "Go!"—not a second before, not a second after. She moved closer to the wide hatch and peered down at the fields in the valley. She found, to her surprise, that she wasn't the least bit frightened.

She leapt from the hatch naturally, relaxed, enjoying the exhilaration of drifting and gliding with the wind, floating for a few minutes between Heaven and Earth.

At the end of December 1943, Hannah finally received the news for which she'd so long been waiting: She had been officially accepted as a volunteer in the British military. In Tel Aviv, she was issued a smart blue-gray uniform of the RAF's Women's Auxiliary Air Force. Her rank was Aircraftwoman Second Class, equivalent to a private in the US Army Air Forces.

Above the uniform's left chest pocket, finely embroidered on brown felt, was the RAF Paratroopers' insignia: two sky blue wings flanking a white parachutist. If Hannah passed MI9's A Force Signals School course in Cairo—and she was confident she would—she'd be issued the "fist-and-lighnting" shoulder badge of a radio operator.

For the first time she fully felt like a soldier, especially when she held the round fiber disc dog tag stamped with serial number 2992382.

From now on, in written communications, she'd no longer be Hannah. The Palmach leadership had ordered that the parachutists not divulge their real names to the British rank and file. For her Palmach code name, she'd chosen a character from a passage she'd always liked in the Book of Genesis, about the young Egyptian maidservant to Abraham's wife, Sarah, whose cruelty makes the young girl flee into the Negev. Found by the Angel of the Lord near a fountain in the desert, she finds out that she's pregnant with Abraham's son Ishmael. The lonely girl. The lost girl. The runaway girl whose name means "flight." The slave girl who's redeemed, who speaks directly to the Lord, who is told that she must return home: Hagar.

14

December 1943
Allenby Street, Tel Aviv

The Histradut labor union headquarters on Tel Aviv's Allenby Street, which also housed the offices of *Davar* newspaper, was bustling and chaotic, reeking of sweat and printer's ink. The nonstop frenetic activity in the place provided a perfect cover for the parachutists to meet one another and their handlers in the Palmach.

The staff of the Mossad L'Aliyah Bet were housed in three small, crowded rooms on the top floor of the Histadrut building. As the Yishuv parachutists' mission developed, the Jewish Agency created a covert committee code-named Plan Het (Infiltration Committee), *het* being the first letter in the Hebrew word *hadira* (infiltration). The committee met in the same cramped offices on the Histradut building's top floor.

Plan Het needed an experienced "fixer," a powerful personality who could serve as a liaison between the British officers and the Yishuv parachutists. David Ben-Gurion realized that there was only one person suited for the job. Enzo Sereni was already a legend in the Yishuv—a diminutive man of great erudition and courage, a natural organizer whom Ben-Gurion envisioned playing a key political role in the future independent Jewish state. Enzo was indefatigable, fast talking, often manic seeming, something of an Italian Jewish whirling dervish.

One of the founders of Kibbutz Givat Brenner, Enzo held a doctorate in philosophy and had already carried out numerous dangerous operations for the Yishuv. In spring 1942, he'd been sent as an undercover agent to Baghdad in response to the Farhud—the 1941 pogrom in which Iraq's pro-Nazi government unleashed mobs that killed several hundred Jews and destroyed their homes and businesses. Enzo established a smuggling network that operated for more than a decade, until almost all of Iraq's 135,000 Jews emigrated to Mandatory Palestine and later to the State of Israel.

Since childhood, Enzo had known with certainty that he was going to be a man of letters. Early in life, he'd conceived a sweeping multigenerational *romanzo* about his remarkable Roman Jewish family, but according to Ruth Bondy, his biographer, instead of writing the great novel that he had always planned, "he lived it stormily" in the forty years of his action-filled life.

He hailed from one of the most prominent and oldest Jewish families in Italy. His father, Samuele Sereni, had for years been the personal physician to King Victor Emmanuel III as well as the doctor attached to the royal court. Enzo had grown up in a large house on Via Cavour in the heart of the old Jewish Ghetto, imbued from his earliest years with the sense that he and his two brothers "were destined for greatness," and all of them, each in his way, had met those lofty expectations. Enzo's older brother, Enrico, became a brilliant neurobiologist and professor of physiology (he died in a freak carbon monoxide poisoning accident while in the bath at the age of thirty), and Emilio, the youngest of the brothers, became a leader in the Italian Communist Party, as well as a politician, historian, author, and one of the drafters of the postwar Italian Republic's first constitution.

The Serenis had been living in Rome for centuries, possibly from the beginning of the Jewish settlement on the banks of the Tiber, even before the destruction of the Second Temple in Jerusalem in AD 70. Enzo became a committed Zionist in 1917, at age twelve. When he was studying for his bar mitzvah, he began engaging in long discussions with Rabbi Angelo-Raphael Chaim Sacerdoti, the chief rabbi of Rome, and was soon swept up in the fervor of Zionist activity in the city. On November 2, 1917, just as Enzo was studying his Torah *parsha* for his formal passage into manhood, British Foreign Secretary Arthur Balfour wrote a letter to Lord Rothschild, the de facto leader of the Jewish community in Great Britain, containing a declaration that sent joyous shock waves through Jewish communities worldwide:

His Majesty's Government view with favour the establishment in Palestine of a national home for the Jewish people, and will use their best endeavours to facilitate the achievement of this object.

Enzo was so excited after reading the Balfour Declaration that he was inspired to write a poem about an unnamed Jew in exile yearning for the lost Homeland:

Do not despair. The day will come and you will see again
The liberated hills of Zion, the Temple rebuilt,
And a free man you will sing to your native air
The song of the exile longing for his Homeland.

Upon finishing his university studies in philosophy in 1927, Enzo and his wife, Ada, left for Eretz Israel, where he worked in the citrus plantations at Rehovot, then joined the group of *chalutzim* at Kibbutz Ha-Meuchad that soon founded Givat Brenner, one of the largest kibbutzim in Israel today.

A gifted, persuasive orator in several languages, Enzo had been dispatched by Ben-Gurion and the Jewish Agency to Weimar Germany in 1932, just as the Nazi Party was growing in strength and its Brownshirts were attacking the Jewish community with impunity. Having served as an officer in the Royal Italian Army and been an eyewitness to Mussolini's rise in the 1920s, Enzo had no doubt that Hitler would soon seize absolute power in Germany.

In the face of great danger, Enzo and Ada moved to Berlin and made their home in a makeshift commune in a large apartment on Alexanderstrasse, in the heart of the workers' quarter. The young Zionists in Berlin who first met Enzo didn't know what to make of him: five feet one, bespectacled, often carrying a stack of books or newspapers under his arm, and wearing a raincoat that trailed down to his ankles and a strange cap far too large for his head.

The members of that tiny German Jewish Zionist community were culturally elitist; they had no patience for anyone who wasn't well versed in Dadaism and Cubism, who hadn't read Søren Kierkegaard, Franz Kafka, and Thomas Mann. Their cultural snobbery might have intimidated the previous Zionist emissaries they'd met, mainly Yiddish speakers from Poland and Lithuania.

Not Enzo Sereni; he went to galleries and museums to see the paintings of Max Beckmann, George Grosz, and Otto Dix and was soon conducting "seminars on the German spiritual giants—Hegel, Kant and Schopenhauer."

In a matter of months, Enzo had organized Berlin's threatened Jewish community, convincing hundreds of young Zionists to make *aliyah* to Mandatory Palestine, and set up a sophisticated clandestine financial network to transfer Jewish capital out of Germany before it could be seized by the Nazis. By 1939, largely due to Enzo's efforts, an estimated $25 million of German Jewish capital ($450 million in 2025 US currency) had been transferred or smuggled out of the Third Reich, only a third of it by official channels.

In 1943, while serving as one of the leaders of Kibbutz Givat Brenner and completing his first book about the origins of Italian fascism, Enzo was also fully engaged in the war effort. He made regular radio broadcasts to Italy on behalf of the Allies and edited an anti-Fascist newspaper that was read by thousands of Italian soldiers and airmen in Allied POW camps.

Now, at Ben-Gurion's insistence, he agreed to accompany the Yishuv parachutists to the third phase of their training in Cairo and then ultimately to the Bari airfield, where in addition to smoothing communications between the British authorities and the Jewish volunteers, he could easily address any problems that might arise with local Italians in his mother tongue.

When he first met Hannah at the Histradut building and learned of her Palmach code name, Enzo smiled. "Hagar—like my own girl." He explained that Hagar was the name of his youngest child, his fifteen-year-old daughter living at Givat Brenner. Hagar was a powerful name, Enzo said, one that he'd carefully chosen because it symbolized the relatedness of the two sons of Abraham, Isaac and Ishmael—the ineluctable brotherhood of Jews and Arabs.

15

On a bleak and rainy winter night, Hannah was reading at one of the tables in the tiny room on the top floor of the Histradut building when she saw a young infantryman in a British Army uniform bound up the stairs.

Three years older than Hannah, born Emil Nussbacher in 1918, in the city of Cluj in Austria-Hungary (now Romania), he had made *aliyah* in 1939, only a few months prior to Hannah. Back in Hungary they'd been active in the same youth Socialist Zionist movement, Hashomer Hatzair.

Hebraicizing his name—he became Yoel Palgi—he joined Kibbutz Afikim, just south of the Sea of Galilee. When the war broke out, he volunteered for the British infantry and by 1943 was a sergeant in the Royal East Kent Regiment (known as "The Buffs") and stationed in the western Sahara Desert.

Palgi was one of eleven thousand Palestinian Jews who enlisted in the British Army during 1941; ultimately, thirty thousand Jewish volunteers from Mandatory Palestine would serve in the British armed forces during the Second World War. For two and a half years he had, as he put it, "bounced around the Western Desert" in the wake of the Desert Fox and his Afrika Korps.

While on leave, driving up from Libya, he stopped in Cairo to see Yonah Rosen and Peretz Goldstein; the three were friends from their youth movement days back in Hungary, all born and raised in the Transylvanian city of Cluj. Palgi had heard whispers that Rosen and Goldstein had volunteered from the ranks of the Palmach for some top secret British mission behind enemy lines. When they had met briefly in Cairo, Rosen had given Palgi a letter to hand deliver as soon as he got to Tel Aviv. Now, amid the clattering of typewriters and the guttural Hebrew shouts of editors at reporters, Palgi climbed the narrow stairway to the top, where he found a slim girl in a Royal Air Force uniform sitting cross-legged in the dusk-shadowed light. "Excuse me," he said in English. "I'm looking for Zvi."

"He'll be back soon."

Palgi lit a Lucky Strike and, through the curling plume of blue smoke, glanced in her direction. She was captivating, no doubt, her beauty residing mostly in her smile. But he also noticed her long, well-shaped legs, the waves of her light brown hair, and the way the blue-gray of her Royal Air Force uniform enhanced the striking lighter blue of her eyes.

Zvi Yehieli, a small man in his midforties, entered the room and Palgi handed him the letter from Yonah Rosen. Yehieli ripped open the envelope, scanned the contents, then called out to Palgi, who was already turning for the staircase, "Wait, don't run off. When're you going back to Egypt?"

"Two weeks."

"You speak Hungarian?"

"It's my mother tongue."

Hannah, only feet away, couldn't keep herself from inconspicuously eavesdropping. Yehieli, pulling Palgi closer so they could lower their voices, asked if he was ready to put in for a transfer from the British Army and take on a dangerous job involving the Royal Air Force.

At the word *dangerous*, Palgi beamed. After over two years in the infantry, he'd given up waiting to see some frontline action. Being a sergeant in a supply company, driving a water truck for hundreds of kilometers under the Saharan sun, he wasn't exactly fulfilling his notions of soldierly heroism—nor contributing much, in his opinion, to Hitler's downfall. It certainly wasn't the reason he had rushed to enlist in the British Army back in 1941.

He felt much as Hannah did, needing to escape from the monotony of nine-hour shifts washing socks, scrubbing floors, or standing guard duty.

The envelope he had hand-delivered contained a letter of recommendation from Yonah Rosen, telling Zvi Yehieli that Palgi, as an experienced soldier, would be perfect for the Hungarian infiltration team. Yehieli quickly gave

Palgi all the crucial details and told him he needed to report to Ramat David Airbase for parachute training.

Hannah stopped eavesdropping and jumped to her feet. "Wait, you're *Yoel*?"

Palgi paused. "And you must be Hannah?" Neither waited for an answer before clasping hands. The Hungarian community on the kibbutzim in the north was tiny enough that by now they'd heard many wildly colorful stories about each other. Some of them were even true. Yonah Rosen, Palgi's close friend since childhood, was the common link, having recruited them both.

Hannah asked if Palgi was spending a few hours in Tel Aviv.

"No, I just found out I've got to go straight to Ramat David," he said. "Tomorrow I'm going to jump."

"Oh, I've done my jump training already," Hannah said, sensing his nervousness. "Listen, it's nothing—really. You go up in the plane, jump, and in no time you're right back on the ground." After a thoughtful pause, as if reliving the moment, she added, "I'll never forget how beautiful Nahalal looked from the air."

She said it offhandedly, as if describing the scrambled eggs and toast she'd had for breakfast. Palgi now felt sheepish. If that young, slim, blue-eyed girl could learn to jump out of a plane at two thousand feet, why the hell was *he* worrying?

A car horn honked loudly and impatiently below: Palgi's driver was waiting on Allenby Street. As he ran downstairs and out into the rain, Palgi started laughing silently. He figured that Hannah was a pretty good actress. She'd been scared when making that first jump at Ramat David—she *must* have been—and was only putting on a brave face for his benefit. Those acting skills should serve her well when she jumped undercover behind enemy lines.

16

December 1943
Tel Aviv

Out of more than 250 volunteers for the parachutists' rescue mission, only 37 were selected; 32 would ultimately jump into occupied Europe, and 5 others would reach their destinations either by plane or by ship.

Hannah waited with undisguised impatience and irritation for further orders from MI9 in Tel Aviv. She walked the city's rain-slicked streets, now crowded with soldiers, sailors, and airmen—not only British, but Canadian, Australian, New Zealander, South African, Indian, French, Polish, Czech, and Dutch. Store windows throughout Tel Aviv posted signs in many foreign languages trying to lure those off-duty servicemen inside: "Polish spoken here." "French spoken here." "Dutch spoken here."

Hannah *hated* Tel Aviv. She recognized its seaside beauty, of course, the aesthetic charm of its thousands of white Bauhaus buildings. Yes, there was the Art Deco Mograbi Cinema on Allenby Street showing the latest Hollywood blockbusters; the Tel Aviv Museum of Art on Rothschild Boulevard, with its recent exhibition of works by Pablo Picasso, Georges Braque, and Juan Gris; the Palestine Symphony Orchestra, where Leonard Bernstein would conduct a program of Robert Schumann, Richard Strauss, and Richard Wagner in 1947.

For Hannah it was too reminiscent of the vibrant cultural life she'd left behind in Budapest. She'd made *aliyah* in 1939 to become one of the *chalutzim*—to study agriculture and do physical labor on the kibbutz.

Even if that vision had turned out to be something of a mirage, even if it meant—as she'd vividly illustrated with a self-deprecating drawing in one of her letters—standing hip deep in a mound of cow dung, she was still a true believer.

Binyan ha'aretz: Building up the Land. That wasn't merely a slogan to Hannah; it had become her entire life. The sophisticates chattering about Marc Chagall or Mies van der Rohe through wisps of cigarette smoke in a sidewalk café on Rothschild Boulevard—that was her past self, her Budapest self. A world once so familiar to Hannah now seemed utterly alien.

Still, as much as she disliked waiting in Tel Aviv, she had come to love the camaraderie that was fast developing among the mission's volunteers, especially the many hours she spent lounging on the roof of the Histradut building, having heart-to-heart conversations with Yoel Palgi, Dov Berger, and Yeshayahu Trachtenberg, better known as Shaike Dan.

They continued to receive lectures and background briefings from British Intelligence's so-called experts. What concerned them most was how they were going to infiltrate their destination countries. Hannah, Palgi, and the other members of their infiltration team were eager to be dropped directly into Hungary. Palgi kept advocating for a nighttime jump close to Lake Balaton. But the British refused on the grounds that the risks were too great. They would not be doing another blind jump into Axis-held territory, as had been tried, disastrously, with Operation Mantilla. In Hungary, there were no safe drop zones controlled by the anti-fascist underground. Indeed, as far as MI9 could tell, there *was* no Hungarian anti-fascist underground.

In Hannah's opinion, the only valuable briefing was given by a British infantryman named Reuven Dafni. Dafni was tall and strongly built and dressed in the khaki uniform of a British warrant officer. So many people said he looked like the movie star Gary Cooper that it later became his operational code name: Agent Gary. He'd been born Ruben Kandt in 1913 in Zagreb, in the Croatia-Slavonia region of the Austro-Hungarian Empire. In 1936, he had emigrated to Mandatory Palestine and become one of the founders of Kibbutz Ein Gev on the eastern shore of the Sea of Galilee. In 1940, he had enlisted in the British Army, becoming an infantryman. He'd fought in the Greek campaign and the Battle of Crete. During the grueling Desert Campaign, he'd been awarded the Africa Star medal for his efforts chasing Rommel's Afrika

Korps out of Egypt, into Tunisia, and ultimately back across the Mediterranean.

Dafni's briefing was about the complex, ever-changing situation in Yugoslavia. He explained to the other volunteers that there wasn't anything that could truly be called Tito's "Partisan territory." On an unfurled table-sized map, he pointed at one section of Slovenia, where a potential parachute jump could be made—but only on a clear, moonlit night.

After sunset these hills belonged to the Partisans, Reuven told them, gesturing with the tip of his pencil. But at sunrise, they belonged to the Nazis.

One by one, first in Tel Aviv and later in Cairo, Colonel Simonds began to personally meet the volunteer parachutists, the thirty-odd men and three women who'd made the final cut. In many cases, he didn't learn their real names—he frankly didn't *want* to know their real names. Fearing that British Intelligence would open files on them, the Jewish Agency had provided all the volunteers with aliases and convincing matching identity papers. "We, too, did not want to complicate matters for their relatives still alive in the occupied countries," Simonds said later. "When the lads and young women reported to me, I could not help but notice the innocence in their eyes. They were all young. Not even Anglophiles. I was especially impressed by their enthusiasm, their faith, and most of all by their courage. They were prepared to sacrifice their own lives for the goal—the rescue of Jews."

If the parachutists needed to conceal information about their real identities from British Intelligence, Simonds, for his part, felt duty bound to withhold at least one hard truth from his young volunteers: "I could not reveal to them what I knew: that the chance of succeeding in the mission and remaining alive was one in ten."

17

January–February 1944
Mandatory Palestine

On January 4, 1944, during her final trip back to Kibbutz Sdot Yam, Hannah had the opportunity to put her affairs into order. Colonel Simonds may not have expressly said so, but Hannah was fully aware that there was a very high probability that she'd never return. For her own peace of mind, perhaps even for posterity, she decided to copy out all her poems neatly and in chronological order in a fresh notebook with numbered pages.

She gave the book a Hebrew title, *Lelo Safa* (Without Language), then signed the cover "Hagar."

There was only one person in Eretz Israel to whom she dared entrust the book: her former classmate at the Agricultural School for Girls at Nahalal, Miryam Pergament—who also went by the name Miryam Yitzhak—the only friend she'd made during her time living in Eretz Israel.

For nearly two years at Kibbutz Sdot Yam, Hannah had never felt accepted by the other members—yes, she viewed them as "comrades" and as fellow pioneers, struggling for the same aims in the Movement. But she had always sensed a coldness toward and distrust of her. "Either they think I'm very naive or take me for a chatterbox who arrogantly talks big about things she can never realize," she wrote. "It seems that estimations of my character pass through three phases: The first impression is very good—but entirely *wrong*. In this one I include all superficial acquaintanceships and unwanted visitors.

In the second phase the impression takes a turn for the worse; and in the third phase they get to know me as I really am."

But very few people in her twenty-two years, either in Hungary or in Eretz Israel, had ever seen Hannah drop her guard, remove the facade of glib joviality or the second layer of seemingly flippant arrogance, to reach the third phase: the true Hannah. "Here in the Land only Miryam *really* knows me," she wrote.

On the first page of her meticulously recopied book of poems she added a dedication in impeccable Hebrew script:

> *To Miryam Yitzhak, my first and dearest reader*
> *and critic.**
>
> *In true friendship,*
> *Hannah*

Then, on January 11, 1944, Hannah dashed off five sentences with a dull pencil in one of her older diaries, on page fifty-five of her nearly full fourth notebook. Her Hebrew cursive was hurried—she scratched out rather than erased the opening two words—and the lettering was not as carefully spaced on the paper as her previous entries had been.

These would be the last words she ever wrote in her diary: "This week I leave for Egypt. I'm a soldier. Concerning the circumstances of my enlistment, and my feelings in connection with it and with all that led up to it, I don't want to write. I want to believe that what I've done, and will do, is right. Time will tell the rest."

• • •

*In 2012, a previously unseen poem was discovered unexpectedly on Kibbutz Hatzor in southern Israel. Hannah wrote the Hebrew verses in Cairo on the back of a letter to Miriam. Titled "Hora to a Girl of the Exile," it conveys Hannah's years of loneliness and isolation in Palestine but also the deep, loving connection between two young women, all in the frenzied moments of a euphoric circle dance around the campfire. "Hora to a Girl of the Exile" can be found in Appendix I.

On the eve of her departure, Hannah received startling news. Her brother, Gyuri, had arrived in Haifa. Gyuri was one of a few hundred Jewish refugees who'd managed to make it to Spain and Portugal during the war. They'd boarded the 10,000-ton ship *Nyassa,* which had set sail from Portugal in January 1944, to Spain, where another four hundred Jewish refugees—one of whom was Gyuri—had boarded. Finally, in February 1944, the *Nyassa* reached the port of Haifa.

Hannah had no idea what travails her brother had been through since she'd last seen him before the war. His textile design studies in Lyons had been interrupted; then he'd been imprisoned by the Vichy French as a POW before managing to make a daring escape and cross the border into Spain.

British officers boarded the *Nyassa* in Haifa harbor and started to process the new arrivals' papers. Upon disembarking, all passengers were funneled by the British into a quarantine area, kept away from anyone who had come to meet them.

Gyuri began to make enquiries about Kibbutz Sdot Yam. Within minutes he was introduced to a burly Jewish longshoreman who turned out to be a member of the kibbutz and offered to tell Hannah that same evening of his safe arrival.

All the would-be immigrants and refugees were transferred under strict escort to Atlit, a secure transit camp behind a barbed-wire fence just south of Haifa. British Intelligence officers from MI6 did extensive screenings, convinced that the Nazis were using both legal and illegal transports to infiltrate Palestine with spies. The process of debriefing could take anywhere from one to two weeks. Gyuri was frustrated, finding himself in Eretz Israel and being greeted with the kind of suspicion he'd experienced in Vichy France and Franco's Spain.

The grapevine in the Yishuv worked quickly; by that evening, the longshoreman had found Hannah in Tel Aviv. She dashed off a welcome card and said she hoped to see her brother the next day.

Gyuri was sitting in the barracks the following morning when a young British captain told him to accompany him to the guardhouse. Under the blinding Mediterranean sun, the captain yanked open an unpainted wooden door, and they entered a small, dark room; before Gyuri could get his bearings, a young woman flew into his arms and squeezed him in a tight embrace. They were both simultaneously laughing and crying. Words began to pour out of Gyuri almost incoherently in Hungarian. Hannah continued to hold him close, as if to make up for the pent-up emotions of the lost years.

When she at last released the hug, Gyuri got a full look at his sister, dressed in a blue British uniform with a small PALESTINE patch on the shoulder and the felt-backed embroidered insignia of a winged parachutist on her left chest. "What's this mean?" he asked in Hungarian.

"Darling, speak in English," Hannah said gently. The British Army captain chaperoning them kept his eyes on the pages of his book but was clearly eavesdropping. Hannah correctly deduced that he was with MI6—the British Secret Intelligence Service. He was monitoring everything they said in case Gyuri was indeed a Nazi espionage agent. "I'm leaving the country in two days, Gyuri. I'm going for training in Egypt. I hope to be back soon."

Gyuri shook his head. "But you've always been a pacifist." He was careful now to use only English.

"I'm with the Women's Auxiliary Air Force. We can't talk now, but believe me, I'm doing everything I can to get a few private hours for the two of us before I've got to leave." She flashed her smile at the British captain. "And it's going to work, isn't it, sir?"

The captain shrugged indifferently. "The rules are very strict here," he muttered. "And I think it's time you two wrap it up."

Hannah gently kissed her brother again before she left.

The next day, a group of representatives from the Jewish Agency came to pick up Gyuri. "Come with me," barked one of the strangers, dressed like a shabby businessman in a somewhat battered gray fedora. Gyuri followed him to an old taxi waiting out of view, already filled with other civilians. They squeezed him into the middle of the back seat. One of them gave his own fedora to Gyuri and forced him to put it on his head, pulling down its brim as the taxi sped toward the gate.

The guard gave them a cursory wave. The taxi sped along the coastal road between Haifa and Tel Aviv. After about half an hour, one of the Jewish Agency officials in the front seat addressed Gyuri in heavily accented English. "Look! A couple of miles off this road is Caesarea, the ancient Roman ruins. If these sand dunes weren't so high, you might see Sdot Yam, the kibbutz your sister is building."

Gyuri looked toward the ocean and saw nothing but mountains of sand, seagulls soaring in circles, massive boulders, and a few pathetically wiry shrubs. He'd read how virtually the whole of Palestine had been sand dunes, arid wilderness, or mosquito-infested swamps, but as they drove south, he marveled at how much had been done to transform Eretz Israel into green livable space—but also how much still needed to be done.

The taxi arrived in Tel Aviv and, screeching to a stop, dropped Gyuri off in front of an Art Deco hotel near the seafront. The decor in the lobby was sleek, the marble floor spotless and gleaming. Hannah was waiting anxiously in a plush royal blue armchair. In Hebrew she thanked the Jewish Agency operative for taking Gyuri out of the detention camp.

Finally, brother and sister could be alone and relaxed and speak in Hungarian, trying rapidly to catch up on the missing years, which in Hannah's case—she calculated—amounted to roughly a quarter of her life.

Gyuri didn't press Hannah for information; she made it clear that she was forbidden to talk in any specific way about her mission. She was allowed to mention only that she was going to Cairo for training first thing in the morning as part of—she claimed—some kind of routine "national service" obligation.

She did promise to write more details in a few weeks. Whenever Gyuri asked a question about their future lives together, Hannah smilingly deflected or spoke in saccharine generalities about the wonderful times they'd all have in Eretz Israel once their mother had escaped from Budapest and joined them and the god-awful war was over.

Shaike Dan had been nearby at the Habima Theatre, watching the hit production of S. Ansky's *The Dybbuk*, starring the great Russian-born actress Hanna Rovina. Dan marched double time into the lobby with Dov Berger, loudly reminding Hannah that they were running late for the farewell party. They hurried over to the Histradut building a few blocks away. Most of the partygoers were high-ranking Palmach officers and Yishuv leaders, including David Ben-Gurion, Moshe Shertok, Golda Meir, Berl Katznelson, and Eliyahu Golomb.

The sight of Hannah entering the room in her Royal Air Force uniform elicited cheers from the other parachutists. Though Gyuri was fluent in seven languages, Modern Hebrew wasn't one of them, and Hannah, conscious that her brother was lost amid all the fast-paced conversations, made a point to introduce him to her Hungarian-speaking *chaverim*: "Gyuri, meet Yoel Palgi, Yonah Rosen, Peretz Goldstein. They're all from Cluj."

The men joked in Hungarian that they knew everything about Gyuri—his sister virtually *never* stopped talking about him.

Hannah arranged for Gyuri to spend his first few months at Kibbutz Maagan on the Sea of Galilee, where the Hungarian *chalutzim* were building their new settlement. He would still be adrift in much of Jewish Palestine, but at Kibbutz Maagan he could at least speak Hungarian and get himself situated until he learned rudimentary Hebrew and was ready to explore the Land.

David Ben-Gurion was a towering leader of tiny stature. Stocky, he stood barely five feet tall in his black wingtip Oxfords, wispy gray hair flaring from his scalp in plumes. He raised his right hand and instantly squashed the din of the party. He kept his speech brief, urging the parachutist emissaries to make sure that the Jews of the Diaspora understood one thing: "Eretz Israel is *their* Land, their haven."

Next, the editor of *Davar*, Berl Katznelson—almost as short as Ben-Gurion, with a head of even bushier and more unkempt hair—reminded each of the volunteers of the importance of their mission, venturing as rescuers and emissaries into the heart of Hitler's Festung Europa. "If no Jews survive this war," he said, "if all our people in Europe should perish, then Eretz Israel and our enterprise here will perish too."

Golda Meir seemed overcome by the gravity of the moment. According to Yoel Palgi, she was speechless and suddenly burst into tears.

Eliyahu Golomb was yet another short Russian-born man, the same height as Katznelson. He had rough-hewn features, piercing eyes, and a broad forehead furrowed by deep lines. He nodded somberly at Hannah and the other volunteers. He was an unpretentious commander in chief of the Haganah, eschewing all regalia or military pomp. His only "uniform" was a Russian *rubashka* buttoned down the side and a pair of khaki trousers pressed to a sharp crease. The room was silent as he stepped forward. His voice was soft but resolute, his parting command to the parachutists terse: "Teach the Jews to fight."

A month earlier, on Christmas Day, when Hannah had had no idea that she'd be seeing her brother before the mission, she'd written him a letter. She'd brought it with her in the pocket of her uniform, already sealed in a stamped envelope, wondering whether to give it to him. Yes, she ultimately decided, he should have it. Gyuri followed her instructions. He didn't open the letter until Hannah was well on her way to Cairo.

December 25, 1943

Darling Gyuri!

Sometimes one writes letters one does not intend sending. . . .

Day after tomorrow I'm starting something new. Perhaps it's madness. Perhaps it's fantastic. Perhaps it's dangerous. Perhaps one in a hundred—or one in a thousand—pays with his life. Perhaps with less than his life—perhaps with more. Don't ask questions. You'll eventually know what it's about.

Gyuri, I must explain something to you. I must exonerate myself. I must prepare myself for that moment when you arrive inside the frontiers of the Land, waiting for that moment when, after six years, we will meet again, and you will ask, "Where is she?" and they'll abruptly answer, "She's not here."

Will you understand? Will you believe that this was more than a childish love of adventure, more than some youthful romanticism that drove me? Will you sense that I had no choice, that I had to do this?

There are events that render one's life meaningless, a worthless plaything, or else compel one to action, even if it means sacrificing one's life. . . .

Enough of this letter. I hope you will never receive it. But if you do, only after we have met. And if it should be otherwise, Gyuri dear, I embrace you with everlasting love.

Your sister,
Anikó

PART TWO

BETWEEN HEAVEN AND EARTH

1

February 1944
Mandatory Palestine

The bronze green Ford Fordor station wagon roared south through the Negev desert, toward Ashdod and the Gaza Strip, following the ancient Roman Via Maris, which went by the Hebrew name Derech Haavot (Way of the Patriarchs). Hannah watched as the stark Bauhaus high-rises and smaller white-washed stucco houses of south Tel Aviv gave way to the dull beiges and dusty browns of the impoverished Arab villages.

It was a twelve-hour drive from Tel Aviv to Cairo. Five parachutists in khaki uniforms had bundled into the Ford: Hannah, Dov Berger, Abba Berdichev, Yoel Palgi, and Shaike Dan. While the rest were laughing—Shaike Dan kept cracking jokes—Hannah's mind was elsewhere: her too brief reunion with her brother, her fears about her mother's safety in Budapest. She and Gyuri had left the farewell party early and had strolled the Tel Aviv beachfront in the cool winter night when they'd heard the whirring of a camera. A photographer had hurried toward them, handing out his calling card and asking for money to develop his picture. He'd clearly taken them for lovers, as they walked in a close embrace. Hannah had thought it would be nice to have the souvenir, so she'd paid the man a few shillings and given him the address of Kibbutz Maagan, to which the picture should be sent.

But in that clunky Ford station wagon, she masked her conflicting emotions, joining in with the mood of forced merriment as everyone sang and volleyed around all kinds of whimsical plans. The parachutists joked that at the end of the war, when their missions were completed, they'd all return in style: A Halifax bomber would fly over Eretz Israel, and each of them would parachute, to great fanfare, into his or her own kibbutz.

Their driver was a British sergeant named Bill, flanked by a second British noncom; neither could understand a word of the boisterous Hebrew conversations in back. "We were soldiers, arrogant and ill-mannered," Palgi later wrote. "We failed to take the Britishers' feelings into account. But Hannah didn't—she was careful to translate all our jokes for the Brits' benefit so they could laugh with us, understand our silly plans, feel involved."

After they crossed the southern border, Hannah surprised everyone by blurting out "I want to learn how to drive." As a privileged middle-class girl in Budapest, she'd never had the occasion to do so; she'd always gotten around on streetcars, buses, taxis, and trains.

The men all protested loudly, fearing that she'd endanger their lives. But Hannah said that it was as good a time as any to learn. She slid behind the wheel and listened as Bill, the British Army driver, gave her a very abbreviated lesson. The boxy Ford Fordor, weighing more than four thousand pounds, with a three-on-the-tree gearbox and an underpowered V-8 engine, was hardly the ideal vehicle for a novice driver; Hannah insisted that she could manage.

After a few hundred yards of unsteady lurching, grinding the gears once or twice, Hannah suddenly accelerated, looking secure and at ease. Palgi stared at Dan; they were both amazed at her ability to pick up everything so quickly, her dexterity with one hand on the wheel and the other on that three-on-the-tree gearbox. She kept picking up speed. All the parachutists begged her to slow down or, better still, let the British driver take over.

But Hannah ignored their entreaties, speeding on furiously through the desert. Whenever another car approached, her passengers winced, preparing for a head-on collision that never came. "Hannah was quite confident and having a wonderful time with her new toy," Palgi wrote. "We soon realized that she knew exactly what she was doing, had a firm hand on the wheel—and we all relaxed." She drove through the Sinai desert for hours on end, without tiring, and handed the wheel back to the British driver only once they'd reached the land bridge at the Suez Canal.

Two hours ahead lay the desert metropolis: the City of a Thousand Minarets.

2

February 1944
Cairo, Egypt

It's hard to imagine a location less conducive to solitary study than Cairo in the winter of 1944. The Egyptian capital was a throbbing hub of distractions—a desert metropolis, at once modern and ancient. By the winter of 1944, as Great Britain's General Headquarters, Middle East Command, Cairo had become something of a Casablanca on the Nile.

Thousands of British and Commonwealth servicemen—British, Canadians, Australians, South Africans—swarmed the streets and piled into the cafés, bars, dance halls, and casinos. For troops who'd been "slogging it out in the Sahara Desert," in the words of the British historian Artemis Cooper, "Cairo meant fleshpots or brass hats."

At the Gezira Sporting Club, officers who'd been educated at Eton and Oxford could play polo, golf, tennis, and croquet. Meantime, battle-weary, parched soldiers could grab a few drinks at Shepheard's Hotel. Randolph Churchill kept a room there during his posting to Cairo. Most nights Colonel Dudley Clarke could be found at the hotel bar, drink in hand, entertaining other officers with his collection of ribald jokes. Shepheard's was famed for its signature wartime cocktail, the Suffering Bastard, originally conceived as a hangover cure for troops weary from the Desert Campaign.*

*Bartender Joe Scialom, experimenting with a hangover remedy, came up with the Suffering Bastard: 1 ounce of London dry gin, 1 ounce of Kentucky bourbon, aromatic

Dubbed the "long bar," Shepheard's was always so crowded that it required enormous patience—or good connections—even to get a drink. During the Battle of El Alamein, Rommel is said to have boasted, "I'll be drinking champagne in the master suite at Shepheard's soon." Apocryphal or not, the quip spread within the British ranks, and before the Second Battle of El Alamein, British servicemen had added a new punchline: "Just wait until Rommel gets to Shepheard's. That'll hold him up."

After years of living the spartan lives of kibbutzniks, Hannah and the parachutists were thrust headlong into a city of wild extremes. Bill, their British driver, pulled the Ford Fordor station wagon up in front of a luxurious high-rise building in central Cairo that was to serve as their undercover headquarters for the training.

Their headquarters was located on Suleiman Pasha Square, around the corner from the famed café J. Groppi—an institution since the 1920s, known for its gourmet chocolate, pastries, cakes, and ice cream. On the ground floor of the high-rise a neon light was flashing: ROBERT'S SCHOOL OF DANCE.

For anonymity, the neighborhood was an ideal choice; the volunteers wore their British khaki drill uniforms, and their presence didn't attract too much attention. Most nights, Lucien Robert's ballroom dance studio was teeming with soldiers, airmen, officers, and professional dancing girls, for whom "hostesses" was the preferred euphemism. Mixed in were a few civilians who wanted to improve their ballroom steps. A gramophone played the latest 78s for learning the foxtrot, waltz, two-step, cha-cha. But most British servicemen, Colonial and Commonwealth troops, and American GIs were more eager to grab the nearest available girl and dance to swing records by Jimmy Dorsey, Artie Shaw, and Harry James, and of course wartime hits such as the Andrews Sisters' "Boogie Woogie Bugle Boy" and Glenn Miller's "In the Mood."

The parachutists made their way through the overheated dance studio to the creaking elevator and up to the fifth floor, where Colonel Simonds had rented space from the Egyptian Radio Institute as a front. Almost around

---

bitters, and the stomach-settling properties of ginger beer. The drink was so popular that British troops reportedly telegraphed the hotel, requesting bulk orders to be delivered to the desert front lines.

the clock, a Greek soldier in uniform let no one out of the lift without a valid pass.

Within days the parachutists were referring to their headquarters as "The Sandwich," due to the unceasing wild activity both above and below. The hardwood floor would vibrate to the thumping of Glenn Miller and His Orchestra, while the light fixtures hanging from the ceiling rattled as servicemen on the sixth floor consummated their rendezvous with "hostesses" they'd met at Robert's School of Dance.

Many of the parachutists, too, became regulars on the dance floor. Zvi Ben-Yaakov—born in Bratislava, Czechoslovakia, as Jindřich Greenhut—was a twenty-one-year-old with dark good looks, the powerful arms of a fisherman, and, by his own admission, two left feet. "I'm now learning to dance," he wrote to his pregnant wife, Michal, on Kibbutz Hahotrim just south of Haifa. "You know that I'm a total ignoramus when it comes to dancing. We've only just begun, but I think I'll learn quickly."

Waltzing and fox-trotting at Lucien Robert's with Haviva Reik teaching him how to lead wasn't for Zvi's amusement. The parachutists' British Intelligence instructors ordered it as part of their mission training. Once they'd been dropped into occupied Europe and were operating undercover in big cities such as Budapest, Bucharest, and Bratislava, the kibbutzniks would need to know restaurant table etiquette, how to order cocktails (taking care never to become inebriated), even the proper way to ask a prospective partner to dance.

Shaike Dan, like most of the parachutists, was overwhelmed by the variety of Cairo's temptations. "As a wireless operator, a parachutist for the Royal Air Force about to leave on a special mission, I had some points to my credit that translated into pay. . . . But I was so naive I even refused to accept the money the British allotted for this. I wanted to show them that we couldn't be bought with such cheap temptations."

His British commanding officers, especially Tony Simonds, expected Dan to join them in exploring the city after dark—going to the Casino Opera, the most popular nightspot in Cairo, a notoriously louche club run by a Syrian-born belly dancer named Badia Masabni. "All part of mission training," Simonds told Dan. The way he saw it, those young, naive Jewish socialists who'd been living a life of near sequestration on communal farms could learn a thing or two by hanging out in nightclubs and casinos, absorbing the seedier side of city life.

Dan stared at Simonds, suspecting that—commanding officer or not—this hail fellow well met merely wanted a drinking buddy for a few nights of carousing. No, Simonds assured him, there was method in his madness: Dan would soon be dropped into Romania and—who knew?—he might find himself negotiating with unscrupulous smugglers, professional criminals, undercover Nazi agents. He might need to disguise himself and believably assume the role of a currency speculator, black-market profiteer, or Bucharest gangster.

Dan refused the invitation to the Casino Opera, telling Simonds that as a dyed-in-the-wool kibbutznik, he had boundaries: "Movies are fine. Museums, okay. Good restaurants, sure. Nightclubs—nothing doing."

The only temptation most of the parachutists fell for was the fine dining in wartime Cairo. There was a dizzying array of options, from casual cafés and brasseries to white-tablecloth restaurants specializing in cuisines from around the world. The cooks dishing out the chow on their kibbutzim had hardly been gourmet chefs. Through a series of Cairo culinary adventures, Dan got to know Enzo Sereni, a remarkable man with prodigious appetites in all aspects of life.

3

That February in Cairo, the cloak-and-dagger intrigue that Hannah had only read about in spy novels became a daily routine. The parachutists needed to develop a sixth sense for enemy agents and plainclothes Gestapo men and know the most effective methods to shake a tail. Since the Nazis were obsessed with official paperwork—traveling permits and identity documents—that meant hours of practice in forging and altering ID cards, permits, and passes.

The lectures began at 9:00 a.m. and, after a lunch break, often lasted until eight or nine at night. Hannah learned that with its narrow focus on E&E, MI9 stressed ingenuity. Brigadier Norman Crockatt, who headed MI9 throughout the war, coined the term *escape-mindedness,* his philosophy that every captured soldier and airman was duty bound to break out of captivity or, at the very least, make his best attempt. In February 1944, in an office in MI9's headquarters on Wilton Park Estate in Buckinghamshire, the eccentric genius Christopher Hutton perfected the prized E&E kits.

A bookish fifty-year-old World War I veteran, Hutton was the first to come up with the idea of printing maps on silk to avoid the rustling sound of paper when a soldier is being frisked. He hid miniature compasses in buttons, collar studs, and pencils. He concealed secret codes in playing cards and the wafer-thin paper in which cigarettes are rolled. He designed regulation-looking

British Army boots that, by simply detaching the leather ankles, could be converted into civilian shoes.

In the early years of the war, before the massive Allied air campaign over Europe, most of MI9's efforts went to helping RAF airmen trapped in dozens of POW camps. The Luftwaffe officers running the prison camps, such as Stalag Luft III in Lower Silesia, made famous in the movie *The Great Escape*, were unusual—for Nazis—in the relatively decent treatment they granted to their inmates. Captured airmen in Luftwaffe camps regularly received Red Cross packages and mail from their families in Great Britain, and they were sometimes allowed libraries and theaters. In several well-documented cases, Luftwaffe officers—observing an unwritten esprit de corps among flyers—disregarded Hitler's direct orders demanding harsher treatment and executions of the POW airmen, a nearly unheard-of act of defiance in Nazi Germany.

Hutton's team managed to smuggle maps, compasses, and civilian clothing into many of the Luftwaffe POW camps. Often they were hidden in packages of factory-sealed board games such as Monopoly and Scrabble.

Hannah and the other parachutists studied under a host of MI9 experts in the classroom. Major Lionel Smiles, an expert in makeup and disguises, taught them how to change their facial structure by placing cotton balls in the pockets of their cheeks when taking photographs for forged ID papers. He provided the three women with kits for dyeing their hair. He told the men to start growing out their mustaches. Why mustaches? The logic was brilliantly simple. When you're undercover in a foreign country, he explained, growing a full mustache would take weeks. "But it takes only a minute or two in front of a mirror to shave it off."

The most colorful lectures were given by Major Jasper Maskelyne, formerly a popular magician, who had joined the Royal Engineers and become MI9's master of tricks and deception. Maskelyne later claimed—without much evidence—to have helped win the Battle of El Alamein with his gimmickry.

Building off Hutton's innovations, Major Maskelyne devised brass uniform buttons that concealed miniature compasses. The fountain pen each man carried also contained a compass. He created a toothbrush in which one could hide a tiny hacksaw and a men's comb into which a thin iron screwdriver was inserted. The best hiding places were clothing: double lining of dresses and skirts, secret pockets in jackets, and hollow boot heels.

The maps and multiple compasses were essential not just for the parachutists once they jumped behind enemy lines but for sharing with downed Allied airmen and escaped POWs. If they did make their jumps successfully, their RAF uniforms could be converted under field conditions into passable men's double-breasted suits.

When Zvi Yehieli spotted Shaike Dan leaving Major Maskelyne's spycraft lecture, dressed in his smart RAF officer's uniform, Yehieli asked, "How come you're walking like that, rocking from side to side?"

Dan laughed. "Must be the compasses. They're pulling me to the north."

Hannah spent most of her time in Cairo at the A Force Signals School; the coding classes for radio operators were the most challenging aspect of intelligence training. She needed to master the Morse code alphabet, using the brass-and-steel key to create messages of dots and dashes without a single error, and learn to take apart and reassemble the Marconi Type A Mark III radio, which could be concealed in a suitcase. When it came to sending, receiving, and accurately deciphering coded messages, speed was paramount.

Poem coding was the system used by all branches of British Intelligence. It was a double-encryption procedure that could be executed with pencil and paper, providing a onetime key for each message, while the master key used to decipher the message was a poem, often committed to memory by the agent. With its double columnar transposition, the system provided—for its era—good security.

The effectiveness of poem coding lay in the agents' ability to commit the verse to memory—thus avoiding the need for carrying a codebook that could be captured and deciphered. In the early years of the war, SOE agents relied on classic English verse—Shakespeare, Tennyson, Keats, Poe, the King

James Bible. But the SOE discovered that the Nazi code breakers included fluent English speakers; through persistence and trial and error, they could identify many English poems, psalms, and passages from Shakespeare's plays. Messages double-encrypted based on well-known lines such as "Now is the winter of our discontent," "Tyger Tyger, burning bright," or "In Xanadu did Kubla Khan a stately pleasure-dome decree" could be cracked within a matter of days, if not hours.

One ingenious solution was to compose new poems. A young Jewish Londoner working as an SOE cryptanalyst, Leo Marks, came up with that novel strategy. The compositions didn't have to be brilliant, merely clear, concise, and easily memorized. SOE headquarters at 64 Baker Street in London was staffed by civilians known as the "Intelligent Gentlewomen." Those "well-bred British girls" would, in peacetime, have been teachers, nurses, or governesses. They were given free rein to exercise their considerable abilities. They sat in rows in the Baker Street office, composing original poems, limericks, and free verse, often comical, silly, and lewd.

Is de Gaulle's prick
Twelve inches thick
Can it rise
To the size
Of a proud flag-pole
And does the sun shine
From his arse-hole?

MI9, unlike SOE, didn't have the resources to staff an office with Intelligent Gentlewomen. But because many Jewish parachutists such as Hannah, Yoel Palgi, and Shaike Dan were multilingual, they could transmit their Morse code messages in codes encrypted by poems in languages other than English. The German code breakers might have had an easy time cracking famous English verses, but it was much less likely that they'd recognize poetry in French, Italian, or Spanish.

During coding class, Hannah was drawn to a slim volume of the great

French romantic poets, including Paul Verlaine, Arthur Rimbaud, and Charles Baudelaire:

Le Poète est semblable au prince des nuées
Qui hante la tempête et se rit de l'archer;
Exilé sur le sol au milieu des huées,
*Ses ailes de géant l'empêchent de marcher.**

*The final quatrain of Baudelaire's "L'Albatros" (1859):

The Poet is like that wild inheritor of the cloud,
A rider of storms, above the range of arrows and slings;
Exiled on earth, at bay amid the jeering crowd,
He cannot walk for his unmanageable wings.

4

It was a warm February evening in Cairo when Hannah, Yoel Palgi, and Enzo Sereni gathered in a fifth-floor room with large picture windows overlooking Suleiman Pasha Square. Most of the other parachutists were out—some at Robert's Dance Studio, others at J. Groppi café. Hannah and Palgi sat in large leather armchairs, studying maps of the Yugoslavian territory held by Tito's Partisans, which was constantly being taken over by Nazi troops and their fascist collaborators.

Enzo, typically, had his nose shoved into a hardcover book. He read aloud one of the wittiest passages of P. G. Wodehouse: "The voice of Love seemed to call to me, but it was a wrong number." He saw no reaction from Yoel or Hannah; both were still deeply engrossed in their maps of Yugoslavia and the overland routes to Hungary.

Hannah suddenly looked up at him with an expression of alarm. "What if we're caught and accused of spying?" she said. "What if I'm caught with a transmitter?"

Silence filled the large, drafty room. Enzo closed the book in his lap, and his breezy expression vanished. "You'll take cyanide." His gaze darted between Hannah and Palgi. "If you're caught, the Nazis will torture you. Without doubt. And be clear. There are *no* heroes, not in the real world. No one can withstand torture. You'll all become traitors. Then, afterward, they'll kill you anyway. The Nazis will show no mercy, not even for a young woman like you, Hannah."

Hannah was startled, looking back at Enzo. Palgi's face flushed; he was furious. "You've got no right to talk like that!" he shouted and stormed out of the room.

Weeks earlier, a Palmach commander named David Shaltiel had given the parachutists a lecture based on his own experiences operating undercover in Nazi Germany. Born in Germany in 1903, he'd emigrated to Palestine after Hitler had risen to power. During the 1936 Arab Uprising, he had returned to Europe undercover on a Haganah operation to purchase black-market arms. The Nazis had captured him in Aachen as he was trying to smuggle 100,000 reichsmarks out of Germany.

He'd been tortured by the Gestapo for days, but they couldn't make him talk. He had spent three years in Dachau and Buchenwald concentration camps. In 1939, the Haganah had managed to secure his release, and he had returned to Palestine.

In blunt terms, he told the parachutists how he'd endured the Gestapo torture. The sadists could break your body, he said, but they couldn't break your mind. Surviving torture required, above all else, mental toughness. Where had he gotten his? He'd honed it in his twenties, when he had spent five years—from 1925 to 1930—in the French Foreign Legion.

No one in British Intelligence had any illusions about the fates of the brave young men and women they were sending behind Nazi lines. By 1942, the lifespan of an SOE radio operator was six weeks. For those who were captured, "the deaths were slow, prolonged, and grim."

Even more graphic than Shaltiel's lecture was a film that British Intelligence had compiled to illustrate Gestapo interrogation methods. Captured Allied agents had their toenails ripped out. Others were branded with a white-hot piece of pipe. Hannah learned about the strappado, a medieval torture revived by Nazi interrogators, and how the Gestapo had managed to devise new tortures never thought of before in history—with a perverse inventiveness worthy of the Spanish Inquisition's Tomás de Torquemada. Rape, she also learned, was almost inevitable for captured female agents.

After the screening, Hannah and several of the other parachutists could barely contain their disgust. For the first time, she spoke to Colonel Simonds in a raised voice. What was the point of showing such graphic and demoralizing scenes? she demanded. No one could withstand that kind of torture.

Colonel Simonds nodded in agreement. Indeed, he said, no one could withstand it. There was, however, one escape route—precisely as Enzo had told them. Major Maskelyne informed the class that they had the option of carrying an "L-pill." Short for lethal pill, it was an oval glass ampoule approximately the size of a pea covered in thin brown rubber, easily concealed under the tongue or in the pouch of the cheek. Maskelyne explained that L-pills could be sewn into the lining of clothing or hidden in a tube of lipstick. Each one was filled with such a high concentration of potassium cyanide that after they bit down on it, death would be instantaneous.

The weeks in Cairo were anxious and tumultuous; departure dates were constantly in flux. Rumors swirled that both the Romanian and Hungarian governments were wavering—would they switch sides to the Allies? If so, would Hitler send in his troops and turn them into vassal states?

Squadron Leader Lawson delivered the unfortunate news to Hannah, Yoel, Yonah, and the rest of their infiltration team that they could no longer be deployed directly into Hungary. They'd planned to parachute somewhere near Lake Balaton—a large freshwater lake where Hannah had vacationed as a girl—then make their way by train to Budapest. Now, because of the fast-changing political developments within the Axis, they were going to parachute into Yugoslavia and meet up with Tito's Partisans. All six members of the Hungarian infiltration team objected, Hannah most vocally. But without the cooperation of the RAF, Squadron Leader Lawson told them, there would be no mission. And the decision was final.

Unlike the first cadre of volunteers who'd come to Cairo in mid-1943, all the volunteers had agreed to enlist in the RAF—in the cases of Hannah, Haviva Reik, and Surika Braverman, in the Women's Auxiliary Air Force.

Squadron Leader Lawson briefed them on what to do in the event they were captured. Under Article 5 of the 1929 Geneva Convention, all downed RAF flyers were required to give only three pieces of information: name, rank, and serial number. With the Nazis, of course, nothing was certain, but Lawson stressed that if they were taken prisoner while wearing RAF uniforms with officers' insignias, they stood a good chance of being accorded better treatment.

For both the British and the Jewish Agency as late as February and March 1944, some fundamental matters had yet to be ironed out. One issue especially rankled the parachutists. During training, the instructors kept referring to them as "agents" rather than as soldiers or paratroopers. The distinction wasn't merely semantic; on it hinged both their military pay grade and their life insurance policies.

On the eve of the first teams departing from Cairo, the tensions between the British Army and the volunteers came to a head. The British needed to know if each volunteer wanted to be registered as an RAF officer or as an espionage agent. Given the inherent risks of parachuting behind enemy lines, MI9 agents were entitled to fortnightly pay in pounds sterling, several times higher than the typical military pay. And in the event of their deaths, their surviving family would receive a larger life insurance payout.

One by one the Jewish volunteers refused to be classified as espionage agents. They'd volunteered for a mission to save the Jews of Europe, to warn their own people—not to serve the British as spies. Among themselves and in the official Palmach records, they called themselves *shlichim*. The word comes from biblical Hebrew, the plural of *shaliach*, meaning "one who is sent forth." In modern Hebrew, its meaning is "emissary" or "messenger."*

Each parachutist took out a life insurance policy that, depending on his or her family status, ranged from £1,500 to £2,000, not an inconsiderable sum in 1944—equivalent to roughly US $133,000 in 2025. Most of the parachutists named their kibbutzim, rather than family members, as beneficiaries.

Hearing that the Yishuv parachutists had turned down the higher pay of espionage agents, a British officer told Surika Braverman, "It's the first time I've met Jews who didn't want money."

Each of the young parachutists had a deep inner reason for volunteering. For them, the urgency was personal. By late 1943, most historians estimate,

*In biblical Hebrew, there is a complex, often loaded meaning to the word *shaliach*. It can, in some passages, mean an angel of the Lord.

five million Jews had been murdered. To the parachutists, those millions of dead—and millions more hiding from the Nazis or trapped in the ghettos—were not faceless statistics; they were their parents, grandparents, brothers, sisters, uncles, aunts, and cousins.

Almost every one of the volunteers had left behind family members whose fate was unknown; they feared the worst. Yoel Palgi had no clue about the fate of his mother, father, and sister in Hungary. Shaike Dan hadn't heard anything about his immediate family in Romania.

Surika Braverman recalled that Hannah was once asked, "Why are you doing this?"

"In my heart I have two great loves," Hannah said, her answer in Hebrew a piece of clever, melodic wordplay: *"Ahava achat l'ami v'ahava achat l'imi"* (One love for my people and one love for my mother).

"My darling Gyuri," Hannah wrote to her brother from Cairo. "At the moment it is difficult for me to write because everything is considered a 'military secret' and I'm afraid the censor will delete something. In short, I am well; there are a lot of soldiers (boys and girls) here from Eretz among whom I can find a good many to be friendly with. During the day I'm busy; at night we go to the cinema, or I stay home and read. Fortunately, I am not in the barracks but in the city, so I can take advantage of my free time."

Most of the parachutists enjoyed taking day trips to the pyramids of Giza and the antiquities museum. There were laughter, joking, and warm camaraderie, but also a sense of fatalism: No one knew if they would ever be together like that again. They captured it all in a series of black-and-white photos: young, smiling British paratroopers in their khaki drill uniforms—shorts for the men, skirts for the women, peaked caps for both—in front of the Sphinx, on the banks of the Nile, and in the shadows of the pyramids.

Haviva Reik posed for a photo next to the statue of King Ramses II, and they all took pictures in front of the Step Pyramid of Djoser in the Saqqara necropolis, dating circa 2670–2650 BC. Haviva and Surika Braverman were dazzled by the beauty of the Japanese park with its swans, water lilies, artificial islands, pagodas, and statues of the Buddha. They spent long hours in the Giza Zoo—one of the largest in the world—where Haviva rode on an elephant.

On another hot afternoon, Haviva and Surika ventured to the Haret el-Yahud—the ancient Jewish Quarter of Cairo—and visited the Bet Knesset Ha-Rambam, a synagogue that had existed since the tenth century and was named for the great Jewish rabbi, philosopher, and medical doctor Maimonides.* The walk through the Haret el-Yahud left Haviva and Surika deeply shaken. They'd brought chocolates and sweets and distributed them to the children in the Jewish Quarter. Haviva suddenly found herself bursting into tears at the sight of a young Jewish mother holding a malnourished toddler, begging her for a piece of candy.

Hannah took a single day trip to the Valley of the Kings to see the temple and the royal tombs of Luxor, but she soon tired of the off-duty tourism, which she saw as frivolous escapism. Many of the other parachutists disagreed. Between the coding classes, while others were sightseeing, Hannah sat alone in her room, absorbed in reading or writing. As she had since childhood, she lived in a world of words: "I feel I couldn't possibly live without writing, even if only for myself, in my diary. A thought that is not put on paper is as if it had never been born. I can only truly grasp a thought when I've expressed it in writing."

She was no longer making entries in her diary; the four exercise books were packed in the suitcase under her bed at Sdot Yam. But she was still composing poems, scribbling on scraps of paper. She was determined to follow her father's path as a successful author, poet, and playwright.

One morning while Shaike Dan was sitting with Dov Berger, Hannah burst into their room, wanting to read them a poem she'd just finished. She'd often heard Dan singing Romanian and Yiddish songs and asked if he could set her Hebrew words to a melody, perhaps a Romanian folk tune.

Dan felt a fatherly affection for Hannah; he later described her as a "highly sensitive girl with a stormy temperament and a poet's soul." She was only twenty-two, while he was thirty-four, so he often felt like the papa among the group of parachutists. "For many of them I was a person they could talk to, a listener to whom they confided their woes," he wrote, "and those were not in short supply."

*Maimonides—Moses ben Maimon—is often referred to by the Hebrew acronym "Rambam."

The poem Hannah wrote in early March 1944—Dan later felt remiss that he had never found time to set it to music—contained two simple verses:

We gathered flowers in the fields and mountains,
We breathed the fresh winds of spring,
We were drenched with the warmth of the sun's rays.
In our Homeland, in our beloved home.

We go out to our brothers in exile,
To the suffering of winter, to frost in the night.
Our hearts will bring tidings of springtime,
Our lips sing the song of light.

February rolled into March. All the thorny details of the negotiations between the British and Jewish authorities were ironed out one by one, and departure dates were finalized. The first teams would be flying off to the Bari airfield in days. The weather reports and lunar phases were all-important: Parachute drops were greenlit only on clear moonlit nights. "The moon was always a symbol of romance," recalled Surika Braverman, "but in Cairo it became a symbol of jumping."

The farewell parties held at various houses in Cairo went on into the early morning. The volunteers ate spaghetti alla Milanese, drank red wine, and sang Hebrew songs late into the night. "And when we raised our glasses with the toast *l'chaim*," Braverman said, "I've never in my life heard it said in just that way. We were drinking to the lives of those who were going off, *and* to the lives of those to whom they were going."

There was raucous laughter, and everyone seemed in high spirits, but for the superstitious among the parachutists, two episodes were later remembered as ominous: One night, Enzo Sereni accidentally dropped a framed photograph from a shelf, its glass shattering all over the floor. And the prior evening, Hannah had spilled a full bottle of red wine on a white tablecloth, leaving a billowing stain that everyone said resembled a pool of blood.

5

March 1944
Bari, Italy

The first leg of Hannah's journey back to Hungary began on board a freezing RAF Douglas Dakota C-47 transport plane from Cairo to Bari with four other volunteers. Enzo Sereni was visibly excited to be returning to his beloved Italy for the first time since 1927.

During the three-hour flight, to pass the time, out of curiosity, or perhaps merely as an intellectual challenge, Hannah began to debate Enzo. His pride and patriotism about returning to Italy mystified her. Since the fascist regime of Admiral Horthy had, in effect, rescinded her citizenship with the passage of anti-Jewish legislation, she no longer felt Hungarian. How could she, when the government had made it clear that not only were Jews unwelcome in society but "racially" they weren't part of the Magyar nation.

How, she asked, could Enzo remain such a proud Italian during the years of Fascist rule? Why had most Italians supported Mussolini's regime for so long? The Italians were such a cultured, artistic, sophisticated people—how could they have stood behind fascism for more than two decades?

Hannah had still been in her cradle in Budapest in 1922 when Mussolini's Blackshirts had marched on Rome; Enzo had become a committed Zionist in 1917. He loved Eretz Israel passionately. He'd thrown all his energy into the founding of Givat Brenner, the kibbutz that was home to his wife, Ada, his son, Daniel, and his daughter, Hagar. He'd come up with its name to honor the pioneering Hebrew author Yosef Chaim Brenner, who'd been murdered along with five of his friends by an Arab mob during the Jaffa riots of 1921. No one could ever question Enzo Sereni's deep love for Eretz Israel. But, yes, he *also* deeply loved Italy.

Hannah couldn't comprehend such ardent dual patriotism. Could Enzo possibly excuse Mussolini's grotesque attempt to conquer Abyssinia? What about the bombing raids on Haifa and Tel Aviv? It was *not* the Luftwaffe, she said, but the Regia Aeronautica that had introduced "terror bombing" to the Yishuv. She well remembered the Italian bombs dropping on the port of Haifa—the sirens would sound at Nahalal, and all the frightened girls would dash for the shelters. Even more horrible was the day—September 9, 1940—when those Z.1007 Alcione bombers had dropped their payloads on Tel Aviv, causing massive damage in the center of the city and killing 137 civilians.

As the C-47 crossed the Mediterranean, Reuven Dafni observed their debate in silence. With each accusation that Hannah leveled, Enzo responded calmly but forcefully, trying not to patronize her. Enzo's bona fides as an anti-Fascist were beyond question; he'd been documenting the rise of fascism in Italy for years and was, in fact, putting the finishing touches to his book on the subject.*

Reuven Dafni paid close attention; it was his first time really observing Hannah, and he was trying to figure out what made her tick. "I'll never forget the discussion between Hannah and Enzo on the subject of whether or not there is a God," he later wrote. "Enzo was an extremely astute man, a Doctor of Philosophy, and he fervently postulated God's existence. Opposing him with clear, penetrating logic was twenty-two-year-old Hannah."

Reuven noted the way Hannah marshaled each argument with uncompromising logic and sent it to do battle with Enzo. She was unwilling to concede a single point, stubborn, completely sure of herself. She was clearly brilliant, Reuven thought, but the type of girl who was always right—even when she was demonstrably wrong.

Reuven tried to visualize what it would be like to work with Hannah once they were dropped behind enemy lines. How could that young girl, so inexperienced, have so much self-assurance? Where did the courage of her

*In Cairo, Enzo had been constantly editing the final chapters of his posthumously published book *Mekorot ha-Fashizm ha-Italki* (Sources of Italian Fascism).

convictions come from? It was admirable, to be sure, but she was so head-strong that Reuven asked himself what would happen in the mountainous war zones of Yugoslavia. Under fire, would she follow the chain of command? Would she listen to orders? Or even to reason?

After they landed in Bari, Reuven took Enzo aside and spoke his mind. He was convinced that Hannah would be *impossible* to work with. "She certainly won't be easy to work with," Enzo said. "But always remember, this is no ordinary girl."

Enzo Sereni was no ordinary man himself. His patriotism for both Italy and Eretz Israel made him a unique figure among the Zionist pioneers. He'd been playing his cards close to his vest. Once he'd sent the various infiltration teams on their mission, he was going to parachute behind Nazi lines in northern Italy. When Ben-Gurion and the other leaders in the Jewish Agency got wind of Enzo's plan, their reaction was unanimous: Under *no* circumstances was he to do so.

Enzo was one of the primary organizers of the mission; he was indispensable. What if he were to fall into the hands of the Gestapo? How much might he divulge under torture? Moreover, the surname Sereni was known throughout Italy, and not only because Enzo's father had been the personal physician to the king's court. Enzo's younger brother, Emilio, was now a leader in the Italian Communist Party, a prominent anti-Fascist fighter who'd been tried and sentenced to eighteen years in prison. Throughout Italy, the name Sereni was simply too well known.

"So what?" Enzo said. "Randolph Churchill's also well known, and yet he parachuted to the Partisans in Yugoslavia."

It was a fair point; in the winter of 1944, after decamping from his luxury suite at Shepheard's in Cairo, Captain Randolph Churchill had indeed parachuted into the mountains of Yugoslavia to rendezvous with Marshal Tito. He was soon joined by his friend the novelist Evelyn Waugh. The two radioed valuable intelligence about Partisan counterinsurgency missions and helped rescue numerous downed Allied flyers.

Churchill's mission to Yugoslavia was no secret. His meeting with Marshal Tito was widely reported in the press, including on the front page of *The New York Times* on February 27, 1944.

Much like Hannah, Enzo was impossible to budge once his mind was made up. Back in Tel Aviv, David Ben-Gurion was furious. He was counting on Enzo to be by his side in the years ahead, one of the intellectual and organizational pillars of the future Jewish state. "There was no replacement for Enzo," he later wrote. "There wasn't another man like him. He was unique. Of course, I knew how important it was to establish contact with the Jews of Europe—but everything has its price."

Golda Meir had tried mightily to dissuade him. Before departing for Egypt, Enzo had visited Meir's office at the Executive Committee of the Histradut labor union. He'd told Meir about his intention to parachute into northern Italy. Behind his thick glasses, Meir recalled, his eyes looked brighter than usual. "I've come to say good-bye," he said cheerfully. "Golda, I'm off."

Meir knew that it was fruitless to debate Enzo, but she tried very hard for about a quarter of an hour. "First of all, Enzo," she said, "you're really much too old and much too valuable here. Please be reasonable, for everyone's sake." But when she was through, he took her hand. "Golda, you must understand. I can't possibly stay behind when I'm the one responsible for sending so many others. Just don't worry. I give you my word of honor that we'll meet again."

6

March 6, 1944
Bari, Italy

In early March 1944, when Hannah arrived, the Bari airfield was buzzing. Almost all the Allied airmen at Bari had been listening to the BBC News reports about the recent bombing raids on the German capital.

On March 6, 1944, the USAAF made its first successful daytime raid on Berlin. General James Doolittle's Eighth Air Force launched a fleet of 672 heavy bombers—B-17 Flying Fortresses and B-24 Liberators—escorted by P-51 Mustang fighters to target industrial and military targets in the capital, aiming to destroy both the Nazis' war production and the German people's morale.

The raid inflicted significant damage on the city, but it was the appearance of the P-51 Mustang in the skies that proved devastating. One of the war's first effective long-range fighters, the P-51 revolutionized aerial combat and strategic operations in Europe. In dogfights, it had enough maneuverability and speed to take out the Luftwaffe's best fighters: Messerschmitt Bf-109s, Junkers Ju 88s, and Focke-Wulf Fw 190s. More important, with two external fuel drop tanks giving it a flying range of almost 1,700 miles, the P-51 was the first Allied fighter that could escort heavy bombers to Berlin and back to their bases in Great Britain.

The P-51 turned the tide of the air war in Europe. Up until March 1944, Luftwaffe fighters ruled the skies from their bases in France, Belgium, and Germany. But now, with skilled pilots in the cockpits, P-51 Mustangs could attack, almost at will, targets of opportunity in Germany and France as they returned from Berlin to England.

March marked the culmination of the five-month-long campaign during which RAF Bomber Command unleashed numerous major air raids. The bombing of Berlin left four hundred thousand people homeless, with the death toll still unknown. By March 1944, the Allied air forces were dropping roughly three thousand tons of bombs on Nazi Germany daily.

Reichsmarschall Hermann Göring—the once dashing World War I ace—had become, according to one contemporaneous account, a "self-indulgent, pleasure-seeking, drug-impregnated bag of lard with whom Hitler had lost patience." In 1939, he'd boasted that the skies over Germany were impregnable. "If just one English bomber reaches the Ruhr, my name is no longer Hermann Göring but Hermann Meier," he said, using a stereotypical Jewish surname.

But on the night of March 6, 1944, Göring looked skyward, witnessed the future, and was chastened. "When I saw the 'Bluenosed Bastards of Bodney' over Berlin," he said, using the nickname of the Eighth Air Force's 352nd Fighter Group, "I knew the jig was up." Most historians dismiss that alliterative remark as embellishment but do attribute to Göring a more plausible quote: "When I saw American fighters over Berlin, I knew the war was lost."

By early March 1944, millions of Germans were cursing the name of Reichsmarschall Hermann Meier.

To tamp down defeatism, Propaganda Minister Joseph Goebbels was forced to go on the air with a mawkish, self-pitying diatribe:

> The English press has called the series of terror attacks on the Reich capital . . . the "Battle of Berlin." The intention of the British war leadership is to destroy the Reich capital with these brutal and horrible attacks, to depopulate it, to crush the war morale of its population, and thus win on the German home front the decisive victory that our fighting soldiers have denied the Anglo-Americans thus far in this war on the front.

Walking on the Bari airfield early one morning, Hannah paused to admire the rows of P-51 Mustangs, their glossy silver paint catching the gleam of the sun. She understood little about the strategic nuances of the air war. She didn't know that the extraordinarily long range of those P-51 fighters had shifted the balance of power in the skies over Europe.

She did know one thing: It was no time to celebrate. This ugly war was very far from over. Heavy bombing might demoralize the German population but alone could never bring down the Third Reich. Strategic railway lines destroyed by British and American bombs were repaired—usually by Jewish slave laborers—in a matter of hours.

The defeat of the Third Reich would require the efforts of millions of Allied infantrymen. The Allies were still months away from an amphibious landing in France, months away from opening the second front that Joseph Stalin had been hectoring Churchill and Roosevelt about. Hannah knew that millions of young soldiers and innocent civilians would die before the Nazis surrendered.

Still, it was heartening to hear that the British and American bombing of Berlin was causing many ordinary Germans to lose faith in the Nazi leadership. It certainly gave Hannah and everyone else about to embark on the parachutist mission a boost.

7

March 13, 1944
Bari, Italy

The Scottish flight sergeant was gobsmacked. Such a slender young woman—a girl, really—with heavily lidded light blue eyes, a cherub's cheeks, in a blue-gray Women's Auxiliary Air Force uniform, had come to him to be fitted into a parachute harness.

It was only hours before Hannah was scheduled to jump. The sergeant hustled her into the storeroom. She spoke to him in English—with a trace of an eastern European accent—as he harnessed her into the MK1 parachute, adjusted the forest green steel helmet, fastened the leather strap under her chin. She never used her real name, of course, only her operational handle: Minnie.

When Reuven Dafni came in next to get harnessed, the sergeant was still shaking his head. "In all these years I've seen hundreds of you chaps," he said. "She's the first girl."

The other RAF and USAAF flyers shared the Scotsman's disbelief. Many who'd seen Hannah around the Bari airfield in the past few days had assumed that she was the wife of one of the British or American airmen, come to say goodbye before he left on a bombing mission.

The sight of her in uniform, harnessed into a parachute, and wearing a steel helmet, set the men gawking. When one young American flyer walked up to her and took her hand, Hannah offered him a smile. The American seemed to want to impart something meaningful, but he became tongue-tied, stammering a few incomprehensible words. Then, before rushing off, he told Hannah, "Thank you."

In the predawn hours of March 13, the landing strips at Bari looked like a jostled hornet's nest. Moonlit uniforms rushed in all directions. The parachutists had one hour before boarding the Halifax heavy bomber. MI9's name for the Hungarian infiltration mission left much to be desired: Operation Chicken. Hannah was hardly pleased at being code-named Agent Minnie, especially when she learned that Yoel Palgi's handle was Agent Mickey. A couple of cartoon mice? No, throughout the operation, Hannah resolved to continue using her Hebrew code name, Hagar. In fact, in that final hour, she wrote a goodbye letter to Kibbutz Sdot Yam.

Dearest Comrades:

In sea, land, in the air, in war and in peace, we are all advancing towards the same goal. Each of us will stand at his post. There is no difference between my task and that of another. I will be thinking of all of you a great deal. That's what gives me strength.

Hagar

As they crossed the Bari airfield toward the waiting Halifax, Enzo Sereni chased after them, dressed in a gray civilian suit. "Remember," he shouted. "Only those who *want* to die, die!"

Moments later, the Halifax bomber glided over the black waters of the Adriatic. The four Rolls-Royce engines thundered as the bomber made its ascent to 20,000 feet, climbing through the cumulus clouds.

Reuven and Hannah faced each other across the front seats next to the hatch; on either side of them sat Abba Berdichev and Yonah Rosen. Reuven surveyed the anxious faces of his team members, lost in thought.

Reuven and Hannah were slated to make the first jump—upon seeing the flash of a round green bulb above their heads. On the plane's second pass over the target, they'd be followed by Rosen and Berdichev.

They crouched inside the crowded Halifax surrounded by large metal drums filled with clothes, food, cigarettes, rifles, pistols, and ammunition for

Marshal Tito's Partisan army. With the MK1 harnesses on their backs and their submachine guns, pistols, and extra ammunition clips packed into their heavy canvas overalls and leather flight jackets, they had almost no freedom of movement. The roar of the four engines killed all conversation.

Hannah's radio transmitter, receiver, headset, and battery were hidden in a beige fabric–covered suitcase. The suitcase was packed in a sturdy aluminum C-type container, to be thrown out of the Halifax with a parachute for a controlled descent.

Reuven's eyes rested on Hannah. Below her oversized steel helmet her face seemed tiny, her expression elfin. Her eyes were aglow, and, far from nervous, she looked excited, obviously happy to finally be on the way. Then, to his surprise, she winked at him. That made him laugh. Her smile reminded him of a little girl jumping onto her first merry-go-round ride. Yonah and Abba soon caught sight of her buoyant expression, and everyone relaxed as the Halifax continued on its bumpy flight. "The air seemed lighter," he wrote. "Fears and black thoughts receded, finally disappeared, and we began feeling peacefully confident. Time ticked by; fatigue and tension took their toll; blessed sleep embraced us one by one."

After two hours, Hannah and Reuven were jolted awake to see the RAF crew tossing parachuted steel supply drums—as well as the aluminum C-type canister containing Hannah's radio set—out the hatch. The plane was making wide circles over the drop zone. Above their heads, the round bulb suddenly flashed from red to green: Go!

Dafni arose, crouching, cautious, fearful that if he straightened up to his full height, his steel helmet would hit the top of the Halifax's fuselage. He glanced out the hatch opening. For the first time in more than five years, he was returning to Yugoslavia—or at least was now a thousand feet above its mountains. Hannah stood close behind him, her face still wreathed in that broad smile. Even on the verge of jumping, she was calm and exultant.

She flashed him a thumbs-up—her favorite victory sign. Dafni's leather-gloved hand returned the gesture, and without a word to her, he leapt from the hatch. She counted off a few seconds, then followed. A freezing gust of air rushed around her. Falling fast, Hannah began counting backward slowly, and then her body jolted back. This felt no different, she thought, from the training jumps at Ramat David. She glanced up; the parachute's silk reminded her of the fleeting beauty of a butterfly's wings as they opened. Her body relaxed as she made a drifting descent beneath that huge white mushroom, falling into infinite blackness above the thickly wooded mountains of Yugoslavia, the wild, untamed land of the Partisans.

She was now at the mercy of the winds.

8

March 13, 1944
Yugoslavia

Even with the best navigation instruments and detailed maps, making a nighttime jump from a Halifax bomber in 1944 was hardly an exact science. The slightest change in weather conditions could make the difference between landing safely among friendly forces and landing in the enemy's clutches.

Fortunately, it wasn't a blind jump. The Partisans were expecting the arrival of the four parachutists and their much needed supply barrels. The drop zone had been lit up with large bonfires, and as Hannah, Reuven, Abba, and Yonah jumped from the Halifax, they had a good view of where they were trying to land.

But the wind that night was much stronger than forecast, and Hannah—whose body weight, even fully laden with weapons and equipment, was far lighter than that of the typical male parachutist—drifted hundreds of feet off course.

During the seemingly endless descent, she braced for the impact, remembering the lessons she'd learned, hearing the voices of those stick-wielding Gurkhas at Ramat David:

Keep your knees clenched together!

When your boots touch down, don't stomp your heels!

Keep your weight on the balls of your feet!

Lean to one side, let your calves and thighs and hips touch the earth.

Breathe!

Stay calm, tumble naturally, roll, roll, keep rolling with momentum.

As she glided down those final moments, all the careful hours of practice proved pointless. Her knees were clenched together, and before the balls of her feet could touch the ground, she found herself crashing noisily through the crown of a massive pine tree. Only her thick nylon jumpsuit protected her from being scratched by the broken branches.

Held up by only a few twisted pieces of wood spiked with pine needles, she dangled above the ground. She held her breath and listened closely. For a supposed war zone, the forest was eerily serene. The only sound she heard was the low *whoosh* of the parachute settling around her. Her gloved hands clutched at the nylon cords that entangled her.

She couldn't stay there long, hanging thirty feet up in a pine tree, farcically, like a human Christmas ornament. She reached for her waist. She unsheathed her Fairbairn-Sykes knife and used the sharp seven-inch blade to cut the thick nylon cords of the chute one by one. As she severed the last cord, she fell with an awkward thud to the hard, cold, icy ground, wincing in pain.

She'd prepared for the dangers of landing from several thousand feet but hadn't anticipated that a much shorter drop could injure her. As she sat rubbing her right ankle, she hit a tender spot and realized that she'd sprained it. After a moment, she stood up, gingerly testing the ankle by putting her partial weight on it. Leaving the parachute conspicuously draped in the tree, she dragged herself on all fours to the nearest snowy mound for cover.

She saw nothing in the pitch dark—certainly no welcome committee of Tito's Partisans waiting to greet her as a liberating hero. She lay still in the freezing silence, listening for a whistle from Reuven or Yonah or Abba. Nothing. Not even a lonesome birdsong.

She took a personal inventory. She was injured but could walk. She had a pistol and a knife, a cleverly concealed compass, and silk maps sewn into the lining of her RAF uniform—but even if she were to try her luck, which way should she go? She might be surrounded by Nazi patrols at any moment.

Footsteps approached, the unmistakable sound of boots crunching on snow. Whoever was approaching must have watched her descend from the Halifax or spotted the bright white silk of the parachute still draped over the towering tree.

She hugged the ground and tried to breathe silently. If it was a German patrol, they'd surely have dogs—German shepherds that would pick up her scent immediately.

She strained to hear the approaching voices and before long could sense that two men had stopped about ten feet from her, on the spot where she had dropped down into the snow. They were obviously trying to decide which way she had gone.

Hannah could understand and speak German with reasonable fluency. But those two men were not speaking German, nor Hungarian, for that matter. It sounded to Hannah like a Slavic language, most likely Serbo-Croatian. From her position she could not see their faces, and it was too dark to make out their uniforms.

She had no choice. Steeling her nerve, she took a deep breath and stood up. Instantly the soldiers turned around, pointing two Nagant carbines directly at her. She stood motionless, her gloved hands open to show that she was unarmed. While one soldier kept his gun barrel leveled at her, the second shone a flashlight up and down her body. After her eyes adjusted to the shine, Hannah could make out his Red Army overcoat without insignia.

Then, suddenly, the man held the light closer. He stared aggressively into her eyes, shaking his head with an expression of disbelief. The other man approached, looking closely at her hair, which fell softly over her jacket collar. Their chatter attracted another pair of soldiers, and as they approached, Hannah saw the *triglavka* hat, a distinctively Yugoslavian olive green beret decorated with a bright red Soviet star. They wore mismatched elements of various uniforms—some from the Yugoslavian Army or the Red Army, some taken off dead German soldiers. They were undoubtedly Tito's fighters.

Within moments, the four rough-looking young Partisans had Hannah surrounded. She braced for a tough questioning—if not a confrontation—but the tension eased as they began laughing, gesturing, and pointing. Hannah couldn't understand a word of it, but it became crystal clear that they were amused by the fact that she was a woman, a parachutist, in a blue RAF uniform. Their laughter grew louder.

Hannah remained still, unsure exactly how to proceed. But then she remembered Reuven teaching her a useful phrase back in Bari—one that could be used as a greeting in Croatian among the Partisans: *"Smrt fašizmu!"* Death to fascism!

Would that work? She calculated the risk and decided to go with something more subtle. Conjuring up her best approximation of a BBC announcer or the well-bred accent of Colonel Simonds, she said, "Hello."

One of the unshaven Partisans, smiling, exhaled a thick cloud of tobacco smoke. "Hello," he said.

Without much fanfare, the four Partisans led Hannah, limping on her bruised ankle, to a nearby encampment, a secure compound lit up by huge bonfires. She was nervous, uncertain, wary—until she saw the others. Standing around the fires, smiling, were Reuven, Yonah, and Abba. They clasped her in their arms, happy to be reunited, all safe and alive. Each spoke hurriedly, wanting to hear about the others' experiences when they'd leapt from the Halifax hatch into the night.

When it was her turn, Hannah sheepishly admitted that she'd crashed through one of the tallest pine trees in the forest during her descent and had to cut her nylon cords, tumbling down and spraining her ankle. Reuven told her that he, Abba, and Yonah had landed on a layer of fresh powder—must've been six feet thick. It had been like falling into a huge feather bed.

Among the Partisan army members, the news spread fast that four British parachutists had arrived to help in the fight against the fascists, bringing containers full of supplies and a radio transmitter. A crowd formed around Hannah. The Partisans simply gazed at her. She saluted them, RAF style, and they responded with the Partisan salute: a clenched right fist raised to the temple, and a sharp *"Smrt fašizmu!"*

"Svoboda narodu!" Reuven replied. Hannah and the others learned the meaning of the Serbo-Croation response: "Freedom to the people!"

Unlike the RAF and USAAF flyboys at Bari, the Partisans' focus on Hannah wasn't due to her gender. Young women fighters had played key roles in Tito's Partisan army, and some were even high-ranking commanders. A few months earlier, in January 1944, the Croatian poet Vladimir Nazor had announced the "birth of a new type of woman," the *partizanka*—female Partisan fighter.

As early as 1943, a schoolgirl named Lepa Radić had become a national heroine in Yugoslavia. The seventeen-year-old, a Bosnian Serb, had volunteered as a nurse transporting the wounded in the Battle of Neretva; she'd grabbed her rifle and emptied all her ammunition clips in a firefight against the 7th SS Mountain Division before being captured by the Germans.

For three days she was tortured by the SS as they demanded information about the Communist and Partisan leaders. She refused to say a word about her comrades and was sentenced to death by hanging, a grim public spectacle that was photographed by the Nazis.

On February 8, 1943, she was led to a large tree, surrounded by German onlookers, and told to stand on a wooden crate. With a noose around her neck and the rope strung over a sturdy branch, she was somber-eyed, her hair falling around her shoulders, facing her execution with immense dignity. "Long live the Communist Party!" she shouted. "Long live the Partisans! People, fight for your freedom! Don't surrender to the fascists! I may be killed now, but my comrades will avenge me!"

In her last moments, she was given one last chance to spare her life in return for providing the names of the Partisan commanders. "I'm not a traitor to my people," she replied. "Those you're asking about will reveal themselves to you when they've come to avenge me—when they've wiped out all you evildoers, down to the last man." With that, the executioner kicked the box from under her feet; the drop was too short to break her neck instantly. She writhed in the air for minutes before dying by strangulation.

In the months after her execution, the courage of the young Lepa Radić entered the realm of myth. A photograph of her standing next to the SS man stringing the noose around her neck—resolute, defiant, without a trace of fear—was disseminated among the resistance fighters of Yugoslavia. Thousands more young women were inspired to pick up rifles and join the ranks of Tito's Partisan army.

But the appearance of Hannah Senesh, a young woman flyer, in a smart RAF uniform, gun holstered on her hip—with a wireless transmitter camouflaged inside a suitcase—was something entirely different. She soon became the subject of wild admiration.

"Having a woman with us, a female paratrooper, made a huge impression on all the Partisans," Reuven later recalled. "In 1944, the parachute wasn't commonplace like it is today, and a female paratrooper in British uniform—well, the news spread like wildfire. Everyone wanted to come to see Hannah.

There were many female Partisan fighters, but there were no female paratroopers."

The Partisans also marveled at how ingeniously British Intelligence had hidden compasses inside brass uniform buttons, how they'd printed detailed maps on silk and sewn them into the linings of jackets and trousers, worn as scarves, or secreted in a hollow boot heel.

On one of those maps, Reuven demonstrated to Tito's officers how well he knew the terrain. He pointed out the route they'd have to take to guide escaped Allied pilots to the Adriatic coast. Depending on the route, it would be about two hundred miles, over difficult mountainous terrain, and would take at least three or four days of marching, Reuven estimated.

What would happen once they reached the Adriatic? Reuven nodded at Hannah. She would send encrypted Morse code messages to headquarters in Bari. From Italy, the Royal Navy could then send speedboats to pick up British, American, and Commonwealth pilots and airmen.

9

March 19, 1944
Čazma, Yugoslavia

Hannah wept. Cloaked in shadows, hunched over her wireless set, ready to send a transmission, tears streamed down her face. She could utter only a few words: "We're too late."

It was five days since they'd left Bari, five short days since they'd made their jumps into the mountains of Yugoslavia—but to all the parachutists, those five days might as well have been a lifetime. They were in the wooded enclave of a Partisan headquarters in the mountains of Slovenia when Hannah received the coded transmission: Hitler had occupied Hungary. "We're too late, too late," Hannah kept repeating.

Operation Margarethe, as the Nazis called it, had been more of a bloodless coup than a military invasion. Not a shot had been fired in anger that Sunday morning. Instead, permission had simply been granted for friendly troops to cross the country and set up a puppet regime. The Wehrmacht and SS units had arrived via train, armored cars, panzers—SS men in full regalia, as if on parade. By that afternoon, German officers in their field coats had been enjoying Budapest's café terraces.

The decision to throw their lot in with the Nazis was no longer popular among the Hungarian people, especially after the Don Disaster at Stalingrad, in which fifty thousand Hungarian troops had been killed or had frozen to death and some seventy thousand had been taken prisoner of war by the Soviets. With the Axis losing the initiative on the eastern front and with units of the Red Army breaching Hungary's borders, Admiral Miklós Horthy and Prime Minister Miklós Kállay secretly sought to negotiate a separate peace with the Allies, promising to surrender unconditionally to them once they reached Hungarian territory.

When word of Horthy's double game reached Berlin, Hitler flew into a rage. He summoned Horthy to a conference in Klessheim Palace near Salzburg on March 18, 1944, and ordered him to make greater contributions to the German war effort and to hand over Hungary's Jews to Nazi authorities. As the two heads of state conducted their negotiations, German forces were already marching from Austria toward Hungary, and by the time Horthy's train returned to Budapest, the nation was effectively reduced to a German protectorate. Horthy was placed under house arrest, and a pro-Nazi former soldier, Döme Sztójay, became the new prime minister, though it was clear that power rested with the German military governor, Edmund Veesenmayer.

The most ominous development by far, however, was the arrival in Budapest of SS Obersturmbannführer Adolf Eichmann—the logistical mastermind of the Holocaust—and six hundred SS officers and Gestapo men. Eichmann was an ambitious former vacuum cleaner salesman born in Solingen, Germany, but raised in Linz, Austria. A fanatical Nazi and anti-Semite, the thirty-eight-year-old had come to Budapest prepared to act ruthlessly and with great haste. On March 10, Eichmann and his main associates had convened at Mauthausen concentration camp in Austria to devise a deportation plan for Hungary's Jews. He now set up his office in Budapest's Majestic Hotel with only one mission: to carry out *die Endlösung der Judenfrage*.

Upon his arrival, further anti-Jewish decrees were enacted and Budapest's Jewish community leaders were called to a conference during which they were ordered to establish a Judenrat (Jewish Council) led by Samu Stern, a respected Budapest businessman, banker, and adviser to the royal court.

The country's Jewish community, numbering approximately one million—including Jews who'd converted to Christianity as well as so-called *Mischlinge* (or "mongrels" meaning people with one or two Jewish grandparents)—had remained virtually untouched throughout the war.*

On the evening of March 19, the Nazis made their first independent move against Hungarian Jewry. They arrested over two hundred Jewish doctors and lawyers whose names had been selected at random from the Budapest telephone book and sent them to Mauthausen concentration camp. Next, the Gestapo moved into hundreds of countryside towns and villages, taking the leaders of community councils hostage and threatening to kill them if their family members didn't bring a ransom of money and valuables.

In the following weeks, all Jews in Hungary were ordered to leave their homes and all their possessions behind and relocate to abandoned barracks, deserted brickworks, and timberyards, which would become de facto ghettos. Continue to comply with orders, the Gestapo said, and no harm will come to you.

Soon after, under the direction of Eichmann from his elegant office suites in the Majestic Hotel, more severe anti-Jewish legislation was enacted. No longer were there quotas; Jews were forced out of the professions entirely. They were ordered to register their property in preparation for immediate mandatory transfers to non-Jewish owners. The Jewish population would soon be cut off from the outside world; all Jews were forbidden to own or use telephones and radios.

For the first time in Hungary, Jewish citizens were ordered to wear yellow stars on all external clothing. Even converts—baptized and practicing Christians who'd been born Jewish—were subject to the anti-Semitic restrictions. To carry out the mass deportations with typical Nazi efficiency, Hungary was divided into six zones:

Zone I: Carpathians
Zone II: Transylvania

*According to the November 1935 first supplementary decree to the Nuremberg Laws, a person with three or more Jewish grandparents was a Jew; a person with two Jewish grandparents was classified either a "full Jew"—specifically a *Geltungsjude*—or a *Mischling* of the First Degree depending on a variety of complex subtests; and a person with only one Jewish grandparent was a *Mischling* of the Second Degree.

Zone III: Northern Hungary
Zone IV: Southern Hungary east of the Danube
Zone V: Transdanubia, including the suburbs of Budapest
Zone VI: Budapest

With the participation of a *Sondereinsatzkommando* (special task force) that Eichmann had brought from Mauthausen and the help of the Hungarian police, the Germans began to round up the Jews, concentrating them within the designated zones. By March 1944, Eichmann had perfected and streamlined the *Aktionen*. Registration, roundup, concentration into ghettos, then systematic and orderly deportation to extermination camps—in Hungary, as nowhere else in Europe, it was all about to happen at an unprecedented pace.

Reuven had never seen Hannah cry, let alone break down like that, shaking and sobbing. She removed her headphones and packed her wireless set into its fabric-covered suitcase. "Reuven, what will happen to the million Jews in Hungary?" she asked. "They're in the hands of the Nazis, while we're just sitting here!"

Reuven knew that there was no easy answer. The Nazi occupation changed everything. All the Partisans' smuggling contacts across the border in Hungary had likely been forced into hiding. And what kind of German travel permits and IDs would be required now? Would civilians without specialized authorization be allowed to travel freely?

Then, once Hannah had dried her tears and regained her composure, Reuven saw something else in her: a steely resolve. Nothing was going to prevent her from crossing the border into Hungary, he realized. Nothing—not even a full-scale Nazi occupation—was going to stop her from trying to rescue her mother and other members of the trapped Jewish community of Budapest. From that moment on, during their months embedded with Tito's Partisans, Hannah knew no rest. "It was," he later wrote, "as if the earth beneath her was on fire."

10

March 1944
Yugoslavia

The first burst of military action that the parachutists saw took place in late March. A tiny Croatian village friendly to the Partisans came under direct attack and bullets tore about the streets, seemingly from all directions. The Partisans made a swift retreat, while the villagers ran about in confusion. The parachutists suddenly found themselves isolated, cut off, and surrounded by unseen sniping Germans.

Hannah and Reuven made a run for it, sliding down a nearby slope, and continued running through an open valley, where they were exposed to ceaseless, interminable gunfire. "All around," Reuven wrote, "we heard cries of fear from clusters of bewildered civilians who stumbled along, clutching pathetic belongings, their children, driving their thinning herds of cattle. The cries of the wounded and the groans of the dying filled the stillness; people dropped like wounded birds."

Reuven stopped running in mid-stride, his survival instinct blinding him to everything but making it out of the village alive. He'd been cut off from Hannah. Had she been gunned down? He glanced around frantically in the melee.

Finally he saw her. She was sprinting, blue eyes glowing, desperately trying to close the distance between them. When she reached him, they turned and ran together toward the sanctuary of the forest at the village's edge.

When they reached the forest, exhausted, they dropped down amid the pine needles and melting snow. For many minutes, they lay silently in the bushes, clutching their rifles and pistols, looking about, "listening to the incessant tattoo of bullets, the moaning of the wounded, praying the German patrol would not penetrate the forest."

A patrol of four or five Waffen-SS soldiers—members of a *Bandenbekämpfung* unit*—began to spread out methodically toward the forest edge, walking directly toward their hiding place. Reuven reflexively brought the barrel of his rifle up. With the Germans' boot steps coming closer, his finger tightened on the trigger. Hannah, calm and in control of her senses, hissed softly, sharply, in Hebrew, "Don't shoot!" They were badly outnumbered, outgunned, and likely surrounded; opening fire would surely be an act of suicide. Without saying another word, Hannah's eyes conveyed everything. They reminded Reuven of all that he'd forgotten in the chaos—that their goal was to rescue their Jewish brothers and sisters in exile and that shooting blindly at the enemy would only endanger their mission.

The Nazi patrol circled closer and closer. Reuven was afraid that they were going to trample the very brush they were hiding in, but unbelievably, the sound of leather boots passed by. He finally exhaled when he heard the German voices fading into the darkness.

A few nights later in the Slovenian mountains, Reuven, Hannah, Yonah, and Abba were marching alone in the forest when they were suddenly separated from their Partisan guides by a fast-moving *Bandenbekämpfung* unit. In the moonless night, they lost all sense of direction, uncertain if it would be safer to stay put or to forge on through the snow into the forest. When they reached the edge of the woods, the Germans began shooting wildly in all directions with rifles and machine guns. The four parachutists took cover behind a few broad tree trunks, ducking deeply into the snow and making themselves as flat as possible.

**Bandenbekämpfung* (bandit fighting) was the official counterinsurgency policy of the Nazis across occupied Europe. The Germans regarded armed rebels such as Tito's Partisan Army, not as legitimate military combatants but rather as *Banden* (bandits), criminal gangs to which the laws of warfare didn't apply. The German policy of deterring "bandits" led to the commission of war crimes, atrocities including mass executions, collective punishment, and the destruction of civilian towns and villages in order to instill "such terror into the population that it loses all will to resist."

Once again, the Nazi patrol came so close that they could have stepped right into the four parachutists' hiding spot. Despite Hannah's lack of military experience, Reuven was impressed by her ability to think clearly, not panicking when gunfire was whistling only a meter or two over their heads. It wasn't the product of the Palmach training, nor the weeks spent with the British experts in Cairo. No, that sense of composure was in her nature.

Only days before, Reuven had expressed to Enzo Sereni his doubts about working with Hannah once they were in combat conditions. No longer. "I'd glance at her from time to time, lying there, gun cocked, a heavenly radiance on her face," he later wrote. "I was overwhelmed by wonder for this unique girl."

11

April 6, 1944
Bari, Italy

Back at the Bari airfield, Enzo Sereni paced, glancing at his watch, then at the runway of the airfield, where Yoel Palgi and Peretz Goldstein were due to arrive on their C-47 flight from Cairo.

He blinked away a pang of exhaustion. As the Palmach's on-site organizer of the operation in Bari, he was constantly working. But in his first weeks in Italy, he'd also spent a great deal of time and energy learning about what had happened to his beloved Jewish community in Rome.

After occupying the city on September 10, 1943, the Germans had imposed a fine of fifty kilograms of gold on the Jewish community of Rome, to be delivered within thirty-six hours. It was difficult to raise that amount. Those without gold contributed silver, which friendly non-Jews converted to gold.

As they had done almost everywhere else they had conquered, the Nazis compiled lists of the Jews in the city from communal offices. For a month, nothing further happened, lulling the Roman Jews into a false sense that perhaps all would end well. But on October 16, 1943, during the predawn Raid on the Roman Ghetto, a total of 1,259 people—almost all from the long-established Jewish community—were rounded up by the SS and Gestapo. Of them, 1,023 were identified as Jews and deported to Auschwitz. Following the warped logic of Germany's Nuremberg laws—first enacted nearly a decade earlier—the deportees were classified as "racially" subhuman. The definition of those with "Jewish blood" included both observant and nonobservant Jews, Orthodox alongside atheists, and even ethnically Jewish Romans whose families had converted to Roman Catholicism generations before.

Since the raid on the Ghetto, Enzo wrote to his wife, "no Jew openly appears on the streets; all remaining Jews are hiding in the homes of Christian friends, some of whom shelter them out of goodness and others for heavy payment."

The news about the fate of the Roman Jewish community deeply depressed Enzo. He had no luck determining the identities of those who'd been rounded up and those who remained hidden but was told by several reliable witnesses that the entire Sereni family had been deported.*

Still, he had to put on a brave face; he continued to bound around Bari, full of his typical manic verve and energy. The wind picked up as the Dakota carrying Yoel Palgi and Peretz Goldstein began to approach the airfield. The plane touched down. As soon as the two paratroopers disembarked, a tall British major greeted them with a salute, while Enzo rushed forward, kissing Yoel and Peretz on both cheeks. Yoel watched with fascination and bemusement as Enzo darted in and out among the baggage, barking rough orders in Italian to the porters, speaking a refined English to the British officer, then chatting in informal Hebrew with Yoel and Peretz.

The newly arrived parachutists wanted to hear about their operational plans, how long they would have to stay in Bari, and when they could expect to parachute into Yugoslavia to join Tito's Partisans and proceed on their mission—but Enzo ignored their questions and instead acted as a proud and peripatetic guide.

Never seeming to slow down, Enzo ran around the Bari airfield without uniform or documents, barging unannounced into MI9's headquarters, crossing into sensitive British and American areas of the airfield, and the sentries barely seemed to notice.

On the rare occasion when some young private asked Enzo to state his business or to show identification, Sereni would stare at the guard with a look of such scornful bewilderment that he was promptly let through. Many British

*Of the 1,259 Roman Jews deported by the Nazis, only 14 returned to Rome at the end of the war.

airmen began joking about it: How did that short, bespectacled man dressed in a gray civilian suit, never carrying proper papers, waltz about anywhere he pleased on the airfield, while every other RAF man in full uniform needed to produce identification? Enzo shrugged. "Self-confidence is what counts, not documents," he said.

He was most ecstatic while showing off the beauty of southern Italy to visitors. No sooner had the two newly arrived parachutists checked into their quarters than Enzo dragged them outside, directing their attention to Bari's buildings, white sand beaches, medieval churches, and cobbled streets. He nodded hello to the old men sitting in the shade sipping a local vintage, smiled at the boys in shorts kicking footballs on the cobbles—yelling and joking along and trying to describe for Yoel and Peretz the inimitable rustic flavor of the Barese dialect.

When a particularly voluptuous young woman passed, Enzo exclaimed, *"Magnifica! Un'aristocratica!"*

Yoel laughed aloud. "Enzo, your aristocratic girls go about barefoot, selling themselves for a can of preserves."

Enzo spun on his heel, enraged. "Understand something, my friend," he said, "Italy has been destroyed by the Fascists—*destroyed*! But we will recover our former glory. We're a cultured and artistic nation with a history almost as ancient as that of the Jewish people."

Yoel raised one palm in apology, chastened. Unlike Hannah, he had no desire to debate a man as feisty and brilliant with words as Enzo.

Like a tiny tornado, Enzo was forever gesturing, arguing, explaining. He didn't bother to ask permission for anything. He snatched a package of American cigarettes from one of Yoel's pockets and started distributing them to Italian pedestrians passing by in the courtyards and alleys; then he urged his friends to buy Italian sweets and distribute them to the children in the street. "Come on! Show some heart! If you don't sympathize with the suffering of others, you won't feel the suffering of our own people either."

12

April 13, 1944
Žumberak Mountains, Croatia

Yoel Palgi and Peretz Goldstein were scheduled to make their drop on the first night of Passover, April 7, 1944, and Enzo had arranged for a portable Seder—matzoh, a small flask of wine, a jar of horseradish, and Haggadahs—on board the Halifax as they flew over enemy territory.

But adverse weather conditions delayed the departure. They had a Seder together on the Bari airfield. Then Yoel and Peretz parachuted into Yugoslavia a week later, on April 13. Their mission was code-named Operation Albert.

They were dropped into the Žumberak mountain range on the border of Slovenia and Croatia. Both men jumped without incident, and a Partisan unit was waiting to greet them. Yoel felt the Partisans surveying him from head to toe. He snapped to attention and saluted crisply. *"Smrt fašizmu!"* he said.

"Svoboda narodu!" the Partisans replied in unison.

On their way to rendezvous with Hannah, Reuven, and the others, Yoel and Peretz joined up with Major General Petar Drapšin, the commander of the Partisans' 12th Slavonian Division. The general was, as Yoel later described him, "a handsome youngster with the face of an educated person; he was the commander-in-chief of the partisan armies in northern Yugoslavia."

With the general was Lieutenant Colonel Stipo—the nom de guerre of Pavle Vukomanović, the most accomplished Partisan saboteur of World War II. Stipo served under Major General Ivan Hariš-Gromovnik—often referred to as Ilija Gromovnik—the commander of a division dedicated solely to sabotage and commando raids. "It was an army within an army," Palgi later wrote.

Almost immediately, Palgi told the Partisan officers about their intention to cross the border into Hungary. General Hariš said that he also wanted to launch a mission into Hungary with a group of saboteurs, but his men lacked the necessary arms and explosives for the operation. General Drapšin had been born into a peasant family in the small town of Srbobran near the border of the Austro-Hungarian Empire. He told Palgi and Goldstein that he knew the border region well and could lead them there.

On the spot, they made a handshake deal: If Palgi would radio his British counterparts and convince the RAF to drop more explosives, the Partisans would help guide the two Jewish parachutists across the border into Hungary.

As they set out to cross the Papuk mountains with the Partisans, Palgi and Goldstein learned the strange rules of engagement in that part of Yugoslavia. The daylight hours belonged to the fascists, the night to the Partisans. When the Partisans passed through any territory, no matter for what purpose, they sabotaged anything that could be of use to the Nazis. After they crossed any railroad, they detonated the tracks. When they crossed a bridge, Drapšin's soldiers expertly used dynamite to topple it.

At one point in their journey, the Partisan convoy came upon a major railway supply line. "Large groups of Partisans scattered and took up positions while one group began to unload shells and explosives from the cart," Palgi wrote. "Feverish activity ensued. Our group was ordered to move on, but we couldn't restrain our curiosity—we stayed where we were. With brisk, calculated movements, the partisans were planting dynamite under the tracks for the length of a kilometer and attaching detonators."

Yoel and Peretz stood a few hundred meters back and took cover. They heard a train in the distance, growing louder, and a nightingale trilling in the forest behind them. Yoel clutched his submachine gun when the train's whistle sounded. He could see that it was a supply train, crawling heavily forward. In a series of chain reactions, dynamite explosions ignited more dynamite; the thunder of overturning engines and carriages and the clang of iron on iron filled the air. For the briefest instant there was deathly silence. Then Yoel heard screaming and cursing in German and roars of pain. More dynamite explosions went off. Machine-gun fire erupted.

The Partisans burst from the forest, swarmed furiously over the train, and, by the light of the burning carriages, began their looting. Within minutes the two horse-drawn carts were loaded way beyond capacity, and many Partisans were needed to help the horses pull the load.

A Partisan commander shouted the order to retreat. They marched at double time into the thickets and dark woods until dawn broke. Yoel and Peretz were exhausted, dragging their boots through the mud, but were deeply impressed by the effectiveness of the Partisans' demolition specialists. They knew that such acts of sabotage against Nazi transport trains were a vital source of supplies and munitions for the Partisans and a key to their strategy. They also knew that now, with the coming of daylight, the Germans were bound to send in hundreds of *Bandenbekämpfung* Waffen-SS men to attempt a terrible reprisal.

13

April 15, 1944
Bari, Italy

In MI9's forward operations base at Bari, Enzo Sereni studied maps of Yugoslavia and tried to pinpoint the whereabouts of the various paratroopers, based on their most recent radio transmissions. After receiving a report from Agent Mickey—Yoel Palgi—describing the effectiveness of the Partisans' army of saboteurs, Enzo proudly marked the spot of the railway demolition on his map. Yoel and Peretz were proving to be a highly effective unit of paratroopers and radio operators behind the lines.

Enzo began to laugh, remembering how *ineffective* Yoel had been just days earlier, trying to use the military chain of command to influence him. "I've brought orders from H.Q.," he had told Enzo sternly. "You're to return immediately to Cairo."

"Out of the question."

"It's an order. H.Q. says that you intend to jump into northern Italy."

"So what? Isn't it our duty to rescue the few surviving Jews in the north?"

Yoel had tried to tell him that there were no more Jews in northern Italy—they'd all been rounded up by the Nazis. In any event, Enzo wasn't authorized to act on his own, a loose cannon.

"Let me tell you something—H.Q. doesn't have a clue what's going on," Enzo had snapped. "Our people have *no* reliable intelligence about the situation in the north of Italy."

"What about following authority? What about discipline?"

Enzo had exhaled loudly. "I follow my own discipline."

Yoel had wondered if Enzo couldn't bear to send so many young people on parachute missions behind the lines if he wasn't willing to jump himself.

"That's nonsense," Enzo had said, and Yoel had had no choice but to drop the matter.

Now, in mid-April, Enzo had a more authoritative surprise visitor. Colonel Tony Simonds arrived in Bari and, uncharacteristically pulling rank, ordered Enzo to return to Cairo. The order came not from British Military Intelligence, Simonds stressed, but from the Jewish Agency. Ben-Gurion himself said that Enzo was urgently needed at Givat Brenner.

Simonds could give no further details. Enzo wasn't so easily fooled. There was no emergency at Givat Brenner. If there was, why hadn't he heard about it directly from his wife? Enzo stared at Tony Simonds and flatly refused to obey the order. Then he dashed off a letter to Ben-Gurion and the leadership inner circle of Committee Het, the Infiltration Committee of the Mossad L'Aliyah Bet:

> *I don't understand the meaning of the stupid message you sent through Tony that I'm needed at my kibbutz. If something has happened that requires my return, write to me about it.*
>
> *If all you want to do is to influence me, you're wasting your time. . . .*
>
> *Just bear this in mind: This will be the end of any relationship between us. Your attempts at preventing me [from jumping] by using administrative pressure have deeply hurt me. . . .*
>
> *This letter is addressed to all of you: Ben-Gurion, Yosef, Eliezer, Dobkin, etc. and it can also be read by the committee.**
>
> *Yours, with love, in*
> *spite of everything,*
> *Enzo*

*Besides David Ben-Gurion, Enzo aimed his displeasure at Yosef Dov, Eliezer Kaplan, and Eliyahu Dobkin, all political leaders of the Labor Zionist movement and members of Committee Het, the committee concerning matters dealing with infiltration of the Jewish communities of Europe.

Enzo's concern for the fate of the remaining pockets of Jewry caught in the Nazis' clutches in northern Italy was real. He'd also been asked by MI9 to contact two Italian generals in the north, who, as Enzo told Moshe Sharrett, "may come over to the Allies if suitably influenced. This could hasten the end of hostilities on this front. I'm confident that I can perform this mission."

There was another, more personal motive—one he didn't share with Ben-Gurion, Sharrett, or anyone else in the Jewish Agency leadership: He wanted to parachute into the north and reunite with his brother. News had reached Bari that Emilio Sereni, the Communist Party representative on the Comitato di Liberazione Nazionale Alta Italia (National Liberation Committee for Northern Italy), had been convicted by a Fascist court and was jailed awaiting sentencing.

Enzo didn't know where his brother was. In fact, Emilio Sereni had by then broken out of jail and was living safely underground in Milan, disguised and using a false name, in charge of the Italian Resistance's department of propaganda.

On April 17, Enzo celebrated his thirty-ninth birthday solemnly and alone, writing and reflecting. The following day, he began an accelerated parachutist's course. Though some of the Italian airmen teasingly called him *il Vecchio* (the Old Guy), he passed the requisite physical and basic training and was green-lighted to jump. On the eve of his first training jump, he wrote a farewell letter to his son, Daniel, at Givat Brenner:

> *Should anything happen to me and I not see you again, I want you to know that I thought of you at this moment—I thought of you and of Mother and Grandma as the most precious possessions I have in life.*
>
> *I wish that you grow up to be what we have not succeeded in being: natural, Jewish working people, and also that you preserve the zeal and the consistency that brought your mother and me to the country and to the pioneering movement. . . .*
>
> *Should I not return, then remember me.*
>
> *Take care of Mother and Grandma. Study well and remain true to yourselves and to me.*
>
> *Shalom to all of you. Shalom to Givat Brenner, for I'm here also for its sake. Shalom to Eretz Israel.*

When one is away from it one feels more than ever that one belongs to it wholly and that all the rest is just so much froth upon the waters.

Two days later, Enzo made his first training jump without mishap. His was an even more accelerated course than that which Hannah and the other Palmach volunteers had gone through at Ramat David; he was required to complete six daylight jumps in four days—no nighttime jumps at all—and was then entitled to attach the embroidered wings-with-parachute badge to his RAF uniform.

"Despite my age I was not among the worst," he wrote in one of his letters home to Givat Brenner. "My height and weight stood me in good stead, and I remained in the air longer than any of the others each time. It's true that every time you have to jump you worry and feel scared all over again, but the sensation when you are in the air is wonderful, and when you reach the ground—well, you feel like a king. Now I feel confident. Now I know for sure that I will make my way."

Enzo's personal mission objectives were clear: to try to rescue as many Jews he could find alive in northern Italy and to locate Emilio wherever he was in hiding. The MI9 side of the operation was just as straightforward: Enzo would go to Florence, meet with two wavering Italian generals, and assist escaped British and American POWs to cross over the Allied lines in the south of Italy. To prepare, he studied detailed maps and saw a spot north of Florence named Campi di Annibale, reasoning that if the great Carthaginian general Hannibal had set up a camp there—with all his war elephants—it would be a broad, flat field, ideal for a parachute landing.

One morning, a transport plane brought a letter from Givat Brenner, written by his thirteen-year-old son, Daniel. Enzo couldn't stop waving it around and reading it aloud to anyone who would listen. "Look, I just got a letter from my little boy! He writes: 'Daddy, even if you die, the main thing is to be brave!'"

14

April 25, 1944
Budapest, Hungary

On April 25, SS Obersturmbannführer Adolf Eichmann summoned Joel Brand, a short, thirty-eight-year-old, red-haired businessman and Zionist leader, to his office in the Majestic Hotel on Schwab Hill.

Brand, a leader of the Relief and Rescue Committee of Budapest, known as "the Va'ada," was thoroughly frisked at the entrance and then escorted upstairs by two SS men. Eichmann's spacious office on the second floor offered a magnificent view of chestnut trees with their white blossoms.

As Brand entered, he saw Eichmann behind the desk, his back to the windows. He was a slight man with narrow shoulders, meticulously dressed in his tailored gray-green SS officer's jacket. His epaulets showed the four stars of lieutenant colonel. The smoke from his cigarette filled the room. Brand later wrote that Eichmann possessed the most unforgettable eyes he'd ever seen: "Steely blue, hard and sharp, they seemed to bore through you. . . . It was only later that I noticed his small face with its thin lips and sharp nose."

Eichmann's revolver and holster lay on the table close to his right hand. His fingers drummed impatiently. "Do you know who I am?" he asked Brand rhetorically.

Brand nodded. Eichmann got up and paced in his polished black boots, until he was face-to-face with Brand. "I know all about you," he said. "You know *nothing* about me." He glared at Brand, hands on his hips. "I've carried out the *Aktionen* in Poland, Czechoslovakia, Austria. They've all been completed. Now it's your turn."

Brand was so taken aback that he found himself squeezing his felt fedora until its brim was twisted.

"If you could decide whom to save, Brand, whom would you choose? Fertile women? Virile men? Children? You've read *Der Judenstaat*. You're a Zionist. What kind of stock do you want?"

"I couldn't—" Brand began.

"You what?"

Every single one of them, Brand wanted to say, but he simply stammered quietly in a manner that caused Eichmann to burst into laughter.

Eichmann proposed an exchange of "useless" Jews for something the Third Reich needed. No, he said, he wasn't interested in gold, jewels, or even cash. He wanted trucks. He coined a phrase that would later become infamous: *Ware für Blut—Blut für Ware.* "Goods for blood—blood for goods. A million Jews, Brand. Consider it. You can gather up a million in Hungary and any other countries which still have Jews."

Brand was stunned to be handed such an awesome responsibility. The fate of a million Jews was suddenly in his hands?

What were the lives of a million innocent Jewish civilians worth? The Nazis didn't expect the Allies to pay a ransom in dollars or pounds—they offered to "sell" a million Jews for ten thousand trucks—properly winterized—along with two hundred tons of tea and eighteen tons of coffee.

Brand said that even with his extensive contacts with the Jewish Agency in Istanbul—he really had none—procuring trucks would be difficult because the Allies might think that trucks were military equipment to be used against them.

"I'm prepared to be reasonable," Eichmann said. He gave his personal promise that the trucks would never be used against the British and Americans, only on the eastern front, against the Bolsheviks.

The scheme was not a fanciful whim of Eichmann. SS Reichsführer Heinrich Himmler had agreed to exchange a million of Europe's surviving Jews for ten thousand trucks. Since Himmler had vowed to make Hungary *judenrein* (free of Jews) those exchanged couldn't remain there. They could emigrate to anywhere except for Mandatory Palestine, as the Nazis had assured the grand mufti of Jerusalem, Hajj Mohammad Amin al-Husseini, that they wouldn't allow more Jewish immigration into Palestine. Perhaps Spain or Switzerland, neutral nations, would take them.

As the negotiations proceeded, Eichmann agreed to a piecemeal deal to demonstrate his honesty. "You'll first deliver one truck per hundred Jews. The trucks must be brand new with spare parts and winterized. A thousand trucks to save one hundred thousand Jews. Then for every additional thousand trucks, an additional hundred thousand Jews." He told Brand that as a sign of good faith, as soon as the deal was consummated, he would not only end the deportations, he'd "blow up" the gas chambers at Auschwitz—a bold-faced lie, since Eichmann had neither the authority nor the inclination to do anything of the kind. "You have the contacts with the Joint and the Jewish Agency!" he shouted. "You go tell them what a great deal the SS is offering."* He ordered Brand to travel to Istanbul and meet with Jewish Agency officials, who would put the offer before Churchill and Roosevelt. Brand's wife, Hansi, would need to stay behind in Budapest, of course, under Eichmann's careful "watch"—the Obersturmbannführer would never use so crude a word as "hostage."

Brand saw the deal for what it was: sheer lunacy. But he also realized that the "Blood for Goods" offer might buy Hungary's Jews the most precious thing in the world right now: time.

•

Elaborate layers of deception were crucial for the Nazis' lightning-paced *Aktion* against Hungary's Jews. On April 29, Eichmann's first deportation trains to Auschwitz left from Kistarcsa, a town with a population of about 12,000, just northwest of Budapest. To keep up the ruse that the Jews were being sent to work for the Reich, these first deportations applied only to "able-bodied Jewish males between the ages of sixteen and fifty."

The leaders of the Judenrat in Budapest were told that the deportees had been sent to a labor camp in Poland known as Waldsee. Waldsee, German for "Forest Lake," was the innocuous-sounding name used by the SS to ensure the smooth transport of nearly five hundred thousand Hungarian Jews

*By "the Joint," Eichmann was referring to the American Jewish Joint Distribution Committee, the largest Jewish humanitarian agency in the world.

to Auschwitz between April and early July 1944. Waldsee, of course, did not exist. To avoid rebellion or escape, to lull those who had stayed behind into a sense of security, the SS arranged for some of those who'd been deported to Auschwitz to send postcards to their loved ones, supposedly from their comfortable new home.

The postcards, written only moments before the prisoners entered the gas chambers, were terse and used the same stock phrases: "I am doing fine," "I'm working," "We've arrived safely," or "Follow us here!" All were postmarked from the mysterious Waldsee.

Eichmann insisted that Joel Brand travel to Istanbul in the company of his handpicked people, such as Bandi Grosz, a convicted smuggler whose declassified American intelligence files list his real name as Andor Gross, though he also went by the names Andre Gyorgy, Antal Giorgi, Andreas Grainer, and a half-dozen more aliases.

Grosz was a Hungarian Jew who'd converted to Roman Catholicism. By 1944, he made his primary income as a handsomely paid espionage asset. Described as short and ugly, with a thatch of red hair, a stooped gait, and grotesquely protruding front teeth, he was a triple agent, working for Hungarian Military Intelligence, the Gestapo, and the Abwehr. Meanwhile, in Istanbul, the Dogwood Network, which had gained the trust of Teddy Kollek and the Jewish Agency, found Grosz to be an effective smuggler who could move across borders in Nazi-occupied Europe with seeming ease.

On May 17, Brand and Grosz left Budapest for Vienna, chauffeured in one of Eichmann's Mercedes sedans. They spent a night at the Hotel Metropole, the Gestapo's headquarters in Austria, then left for Istanbul on a Luftwaffe courier plane on May 19.

Eichmann had promised to discontinue all deportations to Auschwitz for two weeks until Brand got a reply from the Allied governments about his ten thousand winterized trucks. For a fortnight, the Hungarian Jews boarding trains would be held "on ice" in Austria—for "safekeeping," he said—until Brand proved that he was making headway with the Allies.

Eichmann was lying again. "In Hungary in 1944," the British historian David Cesarani noted, Eichmann had behaved "with almost demonic energy"—displaying his fanaticism as he personally saw that the trains bound for Auschwitz were crammed to capacity and departing as quickly as possible. Years later, when Eichmann was on trial in a bulletproof glass booth in Jerusalem, the prosecution proved that he had continued the deportation of Hungary's Jews to Auschwitz-Birkenau unabated, at an estimated eight thousand per day, more than 90 percent of whom had been gassed upon arrival.

15

May 1944
Slovenia, Yugoslavia

Meanwhile, high in the Papuk mountains of Slovenia, the parachutists needed to remain constantly on the move and vigilant not to expose their real identities. Back in Cairo, they'd been instructed that it was imperative to speak only in English—never Hebrew—since anti-Semitism was rampant in the Balkans. Being among Tito's Partisans, however, wasn't as dangerous as being in areas held by the Ustaše, the Croatian collaborators who often outdid the Nazis in the savagery of their pogroms and sadism against Jews, Serbs, and Muslims.

Marshal Tito had absorbed much of his ideology from his Jewish friend and mentor Moša Pijade, popularly known as Čiča Janko (Uncle Janko). They had met while serving time in the Maribor penitentiary for revolutionary activities. Pijade was a highly decorated hero and a leading intellectual among Yugoslavian Marxists. Born Moishe Pijade in 1890 to a Sephardic Jewish family in Belgrade, he was a painter and writer in his youth and made the first translation of Karl Marx's *Das Kapital* into Serbo-Croatian.

Two years older than Tito and politically savvy—he would later serve as president of the Yugoslavian Parliament—Pijade was one of the leading commanders of the Yugoslav People's Army. Throughout the war, Tito considered Pijade his most capable administrator. Pijade's Jewishness also made him a favorite target of Nazi propaganda. Though Pijade never met with Hannah and the other Jewish parachutists, he personally ordered that the Partisans take especially good care of the British paratroopers from Palestine.

The lack of institutional anti-Semitism within Tito's Partisan army was due primarily to its ideological grounding in Marxism. Tito's Partisans, like other Communist-led resistance movements, treated Jews as equals, welcome in the armed struggle. The Communist Party of Yugoslavia saw anti-Semitism as a foreign ideology introduced by the Nazi occupiers and adopted by their Serbo-Croatian collaborators. Rescuing Jews and fighting anti-Semitism was official Party policy, inseparable from the overall resistance against the Nazis.

Senior Jewish commanders included Spanish Civil War veteran Samuel Lehrer, aka Voja Todorovic, and Dr. Roza Papo, a Jewish Bosnian physician and the first woman to ever become a general in the Balkan Peninsula. Among Tito's ranks were more than 4,500 Jews—3,000 of them in fighting units. Tito's Partisans even had a unit called the Rab Battalion, made up of hundreds of Jewish inmates liberated from the Italian Rab concentration camp in September 1943.

On May 1, two days after the deportations of Hungarian Jewry began, the four parachutists—Hannah, Reuven, Yonah, and Abba—were invited by the Partisans to attend a May Day festival. They had no idea that *they* were the star attractions. May Day, for all of them, was a familiar holiday. International Workers' Day had long been celebrated on the left-wing kibbutzim in Mandatory Palestine, and since the 1920s, the Histradut labor union had organized large marches in Jerusalem, Tel Aviv, and Haifa.

The Partisans paraded in their assortment of uniforms, fully armed, filling the streets, their laughter and loud singing adding to the festive mood. As Hannah, Reuven, Yonah, and Abba entered the town hall, the crowd erupted in cheers. Here were four representatives of the British Empire, paratroopers in their blue RAF uniforms. By now, they'd become well known among Tito's rank and file and his high command. Wherever they went, Reuven Dafni wrote, the Partisans and the local villagers were drawn to them—particularly Hannah, "the young British officer in her smart army uniform, pistol strapped to her waist," who in just a few months had become something of a legend, and not only because she was a woman warrior. "Everywhere we went there was a special, mysterious quality about Hannah which excited people's wonder and respect."

Now the top-ranking Partisan officer at the May Day festival singled out

Hannah to address the crowd. She stepped forward, her head held high, her voice echoing through the town hall. She spoke as a British aircraftwoman, of course—in her most proper English—with Reuven acting as interpreter. Her voice was bold as she predicted the ultimate victory of the Allies, the downfall of Hitler, and the crushing of fascism in Yugoslavia. With each line she spoke, the crowd cheered louder. *"Smrt fašizmu!" "Svoboda narodu!"*

After Hannah's speech, rustic food was served, then numerous bottles of slivovitz, the local plum brandy. Several Partisans brought out their stringed instruments—tamburica, lijerica, jedinka—accordions, and tambourines.

They began to dance the kolo, a Slavic circle dance, holding hands or wrapping their arms around one another's shoulders. It reminded Hannah and the others of the hora they'd been dancing for years on the kibbutzim. Partisan men and women danced with Nagant rifles and PPD-40 submachine guns strapped to their shoulders, bandoliers, and RGD-33 hand grenades swinging from their belts.

At one point, Hannah slipped into the main circle, quickly learning the footwork. She danced for hours without rest, until her face was drenched in sweat.

16

May 2, 1944
Serdica, Yugoslavia

"The girl with the sacred fire."

That was how Reuven always thought of Hannah. Since they'd first met during training, her personality had both astonished and confounded him. Despite her talent, charm, and charisma—she could talk with one of Tito's generals just as naturally as she would an unschooled Partisan fighter—she was a very difficult woman to *like*, he thought: headstrong, combative, consumed by white-hot passion, idealism, and self-assuredness beyond her years.

Reuven thought about that as the four parachutists marched through the mountains of Slovenia, hours of hard uphill hiking, until they reached a camp under the command of a young woman Partisan. She greeted them in an oversized Red Army overcoat, a Kalashnikov slung over her shoulder, and an old Soviet revolver on her hip.

It took a few moments for Reuven to realize: He knew her. They'd been childhood friends; they'd lived in the same district of Zagreb, had often played together in its streets. They'd been close as children but had lost touch a few years later, after she had become a Young Communist and he'd joined the Socialist Zionist youth movement.

"Luca," the Partisan commander said, using her nom de guerre, introducing herself to Hannah and the other parachutists. "That's what the Partisans call me."

"You used to have a Jewish name in Zagreb."

"We're not in Zagreb anymore. Now I'm Luca. It's safer, Reuven. Luca doesn't sound Jewish to these villagers."

As Hannah listened to them chat, she found it hard to believe that Luca was Reuven's age—not yet thirty. "The years of terror had left their mark on her face," Reuven later wrote. "She had deep creases around her eyes and despite her youth, her once dark hair was streaked with gray."

That young female commander, that *partizanka,* had already heard about the British paratroopers. Their legend was spreading through stories and songs around the bonfires, and Luca was shocked to learn that Reuven and his group weren't British but Jews who'd left Europe for kibbutzim in Palestine and had now voluntarily parachuted back into the European inferno.

As they talked and began to let down their guard, Reuven learned that all the Partisans in the farmhouse were Jewish, too. The Palestinian parachutists told the Yugoslavian Jews about their new life in Eretz Israel, the Homeland they had been working to build, the kibbutzim and moshavim, and the revival of Hebrew as a spoken language.

As he stirred the crumbling logs in the bonfire with a long green stick, kicking up embers, Reuven told Luca that he had enlisted in the British Army in 1940 and had fought in the Greek campaign, the Battle of Crete, and against Rommel in North Africa—but then Luca cut him short. "See, you left, Reuven. You accomplished something. Now you've come back—a British officer. But here I am—the *partizanka*—yet still a 'filthy Jew' to them."

Luca spoke softly, in an undertone; Hannah listened as she described more horrors, atrocities that beggared belief. Synagogues packed with Jews had been burned alive as SS men had watched and local villagers had howled as if watching a football match. Worst of all, the Ustaše fascist government had constructed its own extermination camp in the village of Jasenovac. In the camp's marshy fields, Jews, Serbs, Romani, and political dissidents were starved, beaten, and murdered by the thousands. Jasenovac had no gas chambers or crematoria like the Nazis' death factories in eastern Poland, but it was known for hands-on, one-on-one killing by Croatian guards using hammers, axes, and a curved agricultural knife called a *srbosjek*. The Ustaše guards would occasionally make bets to see who could kill the most newly arrived prisoners with the *srbosjek* strapped to one hand. In August 1942, an infamous lieutenant named Petar "Pero" Brzica had won the contest by personally cutting the throats of 1,360 men, women, and children in a single rampage.

Suddenly Hannah could no longer listen. A low groan from the depths of her throat turned into a howl of rage. She rose from the bonfire, grabbed her notebook and pencil, and, as she'd so often done in Nahalal and Sdot Yam, began to write by the light of a kerosene lamp. Once again, Reuven saw it: *The girl with the sacred fire* . . . He stared at Hannah. What could she be scribbling so furiously? It would be another month before he would learn the answer.

17

May 3, 1944
Southwestern Romania

Brilliant white silk, billowing, reflecting the moonlight—that was what gave them away. Two members of the Romanian infiltration team, Yitzhak Macarescu and Arie "Rico" Lupescu, both from Kibbutz Sarid, had successfully made a blind jump near the city of Craiova. But after only a few days on the loose, they were picked up by Romanian gendarmes, who'd been alerted by villagers to the sight of two white parachutes descending.

Fortunately, both men spoke good English, and in their RAF uniforms, with dog tags and the insignia of officers, managed to conceal that they were Romanian born, preventing them from being prosecuted for the crime of treason.

Their fictional cover story was that they'd been on a bombing mission to hit the Ploești oil fields and refineries when their Halifax had taken some flak and lost two engines. Knowing that there was no way they could make it back to Italy, the flight crew had bailed out over southwestern Romania.

At the end of a brief military interrogation, they were transferred to a POW camp filled with British, American, and French flyers. To their surprise, they soon met up with Lyova Gukowsky and Arie Fichman, the first parachutists of the Romanian team, who'd been POWs for over a year. With Gukowsky's introductions, Lupescu and Macarescu began working in the established prison underground to smuggle out valuable intelligence as well as aid in the escape of captive airmen.

• • •

Over a thousand miles southeast of Bucharest, Haviva Reik and Surika Braverman were growing impatient, walking the hot, dusty streets of Cairo in their khaki drill shorts, constantly practicing their Morse code skills as they awaited deployment. Haviva and Surika were among the fastest students at the Signals School, completing a course that typically required at least two months in under six weeks. As they strolled through Cairo, they practiced converting each street and store name into Morse code dots and dashes.

Surika, a member of the Romanian infiltration team, should have already been in Bari, waiting to parachute into Bucharest. The only problem was that she couldn't parachute.

While Haviva had loved training at the Ramat David Airbase, for Surika jump school had been traumatic. After Haviva and the three other volunteers had parachuted from the Dakota transport plane, Surika had frozen. At two thousand feet, she'd seen the green light and heard the command to jump. She had followed the others, stood at the hatch, trying to force her legs to move forward. She'd been paralyzed. The instructor had attempted to give her a firm shove, but she'd spun around and forced her way back inside.

Surika was no shrinking violet; she was a natural leader. She'd been handpicked by Yitzhak Sadeh to be one of the first commanders of the Palmach. But she had a phobia when it came to heights. She would never forgive herself for her moment of weakness.

She'd worked as hard as anyone else in training. She'd made all the harnessed jumps from buildings, she'd mentally prepared herself, but then at the sight of the green light, she had frozen. From the back of the transport plane, she had watched as all the other parachutists floated down into the Emek Valley.

Surika was not only embarrassed; she felt disgusted at what she saw as her weakness. She became depressed and withdrew to her room, refusing to see anyone. She stopped attending the training sessions, then packed her few belongings to return to Kibbutz Shamir and resign from the mission.

But Haviva convinced her not to give up, and Surika remained part of the Romanian delegation. She went to Cairo for intelligence training as a radio operator and was determined to make her own contribution behind enemy lines. Yet for the rest of her life she was saddled with a sardonic sobriquet: "The Parachutist Who Didn't Jump."

• • •

Haviva thought back to the farewell party in Tel Aviv for the members of her group departing for Cairo, and she remembered her final words to Yitzhak Sadeh. The commanders of the mission saw it as their duty to speak privately with all the parachutists before departure. Ha-Zaken had a soft spot for Haviva. Back at a convention of kibbutzim in April 1942, when Haviva had heard the charismatic speech of Ha-Zaken—poet, essayist, playwright, soldier—she had been so inspired that she had enlisted, one of the first women in his newly formed Palmach.

After the farewell party, the Old Man had taken an evening stroll alone with Haviva near Rothschild Boulevard. As they walked together in the streets of Tel Aviv, Haviva had described to him her postwar dreams. "I'm convinced that I'll reach my destination," she had told him. "I'm convinced that I'll do what I am supposed to do, and I'm convinced that I shall return. And when I return, I'll remember that I'm a *woman*. . . . Were men meant to fight? Were women built for combat? I will return to my kibbutz; I will have a family; I will have children."

Now, in May 1944, Haviva kept repeating those words in her mind as she walked through Cairo, converting them into Morse code as she awaited deployment to the uprising that was being planned in her native Slovakia.

18

May 6, 1944
Metlika, Yugoslavia

As they hiked through the mountains of Yugoslavia in a convoy, the Partisans told Yoel Palgi and Peretz Goldstein that there was a contingent of British officers awaiting them in Metlika, a Slovenian town roughly thirty-five miles southwest of Zagreb. Yoel thought that they might be meeting Fitzroy Maclean, a Scottish-born officer who'd enlisted at the start of World War II as a private and risen to the rank of brigadier. Prime Minister Churchill had sent him to head the SOE contingent at Tito's headquarters in Metlika.

As Yoel and Peretz approached Metlika, three men on horseback galloped over to them. The pair jumped to attention and saluted smartly. But when the dust kicked up by the horses settled, they saw that the uniformed men on horseback were Reuven Dafni and Yonah Rosen. Yoel dropped his salute and burst out laughing. After Reuven and Yonah dismounted and they exchanged hugs, Yoel glanced around. "Where's Hannah?" Reuven told him that she was out patrolling the northern border with a small band of Partisans, scouting out the conditions for a potential crossing into Hungary.

With them now at Metlika was British Major Robert Eden—said to be the nephew of British Foreign Secretary Anthony Eden—who'd parachuted into Partisan-held Yugoslavia to run Operation Cobweb, a mission designed solely to exfiltrate downed and escaped Allied airmen. Technically, he was now the ranking officer in charge in the field, subordinate only to Colonel Simonds in Cairo and Brigadier Dudley Clarke, the head of MI9 in London.

Major Eden's manners seemed strange and disrespectful to the Partisans, Palgi observed. They may not have understood the English language, but they understood the condescension of an upper-crust Englishman. They found Major Eden patronizing. "The partisans were sensitive to such behavior and paid him back in the same coin, unfortunately lumping us together with him. From now on friendship was out of the question and relations became formal."

The one Yishuv parachutist whom the Partisans trusted was Reuven Dafni, because of his fluency in Croatian and his affinity for the local culture. Soon the Partisans would deal only with Reuven; they ignored Eden completely. The major became incensed. "*He* was meant to be the main intermediary with the Partisans," Palgi wrote, "but Reuven had inadvertently usurped this role. Out of this stemmed disagreements, minor ones at first, but more serious later, and the air became charged."

Eden also had several confrontations with Hannah—after which she openly announced that she would have nothing more to do with him.

Despite Eden's status as their overall field commander within MI9, the parachutists soon lost all respect for his authority; they began whispering together in Hebrew, questioning whether he really was the nephew of Anthony Eden. The crisis came to a head when Eden made several cutting remarks, subtle at first, then more intentionally insulting, about an inherent cowardice in Jews. "I know your lot," he said to Yoel Palgi. "When the time comes for action, you drop out."

Palgi and Peretz Goldstein were dismantling their submachine guns and oiling the parts. Palgi felt a burning anger in his chest. "You *bastard*," he said in a quiet but unsteady voice. "You know very well that we've come to save our brothers from extermination."

The British Empire had *never* been interested in rescuing the Jews who were being exterminated, Palgi said. The RAF wasn't willing to allow the Yishuv to use a single long-range bomber for the paratroopers' mission. "If we could have, we would have done everything ourselves without any help from you. No, you wanted us to come only after you realized there were no British agents capable of speaking the local languages or posing undercover. It's your fault that our departure was delayed until Hungary was invaded by the Germans—and now you've got the nerve to throw slurs at us!" His eyes were inflamed. Peretz Goldstein said nothing, but his eyes also flashed with anger.

After a long, tense silence, Eden finally said, "You Jews have a way of *always* exaggerating. I don't believe those tales of extermination. But it's just as well you've shown your true face. I've always known you Jews from Palestine were hostile to us."

Shortly afterward, the parachutists huddled together, came to a consensus, and decided that it was impossible to work under Major Eden. Palgi radioed Colonel Simonds in Cairo and made their position clear: They were not prepared to carry on with the MI9 escape and evasion aspect of the mission unless Major Eden was removed as their commander.

No sooner had they radioed Simonds than Hannah returned from her survey of the border zone. Yoel hadn't seen Hannah since their training in Cairo. He greeted her with a powerful hug. They were speechless at first; there was far too much catching up to do. Within minutes, he saw how profoundly she had changed. She was not the same girl he'd seen smiling in the streets of Tel Aviv or writing poems in their headquarters in Suleiman Pasha Square. "Her eyes no longer sparkled," he later wrote. "She was cold, sharp, her reasoning now razor-edged; she no longer trusted strangers."

Hannah of the forests and the mountains, embedded with the Partisans for months, was a different woman. She was impatient, unwilling to listen to suggestions that she should delay crossing the border—no matter how sound and reasonable the advice. "Hannah seemed concerned only with her own goals; she was totally lacking in caution and refused to accept discipline."

When she learned about the argument the parachutists had had with Major Eden, she was furious. She said it was foolish to have radioed Colonel Simonds with such an ultimatum. What could be achieved by it, besides jeopardizing the whole rescue operation? In her mind it was simply a clash of personalities. Who cared if Eden made anti-Semitic comments? It was rare to find a British officer who didn't hold such views, even if he was diplomatic enough to keep his thoughts private. MI9 was never going to take the side of a small band of Jews from Palestine over an English officer from such a well-connected family.

As if the rift with Eden weren't enough, Hannah and Reuven began to have heated disagreements about the motives of Tito's Partisans. Reuven believed in the Partisans' promise to help them rescue Jews. Hannah no longer did. She'd concluded that the Partisan commanders were using the Jewish parachutists only to get supplies, munitions, and explosives air-dropped by the RAF.

She'd come back from her solo reconnaissance mission of the Yugoslav-Hungarian border certain that the Partisans had no real intention of helping her cross. They kept making excuses about having lost all their reliable smuggling contacts in Hungary since the Nazi occupation. Whether that was true or not, she demanded that each of the parachutists now follow his or her own path. "For me, this is no longer a matter of military discipline," she said. "It's one of moral clarity—of personal conscience."

Hannah's distrust of the Partisans deepened on May 10, when the parachutists traveled to the ancient Croatian town of Čazma. The local commander, a general of considerable standing, stared at the small PALESTINE patches stitched onto their uniforms. He spoke anxiously to Reuven alone, as he was the only one fluent in Serbo-Croation. "You must remove those," he said. "Quickly."

Reuven was taken aback. "Why?" He couldn't understand why the Partisan general was upset by the sight of their RAF uniforms. So far, everywhere that they'd traveled in that wild countryside, they'd been greeted enthusiastically as the first representatives of the vaunted British Empire, the first British troops that the local people had ever seen in person.

"It's nothing to do with you being British subjects," the general explained. "We can't have everyone seeing that all four of you are Jews from Palestine."

"No," Reuven said firmly, his tone bordering on anger. "We won't comply."

"Sergeant, please don't misunderstand me," the general said calmly. "We know who you are. Those of us who need to know—the commanders and officers—we all know. We appreciate what you're doing here. But the people"—he waved his hand dismissively—"some of these illiterate peasants were hoodwinked by the propaganda."

"What propaganda?"

The general, who, Reuven realized, was a man of considerable education and experience, explained that until recently the region had been under the control of the Nazis and a stronghold of the People's Peasants' Party (PPP), a conservative Catholic faction with a long anti-Semitic history. The Nazis and their fascist allies had drummed it into the heads of the local populace that the catastrophe was entirely the fault of the Jews. "For years they've heard nothing else: 'This war is war caused by the Jews. It's being fought for the Jews. Financed by the Jews. Roosevelt is a Jew. Churchill is a Jew.' Imagine, some believe it! Now this first contingent arrives here to join us—to help us—the first British soldiers they've ever seen, and you're all *Jewish*, all wearing insignia from Palestine? I beg you to understand."

By then Reuven was persuaded by the general's argument. When Hannah learned what had happened, she was once again furious. "We held a stormy discussion about whether or not to comply with the commander's order," he recalled. "Hannah opposed it with all her being. She refused to hide the fact that she was Jewish. She fought me fiercely. For hours she wouldn't accept it. But eventually I prevailed. 'The people's minds have been poisoned,' I said. 'We must face facts. For the mission to succeed, we need to adjust.' Hannah still wouldn't wholly accept the decision that we pose as Britishers, and in the end she said that she was a Jew from England."

Not all the locals were unworldly. One young woman from the city who'd been displaced by the war had traveled to Great Britain and France and spoke good English. She overheard the heated arguments about the PALESTINE patch being shouted in Hebrew. "You Britishers," she said. "What language are you speaking? That's not English."

"No, it's Welsh," Reuven said, thinking on the fly.

"It's what?"

"Welsh. We're from Wales."

"Welsh?"

"Yes, yes, Welsh. From Wales! We all went to school together in Cardiff."

The city girl, mystified, turned toward the bonfire, muttering that she'd never imagined Welsh could sound so utterly different from English.

The next morning was bright and sunny. As Hannah walked along the village street, a young Partisan in uniform stopped her, offering his hand. He was Major General Petar Drapšin, the master saboteur and commander of Tito's Eighth Corps. Behind him walked Major General Ivan Hariš-Gromovnik. Neither wore badges of rank or any insignia to indicate their status as generals.

Hannah invited the two men back to the small quarters shared by the parachutists. They prepared tea and set out their few remaining chocolates for their guests. As soon as Drapšin and Gromovnik sat down, it was clear that they hadn't come to chat over poor-quality tea and stale British chocolates. They knew that the parachutists wanted to cross into Hungary.

Gromovnik also wanted to enter Hungary with a unit of experienced saboteurs but lacked the necessary explosives for the operation—to detonate key bridges, railway tunnels, and other strategic targets. They proposed a straightforward exchange: If the parachutists could acquire explosives from the British, they would ensure that they crossed the border into Hungary.

Gromovnik—a seasoned forty-one-year-old officer who'd fought with the Republican forces during the Spanish Civil War—pulled a typed sheet of paper from his pocket and read a summary of the operations carried out by the units under his command during the preceding three months. The paper listed 1,200 acts of sabotage against railway lines; 840 trains blown up; 400 strikes against bridges, factories, and airfields; the destruction of more than 50 tanks, scores of cannons, and so on. Mines planted by the general's saboteurs had killed or wounded about twenty-seven thousand fascist soldiers, including high-ranking officers.

Gromovnik was dismissive of the British and American bombing strategy in the Balkan theater. By his estimate, if Great Britain and the United States had sent the Partisans one-hundredth of the explosives they'd dropped in the largely ineffectual bombing of Yugoslavia, he and his people would have achieved "a hundred times" those results, while also cutting down on Allied air force casualties.

They made a verbal agreement and shook hands. Then the two Partisan generals departed on horseback, submachine guns strapped to their chests. Hannah opened her wireless and radioed A Force headquarters with the request for explosives.

19

May 12, 1944
Yugoslavia

The next day, May 12, Hannah received a response from Bari, informing her that a British bomber would drop men, supplies, and the explosives that Gromovnik and Drapšin had requested for their sabotage mission inside Hungary.

The six parachutists trudged toward the designated drop zone long after dark, with a cold rain slashing down. Their boots sank deep into the mud, but they appeared as if on parade, wearing revolvers, pistols, and a variety of hats and marching out of step. Hannah humorously recounted her agricultural training at Nahalal, detailing the most minute "secrets of the poultry trade." From time to time, they'd pass a Partisan checkpoint, and "Hannah would respond to [the guard's] salute with a curt yet charming motion, always turning her head to look straight into his eyes."

The sight of the woman parachutist, her blue-gray uniform highlighting her light blue eyes, always seemed to increase the Partisans' respect for the British. "Hannah did more for British propaganda in Yugoslavia than all of Churchill's announcements," Palgi later wrote.

A broad clearing stretched not far from the village, ideal for a parachute drop. A platoon of Partisans busily unloaded logs, kindling, and straw from a cart and prepared beacon fires to mark the area's boundaries to prevent planes from dropping people and materiel onto the village. Then the Partisans and parachutists marked a huge *D* on the ground with beacon fires—the prearranged signal to the British pilots.

The rain pelted down, and the night chill intensified. The Partisans built a huge bonfire and wrapped themselves in coats with the collars turned up. Someone began to hum softly, joined by another, and yet another, until a powerful chorus swelled to fill the night's stillness.

Yoel and Hannah watched as the Partisans sang a wild song, their voices expressing the anguish of an oppressed people. They were simple peasants, Yoel thought, many unable to read, but they'd learned the truest, most profound lesson a nation can learn: "the need to live as free men and to be willing to sacrifice their lives for their liberty."

Immersed in a song whose words she did not understand, Hannah turned to Yoel. He was surprised to see tears welling in her eyes. "If only we had a chance to sit in Hungary with our own people, listening to the songs of our country sung by our own fighters—Jewish freedom-fighters," she said. She paused, taking in the emotion of the Partisans' chorus. "Listen to their song," she continued. "Yes, it's full of pain, yet they're fighting for freedom on their own land. This people's blood will be spilled for its own country, in its own country. If one of them falls, it will be on his own soil." The wildflowers would be his only monument, she said. The Partisans' song was a cry of pain, but it also rejoiced in the day that freedom would come. "And what about us?" she asked. "What will we be fighting for? We're like hunted animals, and the devil laughs at our dying tremor."

Yoel locked arms with Hannah as they slipped away from the circle of Partisans. What were they going to tell the Jews they might still find alive in Hungary? Hannah asked. What could they promise? Freedom? Life in a new land? Compensation for their suffering? "We have no news for them, Yoel," she said. "No. All we can demand is that they struggle, take vengeance, die with honor."

"Don't you believe in the establishment of our Jewish state?" he asked.

Hannah closed her eyes. Yes, she was still a committed Zionist; yes, she still believed in the future Jewish state. But her heart told her that they weren't going to rescue Jews anymore—at least not in Hungary. "When we cross the border, Yoel, what'll happen? We'll pay our final respects to the remaining few on their way to execution." And in the unlikely event that they were able to rescue thousands, perhaps tens of thousands of Jews, and convince them to flee to the Partisan-held lands across the border, would they have the strength to come to Eretz Israel?

She reminded Yoel of David Ben-Gurion's parting words in Tel Aviv: "If Hitler succeeds in destroying the whole of European Jewry, we have no future in Palestine, either."

The Yishuv would clearly wither without the impetus of immigration. And if the movement collapsed this time, it could be another two thousand years before another group of *chalutzim* would arise—young pioneers such as Hannah, Yoel, Reuven, and Peretz—with enough youthful strength and idealism to begin again.

Now that she'd begun—now that *they'd* begun—the journey, there was no turning back—at least for Hannah. If she failed—if the mission failed—"we won't be condemned, Yoel. But we will be *judged*—by our consciences. That's why we've got to act *now*, without weighing the cost or the consequences." She paused. Even if she crossed over into Hungary, was captured and killed, her sacrifice wouldn't be in vain. Perhaps the Jews in the outlying provinces or in the heart of Budapest would hear a rumor that an emissary from Eretz Israel, a parachutist in a British Army uniform from the Yishuv, had tried to reach them, to warn them, to rescue them—and died in the attempt. Perhaps the Jews doomed in the ghettos and camps, those hiding in the forests, would be emboldened. *We need to hang on; we need to cling to life. They haven't abandoned us; they haven't forgotten us—maybe rescue is at hand.*

Who knew for certain? Faith might, indeed, work miracles. "I need to go, Yoel. There's no other way. I need to cross over. I don't want to die. Of course not. I want to live. I still expect a lot from life." But, she added, "I need to repurchase my right to life."

Yoel clenched her rain-slicked, chilly hand. "Let's go," he said.

They returned to the huge bonfire where the Partisans sang, drank slivovitz, danced; Yoel stared into the flames, then back at Hannah. Reuven joined them, and they began to cement their final arrangements. They would take separate routes across the border into Hungary. Reuven made that decision. Better not to put all their eggs into one basket, he said. Two small units crossing the border in different places would double their chances of success. Yoel would travel with Peretz Goldstein, and Hannah would make her own way solo—though Reuven would accompany her as far as the Hungarian border and see that she made it safely across the Drava River.

Once inside Hungary, how would they reconnect? Plan A, Yoel suggested, was to meet at the Great Synagogue on Dohány Street in Budapest after the Erev Shabbat service.

"If there even *are* still Shabbat services," Hannah said.

If there were no longer services—if during the Nazi occupation the synagogues had been shuttered—Plan B was to meet on Sunday in Matthias Church in Buda's Castle District—the Gothic landmark often referred to as the Church of the Coronation because so many monarchs had been crowned there. Matthias Church was always crowded, and they knew they could meet in the pews in relative anonymity.

On May 13, early in the morning, Yoel Palgi and Abba Berdichev set out, accompanied by a single Partisan. They planned to explore the border of Hungary farther east with the intention of creating an alternate route for Jewish escapees via Transylvania. The whole group stood in front of the house to say goodbye.

Hannah and Reuven, set to leave at noon, were busy securing their equipment to a horse. After a long embrace, Yoel and Abba shouldered their guns and started marching along the uneven road. At the turning, Yoel looked back; he could see Hannah and Reuven with the Partisans, all standing there, following them with their eyes. Yoel waved. "See you in Budapest!" he called out.

Hannah, giving her usual thumbs-up, shouted back, "See you in Budapest!"

20

May 15, 1944
Bari Airfield, Italy

Enzo Sereni personally chose his jump partner after an accidental encounter in Bari. Lorenzo Rosselli del Turco was a twenty-eight-year-old Italian soldier originally from Florence who'd served as a communications officer in the Royal Italian Army, despite having an anti-Fascist record. When Italy surrendered to the Allies in 1943, Lorenzo was on the island of Sardinia. He tried to enlist in the Allied armed forces to fight against Germany, but both the British and the Americans were distrustful of Italian would-be volunteers who'd been in Mussolini's army.

Arriving at the Bari airfield on the way back from Sardinia, Lorenzo heard Enzo Sereni giving a passionate speech one night at an officers' club. "I can't understand the young Italians," Enzo told Lorenzo after the speech as they walked across the Bari airfield. "They say they're anti-Fascist yet refuse to risk their lives."

"That's not true," Lorenzo said. "I'm ready and willing. I've tried to enlist. I'll fight, I'll risk my life, if only they'd give me the chance." After several long conversations, Enzo was convinced that Lorenzo was truly an anti-Fascist and recommended him to Major Robert Taylor of MI9. The British did their own screening, then put Lorenzo through an accelerated course with four daytime jumps.

Lorenzo was given a Corsican undercover name so that he could jump in the uniform of a French officer, while Enzo was given the identity of a real

British military officer from Mandatory Palestine, a Jew roughly the same age as Enzo named Samuel (Shmuel) Barda. To avoid charges of espionage, MI9 preferred to use the identity of a real person in case the parachutists were taken as POWs and the Nazis checked their names with the Red Cross.

On May 15, 1944, at 11:00 p.m., the Halifax bomber took off from Bari. Enzo sat in silence, bundled in his parachute. He glanced occasionally at Lorenzo. Neither said a word to the other during the entire flight.

When the red jump light turned to green, Enzo moved to the open hatch and jumped. Lorenzo followed too soon. Taller and heavier, he descended more rapidly, causing Enzo's feet to almost become entangled in the ropes of Lorenzo's chute.

When Lorenzo hit the ground, he thought he heard Enzo whistling their prearranged signal in the distance. Then he blacked out. When he came to, it was two in the morning and there was no response to his whistling. He walked toward where he thought he'd heard Enzo signaling. Two hundred yards away, he found Enzo's parachute open, contrary to instructions. Enzo himself was nowhere around, nor were the radio transmitter and other equipment.

As dawn broke, Lorenzo heard the familiar sounds of a military camp waking up—reveille, whistling, the banging of metal utensils—and realized that he had to get away quickly, without Enzo, without equipment, and without civilian clothes. He buried his two Beretta pistols and went in the direction of a small village on the horizon. If Enzo had broken a leg or been otherwise wounded during the landing, wouldn't he have remained on the spot? And if he were not wounded, how could the open parachute be accounted for? Lorenzo concluded that Enzo, who like himself had had no practice with nighttime jumps, must have lost consciousness upon landing.

But Enzo was not wounded, nor had he blacked out. His light weight had caused him to drift far off course from the site of Campi di Annibale, floating down almost directly into the hands of a unit of Organization Todt, the Nazi civil and military engineering outfit that used concentration camp inmates and Soviet POWs as slave laborers to construct German fortifications.

Enzo was taken prisoner, processed as a British captain, and held for several weeks in a Luftwaffe Stammlager for captured Allied air force officers. As he'd instructed so many of the young parachutists, under Article 5 of the

1929 Geneva Convention, he was required to give only his name, rank, and serial number. "Samuel Barda," he said. "Captain—Royal Air Force." He did not specify his outfit, though on his RAF uniform were affixed paratroopers' wings and a PALESTINE patch.

The most pressing problem for Enzo lay not in the potential that he might be considered a spy but rather in one detail on his RAF fiber disc dog tag.

During World War II, all British and American dog tags stated the religion of the soldier, sailor, or airman in case he was killed in combat so that he could receive the proper religious burial. In general, the religious abbreviations on British dog tags carried no risk: RC: Roman Catholic; CE: Church of England; CI: Church of Ireland; PRES: Church of Scotland; PB: Plymouth Brethren; Q: Quaker. But by 1944, the Nazis often disregarded the protections of the Geneva Conventions when dealing with captured Jewish servicemen. Unfortunately for Enzo Sereni—Captain Samuel Barda—his dog tag was stamped with a *J*—for "Jewish."

21

May 16, 1944
Maruševec, Yugoslavia

Sixty miles of hostile territory lay between Hannah and the Hungarian border. Sixty miles meant weeks of marching, hiking, backtracking—the rest of May and the first week of June—to get within striking distance of Hungary.

Reuven Dafni studied Hannah's ID papers, his brow deeply creased. "No, no, Hannah, I still don't like it," he said.

The Partisans had taken the legitimate papers of a non-Jewish Hungarian woman about Hannah's age and attempted to swap out the photo. (Even in the forested mountains, Tito's Partisan army maintained a department of photography and forgery.) "The average policeman or a gendarme at a routine check-stop wouldn't bat an eye, but a Gestapo man or a real detective—anyone who knew a bit about forgery—could see instantly that the photo had been swapped out," Dafni later wrote.

Dafni had another long argument with Hannah. For weeks he'd tried to reason with her that their efforts were not for nothing; the parachutists were participating in the Partisans' sabotage operations, blowing up trains, destroying bridges, ambushing German patrols. They were rescuing downed British and American flyers, airmen who could go back to Bari and then return to bomb the Germans. Wasn't that more useful to the war effort than a handful of Jewish commandos embarking on a suicide mission into occupied Hungary?

Hannah wouldn't budge from her position. "We're committing *moral* suicide by doing nothing," she said.

• • •

The next morning, she went off with a group of Partisans heading for a Yugoslav village sixty miles to the south, as close to the Hungarian border as they would take her. Reuven, who did not plan to cross the border at that time, decided to go with them as far as the village. The trip took twenty-six days because they had to circle and backtrack around German patrols combing the forests.

Hannah was relaxed, confident, and eager to get going. But she was well aware of the risks she would be taking.

It was seven o'clock and dusk had fallen when the head of the Partisan unit came into the village and found Hannah talking with Reuven. Whatever the risks ahead—and they were manifold—the fact that there was now a green light on her journey back into Hungary visibly lifted her mood.

As she packed up her wireless, guns, and gear, she joked with Reuven, reminded him of some of the lighter moments they'd had in Yugoslavia—the wild circle dance with the Partisans at their May Day festival; the night they'd pretended that their heated Hebrew conversation was Welsh. She talked to Reuven about a day—hopefully soon—when the war would be over and they'd all meet again in Eretz Israel. "She was bubbling with joy, forthright, impish, and amazingly carefree," Reuven later wrote. "She seemed like someone about to embark upon an experience she had been looking forward to for years."

"We'll rent a big bus," Hannah said, "and drive up and down the country. First, we'll visit all the kibbutzim that sent volunteers on the mission. We'll arrange celebrations in those kibbutzim, and we'll tell them everything that happened to us, and we'll spin tall tales. We'll spend an entire month in that bus, touring the entire Land, from Dan to Beer Sheva."*

Reuven and Hannah left the hideout together and, in case anyone from the village was watching, initially walked in the opposite direction: north, away from the border. They soon entered an orchard in full bloom. The smell of the white cherry blossoms was intoxicating.

Hannah glanced over at Reuven and asked if he was carrying any of the

*Hannah, always conscious of her literary sources, was quoting the biblical phrase used to refer to the territories settled by the Israelites, "from Dan to Beersheba," which occurs many times in the Tanach, for example, the Book of Samuel 3:20.

L-pills from Cairo. Reuven walked on for a few strides without answering. His silence told her the answer. "Can you give me one? In case—"

Reuven refused. "You don't send someone on a mission like that saying 'You're not going to succeed,'" he later said. "You need to build up their morale. I knew it was my duty to increase her self-confidence, to encourage her, to remove all doubts."

Reuven and Hannah walked stride for stride in the orchard and agreed on their own cipher—distinct from the ones they were to use for MI9. Not a poem, their cipher would be transposed Morse code letters from a Hebrew phrase, easy for them to memorize, but obviously impossible for the German code breakers to understand, a preface to any message that only they would know: "Hakibbutz Hameuchad Sdot Yam Caesarea."

Now Hannah reached into her pocket. "Here, just in case—"

"What is it?"

"If I don't return, promise that you'll take this to the *chaverim* in Sdot Yam."

She handed him a small slip of paper, carefully folded into a square.

*"L'hitraot."**

Reuven watched as Hannah walked away briskly to join the others. Smiling, she turned and waved a final shalom.

After she'd disappeared, Reuven waited. He'd agreed not to leave the spot until the Partisan guides returned to say that Hannah had made the crossing into Hungary successfully. It took three hours for them to return, telling Reuven in Serbo-Croation that all had gone well at the border.

It was now dawn, and in the dim forest light, Reuven reached into his pocket to read the slip of paper Hannah'd entrusted him with. Thinking that it might be a message to David Ben-Gurion or one of the other leaders of the Yishuv, he unfolded it and strained to make sense of it. A prayer? A *poem*? Four symmetrical lines, neatly written. A Hebrew haiku: "Ashrei hagafrur" . . .

Reuven, unlike Hannah and Enzo, wasn't blessed with literary gifts. He was a soldier, a warrant officer in the British infantry, and now a paratrooper attached to MI9. He exhaled through gritted teeth, feeling frustrated and

*Hebrew for "See you soon."

furious. What was this? *Theatrics?* At such a moment, when he and Hannah were both nervous, when she was crossing the border into the unknown, when she should have been studying maps, she'd decided to hand him some stupid piece of *poetry*?

He clenched his fist, squeezing the paper into a tight wad, and tossed it onto the muddy forest floor, where a strong wind gust tumbled it away.

Ten minutes later, after he reached the Partisans' safe house, sleep escaped him. He was racked by second thoughts. A promise, after all, was a promise. Childishly romantic and foolish as she seemed, who was *he* to question Hannah's parting request? He had no choice; he had to go back. He retraced his steps to the pathway where they'd parted and, risking capture by any daytime German patrol, began his search.

He searched in vain for that little wad of paper. The task was hopeless, he realized. By now the wind had blown it far away. On the verge of giving up, after at least an hour of looking, he saw something in the thick underbrush hanging there white and clean, like an origami flower. He plucked the ball free from the thorny branch, uncrumpled it, and smoothed it out. He folded the paper in half and slipped it into the left breast pocket of his khaki uniform. He kept it there for months.

22

June 4, 1944
Western Romania

On June 4, 1944, Shaike Dan and Yitzhak "Manu" Ben-Ephraim jumped in tandem as the second leg of the Romanian mission Operation Anticlimax Blue.

Arie "Rico" Lupescu and Yitzhak Macarescu had parachuted on May 3, 1944, as part of the first leg of the Romanian mission. Having received no radio transmissions from them, MI9 assumed that they'd been taken prisoner—and might have been given away during their descent by the stark whiteness of their chutes. Shaike Dan and Manu Ben-Ephraim therefore insisted that their parachutes be dark in color.

On board the Halifax, cruising in a formation with several other heavy bombers at 550 miles per hour, Dan reflected on what they'd learned from Major Smiles and Major Maskelyne; he reminded himself how he could quickly remove all insignia from his RAF uniform, make a few simple alterations, and within minutes be wearing a passable double-breasted civilian suit. If Manu did the same, the two, accessorized with a pair of fedoras, could pose as wandering vagabonds.

Dan was wearing a belt into which were sewn numerous gold napoleons, 20-franc coins minted in the time of Napoleon Bonaparte made of 90 percent pure gold. They also had some local Romanian currency, flashlights to signal the plane, and an aluminum container for the radio, onto which they'd strapped a few sandwiches. "If we're not able to transmit with the radio," he said, "at least we'll have the sandwiches."

Along with two cups of hot coffee, a sergeant major from New Zealand brought a few pieces of paper so they could write some last words. Dan nodded in appreciation. "He told us he would give the letters to his commanding officer, Captain Davidson, who was waiting in Bari for the plane to return, and the captain would deliver them to our friends in Cairo."

The two parachutists scribbled away in the dark, keeping their farewell thoughts secret from each other. Manu Ben-Ephraim's farewell note, addressed to his comrades on Kibbutz Shamir, read:

> *Sitting with the parachutes on our backs, chewing gum and eating chocolate.*
>
> *Something is beginning to press in the stomach as we get closer to the jump site.*
>
> *We hope it will be good for us and for you.*
>
> *Antonescu—the Romanian Führer—doesn't even have an inkling of what two enemies are coming to him.*
>
> *11:15—the plane is over the border.*
>
> *See you,*
> *Manu*

Dan took one last sip of coffee as he wrote to his friends at Kibbutz Nir Am, "If only my grandfather could see me now."

The green light soon flashed. Manu jumped first. Dan got up to push the aluminum container out the hatch and felt a tap on the shoulder. He turned to see the New Zealand sergeant major shout, "God bless you!"

Dan nodded. Then he made the blind jump.

"The fourth of June 1944. 12:30 a.m. I'm between heaven and earth," Dan later wrote in his journal. "The words 'God bless you' are still ringing in my ears. Is there really Someone watching over me there above, or am I being watched from below? Where are the great poets—Bialik, Alterman?* Could they give expression to my feelings in this sliver of a second?"

He landed on the spongy earth of a cornfield. The Halifax circled surprisingly low, then gained altitude. According to the instructions they'd received from Colonel Simonds, Dan was to signal by flashlight that they'd touched down safely. But Dan thought better of it. *To signal now with a flashlight? No, that's crazy. We don't even know if we've been spotted.*

Instead, he gathered up his silk parachute, pressed and kneeled on it until it was empty of air, hid it in some bushes. Then he went to look for Manu. Above, he saw the flickering light of the Halifax flying farther and farther away. He felt a stabbing sensation as the plane—the last friendly object—disappeared into the night.

Every movement, every sound, felt like a threat. Luckily, the next sound approaching was Manu Ben-Ephraim. They exhaled, hugging each other in silence. They'd both landed easily: no broken arms, no twisted knees or ankles. That alone was worth celebrating with a gulp from the two pocket-sized whiskey flasks they'd been given. It took them a few minutes, but eventually they found the crate holding the thirty-pound radio. The sandwiches that were lashed to it had been blown away by the wind.

As they were unpacking the radio, they suddenly froze, ducking down. A few meters away was the silhouette of a man. Should they draw their guns? "Wait, no, I'll shut his mouth with a few gold napoleons," Dan whispered.

They drew closer to the stranger, close enough to see: a solitary five-foot-high bush dancing gently in the wind. Dan cursed, then laughed loudly. "Even a bush at night looks like the enemy."

• • •

*Nathan Alterman (August 14, 1910, Warsaw, Poland–March 28, 1970, Tel Aviv, Israel) was a poet, playwright, journalist, and translator who was highly influential in Socialist Zionist politics, both before and after the establishment of the modern State of Israel in 1948. Haim Bialik (January 9, 1873, Ivnytsia, Russian Empire [now Ukraine]–July 4, 1934, Vienna, Austria) is considered to be one of the pioneers of modern literary Hebrew, esteemed for expressing in his verse the yearnings of the Jewish people and for making Modern Hebrew a flexible medium of poetic expression. Bialik is recognized today as Israel's national poet.

After burying the parachutes and wireless set in the field, they hurried as far as possible from the drop site. They were sure that everyone within earshot had heard the roar of a heavy bomber, which had no business in the skies overhead other than to drop foreign agents. Dogs barked as they ran past the peasants' darkened cottages.

Exhausted and hungry, they marched all night, briefly lying down to sleep in the high wheat. By chance, as they continued, railway tracks suddenly appeared in the fields before them. They followed the tracks, and, as it grew lighter, they spotted a small train station. They decided to keep walking, even in daylight, and try to blend in with the crowd of passengers.

Their papers identified them as British flying officers—Dan's English name was Theo, and Manu's was, strangely enough, Franz. They now needed to solve the problem of the RAF uniforms. No expert in Cairo could have advised them; they had to use sheer improvisation. Their military boots were covered with mud. Their blue RAF trousers were so filthy and wrinkled that they could pass for ordinary civilian trousers. Their filthy shirts weren't conspicuous, either.

Dan and Ben-Ephraim sat in the wheatfield and carefully removed the stitching from all the identifying military patches and insignia on their RAF jackets. The brass buttons concealed compasses, and the jacket linings hid silk maps, so the simplest solution was to turn the jackets inside out, fold them, and carry them draped over one arm. They angled their blue berets backward, hoping they would give them the look of local factory workers.

A train arrived, and they joined a group of men disembarking at the station. They were somewhere in the border area between Romania and Hungary, and sooner or later, they realized, they'd be asked to show their papers. After a bend in the road, they spotted a sign: They were entering the city of Arad. They also saw roadside guards and a blockade of Romanian military police. Backing away now would only arouse suspicion. They had to walk straight toward the uniformed police with poker faces.

There were many factories in this suburban section of Arad, and hordes of Romanian- and Hungarian-speaking workers were on their way to the plants. The crowd was too dense for the police to check everyone; hundreds of workers streamed forward in a slow-moving mob. Dan and Ben-Ephraim blended in as best they could and hoped not to hear a shout from the policemen.

Somehow they passed the blockade without being questioned. Dan later recalled, “In a blind drop, nothing is waiting for you on the ground—except perhaps luck.”

Rounding a street corner, the two parachutists heard footsteps, followed by much louder boot steps. “And then,” Dan wrote, “came the sights we traveled all this distance to help put an end to. Two rows of soldiers marched on the main road with rifles, fixed bayonets, and submachine guns. In between were Jews, young and old, being taken to forced labor camps to help the German war effort. We knew there were no extermination camps in this part of Romania, but we heard plenty about the labor camps where thousands of Jews died of hunger and exhaustion.”

From teenage boys to elderly men, Jews were rousted from their homes daily and marched, in silent rows, to forced labor camps, which were lacking in basic hygiene and medical facilities. In most Romanian labor camps, Jewish men were forced to work from sunrise to sunset with at most one half-hour break, while fed starvation rations. “Here are the Jews we came to rescue,” Dan said to himself. “And here we are, emissaries from Palestine, seeing their shame, their hopelessness, and not being able to do a thing. Not yet. I couldn’t have imagined a more tragic encounter than this, although I expected I would also be a witness to more tragic scenes.”

23

June 7, 1944
Slovenia, Yugoslavia

In Yugoslavia, near the Hungarian border, Hannah felt as though she were making a blind jump of her own. After months with the Partisans and in the careful hands of her Palmach comrades—Reuven, Yonah, Yoel, Abba, and Peretz—she was putting her life into the hands of three young men she'd just met. She couldn't rule out the possibility that one or more of her companions might be double agents, compromised by the Gestapo.

Péter Kallós and Sándor Fleischmann were young members of the Jewish underground in Budapest who had come to Yugoslavia from Hungary, seeking ways to smuggle their families into Partisan-held territory and eventually to safety in Palestine.

Fleischmann—short and stocky, with darting blue eyes—was the more confident of the two. Kallós was slightly built, nervous, and had been a member of the same youth movement as Hannah—Hashomer Hatzair. He said he'd spent two years in Palestine and spoke rudimentary Hebrew, but she didn't let down her guard to test him—she continued to only speak English.

The third man, Jacques Antoine Tissandier—everyone called him "Tony"—was a twenty-nine-year-old private first-class with the 236th Artillery Regiment of the French Army. He'd made multiple escapes from Nazi POW camps, joined Tito's Partisan Army, and in June 1944 volunteered for a mission to organize resistance activities in Hungary and smuggle out other French POWs.*

It took Hannah several hours to persuade the Partisans to help her get near the Hungarian border. With reluctance they finally agreed to guide the band of four to the Drava River. Kallós had a reliable smuggling contact in the town of Murska Sobota in the Prekmurje region, previously part of Yugoslavia, which had had a small but thriving Jewish community—until the Nazi invasion of 1941, when the region was annexed by the Kingdom of Hungary. If they could get to the river, a local fisherman might be bribed to take them across. Once over the Drava, they wouldn't be far from the border.

The Partisans would wait a few days at an agreed-upon place in case Hannah and her companions managed to send back some forged papers for their use. But that was all they were willing to do. On the night of June 7, the four set out for the Hungarian border.

Hannah learned over her wireless that twenty-four hours earlier, on the sixth of June, Allied troops had landed in Normandy. The greatest amphibian force in the history of warfare—160,000 British, Canadian, and American soldiers, 1,500 tanks, and 2,727 ships and small landing craft, with more than 1,200 fighter planes providing air cover—had crossed the English Channel and landed on the beaches of Normandy. Although it was too soon to know the outcome, it seemed to be the long-awaited second front in France.

Using one of Hannah's cleverly concealed compasses, they tried to find the border village of Murska Sobota. Kallós had an old Yugoslavian map labeled

*Captured on June 20, 1940, during the Battle of France, Tissandier was imprisoned in the squalid, disease-plagued Stalag IX-A in Ziegenhain, Germany. After two escape attempts, he was shipped east to Stalag 325 and sentenced to the disciplinary "labor commando"—a de facto concentration camp—in Lviv, Ukraine. In August 1942, Tissandier and a fellow French POW broke free of a work detail, crossing the Carpathian Mountains into Hungary, and finding safe haven with the French Legation in Budapest. Escaped French soldiers were treated with kid gloves until March 1944 when the newly arrived Gestapo began rounding up all French POWs and sending them back to stalags in the Third Reich. Tissandier once again escaped—making it to the forests of Croatia and joining up with Tito's Partisan Army. His vocal anti-Communism led to conflict with the Partisan officers and he volunteered for the dangerous mission of returning to occupied Hungary to foment resistance.

with Serbo-Croatian names. They began to argue about where they were and where they were going. Because the territory was so often disputed between the two countries, the Yugoslavs and Hungarians used different names for every village, town, river, and stream. They hiked for more than two days, only to realize that they'd been going in circles. On the night of June 9, they reached a large river— Kallós couldn't recall anything except small streams in the area—that looked like a branch of the Drava. The village they were looking for and the road to Budapest were on the other side, he thought.

They hiked upstream for two more hours in the darkness, hoping to find the narrow bend in the river that Kallós remembered having forded. They saw no bridges, no fishermen, no simple way across. "We'll have to swim," Hannah said.

"Then you'll have to leave the radio," Tony said. If they were caught by Hungarian gendarmes with a radio transmitter, they'd certainly be shot as spies. Hannah argued with him in French: The radio was the most vital part of the mission. How could she relay messages to Agent Gary or Colonel Simonds without it? She was preoccupied with keeping the transmitter in its boxy brown suitcase dry and functional. "I'll take it apart, and we can carry the parts across the river separately," she said.

Tony didn't like the idea, but in the few days he'd spent with that young woman, he'd realized that she was the most stubborn, headstrong person he'd ever met. Hannah removed the radio transmitter from its leather suitcase and dismantled it, just as she'd rehearsed countless times during training in Cairo.

They all stripped down to their underwear and bundled the radio parts and their pistols into their clothes. They'd have to cross the river numerous times, using one arm to hold the baggage above their heads and the other to do a modified breaststroke against the strong current. Holding one another's hands in the dark, they felt their way into the frigid water. It was fresh mountain runoff; the icy cold cut into Hannah's flesh like a razor. It took five or six trips back and forth. Once they'd ferried everything across and put on their clothes, they were so exhausted that they collapsed, huddling on the embankment under the cold moonlight.

Thirty minutes later, they slipped across an unguarded section of the border into Hungary near the town of Drávaszilas—known as Podbrest in Croatian—then forded three more streams during the night. After their final crossing of the Mur River, they were, according to Kallós's map, only four or five miles south of Murska Sabota.

As dawn was breaking, Tony and Kallós began to argue. The Frenchman wanted to turn back and camp in the forest before it became fully light; otherwise they'd be forced to hide from the border patrols for the entire day. Hannah, hunched over her wireless, overruled Tony. There was no way she was turning back. While the men continued to debate, she looked over every piece of the wireless kit. Something was missing. Where were the headphones?

Kallós thought the town was Murska Sobota, but he was wary of entering the town with a woman. "What about her?" he asked Fleischmann.

"What *about* her?"

"If we're stopped and questioned and they see her Hungarian papers, they'll find out she doesn't speak Hungarian. What? She's going to answer the gendarmes in English?"

Hannah had been careful to keep up her undercover role as a Royal Air Force flyer: She'd spoken only in English with Kallós and in French with Tissandier. But no sooner had Kallós finished than Hannah offered him a smile. "Don't worry about me," she told them softly in the educated accent of her mother tongue. "I'll be able to manage perfectly fine in Hungarian."

Fleischmann and Kallós exchanged embarrassed looks: For hours during the march, they'd been using some "colorful" Hungarian language, "expressions not usually used in the company of women."

Kallós was still a bit skittish and wanted to enter the town alone with Fleischmann first—two Hungarian men would look less suspicious. According to Kallós, a train would leave for Budapest each morning at eight o'clock sharp. The plan was to keep Hannah and Tony hidden in the cornfield, then go straight to the station a few moments before departure. In the crush of people boarding the Budapest-bound train, there would be far less thorough scrutiny of their ID papers.

It seemed reasonable enough. Hannah and Tony hid in the reeds by the water. Hannah was shivering with the cold. She set up the wireless and tapped out a Morse code message to Reuven Dafni. It was a simple transmission; there was no need to double-encrypt it using French poetry since she and Reuven had agreed to the prearranged Hebrew line known only to them that would preface any transmission.

24

June 9, 1944
Murska Sabota, Hungary

One—two—three. Hannah paced nervously through the corn. When Kallós and Fleischmann didn't return after an hour, she began to worry. After three hours with no sign of them, it was clear something had gone wrong.

Next to her, Tony Tissandier poked his head up from the high stalks of corn. They suddenly heard loud stomping and rustling. A squad of the border patrol was scouring the riverfront. *"Vite!"* Tony said.

Hannah and the Frenchman crawled on their stomachs through the thick corn stalks to the nearby forest. Digging up the earth with their bare hands, they buried the transmitter parts, her RAF uniform, and their Beretta pistols. They patted down the earth and tried to camouflage the spot with some leaves—it wasn't a great job, they thought, but it would have to do. In a moment they'd be surrounded by dozens of gendarmes. *"Tu dois m'embrasser!"* Tony said. In the tall corn, they threw themselves into each other's arms.

Even with the fear and rush of adrenaline, a corner of Hannah's brain wondered at the irony of it: Only a few months earlier, she'd written of her various suitors in Budapest and Palestine, the four proposals of marriage she'd turned down, her inability to ever meet the "right one." *Who would imagine that I'll soon be twenty-two and I've never kissed a boy?*

Tony Tissandier was no boy. But like an actress in a Hollywood scene, she found herself being forcefully kissed by the rough, worldly infantryman who reeked of cigarettes, sweat, and wet canvas. When the Hungarian patrol came upon them a few moments later, Tony's head was in Hannah's lap and she was playfully tousling his hair, bending over to kiss him and giggling.

The first gendarme to arrive gave them a quick assessment: a blue-eyed girl in slacks with disheveled hair; a young man, very scruffy, unshaven, and unwashed . . . *vagabonds*. "Well, you look harmless enough," he said in Hungarian. He signaled his partner to handcuff the pair. "But we'll still have to take you in for questioning at the station." Hannah asked on what grounds they were being arrested; the gendarme blurted out two words she didn't want to hear: "*Kommunista partizánok*. We've got reports of those damned bastards in this area."

"But we're not Communist Partisans."

"Look, if you're innocent, you've got nothing to worry about. In an hour you can get back to your lovemaking."

By the time Kallós and Fleischmann reached the town, the two smugglers they were looking for had already left for work. Kallós talked to the wife of one of them, who told him to come back in the evening.

As they were heading back in the direction of the river to rejoin Hannah and Tony, they saw two uniformed men heading toward them. Each was wearing a distinctively brimmed, square-top black leather hat with a green cockerel-feather plume. Their uniforms and greatcoats were olive khaki, and their knee-high black leather riding boots were brightly polished. Both shouldered Mannlicher rifles and had pistols on their waists in brown leather holsters.

Fleischmann looked at Kallós. Should they bolt for the woods? Kallós looked straight ahead, shook his head, and gestured to keep going. They continued walking casually. Not surprisingly, the gendarmes stopped them and asked to see their papers, which they scrutinized for about thirty seconds. Kallós and Fleischmann resembled a couple of vagabonds—unshaven, unwashed, rumpled clothes—not an uncommon sight in the wartime countryside of rural Hungary. "Everything seems in order," the younger gendarme said, but the older gendarme, with sergeant's stripes on his epaulettes, told them to come to the local station house for some brief questioning.

Had Péter Kallós been a bit savvier, he would have known that that was a typical psychological ploy of the Hungarian gendarmes; if suspects came along willingly to the station house, they'd generally be told "Never mind" and allowed to go about their business.

In his right-hand pocket, he had a Colt .45–caliber pistol. Fleischmann was carrying two Beretta 9mm pistols, the standard-issue sidearm of the Italian military. As they walked toward the station, the gendarmes were a good thirty feet behind them. Fleischmann signaled to Kallós with his finger, pantomiming a trigger pull—*Look, if it comes down to it, we'll shoot it out*—and then put his hand into his pocket. Kallós reached into his own coat pocket for the Colt .45. But then Fleischmann heard one of the policemen whispering to the other, "Let's let them walk another fifty meters or so and we'll cut them loose."

Fleischmann relaxed and took his hand out of his pocket. Before he could glance sideways to see whether Kallós had heard the gendarmes whisper, a deafening gunshot rang out. The gendarmes tackled Fleischmann. In seconds, both his hands and feet were shackled. As they swung him around, he saw a grotesque tableau. Kallós had blown half his own head off. Blood was trickling down his neck, his skull was gaping open, and his body, somehow, was twitching. The Colt pistol lay in the dust next to his hand.

Why had he done it? Was he afraid that under torture he'd implicate members of the Hungarian underground? Or that he'd doom his family back in Budapest? Neither Fleischmann nor anyone else would ever know.

After a few minutes, several villagers reached the scene. One of them, a Croatian boy of about twelve, told the gendarmes that he'd seen two Partisans hiding in the bushes by the river. The older sergeant sent out a call for reinforcements. He wanted every available gendarme and border patrolman to search the area where the Partisans were hiding so that when the brass came, he would get the credit for having broken up a potential espionage ring.

The gendarmes kicked Kallós's corpse aside, emptying his pockets. To Fleischmann's surprise and horror, they found the headset of Hannah's wireless. It had been in his pocket since they had forded the Drava.

The gendarmes searched Fleischmann next and confiscated the two Beretta pistols. Fleischmann was badly roughed up and thrown to the ground. The contents of his pockets lay scattered on the muddy road next to him. Among a scattering of pengő coins he spotted a folded paper note. Despite the shackles, he wriggled forward, snakelike, shot out his tongue, and swallowed the note.

An elderly Hungarian woman from the village approached Fleischmann and whispered in his ear, "Is there something else you want to destroy, my son?"

"Myself," he said.

25

June 9, 1944
Szombathely, Hungary

As she arrived at the gendarmerie station house, all hope left Hannah. Slumped in a chair, shackled—barely conscious, barely alive—was Fleischmann. Nearby on a table was the sprawled-out corpse of Kallós, unrecognizable, missing a huge chunk of his cranium.

"We found earphones for a radio transmitter in his pocket," the sergeant said to Hannah. "It doesn't matter whether you tell us anything or not. One of the boys has confessed everything and he'll be executed tomorrow."

They beat her while grilling her about the wireless; she denied having any knowledge of it. Then they produced the headset, which they said they'd found on Fleischmann. Despite all the espionage training in Cairo, the practicing for just such a scenario, Hannah fell right into their trap. She could not let Fleischmann take the blame. "He has absolutely nothing to do with the matter," she said. "The headphones are mine."

She admitted that she was a British officer with the Women's Auxiliary Air Force, a radio operator with a mission to connect with the Partisans in Yugoslavia. She was ready to lead them back to the edge of the woods, where her RAF uniform and guns and the wireless set were hidden. The gendarmes agreed. For the first time since the capture, she saw Tony. She couldn't help but recoil in shock. It was impossible to recognize him. He looked *inhuman.* They'd pulled his curly hair out by the roots. The lips she'd been kissing only hours before were now grotesquely ballooned, and when he opened his mouth, she saw that all his front teeth were gone.

The trio were surrounded by gendarmes with bayoneted rifles and led back to the place of their capture. The gendarmes threatened to shoot Hannah on the spot if she didn't help them locate the radio. "When we came to the place, I saw the corn had been trampled down completely," she later recalled. "Searching for the transmitter, they'd destroyed the entire harvest. A car drew up and from it jumped an officer carrying a suitcase with the transmitter. They'd found it without my help."

Hannah, Tissandier, and Fleischmann were taken fifty-five miles northeast to Szombathely, the nearest city with a prison. Hannah knew it well. Szombathely was considered to be the oldest civilized settlement in Hungary, founded by the Romans under Emperor Claudius in AD 45.

When Hannah was a girl, it had been a small city famed for its August carnival a little over a two-hour drive due west from Budapest. But during the war, its railway junction, marshaling yards, airfields, and barracks had given it great strategic value. Since the Nazi occupation in March, the city had become a major military outpost of the Germans, including the Waffen-SS and Gestapo.

It was in that ancient Roman city that the torment began. Confined in a dreary prison cell, Hannah was routinely visited by a Hungarian interrogator who demanded to know the code to the radio transmissions, what communications she had received on the radio, and from whom. She refused to say a word.

Beatings followed. At first they were simple enough: with fists and heavy-soled black boots. But then the jailers stripped her naked and bent her over, striking her with their riding crops. They whipped the soles of her feet and the palms of her hands until they saw blood.

"Your real name!"

"I've told you! Minnie!" She repeated her British identity, her serial number, her rank in the Women's Auxiliary Air Force—that was all she was obliged to do under the laws of the Geneva Convention.

She was bound hand and foot and suspended from the ceiling. Every interrogator was instructed to punch her, kick her, whip her. If she lost consciousness, a gendarme threw cold water in her face and the torment continued. The interrogator repeatedly asked her about the code. She stuck to her story that the codebook was buried in the woods with the transmitter. "You should have found it when you dug up the radio."

"Stop lying!"

"It should be there."

Each answer was accompanied by another round of kicking, punching, flogging. "What is your radio code?"

She knew their game: They wanted to use her wireless to send out false information, transmitting as Agent Minnie, to mislead bomber squadrons so that they could be greeted by fighters and anti-aircraft guns. "It's a table of numbers—it's on thick paper—buried with the transmitter."

There were times during the beatings when she floated away, semiconscious—somehow removed from the pain, imagining that she was walking on the shore of Lake Kinneret with Miryam Yitzhak or swimming in Hungary's beautiful Lake Balaton on summer vacations with her cousin Evi.

Once during a break from the torture, she managed to tear herself away from the gendarmes, running up a flight of stairs with what little remaining strength she could muster, only one thought in her mind: to get to the top floor, where she'd seen a balcony, and make another jump—the *final* jump. Completely naked and half starved, in her bruised and battered condition, she slipped on the stairs. One of the gendarmes grabbed her by the foot. "In that moment, I understood that death was the only way out," she later said. "But I'd failed."

After that suicide attempt, the interrogators handcuffed her to a chair and beat her so badly that they knocked out one of her front teeth. She'd always prided herself on the charm of her smile. She spat the bloody tooth out at their feet.

When the beatings stopped, her conscience was wracked by "what ifs." What if she'd known that the headset had been found on Kallós, not Fleischmann? She could have feigned ignorance and pinned everything on that gruesome corpse missing half its skull. Dead men tell no tales. . . .

• • •

The gendarmes, for their part, believed that they'd uncovered a major espionage ring. Capturing a female Royal Air Force officer with a wireless transmitter? That was a major coup, one for which they might all get commendations from the brass. The arrest was important enough that the prisoners needed to be transferred into the hands of the Hungarian military police in the capital. In fact, the brass in Budapest seemed to have been waiting for their call, expecting the arrival of a female British agent with a wireless.

After three days, Hannah, along with Tissandier and Fleischmann, was handcuffed, placed under heavy guard, and sent to Budapest by train.

26

June 1944
Arad, Romania

By early June 1944, thousands of Jews were making the dangerous crossing from Hungary into Romania, trying to escape from the Nazis' methodical roundups and deportations to Auschwitz. Not all were Hungarians. There were thousands who'd escaped from Poland, Austria, and Slovakia, finding relative safety in Hungary until the Nazi occupation in March 1944. In a western Romanian city such as Arad, hiking distance from the border, weary, scared, bedraggled refugees were a not uncommon sight on the streets. In their filthy RAF trousers and shirts, unshaven and unwashed, Dan and Manu Ben-Ephraim appeared to be two more.

The pair had planned to find the synagogue located on Ştefan Cicio Pop Street but were hopelessly lost. The sun was blindingly bright. Occasionally, sirens blared, alternating between alerts and all clears. They were unsure of their exact location but hoped that they were heading toward the city center. They tried not to quicken their pace to avoid looking suspicious.

Suddenly, at a street corner, they encountered a thick-bearded Jew in a black caftan. *"Kum aheir,"* he said, surprising them both by saying "Come here," openly in Yiddish, inviting them to join the synagogue's minyan—the quorum of ten Jewish males over age thirteen required for public worship.

The bearded Jew led them two blocks and two houses away, to the steps of the old synagogue they'd been searching for. Dan saw that there were more than enough Jews inside to form three or four minyans. It wasn't by chance that the Jew in the black caftan had called out to them in Yiddish; his job was to stand near the synagogue and look for Jews who had escaped the deportations from Hungary.

"That Jew didn't know we were parachutists, but with his sixth sense he did figure we were Jews," Dan recalled. "And as is well known, Jews are guarantors to each other, and if not guarantors, at least they can smell each other out in a crowd."

Soon they were surrounded by Yiddish speakers who began to inquire about their journey. Dan claimed that he was a carpenter and Ben-Ephraim a teacher who'd just escaped from Hungary. When asked if he was from Buda or Pest—the two sides of the Danube—Dan chose Pest, simply because he liked the ring of the word. The answers provided by the supposed refugees weren't convincing—everyone in the synagogue regarded them with suspicion.

The synagogue's live-in caretaker—*shammas* in Yiddish—allowed them to bathe in the mikveh, then sent his wife out to buy them sandwiches. He said they could hide out in the synagogue for a few days until they could strategize how best to get to Bucharest.*

Past the bedroom of the *shammas* lived an old Jewish tailor. He had no more customers bringing him garments, but it seemed he was an expert in patching together various rags to make something resembling clothing.

Dan took the tailor his RAF trousers and asked if he could launder them, undo the seams, and stitch them together on the reverse side, concealing the pleats, so that they'd look like civilian ones. For a price, of course. When Dan went to pick up his trousers, the old tailor gave him a wink. "Top quality English cloth," he said. "Elegant. Fine worsted wool. A twill knit. *Nu*, how does a refugee come by such fancy *hoyzn*?" Dan put on a pair of old eyeglasses and a battered broad-brimmed hat to complete the disguise. He and Ben-Ephraim began to look believable enough.

One morning as they were discussing ways to escape, the *shammas*

*From the Hebrew word *shammash* (servant), the Yiddish pronunciation means both the watchman of a synagogue and the ninth "attendant" candle in the Hanukkah menorah. In America, *shammas* morphed into hard-boiled underworld slang, perhaps most famously used by Humphrey Bogart's character Philip Marlowe in *The Big Sleep*: "What are you, a prizefighter?" "No, I'm a *shammas*—a private detective."

appeared and said the police were doing a mass search for refugees from Hungary. He took Dan and Ben-Ephraim to a small steel door next to the mikveh that led to a narrow niche, where they had to stand with water up to their knees. The *shammas* closed them into the nearly airless hiding place. Once, many hours later, he thrust a hand in with sandwiches and some news; the police dragnet would continue one more day and stop in the evening.

The next morning, Dan found a small item in the local newspaper about two parachutists who had reportedly landed in the area. He showed it to Manu. Anyone with information about two strangers moving about in the Arad region was requested to report to the police for a big reward. “Maybe we should report ourselves and collect the cash,” he said. “After all, we deserve to get something out of this at last.” Manu didn’t smile.

27

June 9, 1944
En Route to Budapest

They were in a private compartment on the passenger train, each flanked by gendarmes. The corridor blinds were drawn to block the gawking of curious passengers. Talking was strictly forbidden.

After about an hour, Hannah broke the silence by asking if she could use the toilet. One of the gendarmes grunted as he stood up and shoved her roughly into the corridor. The train was overcrowded with passengers sitting on their suitcases and standing shoulder to shoulder; it was a struggle to get to the end of the car, and when they did, the sign on the metal door of the toilet read OCCUPIED. Hannah glanced to her right, through the small window of the door where the two cars were coupled. She saw the green-and-brown blur of springtime countryside—the train must have been going forty miles per hour. If only she could pull away, yank open the door, and make a quick jump. No one could survive the fall to the tracks.

She twisted away from the guard and managed to grab the door handle—but the gendarme was too quick, catching her slim body in his strong hands and yanking her back to his side violently by her wrist. He cursed at her. His face flushed with anger. "You are state property," he said. "If you die, you'll die when *we* decide."

Upon arrival, they were taken directly from Budapest Railway Station to the Hungarian Military Prison on Miklós Horthy Boulevard.

Hannah gave up nothing beyond her name, rank, and serial number. The jailers continued to beat her on the palms of her hands and the soles of her feet. They pulled out clumps of her hair. They stripped her completely, bound her to a chair, and flogged her.

Tamás Rózsa, a tall, powerfully built military intelligence officer in a civilian suit, conducted the interrogations with the aid of several uniformed men wielding whips. “We found your wireless,” he said. “Why was there no codebook there?”

“It was with the radio.”

“What is your cipher?”

“I don’t know it,” Hannah said. “It’s a table of random numbers.”

“When I was first arrested, there was one great danger facing me,” she later recalled. “The book of French poetry was the key to the code. I had to get rid of it, whatever happened. On the way to the station, I ‘forgot’ the book in the car. Nobody noticed. Perhaps some lover of lyric verse would now enjoy it.”

A slim blue hardcover book—at most a hundred pages—small enough to slip into a jacket pocket and small enough to fall into a crease in a car seat—left behind, unnoticed. Without that book of French poems—which Hannah now honestly didn’t know the whereabouts of—her wireless was useless. No matter how much her tormenters abused her body and mind, no matter how long they tortured her, she could not confess to something she truly did not know.

The same went for Sándor Fleischmann and Jacques Tissandier, whose screams reached her from the cells below.

The cipher book, unfortunately, was not the only information Rózsa wanted. Hannah still hadn’t confessed her true identity, and her altered papers did not, as Reuven Dafni had feared, stand up to close inspection. Who was she? Rózsa demanded. Whom did she know in Budapest? When she refused to answer, she was flogged with renewed fury.

She thought of Enzo Sereni, sitting serenely in a leather armchair reading aloud from P. G. Wodehouse in the huge room overlooking Suleiman Pasha Square. *You’ll take cyanide.* She pictured Yoel yelling furiously at Enzo and then dashing from the room. She remembered every word of the lecture by

David Shaltiel during Palmach training at Kibbutz Hazorea: *The French Foreign Legion. Mental toughness. Those Gestapo sadists can break your body but never your mind.*

Hannah's mind was tough, but still . . . why had Reuven refused to give her an L-pill? A quick crunch between her molars, and Rózsa could get nothing further from her. Not another word, not another breath.

Before they'd all departed on the mission, Shaul Avigur, the head of Mossad L'Aliyah Bet, had assured every member of the Hungarian team that he'd secure the necessary certificates of emigration and get their parents out of Hungary long before any of the parachutists crossed the border. In her delirium, Hannah began to see her mother reunited with her brother at Kibbutz Maagan on the shores of Lake Kinneret.

Her father was still known by almost everyone, despite the ban on performances of his plays and publication of his books since the Jewish Laws had been passed. She visualized the cover of his illustrated book *Csibi*: the script title in bold canary yellow; the footballer in a scarlet jersey, crouching down and helping a little golden-haired boy learn how to kick properly. Before she'd left Budapest, it had seemed as though every boy under the age of eighteen had carried around a copy.

She remembered the people in the sidewalk cafés reading his humor column "The Coalman" in *Pesti Hírlap*, laughing loudly.

Maybe these thugs would soften if they heard that she was the daughter of Béla Szenes.

"What is your real name?" Rózsa asked again.

Avigur's promise about the certificates of emigration had been made months before in Tel Aviv. Hannah's mother was surely in Palestine already, reunited with her brother, perhaps at this very moment walking the shore of Lake Kinneret at Kibbutz Maagan. . . .

"Your real name!"

"Szenes," she said through her gap-toothed grimace. "My real name is Anna Szenes."

PART THREE

BLESSED IS THE MATCH

1

June 17, 1944
Rose Hill, Budapest

On June 17, 1944, Katherine Senesh awoke at eight o'clock as usual in the large family villa on Bimbó út in the upscale Rózsadomb (Rose Hill) neighborhood of Buda—the same house that had been Hannah's idyllic childhood home. She'd managed to get only a few hours of fitful sleep.

It had been a troubled few weeks; she'd learned that her family in the provinces had been deported. They'd boarded overcrowded cattle cars bound for supposed resettlement and hard labor in a place in Austria called Waldsee. Rumors swirled, however, that "Waldsee" really meant death: extermination in eastern Poland.

She dressed quietly, careful not to wake her housemate. Since her late husband's plays and books had been banned, the royalties that had afforded her family a comfortable living before the war had dried up. She had been forced to rent out her own room—as well as Hannah and Gyuri's rooms—to supplement her income. For the past year, most of her house had been rented by Margit Dajka, the leading Hungarian stage and screen actress of her era. Katherine enjoyed the company of Margit—whom she knew through her late husband's theatrical circle—even if her Bohemian habits were often disruptive. Tradesmen would ring at the door and demand to be paid. Margit was usually in debt, and she'd shout to Katherine from her bedroom, "Tell them I don't have any cash, darling. Ask if they'll take my mink coat."

Like most other Jews in Budapest, Katherine knew that she would need to move soon to the other side of the Danube—from Buda to Pest—where buildings specially designated with a huge yellow star were filling up with thousands of displaced Jews. The Jewish houses were the prelude to some horror that many Jews sensed without knowing precisely what form it would take.

Unlike in the more famous walled-in ghettos in Warsaw, Białystok, and Vilna—which by early 1944 had all been liquidated—the Jews of Budapest had recently been confined to "yellow star" houses put into place by Mayor Ákos Farkas. Only a few days earlier, he had issued the first decree, a list of over 2,600 residences. The deadline for moving to the yellow star houses was midnight on June 21, 1944.

Margit had promised to guard Katherine's most precious possessions—original manuscripts of her husband's novels and plays, pictures of Hannah and Gyuri as kids—but Katherine felt that she had no reason to stay in Budapest. She'd been promised a Palestine entry certificate many times by Va'ad ha-Hatzalah (Va'ada), the Zionist-run Relief and Rescue Committee of Budapest, and she knew that the Va'ada was still issuing them, even if it couldn't secure exit permits for all its clients.

But now she had a second option: A close Jewish friend named János had told her that he'd acquired excellent Aryan papers that she could use and they would travel together to Romania, where there were good smuggling routes to the coast.

Once in the port of Constanţa, on the Black Sea, Jews could get to Istanbul in neutral Turkey, on boats procured by the Mossad L'Aliyah Bet. From Istanbul they would take a train into Syria, then into Lebanon, then be smuggled across the border into Palestine.

Suddenly the bell at the garden gate rang. A stranger in a dark suit and tie was peering up at her through the window. "I'm looking for Mrs. Béla Szegö."

"She doesn't live here."

"Yes, of course, she does." The man took out a piece of paper. "Isn't this Number 28, Bimbó út? Oh, wait—the name's not Szegö: it's *Szenes*. I'm looking for Mrs. Béla Szenes."

"What for?"

"I'm a detective with the state police. Please let me come in."

Katherine opened the door and allowed him to enter. Once in the hallway, he continued, "Mrs. Szenes, you must come with me to the staff headquarters of the Hungarian National Defense."

"For what reason?"

"You've been summoned as a witness."

"What is the case?"

"I really don't know."

"I need to finish dressing," Katherine said. "Please wait here."

As she gathered her things, she was baffled. She didn't know anybody in the military. Jews had been excluded from service since the first anti-Jewish law of 1938. The only possible answer was Gyuri: He was of military age, but he had left the country almost six years before.

As she dressed, she woke Margit. The actress draped a silk gown around herself and went to see what the commotion was about. The detective seemed a bit starstruck at the sight of the screen actress. Margit took the opportunity to launch into her own cross-examination: "What's this all about?"

The detective stammered that he really didn't have a clue about the summons. The women believed him. He was so thrilled to be talking to Hungary's most famous film actress that he would clearly have told her anything he knew.

Katherine came back, her large yellow Star of David prominently displayed on the upper left part of her jacket, as required by law since April 5. Her eyes fell on the dining room table, where the forged Aryan birth certificate was lying openly for anyone to see. That alone was a death sentence. She managed to slip it to Margit for safekeeping.

When Katherine arrived at the Hadik Barracks on Miklós Horthy Street, which housed Hungary's military police and counterespionage unit, she was led up to a second-floor office, where two policemen were having their midmorning snack of smoked bacon and green peppers.

The detective went to announce her arrival and when he returned asked the police to leave. He allowed her to phone Margit. He then asked whether she had any children. When Katherine replied in the affirmative, he asked where they were. There happened to be a large map on the wall, and she smilingly pointed to Palestine.

Just then, a very tall man of military bearing entered the room. His name,

Katherine soon learned, was Tamás Rózsa. He gestured to a chair and settled himself behind a typewriter. The interrogation began.

After taking down the usual data concerning family and background, he questioned her about Gyuri, the elder, but rapidly turned his attention to Hannah. Much to Katherine's surprise, he questioned her repeatedly about her, stopped his pretense of typing, and asked what specific reasons her daughter had had for leaving home. "I can understand your *son* leaving: to see the world, to complete his studies, to prepare for his career. But a *girl* . . . why should a young girl want to leave her home, her mother, her friends?"

"For the very reasons you mentioned," Katherine replied. "Jewish youth has no future in Hungary, no opportunity of making a living. And much as it hurt me to part with her, particularly after having had to part with my son, I'm happy she's not here now to see and experience the terrible suffering of the Jews."

A smile spread over the officer's unpleasant face, and the interrogation continued. The majority of his questions revolved around what Hannah had been doing during the past few years, where she was at present, what she was doing now, and, above all, from where and how often she was in touch with her mother.

It occurred to Katherine that perhaps one of her letters had been intercepted and contained something that displeased the censor. But there was no time for conjecture. The conversation was accelerating and intensifying.

Rózsa now, strangely, wanted to know all about Hannah's activities before she had left Budapest. What had she done at home and in school? Who were her friends? What were her interests, her ambitions. What kind of profession did she have in mind?

"She always wanted to be a teacher," Katherine said.

Rózsa sighed. "God help us. That's all we would have needed."

"I know you would not take my opinion of my daughter's talents as objective, but it would be easy to get confirmation from her former teachers. Why don't you ask Dr. Lajos Áprily," Katherine offered, mentioning the principal of Hannah's high school, one of her early mentors, the famed poet—"or Dr. Boriska Ravasz and Dr. Alice Quant."

Katherine found Rózsa's demeanor crude and dismissive, but she knew better than to object. As the conversation ended, Rózsa instructed the detective to type up a summary of the interrogation. Katherine would have to swear under oath that her testimony was truthful and then sign it.

Katherine summarized her statement, and the detective typed it on a long sheet headed "Szenes Anna." They had barely finished when Rózsa returned, carefully read it over, and made her swear to its veracity and sign it.

"Now, then," he said, "where do you really think your daughter is now? At this minute?"

Katherine repeated that to the best of her knowledge, her daughter was working on an agricultural settlement in the vicinity of Haifa.

Rózsa smirked. "If you really don't know, then I'll tell you. She's here—in the adjoining room. I'll bring her right in so you can talk to her and persuade her to tell us everything she knows."

Moments later, four men brought Hannah in. Katherine turned around and felt as if the floor was giving way under her. She grabbed the edge of the table for balance. She could scarcely recognize the daughter she'd last seen in September 1939.

Hannah's once soft, wavy hair hung in a filthy tangle, her face reflecting weeks of suffering. Her large, expressive eyes were blackened, and there were welts on her cheeks and neck.

Hannah tore herself away from the men and, rushing to Katherine, threw her arms around her neck. "Mother, forgive me!"

Katherine felt the pounding of her daughter's heart against her own. The men in the room stared at them, she noticed, as if watching a scene in a play. Again, the floor seemed to sway. It took all her strength to maintain her self-control and remain silent.

"Convince your daughter to be more talkative," Rózsa said. "Convince her that it's for her own good to tell us everything. If not, I guarantee you: You'll never see each other again."

Katherine hadn't the faintest idea what was happening. Not even in her wildest imagination would it have occurred to her that Hannah, who'd always espoused pacifism, would have volunteered for the British military. She didn't even realize that a woman *could* serve in the British military. But what puzzled her most was how her daughter had suddenly been catapulted from a kibbutz on the Mediterranean coast in Palestine into the hell that was Nazi-occupied Hungary.

One thing, however, was certain: If there was some information that Hannah did not want to reveal, whatever that brute Rózsa was demanding of her, she had good reason. Under no circumstances would Katherine influence her otherwise.

"Dammit," Rózsa said, "why don't you two talk?"

Katherine's voice had a flinty edge. "There's no need to repeat yourself. We both heard you."

Rózsa slammed the door behind him. Mother and child were reunited, alone, for the first time in nearly five years.

What could Hannah possibly say? With no words to explain why she'd done it, why she'd returned to Budapest, she trembled in her mother's arms. It was only then that she understood the full enormity of what she'd done. The only thing Hannah wanted was forgiveness.

"We communicated only with our eyes," Hannah recalled. "Could Mother understand from the fire in my eyes what was happening inside me?"

As her daughter gazed up at her, it suddenly struck Katherine that this could all be her own fault. Had Hannah, hearing about the Nazi occupation and the persecution of the Jews in Hungary, volunteered for a daring, even suicidal mission on *her* account? "Hannah," she said, looking into her child's eyes, "tell me, am I the cause of all this? Did worry and anxiety about me bring you back?"

"No, Mother, no. You're not to blame for anything. Not for anything at all. I can't explain now. But the day will come when you'll understand why I did it."

Katherine finally had a chance to examine Hannah closely. She noticed instantly that one of her upper teeth was missing. "Anikó! What happened to your smile? You were tortured? You lost that tooth here?"

Hannah shook her head. "No, not here," she said truthfully.

Katherine tried to mask her heartbreak. She stroked Hannah's hands, noticing that all the nails were broken; the once soft skin of her palms was like sandpaper. She leaned over to kiss Hannah's bruised cheek tenderly, but at the very instant of their embrace, the door burst open and Rózsa rushed in with

Béla Szenes—né Schlesinger—was one of the most popular playwrights, journalists, and authors in prewar Hungary.

Béla Szenes pictured here with his wife, Katherine (or Katalina, neé Salzberger), an accomplished pianist who would become the keeper of her husband's literary legacy.

3

After Béla's death in 1927, at the age of thirty-three, Katherine Szenes raised their two children on her own in the upscale Rose Hill neighborhood of Budapest. Gyura was born in 1920 and Anna (affectionately known as Anikó) was born in 1921.

4

Anna, Katherine, and Gyura Szenes in Budapest in 1928.

5

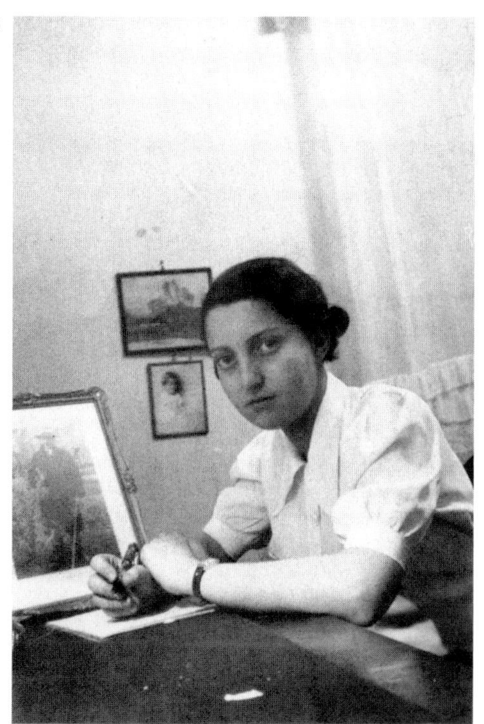

Anna Szenes began keeping a diary at age thirteen. She wrote prodigiously from an early age—poetry, short stories, journalism—documenting her inner transformation and spiritual awakening as a Jew in the increasingly anti-Semitic Kingdom of Hungary.

6

Young Anna Szenes was both athletic and bookish. An avid tennis player, skater, and swimmer, Anna was—as one of her fellow paratroopers later put it—"a poet-tomboy."

7

Anna—now going by her Hebrew name Hannah—in her finest dress on the day she arrived in British Mandatory Palestine. Photo taken on September 19, 1939, in Haifa.

8

Within days, Hannah had fully submerged herself in her new spartan life as a "proletarian woman" in Eretz Israel. She spent her first two years in "the Land" attending the Canadian Hadassah Agricultural School for Girls at Moshav Nahalal.

9

Though Hannah specialized in the poultry industry at Nahalal, here she and her classmates pose with one of the agricultural school's friendlier goats. Hannah (center, fifth from the left) was an exceptional student and gave the valedictory address upon graduation in September 1941.

10

Hannah in the ruins of the Roman capital of Judea, Caesarea Maritima, in 1942. As one of the founders of a new agricultural settlement nearby, Kibbutz Sdot Yam, Hannah regularly wandered in the vast Roman ruins and found inspiration for several of her most famous poems such as "Halicha L'Keisarya" ("A Walk to Caesarea").

11

Enzo Sereni was, at age thirty-nine, the oldest of the Yishuv parachutists. An erudite Roman-born doctor of philosophy, Enzo defied orders by parachuting into Nazi-held northern Italy.

12

Yitzhak Sadeh—universally known by his underground code name "Ha-Zaken" (the "Old Man")—was the founder and commander of the Palmach, the elite "strike companies" of the Haganah.

13

Lieutenant Colonel Anthony Simonds, OBE, one of the commanding officers of MI9's A Force, championed the use of Jewish volunteers from Palestine to his superiors.

14

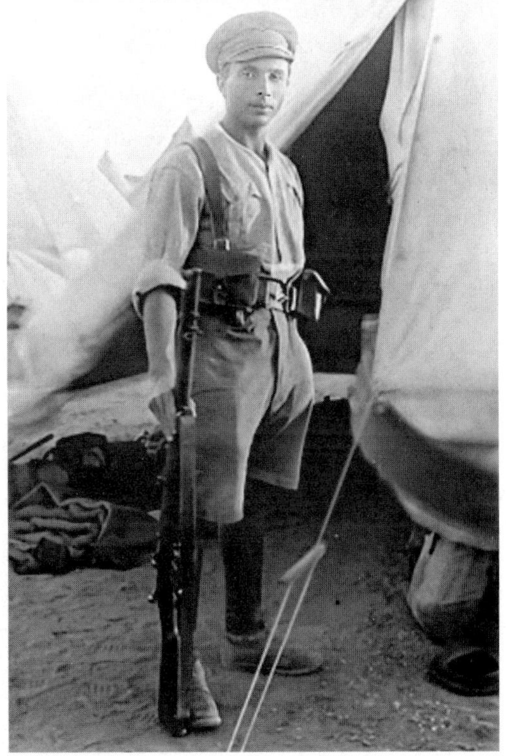

Eliyahu Golomb, the founder and commander of the Haganah—Hebrew for "the Defense"—whose house on Rothschild Boulevard in Tel Aviv was the wartime "nerve center" for the Yishuv's military planning. Golomb had volunteered to serve in the British Army's Jewish Brigade during World War I and is pictured here in uniform in 1918.

15

16

17

Clockwise: Haviva Reik, a charismatic Palmach commander personally recruited by Yitzhak Sadeh who proved utterly fearless when fighting during the Slovak National Uprising in 1944.

Sara (Surika) Braverman, jokingly known as the "Parachutist Who Didn't Jump," was one of the first female Palmach commanders, founder of the Women's Corps of the Israel Defense Forces, and later dubbed the "First Lady of the IDF."

The final photo of Hannah Senesh ever taken in British Mandatory Palestine, during her brief reunion with her brother, Gyura, who'd just arrived on a refugee ship in the port of Haifa. The photo was snapped on the beachfront boardwalk of Tel Aviv in February 1944, just hours before Hannah departed for her radio coding and MI9 training in Cairo.

18

During training in Cairo in 1944, members of the Czechoslovakian parachutists' team, in their British khaki drill uniforms, get some R&R by visiting the famed Step Pyramid of Djoser at Saqqara. Chaim Hermesh is far right; next to him: Zvi Ben-Yaakov and Rafi Reiss. Haviva Reik is second from the left.

19

Reuven Dafni was the most experienced soldier among the Yugoslavian parachutists' team. Known as "Agent Gary," his network smuggling downed Allied airmen and escaped POWs out of occupied Europe was so successful that the Nazis put a bounty of 10,000 reichsmarks on his head.

20

Yoel Palgi, along with Hannah Senesh and Peretz Goldstein, was one of the three parachutists to infiltrate occupied Hungary. Of the trio, Palgi alone survived the war and was instrumental in relating the details of what happened to Hannah after her capture.

21

22

Rafi Reiss (*left*) and Zvi Ben-Yaakov (*right*) of the Czechoslovakian Parachutists' Team. Together with Haviva Reik and Chaim Hermesh, this close-knit group styled themselves "the Simonds Quartet."

At Bari Airfield in the summer of 1944,
from right to left, top row: Reuven Dafni, Zadok Doron, Abba Berdichev.
Bottom row: Sara Braverman, Arie Fichman, Haviva Reik.

 24

 25

Several of the parachutists—including Uriel Kenner and Yaakov Shapira—studying maps and code books onboard an RAF bomber, en route to make their nighttime jumps in the Balkans.

26

Hannah Senesh, in the uniform of Aircraftwoman Second Class, Women's Auxiliary Air Force; photo taken in the mountains of Yugoslavia in spring 1944 while Hannah was fighting with Tito's Yugoslav Partisan Army.

27

Type A Mark III "suitcase radio." This was the smallest transceiver produced by British Intelligence during the war, ingeniously camouflaged, with a range of five hundred miles. Hannah Senesh, Haviva Reik, and the other Jewish radio operators were expert at sending and receiving coded messages in difficult terrain once dropped behind enemy lines.

28   29

Left: Shaike Dan *(right)* and Dov Harari in their jumpsuits awaiting deployment at Bari Airfield.

Right: The parachutists in disguise as local "tramps" while undercover. From right: Yonah Rosen, Manu Ben-Efraim, Shaike Dan.

 30

The only known photo of Hannah Senesh and her fellow parachutists, embedded with Tito's Yugoslav Partisans, circa April 1944. In the front row, seated far right, is Yonah Rosen—the Palmach commander who personally recruited Hannah for the mission. Hannah is seated third from the right. In the back row, standing, are Abba Berdichev at far right, in beret, and Reuven Dafni, fifth from the right, in the uniform of a RAF warrant officer.

31

The only image of the Czechoslovakian parachutists' team during the mission. The photo, taken surreptitiously by a Slovak Partisan, shows the Jewish parachutists huddled together at the Tri Duby airfield during the September 1944 antifascist uprising. From right to left: Zvi Ben-Yaakov (in white trench coat), Abba Berdichev, Rafi Reiss, Haviva Reik (back to camera, in beret), Chaim Hermesh.

32

The repatriation of Hannah Senesh's remains from Hungary to Israel in March 1950 was the largest state funeral in the nation's history.

33

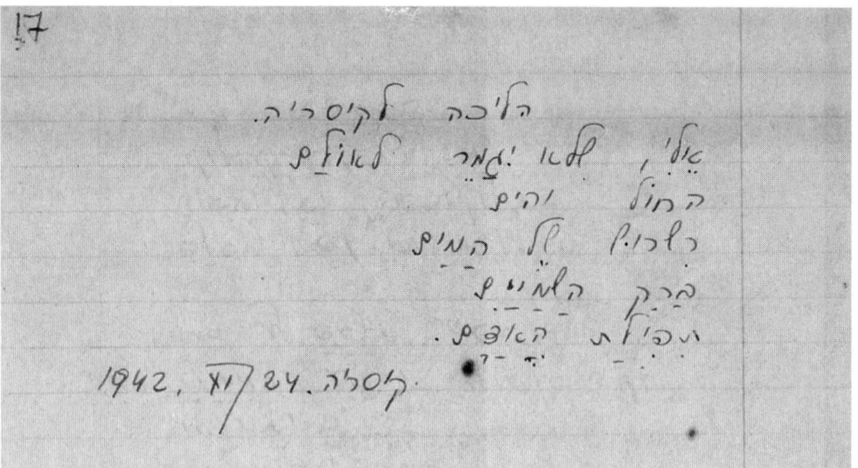

The manuscript of “A Walk to Caesarea”—today better known as “Eli, Eli.” This handwritten version is in a notebook Hannah Senesh left to her best friend Miryam Yitzhak. (Hebrew readers will note that Hannah, who only began learning the language at age seventeen, misspells the word *olam* at the end of the first line, using the vowel aleph instead of an ayin.) Today the poem is one of the most beloved verses in Modern Hebrew.

34

The V-shaped Parachutists’ Plot in the National Heroes Cemetery on Mount Herzl in Jerusalem. Under these headstones are the repatriated remains of three of the seven paratroopers who never returned—Hannah Senesh, Haviva Reik, Rafi Reiss—as well as symbolic graves for the four whose remains vanished in the crematoria of Nazi concentration camps: Enzo Sereni, Peretz Goldstein, Abba Berdichev, Zvi Ben-Yaakov.

his henchmen, who roughly pushed them apart. "Whispering is not allowed here!" he said. "Anyway, that's enough for today."

As quickly as she'd appeared, Hannah was taken away.

"I could detain you as well, but I'll take your age into consideration," Rózsa said. "Go home. If we have further need of you, we'll contact you. Everything depends upon your daughter. But I warn you, you're not to tell anyone anything that has happened here today. Not a word! Not even that you've set foot inside this building. Understand?"

"Yes, I understand. But someone already knows that I'm here."

"Who?" Rózsa asked.

"Margit Dajka."

"Margit Dajka? The *actress*? How is that possible?"

"Mrs. Szenes is her housekeeper," the detective confirmed. "Margit Dajka was there when I picked up the witness."

"Will she ask questions when you return?"

"I'm sure she will. She isn't accustomed to seeing me hauled off by a detective."

"If she asks you anything, tell her you've been forbidden to say a single word."

When Rózsa returned to Hannah's solitary cell, his demeanor had changed. He was soft spoken and apologetic—as if it had all been some misunderstanding. "I'm sorry that we've had to be rough with you, Miss Szenes," he said. "After all, you're the daughter of the great Béla Szenes. I always held your father's work in the highest regard. I enjoyed his plays at the Comedy Theatre. I regret being rough with your mother, too. It's obvious how dearly you love each other. But—"

Hannah instantly saw through the charade, but she listened, eyes wide, waiting for the hammer to drop.

"You've committed a serious crime against your homeland."

"I've committed no crime against my homeland."

"You've committed the crime of espionage."

"I'm not guilty of espionage."

"Miss Szenes, it's not too late," he said. "If you tell me where the codebook is, you'll have made up for it."

Hannah went silent for a long time. When she didn't answer, Rózsa's mask of politeness melted away. "Tell me where your codebook really is! If not, I'll execute your mother in front of your eyes. We'll kill her. Afterwards, we'll shoot you, too. The choice is in your hands."

"No!" Hannah shouted. "No, don't touch my mother."

"In front of your eyes. Do you understand me?"

With that, for the first time, Hannah broke. "Torture me, *kill* me," she pleaded, her sobs echoing in the cell. "Just don't touch my mother."

"Tell me the code."

"Please don't touch her."

"The code!"

"Mother . . ."

"I'll give you three hours," Rózsa said. "If you decide to talk, you can see her again. If not, we'll carry out the sentence. And bear this in mind: You'll have imposed it yourself with your silence and stubbornness."

He left the cell. She was alone, immobile, numb, wishing that she had one of those L-pills hidden in the fold of her cheek or under her tongue. It would be so easy an exit. One bite: an instantaneous escape into nothingness.

Then, as the shock wore off, Rózsa's words took on a terrifying significance. Hannah had a stark choice: become a traitor to her people or condemn her mother to death.

2

Katherine, in her own daze, somehow managed to make her way home. It felt like weeks had passed but it was only one in the afternoon. When she approached the villa, curious neighbors stood in front. They rushed at her. "Tell us what happened!"

"It was all some sort of mistake."

Margit shepherded Katherine inside and gently tried to pry the truth from her. Finally Katherine came clean. "There was no mistake. Something terrible has happened, but I'm not allowed to tell anyone."

The front bell rang. A film director had come to fetch Margit to view the rough cut of their latest movie. Margit had to leave, but Katherine wasn't alone for long—János, the Jewish friend who'd invited Katherine to escape with him and his wife, knocked on the door. The window for them to escape to Romania was closing. They wanted to leave Budapest as soon as possible, within the next day or so. "Kató, are you ready?"

"I've thought about the whole thing," she said. "I've changed my mind."

János was mystified. He didn't know a soul in Eretz Israel, yet he had resolved to leave. Both of Katherine's children were there. Her daughter, Anikó, had worked so hard to obtain a certificate of emigration back in 1939. What possible reason could Katherine have to stay in Budapest?

Despite Rózsa's direct warning, Katherine decided to trust János with the truth. She was taking a big risk, but if he managed to reach Palestine, at least someone could tell Gyuri what had happened.

János listened with horror to her account of the abuse Hannah had suffered at the hands of the Gestapo and the Hungarian police. When she was done, a palpable sadness and tension hung in the room. After a thoughtful silence, he finally said, "I can see why you would want to stay here now with Anikó." He swore to keep the secret but made clear that he didn't think that Katherine should. She needed to tell someone who could help. Why not start with Margit Dajka? She was one of the best-known women in Hungary. She might have connections high up in the military or government. Even if she failed, it was worth a try.

János bade Katherine goodbye, wished her well, and hurriedly left. Within minutes, she noticed from the hallway that a shiny black sedan had pulled up at the curb. Several tall men in gray-green SS uniforms were on the sidewalk. One of them called out loudly to her, *"Wir suchen Frau Szenes. Bitte lassen Sie uns herein."*

Katherine understood and spoke German flawlessly. She replied that she was fetching the key and hurriedly picked up the forged Aryan papers that János had brought her, which were lying in plain view on the table, and hid them in Margit's desk. She then walked casually to the gate, where a plainclothes officer in a leather overcoat was now blocking the way.

After giving his name as Hauptmann Seifert of the Gestapo, he asked Katherine to come with him at once for questioning.

"I can't go with you now," Katherine replied firmly. "I'm responsible for Miss Dajka's apartment and I have to look after her things."

"You can do that when you come back, after you have answered some questions," Seifert said equally firmly. "Please get ready to leave."

Katherine went to her room to pick up her purse and a few things that might be useful in jail, trying not to arouse Seifert's suspicion. He followed her everywhere, asking questions. Which rooms were occupied by Miss Dajka, and which were hers? Katherine replied that only the back room was hers. What about the furniture and the contents of each closet? He wanted to know where each door led. Such information, she knew, was preliminary to a thorough house search, and Katherine used each reply to delay as much as possible. Suddenly Seifert whipped a picture out of his pocket and held it in front of her. "Do you recognize this person?"

The picture in Seifert's hand showed Hannah in the same battered state Katherine had just witnessed. She decided to feign surprise. After all, Rózsa's warning had been clear, and while it could be an orchestrated trap, it was certainly possible that the Gestapo and Hungarian military police were acting independently of each other—conducting their own investigations.

"No, who is it?"

"Haben Sie eine Tochter? Anna Szenes?"

"Yes, I do have a daughter, but I wouldn't recognize her from this photo. How did you get the picture?"

Siefert shoved the photo back into his jacket pocket and told her to hurry up.

At just after five o'clock, Katherine climbed into the black sedan filled with four or five SS men. In a few minutes they'd driven from Katherine's Rose Hill neighborhood to the Castle Hill section near the Danube and arrived in front of the Deutches Polizeigefängnis, an immense red-brick building at Gyorskocsi út-25—No. 25 Gyorskocsi Street—near the Palace of Justice, which, since March 19, 1944, had served as a Gestapo prison. Seifert led Katherine to a room upstairs. For the second time that day, she watched her personal data being typed on a form, which was then stamped with one German word: *dringendste*. Most urgent.

Three others were in the room: a uniformed SS man with a death's-head insignia on his cap, indicating that he belonged to the SS-Totenkopfverbände, the units responsible for the administration of the concentration camps and extermination centers; another young soldier; and a middle-aged civilian who did not appear to be German.

Captain Seifert took her house keys and left. He obviously intended to search the place before Margit returned.

The young death's-head man got straight to business. He demanded to see all her personal belongings and dumped out the contents of her handbag on the table. He confiscated the few coins she had inside, her fountain pen, and her watch—even ordered her to remove the wedding band she still wore despite Béla's death seventeen years before. Then he demanded to know if she had any more money hidden anywhere.

Fastened around her neck on a thin strap was a small leather bag; inside was the maximum amount of money Jews were allowed to carry on their persons. She paused. After a moment, she removed the bag from her neck and handed it to him. "The reward for the momentary delay was a powerful slap across my face," she later wrote. "I spun completely around on my own axis, but strangely enough didn't feel the blow at all. After that morning's encounter with Hannah, I felt nothing, as if a stranger had taken my place, or a mechanized puppet."

During her mother's interrogation, locked in solitary confinement, Hannah struggled with an agonizing dilemma: Should she give up the secret of MI9's coding system? Obviously, the volume of French poetry was lost, but would there be any real harm in telling Rózsa the name of the book or even some of the lines she'd memorized for the double encryption?

German agents would likely try to transmit false information to lead Allied bombers into a trap of anti-aircraft fire, but to MI9, it would be suspicious. Colonel Simonds in Cairo would be expecting messages from Agent Minnie about downed airmen and escaped POWs, not the locations of strategic bombing targets in Hungary. Her British opposite number in Bari was supremely well trained. Surely they'd be able to tell within the first few incoming Morse code lines that Hannah couldn't possibly have been the sender.

Contradictory thoughts ping-ponged through her brain; she felt she was going mad. "If I were only a traitorous spy, that would be bad enough. They'd despise me universally," she recalled. But she was more than a single agent: "I was the representative of a people. *Our* people. We'd all been sent as emissaries in the name of the Yishuv. Our resistance was that of the whole community. My betrayal would be theirs, too. No, I couldn't turn traitor. I couldn't reveal the code."

But what about her mother? Could Hannah betray her? Condemn her mother to death? "Was there anyone in the world who faced such a satanic choice?" she asked.

The three hours Rózsa had given her to decide were up. Two guards came to haul her down to the interrogation room. Hannah gathered her remaining strength. She found that clenching her fists tightly concealed the trembling of her fingers.

"I went along with them stonily, frozen. I'd determined that I couldn't do it. I could not destroy her with my own hands. I had decided to reveal the name of the French book of poetry. That information was meaningless. If they didn't kill me, I'd find a way to put an end to my life. I would not be able to live with myself afterward. But my mother had to remain alive for Gyuri's sake. And they'd understand what had made me turn traitor. There wasn't a single person in the world who would blame me and say, 'In the same circumstances, I would have chosen to kill my own mother.'"

Rózsa threw open the door. "Well, what have you decided?"

Hannah heard her mother's voice: "Don't turn traitor."

"What have you decided?"

"I left the codebook beside the transmitter."

Rózsa jumped toward her. Hannah saw his body twist like a cobra. The wall behind him billowed above his shoulder. She looked for something to lean against but found only air. The blow came. She was suspended as if in flight. And then nothing.

She regained consciousness in the pitch black of solitary confinement. With no watch and no windows in the cell, she had no idea how much time had passed. She couldn't tell if it was day or night.

She wasn't taken back for interrogation right away. She was left alone to ruminate. Sleep became a memory. She refused all food and water, hoping to starve herself to death.

She heard one sentence over and over in her mind: *You killed your mother.*

Sometimes it was a mocking whisper, sometimes a cruel laugh: *You—killed—your—mother!*

She wished for only one thing now: to die.

3

June 1944
Gyorskocsi Street Gestapo Prison, Budapest

Because her husband had been an accomplished Hungarian literary figure, Katherine Szenes was locked in a cell for "notables." The brightly lit communal cell—to Katherine, it almost resembled a hospital room, with six white beds—housed about a dozen inmates, including some high-profile Jewish prisoners whom she'd known in prewar social circles.

Baroness Böske Hatvany was the ex-wife of the left-wing writer and literary scholar Baron Lajos Hatvany, who'd been a good friend of Béla; there was also Mrs. Jenő Vida, wife of a prominent Jewish industrial, private economic adviser to Miklós Horthy and Member of the Magyar Felsőház (the Hungarian Assembly's Upper House) who'd been denounced for supposedly making an anti-Nazi remark; and Countess Clara Zichy, arrested while attempting to hide her valuable art collection. All of them were awaiting Gestapo interrogation.

After a sleepless night, Katherine was ordered out of bed at 5:00 a.m. Sunday was generally a day off for the Gestapo interrogators, but since Katherine's dossier was marked "Most urgent," she was expected at Svábhegy (Schwab Hill) for questioning early the next morning. She was too anxious to keep her situation secret. She confided in Baroness Hatvany, the prisoner she knew best, about everything that had happened. The baroness listened in silence, her eyes wide with shock, and promised to tell no one. Katherine kept repeating her greatest fear: "Is my daughter still alive?"

She understood her daughter's personality better than anyone else did; she was certain that Hannah would never give up any military secrets, she would never begin to talk, even under the worst torture. But she also realized that the Gestapo and Hungarian interrogators would show no mercy. Look at what they'd already done to the once beautiful Hannah's face and body.

Katherine desperately looked around the cell for an escape. "I shuddered at the thought of being questioned and decided it was senseless to endure further torment," she later wrote. "Even if Hannah were alive, I could be of no help to her whatever while imprisoned."

She saw a small shelf on which the prisoners were allowed to keep a few knickknacks and toilet articles. Out of boredom, some of the women would spend hours arranging and rearranging the meager items they had obtained in the outside parcels they were allowed each fortnight. One day, Countess Zichy casually mentioned to Katherine that the most useful gift she had was a tiny razor blade—somehow it had gotten past the guards' notice, and she'd been using it as knife, scissors, and pencil sharpener ever since.

Katherine glanced at it out of the corner of her eye. That night, while half the women were absorbed in the business of arranging their thin mattresses on the floor—more comfortable than sleeping two to a bed—Katherine managed to palm the razor blade without the countess noticing and hid it on the outside window ledge.

The cell had no electric lights, which meant that all the women went to bed as soon as it grew dark outside. When everyone else seemed to be asleep, Katherine quietly retrieved the razor blade. In the darkness, feeling with her fingertips for the radial artery in her left wrist, she slashed deeply into her flesh. She could feel her warm blood—flowing, yes, but it didn't gush forth as she had expected. She tried again on the right wrist but could still draw only a trickle of blood. Perhaps the razor was dull from overuse. Before she could make a third attempt, the prisoners began to awaken. Baroness Hatvany, seeing what had happened, rushed over to Katherine, grabbed both her wrists, and bound them tightly with two handkerchiefs to stanch the bleeding. She spoke quietly, trying to hide her rage. Katherine's foolish suicide attempt could have gotten all of them into trouble, she hissed: The Nazis and their Hungarian collaborators believed fervently in the deterrence of collective punishment.

The baroness told Katherine that when she was taken in for questioning in the morning, she should wear her long-sleeved raincoat to hide the self-inflicted gashes on her wrists.

At nine sharp on Monday morning, a van took Katherine and a group of other prisoners to Gestapo headquarters on top of Svábhegy (Schwab Hill). Formerly an exclusive residential district, the SS and the Gestapo had largely commandeered it, taking over small hotels and villas and converting them into prisons and jails equipped with interrogation chambers.

Katherine saw that Hauptmann Seifert was, as an interrogator, markedly different from Rózsa. His eyes were icy—those of a killer—but his manner was sophisticated and courteous. Between his questions, Katherine decided to risk asking what kind of sentence her daughter was facing.

"According to my interpretation of Hungarian law, your daughter's life is in no danger," Siefert answered drily. "You're very lucky. Our German laws are stricter."

That evening one of the prison trusties—or "domestics," as they were called—a strikingly attractive young German Hungarian woman named Hilda, led Katherine into the corridor and gestured with her eyes toward the courtyard. "When I stepped into the corridor and the door of the cell was closed behind me, Hilda whispered that I was to stand by the window of the cell and look across," Katherine wrote. "Looking out of the window was generally forbidden, but then so many things we ventured to do were forbidden that I did as she bid. At the window directly across the yard, and exactly opposite mine, I saw Hannah. She smiled and waved."

At that precise moment, on the opposite side of the prison, as Hannah was being led down the corridor for her next interrogation session, her domestic escort whispered into her ear, "Quickly, look through the window."

Hannah was startled to see her mother's face across the courtyard, behind the glass. "Using these sort of psychological pressure tactics, they almost managed to drive me crazy," she later said. "They hoped, in vain, that Mother's imprisonment would break my spirit. But it was now clear to me that the fact that I *hadn't* turned traitor had saved my mother's life—and my own. If I'd revealed any secrets, they surely wouldn't have any further need for us."

4

June 13–20, 1944
Arad and Bucharest, Romania

After nine days in Romania, Shaike Dan and Manu Ben-Ephraim were no closer to Bucharest than when they had landed. They decided to go to the train station without forged papers. The station was bustling and chaotic; railroad cars loaded with crates of chickens were attached to the passenger train leaving for Bucharest. The parachutists found the engineer, put a thick wad of cash into his palm, and asked to be placed into the poultry car. It was a surefire way to avoid ticket collectors and random police ID inspections.

The door of the boxcar slammed. The chickens wouldn't stop squawking, and the stifling air reeked of their droppings. "We lay among the crates without being able to straighten our legs," Dan recalled. "Twenty-six hours of physical agony. I imagine that we dozed off now and then, but if so, that was known only to the chickens who alone were in on our secret."

They knew that major train stations such as the ones in Bucharest had constant police scrutiny, but as the train screeched to a stop, they saw that the station was in greater chaos than the one in Arad had been. The disruption of bombings and constant air raid sirens meant that all the gates were open. There were no orderly inspections of documents.

Manu Ben-Ephraim knew Bucharest intimately from his childhood, and he led Dan on a route through the capital that bypassed all the main streets where the Romanian police might have set up checkpoints. They soon arrived at a courtyard filled with young Jews, not unwashed and unkempt refugees from Hungary but Bucharest locals. Several Zionist youth leaders were awaiting their arrival. Or at least the leaders had been told to expect the arrival of two Yishuv emissaries, Theo and Franz. Dan singled out one of the young men, who seemed to have some authority, approached and, in lieu of a greeting, said the prearranged password in Hebrew: "Are you a shepherd?"

"From Kibbutz Yagur," the young man responded.

Using a different, previously agreed-upon code phrase, a message was cabled to the Mossad L'Aliyah Bet office in Istanbul. The telegram was greeted with great excitement, not just in the Turkish capital but also in Cairo, Tel Aviv, and Jerusalem. Operation Anticlimax Blue had cleared its most difficult hurdle: Shaike Dan and Manu Ben-Ephraim were safe, undercover, and operational in Bucharest. They were the first pair of Yishuv parachutists to make it to their destination.

Dan explained to one of the Zionist youth leaders that they needed a safe place to stay for the night. Nowhere in Bucharest was completely safe for Jews, of course, but after some discussion, one of the other young Zionists took Dan and Ben-Ephraim to the apartment of a beautiful Romanian woman who was the mistress of a German officer from a unit stationed about three hours from the city.

For a hefty sum, which Dan paid in advance with napoleons, she agreed to put up the two scruffy-looking strangers for one night. "Clad in our ragged clothes we got into the two soft luxurious beds that were in the room. Even when I'll be in my grave I won't forget the two large pictures that hung above the bed," Dan later wrote. "One was of Hitler, the other of Goebbels. All night it was Hitler and Goebbels who stood watch over us. Our situation can only be described as theater of the absurd—except that the situation was anything but amusing."

The next day, Dan and Ben-Ephraim took the trolley to the Jewish section of Bucharest. In 1941, the capital had been the site of one of the most horrific massacres in the early years of the Holocaust, the Bucharest Pogrom, in which 125 Jews had been murdered in particularly cruel and abhorrent ways. Some had been tortured to death slowly over a period of days.

Another group, including a five-year-old girl, had been hung on meat hooks in a slaughterhouse typically used for cattle, taunted, and tortured; they were disemboweled while still alive, and their intestines were hung around their necks. On the naked hanging corpses, the Romanian killers left inscriptions reading "kosher meat"—mocking the Jewish practice of *shechita,* the ritual slaughter in keeping with the Orthodox rules of *kashrut.*

But by June 1944, the situation of the Jews of Bucharest had changed drastically. In the Jewish ghetto, Shaike Dan and Manu Ben-Ephraim found that life was relatively functional, considering the chaotic wartime conditions. There were restaurants, small stores, and workshops employing tailors and seamstresses. That was because in the "Old Kingdom of Romania"—often called the Regat—the fascist government had chosen to keep over a hundred thousand Jews relatively safe. The Romanian dictatorship knew that as the winds of war shifted—the Nazi defeat now seemed a certainty—they would likely need a large intact population of Jews to use as a bargaining chip with the United States and Great Britain.

There were no deportations to death camps in Poland, but Dan and Ben-Ephraim learned that near the airport, an SS battalion was stationed, poised to liquidate the Jewish ghetto. The most pressing danger was that during a possible uprising in Romania, a civil war, or an attempt by the underground to seize Bucharest, the SS unit might act without orders from above, deporting and annihilating Jews before retreating from Romania.

Shaike Dan and Manu Ben-Ephraim decided that it would greatly increase the odds of their operation's success if they split up, lived undercover in different sections of the city, ceased regular contact, and divided their areas of covert activity. Ben-Ephraim would work solely organizing Jewish self-defense, while Shaike Dan would concentrate on helping Jews make *aliyah* to Palestine and locate the Allied POWs for MI9. Dan took a trolley to one of the wealthiest districts of Bucharest. He correctly assumed that in such an upscale neighborhood, there'd be no random police sweeps for Jewish refugees.

Establishing contact with the underground Jewish leadership of Romania was more challenging. There were several older, wealthy, prominent Jewish men who'd managed to maintain considerable political influence with the fascist regime during the war years—though those resistance leaders would clearly be wary of letting into their confidence an interloper clad in a floppy fedora and rumpled vagabond's clothing, with no one to vouch for him.

Dan knew only one Jew in Bucharest with the necessary political clout to help him: Dr. Abraham Leib Zissu. A journalist, novelist, playwright, and chemist, Zissu, though born into a modest Hasidic home, had become one of the wealthiest men in Bucharest by marrying into a prominent industrialist family. He was considered the unofficial spokesman for the Romanian Jewish community, known for his supreme confidence and refusal to recognize the authority of the Romanian fascists or their Nazi overlords.

Shaike Dan had no personal connection to Dr. Zissu, no letter of introduction, no coded messages from the Zionist leadership in Tel Aviv or Istanbul. But he was carrying in his head one valuable piece of information. The fastest way for Dan to get a meeting with him revolved around a personal tragedy.

Dr. Zissu and his wife, Rachel, had only one child, a son named Theodor "Teddy," born in 1916 in Bucharest. In the 1930s, the Zissus had been living in Berlin just as Hitler had come to power, and Teddy had been schooled at the prestigious Französisches Gymnasium, then sent to England, where he had earned a law degree at Trinity College Cambridge. An ardent Zionist like his father, the younger Zissu had enlisted in the British Army in June 1941 and obtained a commission in the Royal Tank Corps. Stationed in Egypt with the 9th Queen's Royal Lancers, he had fought in the Desert Campaign. During Operation Supercharge, the decisive Second Battle of El Alamein, he had been mortally wounded. He had died on November 3, 1942.

Abraham and Rachel Zissu knew their son was serving in the British Army, but they hadn't had any news about him since he'd enlisted in 1941. They had yet to receive official military notification about his death.

That difficult task fell to Shaike Dan. "When I came to their house, I said I had word about their son and wanted to convey it personally," he later wrote. "Rachel, an impressive woman, entered the room and sat next to him. Dr. Zissu was a Jew of about seventy. I took his hand and told him what happened. His eyes dimmed. He rocked in his chair and squeezed my hand. Those seconds felt like an eternity. Then came silence. He didn't ask how I got to Romania or mention the word parachute. The fact that I was an emissary of the Haganah in Palestine was enough for him."

Zissu understood the nature of the parachutists' mission and quickly saw Dan's weak point: He couldn't risk exposure, couldn't operate openly, but would have to negotiate with black marketeers, smugglers, and less-than-savory shipping agents. "I'm at your disposal day and night," he said. "I'll do whatever has to be done. No danger will stand in my way."

After that first painful conversation, Dan continued to meet Zissu weekly. Through Zissu, he was introduced to an attorney named Jean Cohen. By greasing the necessary palms in Romanian officialdom, Cohen had been obtaining forged papers for Jews and helping escapees board illegal immigrant ships bound for Turkey. Cohen soon gave Shaike Dan a list of all the British and American POWs being held in Romania. Dan was stunned when, among the hundreds of POWs, he saw the fictitious English aliases of Arie Lupescu and Yitzhak Macarescu, the team who'd parachuted into Romania in late May 1944. Nothing had been heard from them since. No one knew if they were alive.

Romanian military officials cooperated with Cohen, hoping that by leaking the information that the highest-ranking British and American airmen were being held in a camp right in the middle of Bucharest, the Allied air forces would stop bombing the city center. They miscalculated. The relentless air raids continued night and day. Shaike Dan also soon learned, to his great relief, that Lyova Gukowsky and Arie Fichman, who'd been captured in October 1943, were in a prison camp for sergeants and enlisted men about three hours from the city.

By bribing diplomatic couriers who traveled regularly between Romania and Turkey, Dan quickly relayed the information to Istanbul and Cairo. He later wrote, "The discovery of the exact locations where the pilots and crewmen were being held and receipt of the list of prisoners was itself cause for happiness in Cairo. Part of our debt to British Intelligence and to our commander, Tony Simonds, was now repaid."

5

June 1944
Gyorskocsi Street Gestapo Prison, Budapest

It seemed strange to Katherine that her daughter's window in the Gestapo prison was so different from the others: right beneath the ceiling, it was a horizontal rectangle considerably smaller than the windows in the other prisoners' cells. In truth, the window was merely intended to let in a sliver of sunlight; prisoners in solitary confinement were forbidden to have any contact with the outside world or a peek out of a window, but even they could be afforded air.

How Hannah managed to look out of that tiny window was something neither Katherine nor her cellmates could fathom, but it soon became her primary means of communication and information. Each morning, she would painstakingly write her various questions in the air and wait for her mother to respond in kind. Her first question was about the yellow Star of David, which she had never seen. What did it signify? she asked.

Katherine, tracing Hungarian letters slowly in the air, explained when and how wearing the star had become mandatory for all Jews in Hungary. She asked her daughter if she was excused from wearing the discriminatory emblem.

Hannah answered that she no longer considered herself to be a Hungarian citizen and was not bound by such "laws."

One of Katherine's cellmates interrupted, writing in the air, "You're lucky not to be branded."

Hannah then used her finger to draw an enormous Star of David on the dust-coated window. A delicate and fleeting sign of solidarity, it remained there for several weeks until the window was washed.

Not long after she drew the star, Hannah disappeared from the window; Katherine watched for her all day, but her daughter didn't appear again.

The next evening, Hilda, the German-born domestic, called sharply to Katherine to come out of her cell. In the corridor, however, her tone changed, and she whispered that Katherine could talk to her daughter for a few moments in the bathroom nearby while Hilda stood guard. "At last, I could hold her close, kiss her," Katherine wrote, and once they had greeted each other, Hannah finally, rapidly, told her mother the truth: She was a radio officer in the British Royal Air Force and had volunteered for a mission that, unfortunately, she could not complete. "I'm now reconciled to my fate. But the thought that I've needlessly involved you in all this is unbearable."

Katherine convinced her daughter that she was perfectly all right, that she hadn't been harmed in prison. The one consolation in the entire tragedy, in fact, was that Katherine could be close to her and see her now and again, even talk to her. Had Katherine not been arrested, she would probably never have obtained visiting privileges.

Hannah smiled sadly. For a moment, Katherine noticed, she almost looked like her old self. The visible marks of the beatings had begun to heal and fade. Her hair had been washed and neatly combed. Her expression was calm. But the gap in her once beautiful smile still disturbed Katherine.

How had Hannah lost her tooth? When she asked, Hannah said that she'd taken a course in parachute jumping while still in Palestine and lost the tooth, tumbling awkwardly on rocky ground during a bad landing.

Katherine knew that her daughter was lying.

To cover the lie and change the subject, Hannah added brusquely, "We should both be so lucky, Mother, if the biggest price we pay is a single tooth."

Katherine asked again if she had been tortured and how severely, beyond the obvious missing front tooth.

"Believe me, Mum, compared to the mental and emotional anguish, the physical suffering is negligible."

At that point Hilda knocked loudly on the door. Time was up. The women had to say a hasty goodbye.

In the following days, Katherine hardly saw Hannah; there were stretches when she did not appear in the window at all. Soon she learned that her daughter was being taken to Svábhegy daily for interrogation, rarely returning until nightfall.

On days when she could appear at the window for a few moments early in the morning, Hannah would begin the "air correspondence" but then might suddenly duck down in the middle of a word or sentence.

Over time, Katherine spoke to other prisoners and learned the steps Hannah went through to communicate. She could reach that sliver of window only by putting her table on her bed—and on top of the table, she balanced her chair. It was a precarious arrangement, requiring the poise of an acrobat, and often she had to jump down from her perch quickly and rearrange her room when she heard the guards' footsteps.

6

June–July 1944
Budapest, Hungary, and Slovenia, Yugoslavia

On June 13, 1944, guided by the experienced Partisan saboteur Lieutenant Colonel Pavle Vukomanović aka Stipo, Yoel Palgi and Peretz Goldstein entered Hungary, crossing the Drava River by rowboat. Yoel had decided that it would be best not to travel with his suitcase radio and had left it behind with the Partisans. He planned to send for it only if the situation in Budapest was safe.

Within just a few hours on foot, they realized the bleakness of the situation. The Nazis had already purged several Hungarian communities of their Jewish populations. Fearing the worst, they proceeded by train to Budapest to see if there might be anyone left to save.

As they were walking near Budapest's Central Station, Palgi saw a girl coming toward them, wearing a blue coat. She walked with hurried steps, her dark eyes darting from side to side. On the chest of her coat, Palgi saw a fist-sized Star of David made of yellow cloth. He gripped Peretz tightly and tried to mask any emotion. Peretz also looked at the girl but at once glanced away. There were still some Jews alive. Not all of them had been deported from Hungary. "Maybe we're *not* too late," Palgi whispered.

Before they'd left Cairo, Reuven Zaslani had provided Palgi with three underground contacts in Hungary—by that time, Palgi had received word that only one was still active. Palgi dialed the number. A woman picked up. Calmly, he spoke the Hungarian password—"I'm with the labor union"—and asked for Moshe Schweiger. The woman said that she did not know anyone by that name and hung up.

Confused and anxious, Palgi made a risky decision to visit the house of Dr. Rudolf Kasztner, a leader of the Relief and Rescue Committee of Budapest. Kasztner was a brilliant lawyer, journalist, and Zionist organizer whom Palgi had considered a family friend—both had been active members of the Hashomer Hatzair movement during their days in Cluj, Transylvania.

Kasztner was anything but pleased to see Yoel Palgi—whom he remembered as Emil Nussbacher—and his young, doe-eyed companion, Peretz Goldstein. While Joel Brand had been off in Istanbul, trying to convince the Allied leadership to swap ten thousand trucks for a million Jews, Kasztner had been negotiating his own deal with SS Standartenführer Kurt Becher, who was acting under the direct authority of Heinrich Himmler, to create a "Train of the Privileged." Later known as "Kasztner's Train," it was aimed to rescue carefully selected members of the Jewish community. Himmler saw the train as a good-faith gesture and, pending word about the "Blood for Goods" proposal, knew he could use it as a potential bargaining chip in negotiations with the Western Allies.

Among those selected by Kasztner and the Relief and Rescue Committee were the future Satmar Rebbe, Yoel Teitelbaum; Zionist leaders; members of Budapest's intelligentsia; and, most controversially, many of Kasztner's friends and family. A total of 1,684 passengers would leave Budapest for either neutral Switzerland or Spain.

Kasztner feared, correctly, that Palgi and Goldstein were being followed by the Gestapo or the Hungarian military police—or both. If the Germans thought that the two Jewish parachutists were British spies, he worried, it would kill the agreement he was hammering out with Becher and Himmler.

Kasztner told Palgi that his only option was to visit Gestapo headquarters and tell them he'd been sent as an emissary from the Jewish Agency, intending to help in the "Blood for Goods" deal. Palgi reluctantly agreed and went to Gestapo headquarters. To his surprise, he was interviewed and let go but then picked up by the Hungarian military police under suspicion of espionage and put in jail, awaiting interrogation.

Meanwhile, Peretz Goldstein was on a new mission. As part of the

Kasztner-Becher negotiations, the "privileged" Jews were concentrated in a loosely guarded camp on Kolumbusz utca—Columbus Street—in the upscale Fifth District in the center of Budapest. Goldstein entered the camp without problem, looking for his parents. He tried to hide out, hoping to sneak onto the train to safety, but word got out that the Hungarian police were searching for a second British parachutist from Palestine who'd entered Budapest as a spy. Not wanting anything to jeopardize the negotiations over his train, Rudolf Kasztner visited the Columbus Street camp, found Goldstein, and gave him three options: He could continue to hide out somewhere other than the Columbus Street camp, attempt to escape from Hungary, or surrender to the police.

Goldstein's exact motives for surrendering—to protect his parents or the departure of Kasztner's Train—remain unknown. But after he turned himself in, the Hungarian police arrested him for suspected espionage. He was put into the same jail cell as Yoel Palgi.*

High in the mountains of Yugoslavia, having lost all radio contact with Hannah, Yoel, and Peretz, Reuven Dafni continued to run his own mission, saving Allied pilots and escaped Jews. He fought alongside the Partisans, blowing up trains and bridges amid firefights with Nazi units.

By the summer of 1944, with the massive American and British air attacks continuing over Hungary and Romania, destroying resources critical to the German war machine, it was more crucial than ever to help flyers downed during various raids reach safety. Reuven printed maps showing how to pass through no-man's-land and avoid the sections of the mountains controlled by the fascists, which proved invaluable to many flyers. Allied planes also

*Rudolph Kasztner undoubtedly risked his life in 1944 by negotiating with high-ranking SS officers as he managed to get his train of 1,684 Jews safely from Hungary to Switzerland. Rather than being seen as a hero, however, Kasztner became a reviled and divisive figure in the young State of Israel. By the early 1950s, accused of being a venal collaborator, he was judged—like Doctor Faustus—to have "sold his soul to the devil," in the verdict of Judge Benjamin Halevy in 1955. Numerous books have been devoted to the Kasztner Affair—beginning with Ben Hecht's furiously polemical *Perfidy* (1961) and continuing through several more balanced and carefully researched recent titles, which you can find listed in the bibliography.

dropped leaflets in Croatian urging local civilians to organize search parties to aid downed aviators.

Before long, stranded Allied airmen and escaped POWs in Romania, Hungary, and the Balkans knew that if they made it to the British Intelligence operative known as Gary, he would safeguard them and smuggle them back to Allied lines.

Though the Nazis didn't know Reuven's real identity, the Gary Network had become so successful that they reputedly put a bounty of 10,000 reichsmarks on his head.

He would march the airmen to the Adriatic coast at night with a small Partisan escort, then radio the British and pinpoint a place on the coast for Royal Navy speedboats, typically a harbor in a small fishing village. The latter part of the operation took only minutes.

Later, as the Partisans became bolder, they used the ports of cities such as Rijeka, Pula, and Zadar, where the German forces, on the defensive, generally had only small garrisons. The Partisan forces made noisy frontal assaults on the Nazi garrisons, using grenades and triangulating their machine-gun fire, and, while the Nazi troops were scrambling, Reuven Dafni sneaked the Allied airmen into the harbor, where Royal Navy speedboats picked them up and within minutes were en route to Italy.

As the Partisans liberated more swaths of territory in Yugoslavia, large, flat fields were converted to proper landing strips for the RAF. A British plane—typically a Douglas C-47—would land, and Reuven would oversee the rapid unloading of crates of guns, ammunitions, explosives, and vital medications that the Partisans needed. Then, just as quickly, all the rescued Allied airmen would pile into the empty transport plane, along with any Jews who'd managed to escape from Hungary, Greece, Slovakia, or even Poland.

Along with the airmen, a trickle of Jewish refugees managed to make it across the border into Yugoslavia. Reuven and his team shepherded them to safety. It was grueling, gratifying work. By the summer of 1944, Dafni later said, he had saved countless lives, but to his great regret, there were very few Jews left to rescue. "We'd come too late," he recalled. "Had we come one year earlier, we could have saved hundreds and hundreds—perhaps even thousands."

7

July 1944
London, England

Meanwhile, the truth about the Holocaust was becoming ever more public due to the dissemination of the Auschwitz Protocols, a spring 1944 report compiled by the Bratislava Working Group—the leading Jewish underground organization in Slovakia—recording the eyewitness testimonies of two pairs of Jewish prisoners who'd escaped from Auschwitz-Birkenau: Walter Rosenberg (later known as Rudolf Vrba) and Alfréd Wetzler; and Arnošt Rosin and Czesław Mordowicz.

By March 1944, the SS had expanded its machinery of death, extending the rail tracks directly to the gas chambers and crematoria in Birkenau in anticipation of the massive numbers of Hungarian Jews they'd need to "process" daily.

On June 26, 1944, President Roosevelt told his secretary of state, Cordell Hull, to send a personal message to Admiral Horthy about the issue:

> *The United States demands to know whether the Hungarian authorities intend to deport Jews to Poland or to any other place, or to employ any measures that would in the end result in their mass execution. Moreover, the United States wishes to remind the Hungarian authorities that all those responsible for carrying out those kinds of injustices will be dealt with.*

Despite his royal title, Horthy was a mere figurehead—many Hungarians jokingly referred to him as "the admiral without a navy and a regent to a meaningless crown." The day after he received Roosevelt's telegram, 12,421 Jews were sent to Auschwitz in four separate transports of overcrowded cattle cars.

A power struggle broke out inside the Hungarian government, with many determined to continue to do the Nazis' bidding and rid the country of its Jews. The military forces themselves split: One Hungarian tank division stayed loyal to Horthy, while battalions of provincial gendarmes followed the orders of the SS.

By July 1944, 434,000 Hungarian Jews had been deported to Auschwitz-Birkenau on 147 trains. Adolf Eichmann was disappointed when he saw that total; he'd set a target of 500,000. With the newly installed rail spur at Birkenau leading straight to the gas chambers, the extermination process had never been more rapid and efficient. Of the 434,000 deported, more than three-quarters were murdered within an hour of their arrival.

On July 2, 1944, as part of the British and American strategy to drop mines into the Danube River, American aircraft unleashed bombs on Budapest. Hungarian oil refineries and storage tanks, crucial to the German war machine, were destroyed during the air raid. Along with the bombs, leaflets in Hungarian threatening retribution for those responsible for the deportation of the Jews were dropped on Budapest. Faced with the ever-worsening military situation and the now open Allied threats of war crimes trials, Horthy ordered a halt to all deportation of Jews on July 7, though the trains stopped moving only on July 9.

By midsummer, the scope of the Nazi atrocities against the Jews of Hungary was well known to the Allied command. In Poland, the country with Europe's largest Jewish population, it had taken the Nazis nearly five years to deal with the *Judenfrage*; in Hungary, it took them less than four months.

Determined to wipe out the Jewish population before the arrival of the Red Army, the Nazis and their Hungarian collaborators subjected the Jews of the Hungarian provinces to the most rapid process of destruction in the entire Holocaust. An average of twelve thousand Jews per day were gassed at Auschwitz between mid-May and July 1944, the fastest-paced extermination of any major Jewish community in Europe.

On July 11, 1944, Winston Churchill wrote to Anthony Eden:

Foreign Secretary:

*There is no doubt that this is probably the greatest and most horrible crime ever committed in the whole history of the world, and it has been done by scientific machinery by nominally civilized men in the name of a great State and one of the leading races of Europe.**

It is quite clear that all concerned in this crime who may fall into our hands, including the people who only obeyed orders by carrying out the butcheries, should be put to death after their association with the murders has been proved. . . .

Declarations should be made in public so that everyone connected with it will be hunted down and put to death.

W. S. C.
11.7.44.

*In the letter, Churchill avoided being too specific, but his use of "this" in the first sentence is obviously a reference to the ongoing mass murder of Hungarian Jewry.

8

July 1944

Gyorskocsi Street Gestapo Prison, Budapest

When Katherine and Hannah weren't being interrogated by the Gestapo, Katherine could sometimes glimpse her daughter in the courtyard below, taking her allotted ten-minute exercise after lunch. The entire courtyard was not visible from her window, so she could see only Hannah at the end of the line, walking by herself, while the other prisoners were paired.

On the rare occasions when their exercise periods coincided, the supervising matron did her best to keep them separated, ordering Katherine to the front of the circling line and her daughter solo at the back.

The matron stood in the middle, whip in hand, and armed guards were posted at strategic points in the courtyard. Hannah would step out of the line, pretending to tie her shoelace; at the right moment, she would jump back into the line next to her mother. The prisoner originally next to Katherine would step back one row, and the whole line would realign behind them. If the matron on duty noticed that breach in discipline, she turned a blind eye for a few moments.

Mother and daughter walking near each other for nine or ten minutes was one thing; but talking in the ranks was strictly forbidden. Katherine was anxious about getting her daughter into further trouble, but Hannah refused to stay silent. "Mum," she said, "we're in the greatest possible danger here anyway, so we might as well take the few chances we can to talk."

Katherine agreed and tried to use those brief conversations to gain answers to questions she was still puzzled about—most importantly, what could have induced her lifelong pacifist daughter to return to Hungary in a British uniform?

"It's a military secret, Mum," Hannah responded. "And I wouldn't tell you even if I could because they might try to get it out of you. Best you know nothing. You know what they say: 'You can't tell what you don't know.' In any case, we'll win this war soon, and then you'll find out everything."

Katherine nodded, but she couldn't help but speculate. "I can't believe that some kind of enthusiasm for the *British* had you sign up, to volunteer for their military. . . . There must be a Jewish angle, a Jewish motive behind all this."

Hannah squeezed her mother's hand. "You're on the right track there, Mum."

Many years later, Katherine remembered her own rather blunt and scolding reply: "Then, Anikó, the only question is whether it's worth risking your *life* for this boundless enthusiasm of yours."

Hannah smiled. "Mum, it must be worth it to *me*." Then, as if to soften the tone, she continued, "Believe me, Mother, I've done nothing at all to harm Hungary—I've done nothing traitorous, despite what these fascists are falsely alleging."

They walked on, quiet footsteps on concrete, glancing warily at the stern-faced matron and the armed guards. Katherine had no reply; she merely stared at her daughter. Hannah whispered, "On the contrary, Mum. What's considered a sin today will be honorable tomorrow.* It depends on the outcome of the war, of course. But I'll be vindicated soon."

*Hannah's Hungarian phrase, *Ami ma bűn, holnap érdem című* (What's a sin today will be honorable tomorrow), would be the title of Katherine Senesh's memoir, published in 1991.

9

July 1944
Bucharest, Romania

In Romania, as the clock ticked down, Lyova Gukowsky—the blue-eyed shepherd from Kibbutz Yagur in the Carmel Mountains—Shaike Dan, and the other Romanian Jewish emissaries feverishly worked for both the MI9 aspect of the mission and their own goal to save Jewish civilians.

With forged identity papers of a Christian, civilian clothes, and the flawless accent of a native Romanian speaker, Shaike Dan was able to move around Bucharest freely, making it part of his routine to case the POW camp where the British and American airmen were being held. The camp was surrounded by barbed wire and heavily guarded by Romanian soldiers. Loitering near the building was forbidden, and any unnecessary glance was liable to arouse suspicion, so Dan found a small café with a clear line of sight. He could order an espresso and sit for a short while, pretending to peruse a newspaper while surveilling the camp.

Via encoded message couriered from Istanbul, Colonel Tony Simonds had recently conveyed to Dan and his team that a worst-case scenario was developing. The Nazis' military situation was deteriorating, which meant that the captured pilots' chances of survival would, too. Backed against a wall, the Germans might very well take the Allied airmen deeper into the Reich—not as Luftwaffe POWs but to concentration camps run by the SS. MI9 knew that other Allied airmen, who should have been protected under the Geneva Convention, had already been sent to Mauthausen and Dachau.

Colonel Simonds gave Dan an urgent order to convey to the fascist leadership of Romania; they needed to be told the consequences should any harm befall Allied prisoners of war. Again, Dan would need the aid of Dr. Zissu, probably the only Jew in Romania with the clout to help directly. Using his covert contacts, Zissu could get a face-to-face meeting with Prime Minister Ion Antonescu, the man who wielded ultimate power in Romania, the country's wartime *conducător*.* There was no time to lose.

Dan promptly met with Zissu and laid out the specific wording that needed to be conveyed, as coming directly from Churchill and the British high command in London, to Antonescu and his fascist inner circle: "I told [Zissu] to warn them that any harm done to the British and American pilots would not be forgiven, and that there's no envying those who would have to pay the ultimate price for that."

The strategy worked. Zissu quickly relayed the message to Antonescu, who promised that all the Allied pilots would remain safe and would not be transferred into Nazi Germany. As a show of good faith, the Romanians even relaxed the guard around the POW camps.

While Shaike Dan focused on protecting Allied POWs, Manu Ben-Ephraim organized Jewish self-defense in Bucharest. The overcrowded Jewish quarter was a powder keg. The cramped conditions meant that in the event of a liquidation order, it would be impossible to organize escape routes. There would be total annihilation. The SS unit posted on the city's outskirts was poised to strike at any time.

Manu Ben-Ephraim couldn't organize an army with real weapons—there simply weren't any guns, grenades, or even gasoline with which to make Molotov cocktails—so he was left, as Dan recalled, trying to do "something that today maybe sounds bombastic: preparing Jews to die with honor." Ben-Ephraim trained the young, fit men and women to fight with knives, hatchets, homemade bats, and even hand to hand if the Gestapo came to liquidate the Jewish quarter.

*The Romanian fascist title for "leader," akin to Mussolini's *duce*, Hitler's *führer*, and Francisco Franco's *caudillo*.

10

July 16, 1944
Gyorskoscsi Street Gestapo Prison, Budapest

"If it were up to you," Hannah asked one of the German guards escorting her to her daily interrogation, "what kind of punishment would you give me?"

"I wouldn't punish you at all," the guard said. "I have never met a woman as brave as you."

Hannah's prison window became a sort of broadcast center where other prisoners could get the latest news. Signaling war reports entailed constant risk, but now that she had endured the worst weeks of both physical and psychological torture, she felt it was a risk well worth taking.

She felt she'd won the trust of several of the matrons, but the Gestapo prison commandant, SS Hauptscharführer Werner Lemke, was an unpredictable sadist known for personally beating his prisoners for the slightest infractions. Lemke had been nicknamed "Flammke"—from the German word *Flamme* (flame)—because of the white-hot intensity of his rages. He would often beat a prisoner—male or female—unconscious with his black-gloved hands and use the toe of his knee-high boots to kick them in the ribs once they were on the concrete floor.

Making his rounds one day, he caught Hannah cutting out paper letters with a small pair of scissors. Lemke rushed into the cell with his gloved fist raised. He expected her to cower, but according to one matron's eyewitness account, Hannah looked at him calmly, without interrupting her work. "Take a seat," she said in English.

Lemke stared at her in disbelief. *Where did this waif of a girl get the audacity?* He looked around at the simple decorations that Hannah had made to turn her solitary confinement cell into a pleasant room. His eyes paused on the bed, where a pair of paper dolls lay like lovers embracing. "What are those?"

"Just paper dolls," Hannah said.

"You are forbidden to make dolls!" Lemke shouted. "If I see another doll here, I'll punish you severely!"

From then on, Hauptscharführer Lemke visited Hannah's cell daily. He treated her with a level of respect no one in the Gestapo prison had seen before. Perhaps it was Hannah's status as an RAF paratrooper, her credentials as a British prisoner of war. Hannah, though fluent in German, cleverly pretended not to understand a word of the language, always speaking to Lemke and the other German officers and guards in English. Whatever the reason, Lemke's demeanor would change the moment he stood in her doorway. He'd ask whether he could sit down and then listen intently to her calm and logical analysis of the war's progress.

The Kingdom of Romania, the staunchest member of the Axis, was, in Hannah's estimation, on the verge of switching sides; its still powerful army would soon be fighting against Nazi Germany. And it was one of the worst-kept secrets in Budapest that Admiral Horthy had been trying to negotiate an armistice with the Western Allies and pull Hungary out of the disastrous war.

After Mussolini was deposed and arrested by his own people, after the humiliating defeat and surrender of the German Sixth Army at Stalingrad, who could fail to see that it was only a matter of time before the war was lost for Hitler? How could Hauptscharführer Lemke, at that point, still have faith in Hitler's catastrophic war of conquest?

Several of the prison matrons—who eavesdropped outside the cell—heard Hannah frankly describing, in her proper British accent, the retribution that would come to SS officers like Lemke for their complicity in war crimes. After those visits, the matrons later recalled, Lemke would leave Hannah's cell in silence, lost in thought.

On July 17, Katherine Senesh wrote, "I knew that Hannah's birthday was drawing near. I wondered what little gift I could send her. I had already shared my last parcel with her but had providentially put aside a jar of marmalade. When my cellmates saw me preparing the carefully guarded bottle, they contributed gifts from their own precious stores: a handkerchief, a sliver of soap, a sponge—in prison each a cherished, rare possession. One of the matrons agreed to deliver the gifts."

That afternoon, the matron summoned Katherine to the peephole and dropped in a piece of paper on which Hannah had written a few lines to thank them for their thoughtfulness and generosity. She said she especially liked the marmalade; it reminded her of Palestine. In her brief note, she summed up and weighed the events of her life and, looking back over her twenty-three years, decided that they had been very colorful and eventful, her childhood happy and beautiful. Hannah's accounting with life at such a tender age was, Katherine wrote, "like a dagger in my heart."

One day during the exercise period in the yard, Katherine noticed a pair of small children on Hannah's left and right, tugging her arms, clinging to her: a Polish boy and girl, ages four and six. They had been wandering for years with their mother from camp to camp, prison to prison. They seemed to have recently lost her; the rest of their family had vanished in the flames of Auschwitz.

They sensed that they'd found a friend in Hannah and wouldn't leave her side. Sometimes they played tag, and the guards pretended not to see. Hannah began making dolls for the two children, crafting them ingeniously from bits and pieces of string, paper, rags, and foil. Eventually Katherine heard, via the jailhouse grapevine, that Hannah had been placed in the communal cell where the children were—no one was quite sure what the reason for such leniency was.

Hannah began teaching the children to read and write and told them whimsical stories. Before long she fulfilled her lifelong dream of being a teacher: giving daily lessons to both children and adults in Hebrew. "She was soon back in solitary confinement, but the manufacturing of dolls continued, and our 'window correspondence' flourished once again," Katherine later wrote. "Hannah had even won over the cruelest matron with the bullwhip and began making dolls in a furious fashion."

One day Katherine received some paper dolls: a boy and girl walking hand in hand. Her cellmates were delighted, so much so that Katherine sent Hannah a note to thank her: "Though I have always dreamed of the day you would present me with grandchildren, for the time being these substitutes will do."

Gradually more and more of Hannah's dolls turned up among the women prisoners, and the more she made, the more varied and colorful they became: Biedermeier dolls, Rococo dolls, ballet dancer dolls, Carmen dolls, Madame Butterfly dolls, Tosca dolls, and so on. She sent them not only to the prisoners but also to the matrons, who cherished them equally. But among the prisoners, the most popular were her dolls of little pioneers in Palestine, likenesses of boy and girl kibbutzniks shouldering picks and shovels. As she told Katherine, "I'm glad my time here isn't entirely wasted. I've converted a good many people to Zionism."

11

July 20, 1944
Budapest, Cairo, London

In his spacious office at the Majestic Hotel, Adolf Eichmann grew increasingly irate at the lack of response from Joel Brand regarding the "Blood for Goods" proposal. For weeks, there had been no word from the Zionist leadership in Istanbul. Eichmann interpreted that communication gap as a stalling tactic by the Zionists and the Allies.

In reality, Brand had been unable to communicate at all. The warm welcome he had expected in Istanbul had turned into a fiasco. He had been denied the proper entrance visas for Turkey, held in quarantine, and quickly escorted out of the country with diplomatic papers by Moshe Shertok. He had then been arrested by British authorities while on a train from Istanbul to Mandatory Palestine and held in a police jail in Aleppo, suspected of being a double agent—his "true" mission supposedly being espionage for the Gestapo.

By the time Brand's Zionist credentials were confirmed and the British authorities finally accepted him as an official representative sent by the Jewish Leadership Council in Budapest, months had passed. The beleaguered Brand was taken by train to Cairo, where he met with Lord Moyne, minister resident for the Middle East and Churchill's only war cabinet member stationed in Egypt.

They met at Moyne's private club, where Brand reiterated Eichmann's offer to sell the 1 million Jews supposedly still alive in Hungary in exchange for 10,000 brand-new winterized trucks, 800 tons of coffee, 200 tons of tea, 2 million cases of soap, large quantities of tungsten, and other goods. Most important, he emphasized, quoting Eichmann directly: Those ten thousand trucks would be used by the Waffen-SS only against the Red Army on the eastern front.

According to Brand's recollection of the day, Lord Moyne abruptly interjected, "But Mr. Brand, where could I possibly put these million Jews?"

His vocal opposition to allowing any further Jewish emigration to Mandatory Palestine, even once the horrors of the Holocaust were publicly known, and his outspoken views, which seemed to heavily favor the Arab majority under British colonial rule, made him a lightning rod for Jewish public opinion and would soon have deadly and far-reaching consequences.

By the middle of July 1944, Eichmann's "Blood for Goods" offer had made it all the way to the desks of Churchill and Roosevelt, who quickly saw the deal for what it was: a cynical effort to drive a wedge between the Western Allies and Stalin. The story was leaked to the press and made explosive headlines. On July 19, the *New York Herald Tribune* described the proposal as a perverse German scheme to undermine the unity of the Allies. On July 20, *The Times* of London, in a scathing assessment, clearly espoused the position of Churchill's government:

> **A MONSTROUS "OFFER"**
> **GERMAN BLACKMAIL**
> **BARTERING JEWS FOR MUNITIONS**
>
> It has long been clear that, faced with the certainty of defeat, the German authorities would intensify all their efforts to blackmail, deceive, and split the allies. In their latest effort, made known in London yesterday, they have reached a new level of fantasy and self-deception. They have put forward, or sponsored, an offer to exchange the remaining Hungarian Jews for munitions of war. . . .
>
> The whole story is one of the most loathsome of the war. It begins with a process of deliberate extirpation and ends, to date, with attempted blackmail. . . .

> The British Government know what value to set on any German or German-sponsored offer. . . .
>
> The German "offer" seems to be simply a fantastic attempt to sow suspicion among the allies.

It was a stunning development, but its impact was short lived. Eichmann's monstrous "offer" was knocked out of the headlines within a day. On July 20, Hannah overheard wild rumors being whispered in German, many conflicting reports among the Gestapo and SS guards, and no one was sure quite what to believe. There was a tone of confusion and fear that she had never heard in the voices of these haughty, brutal members of the "master race." But one thing was clear: Everyone was murmuring that the war might soon be over.

The BBC's German-language service broadcast a series of news bulletins on the evening of July 21, 1944: "A German radio report says an attempt has been made on the life of Adolf Hitler. The report states that the attempt was made at the Führer's headquarters in East Prussia."

The prisoners learned the news through Hannah, who climbed her rickety setup—chair on top of table on top of bed—to reach her window, placed two fingers over her upper lip to form a Hitlerian toothbrush mustache, and then quickly slashed them, bladelike, across her neck.

Confused reports kept coming from Berlin—no one was sure if there'd been a successful coup lead by high-ranking Wehrmacht officers and the anti-Nazi resistance or whether the BBC German-language broadcast had it right that Hitler had survived the bombing. On July 22, *The New York Times* confirmed on its front page the fact that Hitler had, miraculously, walked away unscathed:

NAZIS BLOCK PLOT TO SEIZE GOVERNMENT

HITLER HUNTS FOES

THOUSANDS OF OFFICERS REPORTED ARRESTED IN PURGE OF ARMY

MUTINY IS RUMORED

In the days ahead, the world learned more details: A briefcase bomb had been planted by Colonel Claus von Stauffenberg at the Wolfsschanze (Wolf's

Lair), Hitler's eastern front headquarters. Stauffenberg was a wounded and decorated war hero, and the mutiny had been led by many old-school Prussian Wehrmacht officers. Hitler's revenge against the plotters was swift and terrible, but the very fact that there *had* been an assassination attempt, a deeply rooted military conspiracy to overthrow the Nazi government, gave many people, especially the Gestapo's prisoners, reason for hope. They speculated in whispers in their cells: Were the Germans *finally* turning against Hitler and the Gestapo terror state?

Susan Beer, a fellow Hungarian Jewish prisoner who had met Hannah in June, watched her working hard to be the chief morale booster in the grim prison that summer. She constantly spread news she had overheard about the Soviet Army's rapid advances, the D-Day landing, and the successes of the Second Front in France.

Hannah kept herself occupied constructing homemade gifts, especially for the prisoners' birthdays. Her almost constant smile, her colorful stories of life in Eretz Israel and the prospects of a better world—a world free of Nazism and fascism, anti-Semitism and racial bigotry—spread an air of optimism. "In that prison it was good to hear things like this," Beer recalled, "something beyond our misery."

On July 23, 1944, the Red Army, advancing rapidly across Poland, liberated the first *Vernichtungslager*: Majdanek, near the city of Lublin, which had, according to reports, been the site of the murders of 1.5 million people.

Initially, most of the world did not believe what the Red Army claimed to have found there: gas chambers, crematoria, human remains. Konstantin Simonov wrote a full description of Majdanek for *Krasnaia Zvezda*, the official newspaper of the Soviet Ministry of Defense. It was Simonov who first gave an eyewitness journalistic account of a Nazi gas chamber and imagined the agony of the victims; he was the first to write about the canisters of Zyklon B pesticide and the enormous piles of children's shoes:

> *At some period in the future, after thorough and painstaking inquiry, the full immensity of the crime against humanity committed here by the Germans will come to light. I myself am at present in possession of only a fraction of the facts; I have spoken to perhaps only one-hundredth of the witnesses and have seen*

maybe only one-tenth of the traces. But a man who has seen what I have seen cannot hold his peace. He cannot wait to speak. I desire this very day to tell what I have heard with my own ears and seen with my own eyes of the discovery of the crime.

Many British and American newspaper editors—suspicious of Soviet propaganda—refused to pick up the story. *The New York Times,* for example, sent its previously skeptical correspondent, W. H. Lawrence, to Lublin so he could see the evidence for himself. His report, which was datelined August 27, ran on the front page on August 30 under the headline "Nazi Mass Killing Laid Bare in Camp." It was the first such report to reach a broad American audience. Lawrence's lede for the *Times* was indelible:

I have just seen the most terrible place on the face of the earth—the German concentration camp at Maidanek, which was a veritable River Rouge for the production of death, in which it is estimated by Soviet and Polish authorities that as many as 1,500,000 persons from nearly every country in Europe were killed in the last three years.

Although today historians place the number of victims murdered at Majdanek at several hundred thousand, it was the first widespread confirmation—other than the eyewitness reports of escapees—that the Nazi regime had created an industrialized machine for the genocide of the Jewish people.

12

August 1944
Gyorskocsi Street Gestapo Prison, Budapest

As a widow of nearly twenty years, Katherine had long since stopped observing her wedding anniversary. But during the first week of August in prison, Hannah marked what would have been Béla and Katherine's silver anniversary in a most loving manner: After weeks of scrounging materials in the jail, she covered an empty talcum powder tin with foil, attached white buds made of tissue paper onto twenty-five blades of straw pulled from her mattress, and fitted them into the holes in the top of the can, which then looked like a little bouquet of white roses. She glued a lace doily, also made of tissue paper, to the bottom of the can. Accompanying the "flowers" was an exquisite little paper doll bride with a long veil carrying a minute bouquet of tissue paper roses. The gift was accompanied by a poem. After reading it, in an effort to keep her daughter safe, Katherine tore the paper into tiny shreds. But for the rest of her life, she could cite its simple Hungarian words:

Memories, like paper flowers,
Do not wither;
They remain fresh.
How often we look at them with longing,
All the while forgetting—
They are not alive.

• • •

In mid-August, Hannah was given a new cellmate: a woman in her midtwenties, hair bedraggled, eyes swollen, showing the signs of bruising that reflected the torture she'd been undergoing daily at the hands of the Gestapo.

Her name, she told Hannah, was Matilda Glattstein. Originally from a small town in Slovakia, Matilda, her husband, Eliezar, and their young daughter, Tova, had been in hiding for more than two years. In March 1942, when the Nazis had begun rounding up Slovak Jews and deporting them to Auschwitz and Majdanek, Matilda and her family had fled into the forest.

They couldn't survive outdoors long—Tova being only two years old at the time—so the Glattstein family, along with Matilda's sister, Hilda, had obtained forged identity papers and had arrived in Budapest in late 1942. Budapest had proven to be a fairly safe refuge. That was, until March 19, 1944, when the Germans had occupied Hungary and Adolf Eichmann had arrived in the capital to organize the rapid liquidation of Hungary's Jews.

Matilda had decided to put Tova, now almost five years old, into a convent, pretending that she was a Roman Catholic orphan; she and Eliezer had found separate hideouts, constantly moving and meeting only infrequently in a public park. One morning in July 1944, Matilda had been stopped by gendarmes for questioning; her forged papers and broken Hungarian had been an instant giveaway. She'd been taken to the Gyorskocsi Street Gestapo prison for questioning and roughed up by the guards.

The Gestapo saw her as being possibly more than another frightened Jew in hiding; they suspected her of espionage. But Matilda Glattstein was no spy. No matter how much they interrogated her and threatened her, she had no military intelligence to divulge. She did, however, have a secret that she'd managed to conceal from the Gestapo now for two weeks. It was a secret she wouldn't be able to keep for much longer, a secret she felt she needed to now confide to Hannah: She was pregnant. She said she was expecting the baby in February. Hannah grimaced when she heard that. There was no way the Gestapo would allow that woman to give birth to a baby in prison. If they found out, she'd be killed instantly.

By now Hannah was an expert in the methods of the Gestapo and the Hungarian military police. She'd experienced and survived the worst physical and mental torture. She also knew all the Gestapo's threats and bluffs.

In their communal cell, with its barred windows, the two women huddled together. As they talked, Hannah showed off her many handmade dolls. She pretended to be giving Matilda lessons in dollmaking, but she was secretly giving her lessons on how to behave during interrogations.

Unfortunately for Matilda, Hannah's initial piece of advice proved to be a very poor strategy. The next time they took her for questioning, Hannah said, before the Gestapo men were fully focused, she should palm the forged identity document from the table, ask to use the bathroom, and destroy the paper in the toilet. That way, Hannah reasoned, the Gestapo couldn't legally incriminate her. Matilda followed the advice, but it backfired: By destroying her incriminating forged papers, she looked even more guilty of espionage.

Now Matilda was subjected to daily torture, the same sorts of merciless beatings and floggings Hannah had endured. After the torture and interrogation sessions, she'd be shoved back into the cell, covered with welts and cuts.

Hauptscharführer Lemke had laughed at Matilda's feeble attempt to trick him. "You think I need some *document* to execute you?" he snarled. "I can execute you anytime I like."

"You can't stay here," Hannah now told Matilda. "We'll have to get you out."

"Get me out?" Matilda thought Hannah must be making a cruel joke.

"You'll need to go through the window—it's risky but with some luck, you'll make it."

Matilda stared at Hannah as if she were a madwoman. Who could pry open those iron bars? No, Hannah, whispered. Not from that communal cell. Above them, on the third floor, was an infirmary. The windows there weren't barred. "And in your sickbed, you won't be watched around the clock. Yes, it's possible to escape through the window." Matilda listened to Hannah laying out the plan in slow, logical detail. The trickiest part of the plan was the first step: Matilda would have to suffer a real injury. "When you're taken for questioning, you'll fall down the stairs. Of course, land on your backside—protect the fetus—but you'll need to twist or sprain an ankle, a wrist, a knee."

As Hannah spoke, Matilda began to panic. The scheme sounded too complex, too convoluted, its odds of success too low. "Odds?" Hannah said. "And what are your odds if you stay here? A *pregnant* woman? Beaten daily? Even if you don't miscarry, do you think they'll let you bring a Jewish child into the world?"

Matilda agreed. She asked Hannah to repeat herself, memorizing the steps again. But she wondered: Wasn't the plan one Hannah could use to save herself? Why had she not tried to break out of a window in the third-floor infirmary? "They know I'm a British paratrooper—but they're accusing me of espionage and of treason—unlike you, I was born here. They'll likely put me on trial before a military court. It's a matter of time. I just don't know when."

But with the Red Army rolling relentlessly westward, with the Americans and British having landed in Normandy and liberated much of France, with the attempted assassination of Hitler in July, even the most die-hard Nazis knew that the German military could no longer win the war. Even their SS commandant, the fanatical Hauptscharführer Lemke, didn't live in a complete fantasy. Many high-ranking Nazis were already scheming ways to enrich themselves and line up fake identities, escape routes, alibis, and other ways to save their own necks.

Hannah also explained to Matilda how different their lives were, that her father had been a famous Hungarian playwright and author, that the name Szenes was well known in Budapest. Between that notoriety and Hannah's rank in the RAF, her captors had likely earmarked hers a "high-profile" case. In any event, she felt no need to break out of prison. She'd make it through—somehow. The infirmary escape was Matilda's now. "You must get out of here," she insisted. "If not for yourself, save your unborn child."

13

August 1944
Bucharest, Romania

During the last week of August 1944, the Romanian infiltration mission working undercover in Bucharest began to hear reports over BBC radio that the Red Army was advancing toward the Dniester River—the border between the USSR and Romania. The news was welcome, though many, including Shaike Dan, thought that the hour of liberation was coming far too late.

Outside Bucharest, in northwestern and eastern Romania, most Jewish communities had been destroyed, primarily by the Romanian fascists. Entire towns had been wiped out, synagogues and homes burned to the ground, under the direction of Prime Minister Ion Antonescu, a unique figure among Holocaust perpetrators in that, without Nazi pressure, he had independently implemented policies responsible for the deaths of as many as four hundred thousand Romanian, Bessarabian, and Ukrainian Jews, as well as thousands of Romani. ("As far as the Jewish Question is concerned," Hitler had told Goebbels about his Romanian ally in August 1941, "it can now be stated with certainty that a man like Antonescu is pursuing much more radical policies in this area than we have so far.")

Prior to the Second World War, the Jewish population in Romania had numbered approximately 850,000. By the conclusion of the conflict in August 1944, the figure had dwindled to around 450,000. The Jews of Lipcani, Shaike Dan's hometown in present-day Moldova, had almost entirely perished in concentration camps and during a death march that had begun on

July 20, 1941. Out of the 150,000 Jews banished to Transnistria—a largely desolate area, part of today's Moldova that had been under Romanian military rule since 1941—only about 50,000 managed to endure the harsh conditions. Thousands had died doing slave labor or succumbed to disease and starvation.

A significant number of the survivors were Jewish orphans, left abandoned in Transnistria. The Soviet Union made it clear that any orphans originally from Bessarabia and northern Bukovina who'd been exiled to Transnistria would revert to Soviet jurisdiction. Many Jewish survivors of the Transnistrian ghettos and camps were conscripted into the Red Army, with children as young as thirteen being enlisted. Some orphans were subjected to forced labor in work camps located deep within the Soviet Union.

The suffering of Romania's Jews particularly afflicted Shaike Dan. Like almost all of the other volunteer parachutists, he had lost all contact with his immediate family after the outbreak of World War II, and thoughts of his father, mother, sister, two brothers, and the other members of his large family haunted him nightly. "Entering the orphanage, I saw the brands snatched from the fire: the orphans from Transnistria," he later wrote. "Blank-faced. Children whose eyes screeched with the horrors of the Holocaust." Asking about his hometown, he called out in Yiddish, "Anyone here from Lipcani?" A young man named Eliezar answered in a weak voice. "I didn't know him; he was just a child when I left Lipcani, but I remembered his parents very well," Dan wrote.

Without giving away his identity, Dan began to question Eliezar, mentioning the names of people from Lipcani, including the members of the large Trachtenberg family. Eliezer nodded—he remembered that years back there had been a well-known football player in Lipcani named Shaike Trachtenberg. Dan smiled with his eyes; but he didn't let on that before emigrating to Mandatory Palestine, he'd been a star footballer for Lipcani's semiprofessional Jewish team.

Eliezer added that he'd seen Shaike Trachtenberg's sister and her two children before he'd left one of the camps in Transnistria. The mother and two daughters had been wandering across Bessarabia on foot, looking for a way to get back to their hometown—a town that was no longer on the map, completely burned to the ground.

Shaike Dan was startled. Someone from his family had survived. He didn't know where his sister or nieces were, but just the news that they were alive somewhere gave him added strength. Over time, the word *rescue* took on a more profound meaning for him than the rescue of his immediate family. Especially after seeing the piteous faces of the Transnistria orphans, he felt he was engaged in rescuing another family, an extended family: the Jewish people.

Dan and the other Jewish parachutists in Bucharest knew that they would have to find some way to smuggle those orphans out of Romania before they died of malnutrition or disease or fell into the hands of the Red Army. They didn't have much time. The rumble of the Soviet tanks and the thudding of the army's artillery could already be heard in the border region.

In Bucharest confusion reigned. As the Germans lost their grip on the city, gunfire and explosions erupted in all directions. Planes from the airfield that the Luftwaffe still controlled bombed Bucharest from the air. Shaike Dan and the other members of the Romanian infiltration team found themselves under a triple bombing threat: the RAF, the US Army Air Forces, and the Luftwaffe. The Americans and British divided the work between them: the USAAF in the daytime and the RAF at night. The Luftwaffe bombed Bucharest around the clock.

Any Jewish refugees—including the thousands of orphans—would need to set sail from Costanţa, Romania's biggest port on the Black Sea, and navigate the still treacherous waters mined by the Kriegsmarine and patrolled by U-boats, not to mention the corrupt officials, gangsters, and seafaring men Dan called "pirates." "Romania in the summer of 1944 was in chaos, ruled by men with rifles, underworld kingpins, and especially anyone with cash," he later wrote. "Nothing was achieved without payoffs."

Hiding his true identity, playing the role of a gangster and black marketeer, Dan made good use of the gold napoleons he'd secreted away to "grease the palms of shady underworld actors," including an unscrupulous, obese Greek shipping agent named Jean D. Pandelis. Since 1939, Pandelis had had a murky financial relationship with L'Aliyah Bet organizers in Istanbul—his Hebrew code name was Ha-Shamen (the Fat Guy)—to smuggle Jewish refugees out of Romania's ports.

Without much difficulty, Dan bribed Pandelis to procure boats on which

Jewish refugees could be smuggled to Istanbul. In turn, Pandelis used some of the money to bribe Romanian officials to provide the necessary permits, provisions, and an experienced crew of sailors. "More than anything else, he was expert in getting what was due him for his services—in gold napoleons—from our people in Istanbul," Dan wrote.

He also managed to use his connections and napoleons to purchase three boats of varying degrees of seaworthiness, the *Morina, Bulbul,* and *Mefkure,* each of which could carry no more than 150 Jewish refugees. Soon the number of candidates swelled to well over a thousand.

Things turned complicated when, on August 1, 1944, Turkey broke off diplomatic relations with Romania, violated its neutrality, and joined forces with the Allied powers. Overnight, the Black Sea became a battlefield filled with Nazi, Soviet, British, and Turkish warships and submarines.

The members of the Zionist executive met with Shaike Dan to decide whether to go ahead with sending the ships to Turkey. Foremost in everyone's minds was the sinking of the *Struma,* one of the worst civilian maritime disasters of the war. On December 11, 1941, the *Struma,* a two-masted steamer over seventy years old owned by none other than Jean Pandelis, had set sail from Constanţa carrying almost eight hundred Jewish refugees. Three days later, she had reached Istanbul's harbor, where the authorities had kept her quarantined for more than two months. Turkish authorities had denied the passengers permission to land without British agreement to their continued journey to Palestine. On February 23, 1942, the Turks had towed the *Struma* from Istanbul through the Bosphorus and into the Black Sea and cast her adrift without engine power.

The next day, a Soviet submarine, for reasons still unknown, had torpedoed the *Struma.* Most on board had died, trapped belowdecks. Others had survived the sinking by clinging for hours to floating wreckage, only to drown or succumb to hypothermia. There was one survivor of the *Struma*: nineteen-year-old David Stoliar, a Jewish refugee from Kishinev.

Nightmares about the *Struma* "still hung like a black shadow over the activities of everyone involved in rescue work," Dan wrote. Many of the Jewish refugees in Bucharest had begun to voice concerns about the ships' seaworthiness and the risk of submarine attack. But most of all, people began to panic about overcrowding. Even though the combined capacity of the ships was 450 people, the number of passengers would easily surpass a thousand—mainly the orphans who'd reached Bucharest from the camps of Transnistria. Some who'd paid for emigration documents demanded their money back.

Despite that widespread trepidation, Shaike Dan knew that the evacuations had to be sped up; the danger that the SS would enter the Jewish quarter and begin roundups and deportations was imminent. If the Jewish refugees weren't moved out of Romania and into Turkey right away, the chance to do so could be lost.

On August 3, the three small old merchant ships, the *Morina, Bulbul,* and *Mefkure,* set sail, carrying over one thousand Jewish refugees. For the first forty-eight hours, the operation seemed to be a success. And then disaster struck.

On August 5 at 1:00 a.m., twenty-five miles northeast of Igneada, Turkey, the *Mefkure* was hit by torpedoes and gunfire. Hundreds of Jewish refugees drowned as the ship went under; the survivors were machine-gunned to death while struggling to swim. Only five Jewish refugees and six crew members survived, lucky enough to be picked up by the *Bulbul.* Among the dead were the parents of Manu Ben-Ephraim.

To this day, there are conflicting theories about the *Mefkure* disaster; no one is certain whether the torpedo came from a Kriegsmarine U-boat or a Soviet Navy SC-215 submarine. But in early August 1944, any investigation into who was to blame for sinking the *Mefkure* didn't concern Manu Ben-Ephraim. There simply was no time for arguments and accusations. Even as he was grieving the loss of his parents, the rescue mission took priority. Thousands of refugees, orphans, and Holocaust survivors depended on Manu and Shaike's work.

"Manu was my closest friend and suddenly we were in the middle of a calamity," Dan later wrote. "Even in those tragic days Manu acted and functioned with supreme heroism." He felt that Manu and all the other Romanian parachutists derived "a kind of spiritual power" from their work, "the power that impelled us to tell the Jews they should sail," despite their understandable fears about the maritime disaster. "The *Mefkure* was one more embodiment of the tragedy of the Jewish people," he wrote. "Jews suffered many disasters along the roads of rescue. But we knew that immigration to Palestine mustn't stop. Manu continued his activity with an inexplicable drive to act that only a person like him—with his kind of belief in what he was doing—could have."

• • •

On August 23, 1944, opposition parties and pro-Allied elements in Romania staged a coup d'état, led by Romania's young King Michael I. The king met with the "Romanian Führer," Antonescu, and his ministers and asked the prime minister to sign an armistice with the Western Allies and the Soviets. Antonescu refused to be party to any such armistice. In response, a colonel and four soldiers arrested him. At 10:00 p.m., King Michael announced over the radio that Antonescu had been deposed. Bucharest was declared a liberated city.

The news hit Hitler and the remaining members of his Axis like an earthquake. Romania's anti-fascist opposition had executed "the most remarkable and successful coup d'état of World War II," according to John Lukacs, a Hungarian-born American historian. "With an entire German Army in their midst, they turned around within twenty-four hours and proclaimed their alliance with the Soviet Union, Great Britain, and the United States."

After Romania's overnight switching of allegiance, the Luftwaffe began intensive bombing of the capital, unleashing confusion and chaos. In order to survive, the newly installed Romanian government turned to the thousands of British and American POWs in their custody, seeking military advice and insight.

All that time, Shaike Dan and Manu Ben-Ephraim had been in contact with the two previously captured parachutists, Lyova Gukowsky and Arie Fichman, in POW Camp 14, north of Bucharest.

While still in his hospital bed recovering from a fractured and infected leg after his disastrous landing in 1943, Gukowsky had managed to contact the Jewish underground in Bucharest, which had eventually connected him with Allied and Jewish Agency officials in Istanbul and Cairo. He had helped secure supplies from the local underground, and before long, his international contacts had relayed messages to all Allied POWs in Romania saying that they were to obey Gukowsky regarding escape plans.

From there Gukowsky and Fichman enlisted the help of a non-Jewish nurse from Bucharest who pretended to have fallen in love with Lyova—she served as the contact between Gukowsky and a member of one of the youth movements, and after the youth was arrested, she kept up her contacts with the POWs underground through a dentist who worked in the camp and reported regularly on the prisoners' condition.

After the coup d'état, when the Germans began to retreat and the POW camp was abandoned, Gukowsky and Fichman reached Bucharest. Rico Lupescu and Yitzhak Marescu were also in a POW camp, having stuck to their cover story of being British officers. In the pandemonium of Bucharest, they simply walked out through the gates of their prison in RAF uniform.

As grim as the summer of 1944 was for the Jews of Hungary, in liberated Bucharest, there was a happy reunion. A sizable band of parachutists had made it to the city: Rico Lupescu, Yitzhak Macarescu, Arie Fichman, Lyova Gukowsky, and Shaike Dan were soon joined by Baruch Kamin and Dov Berger, who'd successfully made their own jumps.

The hundreds of British and American pilots in the unguarded detention building were waiting for the parachutists and the underground to help them flee. They were in no condition to escape—since their warders had fled, the camp had no more food and no potable water. Nor could any of the British and American prisoners communicate effectively in Romanian. Day by day, the situation of the pilots was getting increasingly desperate.

Rico Lupescu swapped his RAF uniform for civilian clothes, received forged papers and a truck from the underground, and began to make daily deliveries of food and water to the airmen with whom, until days before, he'd been behind the barbed-wire fence.

The hundreds of British and American pilots were amazed to see Rico, a fellow prisoner, suddenly unloading the necessities for staying alive from the back of his truck. Beyond food and water, he brought fresh clothes, blankets, and flashlights in case the jailhouse lost power—all while driving back and forth in the chaos of Bucharest, through sniper fire and bombing raids.

14

Late August 1944
Italy, Germany, and Yugoslavia

On August 23, from MI9 headquarters in London, Brigadier Norman Crockatt, the overall commander of A Force, authorized Squadron Leader Robert Taylor to green-light Haviva Reik and Zvi Ben-Yaakov's departure from Cairo for the Bari airfield in the Operation Amsterdam part of the Slovakian infiltration mission.

Taylor issued the pair RAF uniforms that would serve them well in Europe, with all the clever survival devices dreamed up by Major Maskelyne: a small hacksaw undetectable in a fold of their uniforms, silk maps hidden in the cuffs, spaces in heels for hiding gold coins, watches, and jewelry. Each of them was given 1,000 Hungarian pengós, 30 napoleons, US $50, and jewelry worth £60 to be concealed on their persons—courtesy of Major Maskelyne.

They were given a compact transmitter in Cairo identical to the one Hannah Senesh had been captured with—concealed inside a small suitcase. They'd be given batteries in Bari at the last moment, together with rations, personal weapons, and their parachutes.

Meanwhile, during a roll call on August 25, 1944, Enzo Sereni was taken from the Luftwaffe stalag in Germany. As a "high-profile political prisoner," an RAF captain from Palestine, he would be transferred back to Italy and jailed in Verona—*Shakespeare's* Verona, as Enzo thought of it. After a long train ride, he was incarcerated in the ancient city prison Gli Scalzi, formerly a monastery.*

Enzo's true identity was a secret, but not for long. Giovanni Dean, a professor and political prisoner who had been condemned by a special tribunal for his anti-Fascist activity, later testified that he'd seen "the British captain" when the prisoners were huddled together during one of the frequent British and American air raids and had been informed by his wife—visiting him on behalf of the National Liberation Committee of the Veneto district—that the captain was really an Italian Jewish commando from Palestine.

The news was relayed to the political prisoners and the anti-Fascist resistance. On August 25, Dean saw Enzo being taken out of the prison, together with members of the National Liberation Committee. As a professor, Dean had been granted special permission to keep books in his cell and, after witnessing the departure, wrote the names of thirteen of the prisoners, including that of Captain Samuel Barda, between the lines of a volume of Italian poetry. The group was taken for a short trip, from Verona to Bolzano in the foothills of the Alps, an area of Italy that had been annexed by the Third Reich.

Bolzano transit camp, in a suburb called Gries, was the largest concentration camp established by the Nazis in Italy. It held three thousand prisoners, and though security was in the hands of the SS, internal administrative functions were assigned to the prisoners, who were divided into three categories: political prisoners, forced laborers, and Jews.

Enzo was included among the political prisoners, each of whom wore a red triangle stitched to his prison uniform. In the same room with him were an American officer and twenty-three Italians. They were kept apart in a fenced-in area and never sent outside to work for security reasons.

Most of the prisoners were issued prison uniforms and wooden clogs, but Enzo continued to wear his RAF uniform and, in addition to the inverted red triangular patch over his breast, a second yellow triangle was sewn under the red one to form a Star of David. Meals consisted of a watery soup twice a day

*Gli Scalzi was a convent of the Order of Discalced Carmelites adjacent to the Church of the Scalzi in Verona built between 1666 and 1750, suppressed in 1806 by Napoleonic decree, and used as a prison from 1883 to 1945.

and a ration of 150 grams of bread, but some of the Italian prisoners, especially the skilled workers, were allowed to receive packages from outside and to buy additional food with their own money.

Enzo was not officially permitted to have any contact with the other inmates, but by August 1944, discipline within the camp wasn't strictly enforced by the largely demoralized Italian guards. Soon he struck up an unlikely friendship with a Roman Catholic priest named Mauro Bonci. They discussed the progress of the war and held out hope that because of the Allies' rapid advance northward, the Germans might not be able to transfer the prisoners from Gries.

Father Bonci was impressed by Enzo's inner peace and felt encouraged when in his company: "We frequently quoted verses from the Bible to encourage one another," he wrote. "He'd committed much of the Hebrew Bible and the New Testament to memory. He often surprised me by his extensive knowledge of the Holy Scriptures, which he could quote in Hebrew, Greek, and French."

By late August 1944, the landing strips in the Partisan-held territory of Yugoslavia, where Reuven Dafni was busily working his missions, saw constant activity. British and American warplanes landed daily, filling up all available space with the Allied airmen and escaped POWs who'd made it to the protection of the Agent Gary network. Each incoming flight delivered crates of food, munitions, medical supplies, and the commodity most desired by the Partisan saboteurs: explosives such as TNT, dynamite, and C-3 "blasting gelatin."

On one incoming Douglas C-47, Reuven was surprised to see the smiling face of Surika Braverman. Surika was kitted out in the blue-gray uniform of a WAAF non-commissioned officer, complete with sergeant's chevrons. Yes, she'd been too terrified to jump at Ramat David, but she had finally managed to start her mission. She'd been trained with the Romanian infiltration team, but with the situation on the ground in Bucharest now so chaotic, Colonel Simonds had decided that she could be more useful helping Reuven and the Partisans rescue Allied airmen.

Reuven wanted to hug Surika, but that would have blown her cover story. She was supposedly Sarah O'Connor, a flight sergeant in the WAAF, now on assignment as a war correspondent covering the Balkans theater for *Union*

Jack. She said her readers were closely following the successes of Tito's Partisan army and the role that the RAF and USAAF were playing in assisting the guerrillas. They saluted each other instead.

Every day, Surika and the other British and American soldiers would see a young Partisan girl who led a cow down a path. She spoke no English but smiled at the airmen and offered them fresh milk. One morning, Surika spontaneously showed her the skills she'd learned during her time studying agriculture and working on the kibbutz. She expertly milked the cow, filling a pail to the top. The young Partisan girl was shocked to see that proper Englishwoman in uniform on her knees, milking the cow as deftly as a girl raised on a dairy farm. "Whoever heard of an educated English lady who doesn't wear makeup and knows how to milk Partisan cows?" Surika later recalled with a laugh.

15

September 1944
Bucharest, Romania

On the morning of September 1, 1944, at 10:00 a.m., the lead tanks of the Red Army rumbled through the streets of Bucharest. The Soviet troops, drunk on victory—and vodka—waved machine guns and red flags. "All of Bucharest was out on the streets," Shaike Dan wrote. "People who until the day before had fought alongside the Germans suddenly changed their skin and fell on the necks of the Red Army with hugs and kisses. About one hundred fifty to two hundred youths came marching from the Jewish district displaying the Romanian flag and our national flag."

Shaike Dan didn't join the march but walked along the edge of the pavement, observing as hundreds—if not thousands—of Jews left the entrances of their houses and spontaneously joined the procession. "It was a thrilling sight to see the outburst of joy that grew and grew as more and more Jews, and more and more flags, joined the demonstration . . . singing 'Hatikvah,'" he wrote.*

*At the First Zionist Congress in Basel in 1897, a white flag with thin blue stripes—based on the tallit, the traditional prayer shawl—with a blue Shield of David (or Star of David) in the center was adopted as the "Jewish national flag"—the Israeli national flag since 1948.

"Hatikvah"—Hebrew for "The Hope"—is considered the most powerful Zionist song ever written. The popular poem was written in 1878 by Naftali Herz Imber, and in 1887, the violinist Shmuel Cohen set the lyrics to a traditional Romanian folk

> A mighty force of hundreds, thousands of tanks rolled through Bucharest day and night. I must admit that after I returned to Palestine and was asked about the soldiers of the liberating Red Army, there wasn't much I could say to their credit. The joy of victory and the welcome given the Russian soldiers was overshadowed by acts of robbery, drunkenness, and rape that didn't add honor to the "Red heroes."

Though Romania was now free of fascist rule, thousands of Jewish refugees and orphans were still in peril. During the curfew the Soviets imposed on Bucharest, Shaike Dan and the other parachutists met and planned their next steps. With over a thousand British and American POWs now liberated, the priority for Colonel Simonds was to get them to Bari. First, via Cairo, the Romanian team called for several Allied heavy bombers, which landed in Romania with Soviet permission and took off laden with freed Allied POWs. Hundreds of well-trained pilots, eager to return to action, were once again ready to bomb strategic Nazi targets.

Lyova Gukovsky, Arie Fichman, and Yitzhak Macarescu returned on flights with the Allied airmen and went for MI9 debriefings in Bari, while a core team of parachutists stayed operational in Bucharest: Manu Ben-Ephraim, Dov Berger, Baruch Kamin, Shaike Dan, and Rico Lupescu. They were soon joined by Uriel Kaner from Kibbutz Ruhama, who'd made a solo parachute jump into Romania two weeks earlier.

Now the focus shifted to the thousands of Jewish orphans who had somehow made it out of Transnistria alive. Most had been nursed back from starvation and illness and were in reasonably good health. But flying them out of Romania on British or American heavy bombers was not an option—they'd need to leave the Port of Costanţa by ship.

With Romania liberated, Shaike Dan could now openly reveal his identity to Jean Pandelis, and by early September, he began negotiating with the Greek to procure two more ships, the *Turos* and the *Saladin*. Pandelis demanded an up-front partial payment in US dollars and napoleons.

---

melody. Imber's line *"Lashuv le'eretz avotenu"* (To return to the land of our forefathers) succinctly expressed the aspirations of millions of Jews in the Diaspora. "Hatikvah" is the State of Israel's national anthem.

Dan was concerned that after the torpedoing of the *Mefkure,* no Jewish refugees would want to risk sailing in the still treacherous waters of the Black Sea. He and several of the other Romanian parachutists met with Dr. Abraham Zissu as well as the leaders of the Zionist youth movements, urging them to spread a clear message at synagogues and other Jewish gatherings: Despite the disaster in August, the Aliyah Bet immigration to British Palestine would not stop. The enthusiasm of the young Zionist emissaries was so great that the waiting list for passage would have filled several more vessels.

"We sped up the handling of the sailing of the *Turos* and the *Saladin* as much as we could," Dan recalled. "Evacuation of the orphans from Transnistria was our number one concern." Deeply distrustful of Pandelis, he made it a point to personally supervise the Greek's work, checking the safety conditions and the seaworthiness of both ships, as well as the assembling and screening of the crew members, and getting the necessary permits from Romanian authorities. He calculated that the *Saladin* could carry close to five hundred passengers and the *Turos* perhaps eight or nine hundred. Almost all the available spots would be set aside for the Transnistrian orphans, those gaunt, piteous young people Dan had called "brands snatched from the fire."

16

September 1, 1944
Bari Airfield, Italy

On September 1, RAF Squadron Leader Taylor called Haviva Reik, Zvi Ben-Yaakov, Rafael "Rafi" Reiss, and Chaim Hermesh into the MI9 headquarters in Bari. The Simonds Quartet—as they jokingly called themselves—thought it was a routine briefing about their upcoming mission, code-named Operation Amsterdam.

Just days earlier, on August 29, 1944, Lieutenant Colonel Ján Golian had given the order to start the Slovak National Uprising in Banská Bystrica, Slovakia. A response to the fact that SS *Bandenbekämpfung* units had entered Slovakia to "eliminate Partisans," the Slovak National Uprising would develop into the second largest anti-fascist uprising during World War II, with some eighty thousand fighters. They liberated more than eight thousand square miles of territory with approximately 1.7 million inhabitants.

Squadron Leader Taylor shared an encrypted telegram he'd just received from Colonel Simonds in Cairo:

> ZASLANI ALSO COMING ON 5 SEPT TO ASSIST YOU IN HANDLING ALL BATS FORKS NOW IN BARI MUST LEAVE TO YOU DECISION AMSTERDAM PERSONALLY SUGGEST WE CONTINUE PLAN OF DROPPING ONLY MALE FORKS IN SLOVAKIA SHOULD STILL BE POSSIBLE IF YOU PICK A SUITABLE AREA AWAY FROM PRESENT FIGHTING

"Bats" was the code word for the emissaries from Palestine; "Forks" referred to parachutists. Whenever Simonds used the phrase "personally suggest" in a telegram, Taylor knew it was a direct order. Haviva would not be allowed to jump. Hearing that, all four of the paratroopers were stunned and began chattering heatedly in Hebrew.

"And why not me?" Haviva finally asked in English.

All Taylor could say was that in a day or two, Reuven Zaslani would arrive in Bari and explain it to her in person. MI9 learned that the Germans had copies of the British military's standing orders prohibiting females from crossing enemy lines, and no one had heard anything from Agent Minnie—Hannah Senesh—since June. She was presumed to be either captured or killed. Simonds couldn't afford to take more risks.

Since they were making a blind jump very close to combat lines, Haviva might fall directly into German hands. If she were captured, the Nazis would not take her uniform into consideration, nor her dog tags identifying her as a WAAF sergeant named Ada Robinson. She would be treated as a spy and almost certainly executed.

"And what about the men?" Haviva countered. "Don't they face just as much risk?"

Taylor said that if captured, the men would be taken for RAF officers and treated as prisoners of war. The three men had a good cover story; they'd say that they had been sent to serve in the Soviet headquarters in eastern Poland and due to an aircraft malfunction in midflight, the pilot had ordered them to jump. Their Luftwaffe captors would almost certainly treat them decently.

Recent developments in Bucharest backed up his speculation. On August 23, the day of the Romanian coup d'état, all Allied POWs had been released; the first among them had arrived in Bari on their way home to Palestine. Arie Fichman, Lyova Gukowsky, and Yitzhak Macarescu had told their comrades what had happened to them in Romania—how they'd been held in a POW camp with British and American flyers, treated humanely, and fed well, by and large.

Haviva tried to explain to Taylor that from the very beginning she had taken the risk of falling into Nazi hands and being shot as a spy. Taylor frowned; he wouldn't budge.

What was so different now? As a Palmach commander, she knew full well the inherent dangers of falling into enemy hands and that, if captured, the Nazis would not treat her under international law, they wouldn't observe the Geneva or Hague conventions.

For the first time since her enlistment, she raised her voice to a British officer. "I'm not some immature child!" she shouted. "I'm a thirty-year-old woman who embarked on her mission with a clear mind and my eyes wide open."

Why had she trained as rigorously as the men, gone through the parachuting course, practiced judo, jiujitsu, hand-to-hand combat, how to read a compass in the dark, how to slit an enemy's throat with a knife and fire a Sten gun and a submachine gun—only so that at the last minute, she'd be ordered to remain at the base in safety? If she didn't jump, she argued, Operation Amsterdam would be losing its best intelligence asset. Haviva knew the people and terrain at the epicenter of the Slovak rebellion, Banská Bystrica, better than the three male parachutists combined. "I grew up there! I know Banská Bystrica like the back of my hand."

Her arguments were cogent and logical, but to avail. "Those are my orders," Taylor said.

When the parachutists left Taylor's office, Haviva was at once incensed and distraught. Chaim Hermesh was shocked to see that strong, fit, brilliant woman suddenly seeming broken. For the first time, he saw her crying. "We had an agreement—we had a *plan*," she said. "We trained for this together! We promised that all four of us would jump together."

Chaim had no answer. He knew that Haviva was right.

The tears were hot in Haviva's eyes. "What'll become of me now? What am I supposed to do?"

For hours in their quarters, she paced and fumed, but to whom could she turn? She desperately needed help from Enzo Sereni—that whirling dervish of a fixer, dashing around Bari, giving commands in Italian, English, Hebrew, German—seemingly able to organize *anything*, persuade *anybody*, navigate effortlessly between the British and American brass and his friends, the heads of the Jewish Agency.

But Enzo had long since left Bari on his own parachuting mission to northern Italy—and no one had received a radio transmission from him yet. Reluctantly, apologetically, the other three—Rafi Reiss, Zvi Ben-Yaakov, and Chaim Hermesh—decided that they'd have to break up the Simonds Quartet. They would make the blind jump into Slovakia without her.

Haviva was on her own.

17

September 11, 1944
Gyorskocsi Street Gestapo Prison, Budapest

In the early hours of September 11, 1944, an SS guard barged into Yoel Palgi's cell and told him to pack his belongings quickly.

"Where to?" Palgi asked.

The guard muttered something guttural in German about the Hungarians taking charge of all prisoners. Palgi snatched up his toothbrush and soap and with a nail file scratched on the door, "11 September 1944—I have been released!"

Palgi went into the corridor, where he was suddenly joined by Peretz Goldstein, who was pale and noticeably thinner. When Palgi offered a thumbs-up, Peretz smiled sadly and made a dismissive gesture, indicating his doubts. His long-fingered hands were like those of a pianist. He didn't know where they were being taken. Sándor Fleischmann also turned up, as did Jacques Tissandier. The four of them stood in a line with their faces to the wall. Suddenly the barred gate opened with a creak.

"Hannah was coming down the stairs," Palgi wrote. "She had grown thinner, but she had become startlingly more beautiful. She was wearing a blue skirt and a white silk blouse. She had a light raincoat over her arm and carried a small black suitcase. She smiled at us as though she had come from a long journey and was stepping out of a railway carriage. She came and stood beside me, walking lightly. I put out my hand, which she clasped warmly."

"This isn't a café!" a Gestapo officer shouted, pulling out his Walther PPK for emphasis.

When they called out the names of Hannah, Goldstein, Palgi, and Tissandier, Palgi turned to Tissandier and saw for the first time that all his front teeth were missing. Surrounded by Gestapo men, they walked silently down to the courtyard. Three transport vans awaited them, each containing three single cubicles—two side by side and one facing the others, along with a large cubicle.

Hannah and Peretz were placed in the adjoining single cubicles, while Yoel and the others occupied the large one. As the van started to move, Yoel used Morse code to lightly tap out "Shalom" to Hannah on the metal division.

"What now?" Hannah quickly tapped back in Morse code.

Yoel answered with the opening four notes of Beethoven's Fifth Symphony.

The van came to a screeching halt. The guards lined the width of the pavement, closing it off, and took them out in pairs. Yoel and Hannah looked out in front of them. They had returned to the same Hungarian prison where they'd been so severely tortured. The officers they knew well were at the front, though they didn't see Rózsa. "They extended their hands one by one and greeted us, gathering around Hannah with affection, inquiring after her well-being and that of her mother," Palgi later wrote. "It was as if the evil spirit of the place had passed away."

He harbored no illusions about the turnabout in the guards' demeanor. "The little rats already sensed that it was worth being friendly. One of those who had arrested me whispered in my ear: 'Will you remember that I was good to you?'"

They were led back to their cells. The sergeant and the guards were polite. "In a day or two you'll be taken to a military prison, where you'll be made comfortable," they explained. "You won't be in prison much longer."

Palgi had managed to hold on to a package of American cigarettes—an invaluable currency in wartime Europe—and, offering a Lucky Strike to the sergeant, said he wanted to talk to Hannah. The guard nodded. Moments later, there she stood.

"Sit here, by the door," the guard said. "When anyone comes, get up as if you're waiting to be frisked."

They were left on their own; silent for a few moments, simply holding hands and staring into each other's eyes. "Is this how we arranged to meet?" Hannah finally said with a quiet laugh. As her lips parted, Palgi noticed her damaged smile. "What happened to your tooth?"

"I lost it in Szombathelyi. One of the gendarmes was positively impolite."

"Tell me everything that happened to you after we separated."

As quickly as she could, she recounted all that had transpired since she'd flashed him her farewell thumbs-up in the mountains of Slovenia: the monthlong trek to the border; the multiple crossings of the Drava River and numerous streams so she could keep her wireless radio intact; the dragnet of gendarmes; how she and Tony Tissandier had pretended to be lovers in the cornfield; and how Kallós—for reasons no one could fathom—with the headphones in his pocket, had lost his nerve and blown his brains out with his Colt .45, bringing down the house of cards.

And then she got to the torture, the grim specifics of which she glossed over; and her two attempts at committing suicide, racing to fling herself from the window of the gendarmerie headquarters and trying to jump beneath the wheels of the moving train.

She moved on to the way she'd left the book of French poems on the train and the most painful moment of all: the psychological torture of seeing her mother paraded before her in jail.

Yoel, too, had suffered days and nights of torture at the hands of the Hungarian police and the Gestapo; they had suspected that, like Hannah, he was a radio operator for British Intelligence, though they'd never recovered his wireless transmitter. He told her everything, too. Unable to bear the torture, at one point, he said, he'd also attempted, unsuccessfully, to take his own life. Then, seemingly as quickly as he'd left, the compliant guard was back. "Time's up," he said.

They'd been betrayed. There was no doubt about that. But by whom?

For weeks, Hannah and Yoel had both been ruminating in their cells. The Hungarian authorities had clearly been waiting for Hannah—or rather, waiting for the arrival of a female British paratrooper crossing the border from Yugoslavia, carrying a wireless transmitter. They didn't know her real name, of course, only her code name, Agent Minnie. But they'd been expecting her arrival and that of her comrade, Agent Mickey, as well.

Yoel speculated that some of the smugglers along the border had been the traitors. They were all dubious types, mercenary in motive, and for the right amount of cash, treachery was second nature to them.

In Istanbul, meanwhile, Agent Dogwood, the Czech Jewish businessman Alfred Schwarz, while in the pay of Teddy Kollek and the Mossad L'Aliyah Bet could have passed information about the Hungarian infiltration team to both his Nazi handlers and Hungarian Military Intelligence. Yet how much Kollek himself, and therefore Agent Dogwood, knew about the logistics of Hannah's mission remained unclear. Betrayal may, in fact, have come from several sources simultaneously.

One new possible source came to light in 2010 when, within in the archives of the Yugoslav Army in Belgrade, Serbia, previously unseen documents shed light on what the Partisans had known about Hannah and her fellow paratroopers. The documents reveal the extent to which Marshal Tito closely followed the Jewish parachutists' mission, wanting to know every operational detail, right down to the personal characteristics of each paratrooper. Another document indicates that a Nazi mole had likely infiltrated the Partisan high command, learning every secret known to the inner circle of Tito's leadership.

Though she never revealed her true name during her months with the Partisans, by June 1944, Hannah had become something of a mythic figure: a blue-eyed girl who'd floated down from the heavens with a beatific smile and a Colt .45 pistol strapped to her waist. No one in the forests and villages of Slovenia and Croatia had ever seen anyone like her.

The Nazi espionage agent in Tito's headquarters would surely have told his German handlers to expect the arrival in Hungary of several British paratroopers from Palestine, including an attractive, highly intelligent young woman trained as a wireless radio operator by British Military Intelligence in Cairo, who'd parachuted into Yugoslavia from an RAF bomber in March 1944.

The day after their brief meeting, Hannah and Yoel were back in the prison vans: The Gestapo was handing off their entire group to the Hungarian military authorities, and the first stop was the Conti Street prison. An officer appeared at the gate and announced that only Hannah was to be imprisoned there; there wasn't room for anyone else.

When it came time to part, she set down her small brown suitcase and gave her hand to each of the men in turn. "I'll be seeing you," she said. "Come and visit me at my mother's house, 28 Bimbó út. If the house has been destroyed, ask for me at number 30."

"We'll be seeing you," Yoel said and got back into the car.

For the rest of his life, Yoel would remember her silhouette at the open gate, how her eyes had followed them with a cheerful gaze. And how, as the car pulled away, Hannah raised her thumb with a mischievous laugh.

18

September 16, 1944
Tel Aviv

Arie Fichman—the parachutist who'd been captured in 1943 in Bucharest and survived torture at the hands of the Gestapo before being sent to a Romanian POW camp—arrived in Tel Aviv via Cairo and Bari on September 16, 1944.

Fichman was one of the first of the emissaries to reach Eretz Israel safely. In the upper pocket of his khaki uniform, he carried a treasure: the well-worn scrap of notepaper Reuven Dafni had given him, the paper on which Hannah had scribbled "Ashrei Hagafrur" on May 2, 1944, by kerosene lamplight, in the Partisan camp in Serdica, Yugoslavia.

Fichman carefully opened the rectangular slip of paper, flattened and neatly folded into quarters, and read the four lines again, noting how the ink in Hannah's Hebrew script had in places been washed away by melted snow water. The first line was nearly gone. Was it an act of providence, he wondered, that the entire thing hadn't bled into illegible inkblots? Or dissolved away completely during those many hard months in the Yugoslavian mountains?

He handed the slip of paper to Zvi Yehieli, who passed it on to the editors of *Davar*.

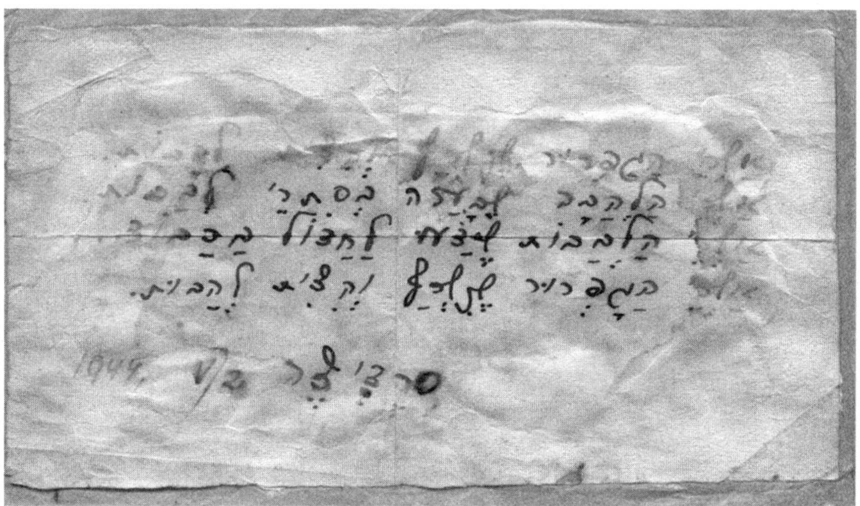

הלהבה שבערה בסתרי לבבות
הלבבות שידעו לחדול בכבוד
הגפרור שנשרף והצית להבות.

In late September 1944, while she was languishing in various Hungarian and Gestapo prisons in Budapest, Hannah Senesh achieved her first moment of literary recognition. She was now, albeit anonymously, a published poet.

The poem appeared on the front page of *Davar Hapoelet*—the Labor Union newspaper's women's supplement—under the cryptic note "A member who set out on a special mission wrote these lines before she left."

Before long, readers throughout Eretz Israel were showing one another copies of the newspaper, quoting those four simple lines. No one could have possibly known that "Ashrei Hagafrur" (Blessed Is the Match) would soon become one of the most famous poems ever written in Modern Hebrew:

Blessed is the match consumed
in kindling flame
Blessed is the flame that burns
in the secret fastness of the heart
Blessed is the heart with strength to stop
its beating for honor's sake
Blessed is the match consumed
in kindling flame

19

September 16, 1944
Bari Airfield, Italy

Haviva was still in shock, devastated by her team's decision to leave her behind, when one day she was called urgently to Squadron Leader Taylor's office. She feared the worst: The first group of parachutists who'd returned from Romania—Lyova Gukovsky, Arie Fichman, and Yitzhak Macarescu—had met with Colonel Simonds for official debriefings in Cairo and were being discharged from the British Army. Haviva was certain that Taylor was about to tell her that she'd be going back to Cairo with them. On the contrary, in a recent telegram Colonel Simonds had left instructions for Taylor: CONCENTRATE ON FINDING NEW TASK FOR MARTA.

Within days, US Intelligence in Bari informed British Intelligence that the USAAF was about to fly an American delegation of OSS agents to Slovakia. The British requested that the flight include its own delegation headed by SOE Major John Sehmer and including RAF Flight Sergeant Ada Robinson—Haviva Reik's undercover name.

Haviva entered Squadron Leader Taylor's office and saluted. "Good news," Taylor said. "Tomorrow you're flying to Slovakia."

Haviva would have to prepare herself quickly, get the suitcase transmitter—which she had returned to the MI9 storeroom for her drop—then check and clean her pistols and the rest of the necessary gear. "And the parachute?" she asked. Where was the drop zone in Slovakia?

She wouldn't be parachuting at all, Taylor explained. She'd be flying on an

American bomber with a British and an American delegation and would land at a recently captured military airfield under the control of the Slovak Army, ten miles south of Banská Bystrica.

Haviva smiled. She didn't ask Taylor to explain anything more about the airfield. She had fond memories of the spa village of Sliač, where she had often gone with friends as a teenager on long summer afternoons; she would ride her motorcycle alone out to the old airfield called Tri Duby (Three Oaks). Tri Duby was now the crucial landing strip fueling the ever-growing Slovak National Uprising.

Just before 8:00 a.m. on September 17, Squadron Leader Taylor accompanied Haviva Reik to the busy landing strips of the Bari airfield. The US Army's Fifteenth Air Force had two heavy bombers waiting on the tarmac, revving up their four turbocharged engines; Haviva recognized the famous Boeing B-17 Flying Fortresses, the aircraft that had been unleashing devastation on the heart of Hitler's Reich and its fascist allies.

As they approached the bombers, Taylor introduced Haviva to Major John Sehmer, the head of the British military delegation, and Bill Wilson, a wireless operator, leading the team on Operation Leadburn. "Sergeant Ada Robinson," wearing her three chevrons proudly on the arm of her blue WAAF uniform, saluted them. Then it was time for Taylor to say his farewell. "Good luck, Marta," he said.

On board the Flying Fortress were six American officers and OSS agents, led by Lieutenant James Holt Green, a navy reserve officer and the head of the American delegation to the newly liberated zone of Slovakia.

Sending heavy bombers and their fighter escorts into Slovakia, as opposed to making parachute drops, he explained, had become possible only after Banská Bystrica and the nearby Tri Duby airfield in Sliač had been captured by General Ján Golian and his rebel troops. General Golian had turned Tri Duby into the key airfield for the Allied efforts to assist his rebel Slovak Army in their fight against the Nazi occupied forces.

Now a dozen USAAF and three RAF airmen—including one Czech pilot—were awaiting evacuation. Most had been shot down by German anti-aircraft batteries or Messerschmitt Bf 109s; others had escaped from POW camps and wandered in the Slovakian mountains, until, with the help of anti-Nazi locals and Partisans, they had reached the safety of the liberated enclave. Given the shortage of trained pilots and experienced aircrews in September 1944, it was a top priority for MI9 and OSS to take them to Bari so that they could resume bombing missions. Haviva was to aid in the evacuation and then locate the dozens of other Allied pilots and flight crews stranded in Slovakia.

At 8:25 a.m., the two B-17s lifted off the runway in Bari, escorted by forty-one P-51 Mustang fighters, which would protect them from Luftwaffe fighters and neutralize anti-aircraft guns. The bombers were packed with eight tons of military equipment—guns, grenades, ammunitions—as well as badly needed medical supplies for Golian's rebel forces.

Once they were in flight, Haviva felt the airmen gawking, repeatedly looking her up and down. A sudden loneliness took hold of her. As the only woman on the plane, the only non-American, she had no one with whom she could share her true feelings about her mission. After the Flying Fortress had been airborne for two hours, she took pen and paper and wrote a note to the parachutists who had remained back in Bari:

My dear friends—

It's about an hour from my destination and I'm thinking about you and that gives me strength. During the first two hours I was somewhat excited. Now I'm totally calm and am looking to the future with a lucid mind.

Give my regards to our comrades. The men who accompanied me took good care of me.

We will see one another soon. Have a drink for me too.

Thank you for everything.

Yours,
Haviva

After jotting down the brief note, she ran through a mental checklist: Dog tags, identifying her as Sergeant Ada Robinson, were around her neck. Brass uniform buttons contained hidden compasses. In her knapsack, she had her prized possession, the hardcover book *Women Members of the Kibbutz*, which she'd been reading during her free time since the beginning of her training in Cairo. Around her waist, she wore a tight money belt that held US $1,000, several gold napoleons, and the Slovakian bills that Colonel Taylor had given her before departure. The Jewish Agency had allotted $1,000 for Agent Martha—Haviva—and $3,000 for Agent Willis—Abba Berdichev—who'd reached Banská Bystrica, traveling overland from Yugoslavia a week earlier. There were more napoleon gold coins nestled in the hollowed-out heels of her boots.

Just after 11:00 a.m., the two Flying Fortresses touched down at the Tri Duby airfield. The bombers stayed on the ground for barely forty-five minutes, refueling, picking up the seventeen rescued USAAF and RAF flyers, and dropping off the six American OSS officers, along with Haviva Reik, as well as the eight tons of weapons, ammunition, food, and medical supplies for the Slovakian rebels.

She left the note she'd dashed off in midflight with a B-17 crew member, who promised that he'd deliver it to her friends back in the heel of Italy. Within a matter of hours, the Flying Fortress landed at the Bari airfield and the note was handed off by the USAAF crewmember to one of the Jewish emissaries in Bari.

Haviva's timing was perfect. The sun had set, and the parachutists in Bari were celebrating the start of the Jewish New Year. At their small Rosh Hashanah party—with glasses of full-bodied Primitivo red wine and shouts of *"L'Chaim!"*—her friends read the message aloud, toasting to the health of Haviva Reik and the two dozen other parachutists operating behind enemy lines.

Haviva was home, walking the familiar streets of Banská Bystrica, the city in which she'd grown up and gone to school. People called out to her, remembering her as Marta—or, if they didn't know her first name, as "the girl on the motorcycle." In those prewar years she'd been unmistakable with her bobbed hair, tearing through the streets on her Jawa 175 motorcycle, known to everyone as a daring, free-spirited tomboy.

As she passed through town in her distinctive blue WAAF uniform, wearing dark sunglasses, she saw a huge poster depicting a Slovak partisan crushing a German helmet under his boot. In one hand he held a gun and in the other, an ax with which he was chopping down a flagpole flying the flag of the Third Reich, with text below:

FOR DEMOCRACY!
FOR CZECHOSLOVAKIA!

Haviva didn't know it at the time, but the poster had been designed and drawn by Sanyo Wollner, a member of Hashomer Hatzair who'd known Haviva in her youth.

Banská Bystrica was now the heart of the Slovak National Uprising. Eighteen days into the uprising, the ranks of the rebel army had swollen to forty-seven thousand troops. Many were Slovakian soldiers and reservists who'd defected to General Golian's side. There were also the irregulars—Slovak partisans, Jewish prisoners who'd escaped from camps, and other political dissidents.

Before the war, Jews had accounted for only 4 percent of the population in Slovakia. Of the Jewish community of eighty-nine thousand in 1940, an estimated sixty-nine thousand had been deported to the camps in Poland—Sobibor, Treblinka, Chełmno, Majdanek, Auschwitz—beginning in 1942 or had died from disease and overwork in forced labor camps. Of the sixteen thousand Slovak partisan fighters, somewhere between sixteen hundred and two thousand were Jewish, including 169 young women, many of whom had come from the Zionist youth movements.

The car stopped in front of a five-story building with a gray slate roof. Haviva remembered it well: the garrison force headquarters. Her eldest sister, Nelly, had once pointed at one of the windows and said that it was the office of the general in whose home she worked as a housemaid.

Now, Haviva assumed, General Golian, the military commander of the rebels, was occupying that office as the resistance headquarters. It was where she would transmit to British Intelligence in Bari.

The Slovakian soldier who drove the military vehicle didn't know a word of English, so Haviva spoke Slovakian with him. He must have been intrigued by the female British sergeant's fluent Slovakian but didn't ask any questions. Banská Bystrica was teeming with soldiers and partisans of various nationalities wearing diverse uniforms, but of all the Jewish emissaries from Mandatory Palestine who landed in Slovakia, Haviva was seen, undisputably, as the emotional leader, which at that moment seemed more of a curse than a blessing.

Not only was she recognizable—even at age thirty many people in her old hometown remembered how she'd looked a decade earlier—but her blue British uniform drew far too much attention. She needed to disguise herself, and quickly.

She walked into a department store she'd known as a schoolgirl and used some of the Slovakian cash secreted in her money belt to purchase a green woolen skirt, bulky off-white shoes, a stylish broad-shouldered Austrian loden all-weather coat, and a dark olive French-style beret, which she tilted over her forehead so that it shadowed part of her face.

The sunglasses she'd brought from Cairo would've made excellent camouflage in midsummer, but the late-September days were overcast and rainy, and a young woman wearing dark glasses would look ludicrous, like a Hollywood starlet desperately trying not to be noticed.

She went straight to her hotel room and changed her outfit, finally able to practice what Major Maskelyne, that eccentric mustachioed magician, had taught her in Cairo: She stood in front of the mirror, hunching her shoulders, walking back and forth, shuffling. If she carried a canvas tote bag, the transformation was complete: She looked like an old peasant woman from a village who'd come to Banská Bystrica to do her shopping.

While she awaited word about her three still missing comrades—Rafi Reiss, Zvi Ben-Yaakov, and Chaim Hermesh—she set up her suitcase radio, contacted Squadron Leader Taylor in Bari, and got to work on the MI9 aspect of the mission: rescuing downed Allied airmen. The instructions she had given to several of the young Slovakian Hashomer Hatzair underground fighters were crystal clear: "If you see three young dark-haired men with mustaches, walking together, first speak to them in Hebrew."

In the end, it wasn't at all hard to spot them: Zvi Ben-Yaakov, Rafi Reiss, and Chaim Hermesh stood out conspicuously in their blue RAF uniforms, their thick mustaches, and the white scarves that peeped from their collars.

Suddenly Hermesh and the others heard the soft voice of a man behind them, speaking in Hebrew: "Rafi, Chaim, Zvi—shalom!" They turned to see a light-haired Slovak partisan carrying a pistol. "Follow me," he said, "Ada Robinson sent me. She's waiting for you."

When they arrived, they were surprised to see an elderly peasant woman, frail and stooped over. "Haviva showed no signs of recognizing us," Hermesh later wrote. "As if she were a stranger, she passed us without looking at us and we understood the game: We also acted as if we didn't know her. Only, later, in Egon Roth's room did she let herself show emotion."

The three men were no less emotional. There were hugs, kisses, and some tears. Haviva finally let out a relieved laugh. "Well, the Simonds Quartet is reunited!"

They told her about their blind jump, how their British pilot had dropped them some thirty-five miles northwest of the designated landing spot on Mount Križna. They'd come down near the city of Vrútky; far from being held by the Slovak rebels, it was deep in Nazi-held territory, and they had searched for one another for two days before they eventually met up. Their radio transmitter and the rest of their cache of weapons and equipment were lost. More than once they had almost been captured by the Nazis or the Hlinka Guard. It had taken them four days to reach Banská Bystrica.

Haviva took charge of setting up the Jewish rescue operations. She had access to considerable funds if needed to bribe corrupt officials—the Jewish Agency had transferred US $150,000 through an emissary in Istanbul to Gisi Fleischmann, a Zionist leader of the Bratislava Working Group, one of the most successful Jewish rescue operations during the Holocaust.

Haviva had only to say the agreed-upon password—"Merhavia Degania," the names of two kibbutzim—and Gisi Fleischmann would give them the money designated for the rescue operation.

During the chaotic uprising, more than five thousand Jewish refugees—mostly women, children, and elderly—began to arrive, starving and freezing, in the liberated stronghold. Within days, Haviva set up a communal soup kitchen and distributed blankets and provisions. She and the other parachutists helped the Jewish underground by using skills they had learned in Cairo: forging non-Jewish identification papers and plotting escape routes overland through Hungary into Romania. There, the parachutists would connect with the Bucharest team of parachutists to arrange ships on the Black Sea to take refugees to Istanbul and eventually to Palestine.

Like Hannah in her Budapest prison, Haviva entertained Jewish refugees with stories of life on the kibbutzim and the beauty of Eretz Israel. The refugees saw her not just as an inspiration but as a strange apparition descended from the heavens. With Haviva's training as a Palmach commander and natural leadership skills, one survivor of the Slovak National Uprising remembered her as a "magnet" who "gave us advice, information, instructions."

The partisans eagerly listened to her foretelling the rebirth of a nation on ancestral ground. Some of the more religious refugees "viewed Reik as a messenger from God, and one Orthodox rabbi referred to her as a saint." For the next six weeks, the reunited quartet carried out their dual mission: helping Allied pilots and POWs return to their squadrons and organizing the escape of thousands of Slovakian Jews who had found refuge in the enclave.

20

October 8, 1944
Bolzano Transit Camp, Italy

On October 8, six weeks after Enzo arrived at Gries, the Nazis emptied the camp, sending two large train transports of prisoners deeper into the heart of the Reich. Three hundred men, including the Jewish Italian parachutist, were jammed into cattle cars, roughly eighty men in each. At one point in the ride, through tiny slits covered in barbed wire, the prisoners could see that they'd crossed the Brenner Pass. They'd left Italy and entered Austria, part of the greater Reich.

All hope faded. While being held behind barbed wire in Italy, they could at least dream—imagine—that the advancing Allied battle lines might overtake them. But now, entering the heart of the Thousand-Year Reich, few had any expectation that they'd survive whatever ordeal lay ahead.

When the train finally reached its destination and they piled out of the cattle cars, they saw the stark reality. They had arrived at the oldest and most infamous of all the Nazi concentration camps—the camp where almost all of the commandants of the other SS death camps had done their training: Dachau.

Unlike the death camps—Auschwitz, Treblinka, Sobibor, Belzec, and Chełmno—whose existence had for years been top secret, the existence of Konzentrationslager Dachau had been well publicized to the German people since it had first opened as an instrument of political terror in 1933. The name meant little to the Italian prisoners apart from Enzo—having been a Zionist organizer in Berlin in 1932 and 1934 during Hitler's rise to power, he knew very well that Dachau was no POW camp.

It was a grim, drizzly morning. They marched into the camp through a gate bearing the cruel inscription ARBEIT MACHT FREI (Work shall set you free) and were ordered to assemble in the Appelplatz for roll call. Around them they saw electrified barbed-wire fences, a guard tower with riflemen ready to shoot anyone who crossed the line of death, the notorious "trip wire."

Suddenly one of the SS sergeants called out a name: "Barda!" Enzo stepped forward and faced the SS man with a smile. The sergeant struck Enzo full force in the face with his fist. Enzo reeled back, regained his balance, and remained standing at attention. For all the Italians, it was a shock: a first encounter with and warning of the brutality to come.

The men were ordered to undress and marched, naked, to the shower rooms near the entrance to the camps. As they shivered with cold, their heads and bodies were shaved with a straight razor and their skin painted with a burning greenish disinfecting fluid.

Enzo was registered as Captain Samuel Barda—British, Jew—and issued number 113,160. The date of his arrival in Dachau, 9.10.44, was stamped in red in his file.

In a short time, Catholic priests, social democrats, labor organizers, and even a professor of philosophy were transformed from individuals into what the SS guards viewed as the lowest form of life: *Lagermenschen*. Shivering from the cold, weariness, and tension, they were given their first Dachau meal: a foul-smelling, grayish, cold liquid—"soup," they were told it was, but many of them could not swallow a spoonful of it without gagging.

In Block 25, which served as a kind of quarantine station, the Italians made their first acquaintance with the kapos categorized as *Berufsverbrecher* (career criminals)—convicted murderers, rapists, hysterical psychopaths—wearing inverted green triangles, who, as block leaders, employed unrestrained cruelty to control their fellow prisoners.

The Italian prisoners were assigned to bunks arranged in three tiers, three men to a bunk wide enough for one. They spent the first days locked in the barracks, learning the ways of the camp, and in interminable roll calls morning and evening. All illusions of being treated as POWs vanished. There would be no letters from home or food packages or any contact with the outside world. Bolzano seemed like a remote paradise.

In the Dachau barracks at night, Enzo could hear the USAAF planes dropping their payloads on Munich, the symbolic stronghold of Nazism. Whenever the air raid sirens sounded, the Germans ordered a complete blackout of Dachau, then shone floodlights on an empty field far from the camp to try to confuse the bombers.

One night the Italians were awakened and issued striped prison uniforms. After a roll call, they were loaded onto cattle cars and taken ten miles to the outskirts of Munich, where they were ordered to repair a railroad station that had been hit by Allied bombs. Enzo and the other Italian Jews had to march through the center of the city to reach their destination. Some residents of Munich averted their gaze, but others—enraged at the Allied bombing raids that had been laying waste to so many German cities—spat on the prisoners, cursed them, and threatened them with their fists.

In the evening when the Italians returned from Munich, they were taken to the shower room instead of to their barracks. After showering, they were subjected to a superficial medical examination, and the stronger ones, including Enzo, were transferred to one of the numerous slave labor camps that were satellites of Dachau.

21

October 15, 1944
Budapest, Hungary

On October 15, no doubt influenced by the successful coup d'état staged in Romania, Admiral Miklós Horthy, who'd been secretly negotiating a separate peace with the Allies for some time, made a radio address to the Hungarian nation announcing his intention to disengage from his alliance with Nazi Germany:

> Today it is obvious to any sober-minded person that the German Reich has lost the war. All governments responsible for the destiny of their countries must draw pertinent conclusions from this fact, for, as a great German statesman, Bismarck, once said: "No nation ought to sacrifice itself on the altar of an alliance."
>
> Conscious of my historic responsibility, I have the obligation to undertake every step directed to avoiding further unnecessary bloodshed. . . .
>
> I informed a representative of the German Reich that we were about to conclude a military armistice with our previous enemies and to cease all hostilities against them.

Hitler was furious—but he'd been anticipating Horthy's betrayal, and his elite SS reacted swiftly. While Horthy was still addressing the nation, Hitler launched Operation Panzerfaust, sending his favorite commando, SS Obersturmbannführer Otto Skorzeny, to abduct Horthy's son Miklós Horthy Jr., who was in the process of negotiating a surrender to the Soviets. The younger Horthy was caught unaware, beaten, wrapped in a carpet, flown out of Hungary, and taken to Mauthausen concentration camp in Austria for safekeeping. With SS troops and a contingent of Tiger tanks outside his official Castle Hill residence in Budapest, Admiral Horthy was given the choice of saving his son's life or signing papers of abdication and naming as his successor Ferenc Szálasi, the leader of the vehemently anti-Semitic Arrow Cross Party.

But before the admiral could make his decision, the Nazis reneged on their pledge to release Horthy's son and took the admiral himself prisoner, guarded by over a hundred Waffen-SS men, to sit out the war under house arrest in Schloss Hirschberg in Bavaria.

Within hours a new government was formed, this time under the banner of the Arrow Cross. Szálasi was both prime minister and regent, the de facto Hungarian Führer. He was a fanatical anti-Semite and believed in the Nazi plan for the total extermination of the Jews. Under his hordes of thugs in their black uniforms with red armbands that closely resembled that of the SS, a new reign of terror began in Budapest. "Szálasi came into power, and whatever hardship or atrocities the Jews had hitherto endured were nothing compared to the atrocities and bloodbath that ensued," Katherine Senesh later wrote.

Besides being forced to live in the yellow star houses, all Jews were subject to a twenty-two-hour curfew, permitted to be on Budapest's streets only between the hours of 10:00 a.m. and noon. Any Jew caught in public without the requisite yellow Star of David badge visible on his outer clothing was liable to be shot.

The two hundred thousand Jews remaining in Budapest may have escaped the gas chambers of Auschwitz, but now the city fell into the grip of a medieval pogrom. Arrow Cross men took over the streets of Budapest, punching, clubbing, beating, robbing, and killing Jews. Following the government restrictions was not even a guarantee of safety. On October 15, Arrow Cross gunmen opened fire into a yellow star house, and a Jewish man, picked randomly from a street corner, was shot dead. On October 16, forty Jews were shot in the streets; on October 17, more than a hundred. The banks of the Danube River were the preferred killing ground—shooting Jewish civilians next to the Danube was convenient, and the river quickly washed the evidence away. An estimated twenty thousand of Budapest's Jews were executed by the Arrow Cross on the bridges and riverbanks. By the winter of 1944, Arrow Crossers were jokingly referring to the Danube as "the Jewish cemetery."*

*Often, Arrow Cross members would force their Jewish victims to remove their shoes before pushing them into the Danube—footwear was a valuable commodity on the black market. To conserve ammunition, the Arrow Cross men would often pull the shoestrings out of children's shoes, then bind together the hands of two or sometimes three Jews. In 2005, on the Pest side of the river, a memorial called *Shoes on the Danube Bank* was unveiled, consisting of sixty pairs of 1940s shoes cast in iron to commemorate the Jews who were taken to the spot by members of the Arrow Cross and shot.

22

October 20, 1944
Dachau Concentration Camp, Germany

On Sunday, October 20, less than two weeks after they'd been taken to Dachau, Enzo and the rest of the Italian contingent were loaded onto a truck and taken to the subcamp at Mühldorf, fifty-five miles to the east. Because there was a smaller turnover of prisoners at that time, the official records were more thorough.

Name: Samuel Barda
Rank: RAF Captain
Born: Jerusalem, 22 June 1905
Profession: Professor of philosophy
Married, father of three children.
Last known residence: Tel Aviv.

New prisoners were a rarity in Mühldorf, and since they arrived on a Sunday, when the inmates typically didn't work, old-timers crowded about the fence surrounding the roll call area, hoping to hear something of what was going on in the world. The commandant of Mühldorf, SS Oberführer Walter Langleist, and his assistants walked among the new prisoners.

SS Hauptscharführer Georg Schallermair, the master sergeant in charge of roll call, stood out by the brutal standards of SS men at Dachau. Though a small, thin man—five foot six, 145 pounds—ruddy-faced and blond, Schallermair took pleasure in beating prisoners to death with his bare hands; he'd later visit the morgue with a prisoner who was ordered to yank out the gold teeth of the men he'd killed.

The next day, October 21, the Italians were divided into groups. The skilled workers remained in Mühldorf, and the others were taken to a tent camp in the forest—the kapos appointed Enzo as interpreter in Mühldorf, since he was the only Italian who spoke German fluently. Most of the others brought from Italy were assigned to construction work, carrying heavy stacks of cement to the mixer for twelve hours at a stretch, day and night shifts, with a break of half an hour for lunch—that lukewarm, foul-smelling liquid purporting to be soup.

In his role as interpreter, Enzo maintained his sense of pride. One day, a Lithuanian Jew who was assigned to work with the Italians heard a curious German guard ask *il Capitano* what his nationality was. *"Engländer? Italienisch? Was bist du?"*

Enzo turned and answered resolutely, *"Ich bin Jude."* He said the words loudly, not averting his eyes. He knew that he was risking another fist to the jaw. *I'm a Jew.* It was a small gesture, a few words. But in a place like Dachau, it was a bold act of defiance.

Another morning, one of the top-ranking SS men—supposedly from a German Templar family who'd lived in Palestine and could speak Hebrew—stopped and asked, "Who is the Jew who came to drop British bombs on us?" The old-timers, mostly Jews, could not believe their ears.

A small, swarthy, bespectacled man stepped out and declared in German, *"Das bin ich."*

The SS man wanted to know all the details, where he was from, what branch of the British military he served in, his rank. Enzo told him that he'd not dropped bombs on any German cities, that he was a parachutist and a captain in the Royal Air Force.

A few minutes later, when the SS guards left the area, longtime Dachau inmates approached the strange Italian newcomers. David Srulovitz, a man of about thirty who'd been brought to Mühldorf after the Vilna ghetto had been liquidated in September 1943, struck up a conversation with Enzo, first in German and then in Hebrew. Enzo was intrigued. "Where did you learn to speak Hebrew?"

"I attended a Talmud Torah in Vilna."

Enzo told him that he'd been born in Rome but had gone as a *chalutz* to Eretz Israel back in 1926, living on a kibbutz he'd helped to found: Givat Brenner.

"And how did you end up here?" the Lithuanian asked. "Why are you in this hell?"

Enzo explained that he was a parachutist who'd been captured during a rescue operation, a Royal Air Force mission from southern Italy.

Srulovitz stared, uncomprehending.

Enzo repeated, *"Ani tzankhan."**

"What?" Srulovitz was stumped. *Tzankhan.* The word meant nothing to him.

In the stinking hell of the Nazi slave labor camp, Enzo reverted to what he knew how to do best: He became, once again, a teacher.

"Tzankhan," he repeated, explaining that the plural form was *tzankhanim.* Srulovitz marveled at the word, arching one eyebrow. Enzo smiled: The young slave laborer was a classic Litvak—probing, curious, skeptical.

"Okay, *tzankhan,*" Srulovitz asked, "what root is it derived from?"

Enzo paused to think about it. The creators of Modern Hebrew had taken an ancient biblical verb—*litznoach,* meaning "to drop"—and given it a contemporary twist. With each of Enzo's explanations, Srulovitz grew more animated. He wanted to hear all about life in the Yishuv—the kibbutzim and moshavim, the cosmopolitan Hebrew-speaking metropolis called Tel Aviv. He was so excited that he switched to his mother tongue, Yiddish: What did they know in Palestine? How much had they heard? "In Tel Aviv and Haifa, do they know what's being done to us here? Do they know the catastrophe that's befallen the Jews of Europe?"

Enzo was silent for a moment, realizing that no answer he could give would be satisfactory. "Yes," he said, "we know everything."

Srulovitz ran back to his friends—the survivors, the toughest longtime

*"I'm a parachutist."

slave laborers of Dachau—to tell them of the miracle of this *shaliach,* this emissary, an Italian professor no less, a small, aristocratic-seeming volunteer from British Palestine and captain in the RAF who'd drifted down to Earth under a massive halo of silk.

There were many Zionists among the Jewish prisoners; most of them were, like Srulovitz, from Lithuania, Latvia, and White Russia. The news struck them as unreal—*surreal*—like a tale conjured up by a writer of fantastical fiction.

"The arrival in Dachau of this parachutist, this professor from Palestine," Ruth Bondy wrote, "was as if an angel had floated down from a long-forgotten world."

23

October 20, 1944
Conti Street Prison, Budapest

In late September—on Yom Kippur—Katherine Senesh was now living in one of the yellow star houses on Alkotmány Street with her sister. She desperately wanted to visit Hannah, who was still in the Conti Street prison.

Katherine went to the family home at Number 28 Bimbó út, the home in which it was now illegal for her, as a Jewess, to live, and found that her good friend and tenant, Margit Dajka, had a surprise for her. "When I went to visit my home, Margit gave me an envelope that, she said, had been brought to her dressing room in the theatre the previous evening by two young men," she wrote. "There was a considerable sum of money in it, and Margit said the men had asked her to see that Hannah lacked for *nothing* in prison." Someone named Gary had sent the money, Margit said, along with warmest regards to Hannah. "Of course, at the time I had no idea who the mysterious Gary was, but later I discovered he was Reuven Dafni, her parachutist comrade who had been with her in Yugoslavia among the Partisans."

A non-Jewish lawyer friend of the family, Dr. Nánay, promised that he would arrange a visitor's pass for Katherine—but only if she agreed to remove the yellow star from her coat. He accompanied Katherine to the Conti Street prison, where she was allowed a ten-minute visit with Hannah. When Hannah appeared in the tiny room—flanked by two guards—Katherine was surprised at how good, how healthy she looked. "Naturally, our conversation was circumscribed, but at least we could embrace, and she opened the package I brought."

In that fifth year of war, there were food shortages and rationing, but when friends heard that Katherine was now able to visit Hannah, they rushed over with articles of clothing, cakes, pastries, and whatever other odds and ends might be helpful.

In addition to her passion for writing and photography, as a girl Hannah had always loved to sew. Katherine had found the small sewing kit Hannah had received as a child and included it in the parcel. "As an experienced ex-prisoner," Katherine wrote, "I knew the importance of such a thing. Everything delighted her," but the small black sewing kit "pleased her above all. It brought tears to her eyes."

"Does this thing still exist?" Hannah said. "Was there ever such a time—a time of childhood and carefree happiness?"

Katherine asked her daughter what she most needed while behind bars on Conti Street.

"Books—*good* books," Hannah said, "as many as you can send. Reading is allowed here, Mum. You won't get the books back because they're confiscated and put in the prison library. Books, books, books." Then she added, "But more than anything else, I'd like a Bible. A Hebrew Bible."

Overhearing that, one of the guards interrupted, "Wait, how is it that your daughter is Jewish and you're a Gentile?"

"I'm Jewish, too," Katherine said.

"Then where's your yellow star?"

"I'm now exempt from wearing the yellow star in view of the literary activities of my late husband."

A recent government regulation granted exemption from wearing the ignominious yellow star to Jews responsible for "important cultural achievements" and those "who merited special consideration for enhancing Hungary's prestige in the world." In view of her late husband's literary achievements, Katherine had been recommended for such an exemption. The application had received the endorsement of various theaters as well as of *Pesti Hírlap*, the newspaper for which Béla Szenes had written his humor column. Due to the snail pace of bureaucracy, she'd not received the necessary paperwork yet.

One of the other guards smiled. "But of course! I remember Mr. Szenes—in fact, I knew him well. I was a waiter in the café he often went to."

Knowing that her visiting time was limited, Hannah changed the subject. Now that it was October and temperatures at night were dropping, she said, "If possible, Mum, I'd like some warmer clothes—it's cold in the cell."

Katherine promised to return with sweaters and a coat.

"Mum," Hannah said, "I'm going to be tried soon."

"On what charges?"

"Espionage and treason."

"But you said you've done nothing to harm Hungary—"

"I've done nothing to harm the Hungarian nation, Mum. I assure you of that. But, still, the charges are serious. I'll need a lawyer—a good lawyer—to defend me. Decide on someone as soon as possible."

Even before she began searching for a defense attorney, Katherine scoured Budapest for a Hebrew Bible. In the prewar years, it would have been an easy task to find one—Budapest's population, after all, was roughly one-third Jewish. But in recent months, all bookshops dealing in Jewish literature had been shuttered. "I even called at the home of the former proprietor of the largest shop of this kind in Budapest, but he had fled the country," Katherine later wrote. "In the well-known shop dealing in religious books in Deák Square," her request was met with surprise; they had copies of the Old and New Testaments in numerous languages—Hungarian, German, French, Italian, but certainly not in Hebrew. "To my everlasting sorrow," Katherine wrote, "I was unable to fulfill Hannah's last wish."

24

October 23, 1944
Banská Bystrica, Slovakia

The Germans had been surprised by the military strength of the Slovak Resistance, not expecting the Allied materiel support or the strategic assistance provided by the OSS and British Intelligence. Initially, under the command of Waffen-SS General Gottlob Christian Berger, the German response had been ineffectual. When Berger hadn't crushed the uprising by mid-September, Himmler had replaced him with SS General Hermann Höfle, a World War I veteran and Alter Kämpfer (Old Fighter, meaning one of the earliest members of the Nazi Party).

By mid-October, the Germans had mustered forty-eight thousand experienced, well-armed soldiers—eight German divisions, including four Waffen-SS and one pro-Nazi Slovak division.

By late October, Banská Bystrica, the center of the uprising, was on the verge of being overrun. The rumbling of Nazi artillery could be heard on the outskirts of the city. There was an unmistakable thunder to the dreaded German 88s.*

The Zionist youth leadership called an emergency meeting at a house

*The German 88mm anti-aircraft artillery gun was also used as an anti-tank gun. It is considered by many historians to have been the most effective artillery gun of the Second World War.

whose windows had been blacked out due to the threat of nighttime Luftwaffe bombing. In preparation for a quick retreat, Haviva was handling logistics: assigning tasks for the Jews who'd be escaping to the mountains; collecting canned food, warm coats, blankets, and all available medicine.

The most pressing question was: Who would they take with them to the mountains? Haviva was by now highly respected as the leader of the parachutists. Quieting the din of the emergency meeting, she announced her decision. "We'll go up into the mountains and continue fighting as an independent unit—a Jewish unit," she said. "Half will be members of the [Zionist] youth movements and the other half some of our older comrades. Even if they're not fighters, we can't abandon them."

Zvi Ben-Yaakov, the youngest of the parachutists but an experienced Palmach commander, seconded the strategy. The only possible option, he opined, was relocating in the peaks of the Carpathian Mountains. If they could link up with some non-Jewish partisan units there, they could continue their guerrilla warfare against the Nazis.

At first Haviva's intention to include the "older"* Jewish activists was met with vocal opposition by the members of the two Zionist youth movements—Hashomer Hatzair and Maccabi Hatzair. "We wanted to establish our own partisan unit made up only of young people," Hansi Weiss, a local Zionist leader, remembered. "But the parachutists wanted to have older people join us, people who we knew could not offer any help."

Taking the floor, another local Zionist organizer, Putso Goldstein, argued loudly against Haviva. "In those mountains, only healthy young people can survive. It's better to take men than women. The elderly, the sick, small children—no, taking them with us is out of the question."

Haviva rose again and spoke in a fiery voice, looking first at Egon Roth, the unquestioned leader of Hashomer Hatzair in Slovakia. Roth was in his early twenties, curly haired, brooding and bookish in his thick, circular glasses, and an experienced fighter—a member of the 6th Working Battalion of the Slovak Army and the First Czechoslovak Army. Though young, he'd fallen gravely ill and spent almost the entire past year in various hospitals. "Would any of you

*"Older" in this context referred to civilians and Zionist activists who were in their forties and fifties.

think of leaving Egon behind just because he's sick and weak?" she asked. No one had a rebuttal.

"Better to take men than women, Putso?" she said, her voice searing with sarcasm. "I'm not a man—but I'm ready to compete with any of you in marching, shooting, even in judo. Are you *men*? Who are you to underestimate us—who are you to underestimate a woman's ability? All the years in the Movement, you advocated for women's equality and now, when the test comes—what? You *forgot* it all? Were the years in the Movement simply child's games to you? You've suddenly grown tired of fighting for justice and honor?

"None of us was drafted," she continued. "We all volunteered. This was our choice. We chose to come here—we chose to come back to Europe. We could have remained on the kibbutzim. We could have built our homes, raised our children, worked in the fishponds or the orchards harvesting grapes. But we came here to do our bit—to make our contribution, on behalf of the Yishuv, for all our Jewish brothers and sisters.

"Even today, those of us in British uniform can still evacuate—we could still fly out to safety in the Soviet Union or Italy and avoid whatever catastrophe may lie ahead. But we choose to tie our fate to yours.

"And no—we're not doing this as some 'noble' act. We're simply obeying our consciences. Consciences that tell us that in the darkest hours you don't abandon your fellow brothers and sisters, that all Israel is responsible for one another."

Haviva's argument carried the day. As they escaped from Banská Bystrica, they took as many Jewish refugees along as possible—women, middle-aged civilians, and the sick. It was a tough thirty-mile march west, but Haviva could envision them building an independent Jewish partisan stronghold in the Carpathian Mountains, established near the village of Bukovec.

In the hours before their retreat, Haviva Reik and Zvi Ben-Yaakov had been the only ones awake; neither had slept all night. With the rapid German advance, the parachutists decided to burn all identification cards, papers, letters, and books—anything that could betray them as Jewish. Zvi was busily burning documents and letters in Hebrew by tossing them into the potbellied iron stove. He reached for the thick book *Women Members of the Kibbutz*. He knew how precious it was to Haviva but demanded that she get rid of it.

"Never," she said.

"It's in Hebrew," Zvi said. "It weighs at least a kilo!"

She refused again. She loved the book, had drawn strength from it when she read passages written by women who had gone through experiences similar to hers in the Movement, draining mosquito-plagued swamps, building the kibbutzim, training in self-defense.

Zvi accused her of being sentimental. Their argument was loud and passionate—they had briefly been lovers in Cairo—but Haviva would not back down. She carried her copy of *Women Members of the Kibbutz* with her until the bitter end.

Before their departure the next morning, Haviva wrote a final letter—unsent and discovered only after the war—reflecting on the impact the parachutists had had on the beleaguered Jews of Slovakia. "It's a shame we couldn't arrive a little earlier. But we have brought some light and hope into their gray lives," she wrote. "Every day we're alive is a gift from the heavens."

25

October 28, 1944
Budapest, Hungary

In the final days of October 1944, the Red Army launched its Budapest offensive. More than a million Soviet and Romanian troops split into two operating groups, encircling the city and isolating it from the German and Hungarian forces. The resulting Siege of Budapest, which lasted fifty days, would see some of the most brutal urban combat of the Second World War.

One late-October night after 2:00 a.m., the alarms in the Gestapo prison went off, and a great commotion spread through the prison. There'd been an escape. Matilda Glattstein, the Slovakian Jew who'd been Hannah's cellmate in July, now seven months pregnant, had evidently followed Hannah's escape instructions precisely.

On her way to her daily interrogation on Schwab Hill, she'd intentionally tumbled down a half flight of stairs, sprained her ankle, and been taken to the infirmary on the third floor. Since she seemed immobile—hobbling on a crutch, her left ankle heavily bandaged—she hadn't been watched twenty-four hours a day. Feigning sleep, she had waited until the night nurse left her unattended, then tied several bedsheets together, knotting them tightly, and secured one end to the base of the radiator.

Just as Hannah had said, the infirmary windows in the prison were neither locked nor covered by iron bars. She had pried the window open and in spite of her pregnancy and injured ankle managed to scale down the bedsheets to the street. Her greatest fear wasn't being recaptured; it was falling and losing her unborn child. But luck was with her. She landed safely on the pavement. The street was nearly deserted at that late hour: no policemen or soldiers, no gangs of Arrow Cross men roaming about. And before anyone in the prison infirmary noticed that she was missing, she escaped into the frigid night.

Just before the capital came under furious siege, Hannah received her trial date. Though she wasn't given the formal legal paperwork, she understood that she was charged with being a British spy. Since Jews were forbidden to own telephones, Katherine called Hannah's lawyer, Dr. Andor Szelecsényi, from the home of some non-Jewish friends, desperately anxious to understand how things stood now that Prime Minister Szálasi's Arrow Cross Party had seized power.

Dr. Szelecsényi told her that, yes, the political situation was volatile, but based on existing law, if Hannah were convicted of espionage and treason, she could potentially get a ten-year, twenty-year, or even life sentence. But with the USAAF bombing Budapest daily, with the Red Army on the verge of entering the city, he assured her, the military reality trumped the political one. "Whatever the sentence," he said, "it will be essentially meaningless."

"What do you mean, Doctor?"

"Even if your daughter is convicted," he said, "the sentence will be quashed when Budapest is liberated."

On the morning of October 28, Katherine arrived early at the massive courthouse and military prison at 85 Margit Körút and made her way through the noisy mob milling about. Dr. Szelecsényi had urged her to be there promptly; there was a chance she might be able to speak to Hannah during a recess. Unable to enter the courtroom itself—no spectators were allowed—she took a seat in the antechamber. When she glanced up, she saw a sign: ANNA SZENES AND ACCOMPLICES.

With Soviet artillery rumbling in the distance, the trial of Hannah and her two codefendants began. Sándor Fleischmann, a Hungarian citizen, was charged with giving aid to an enemy agent: Anna Szenes. Jacques Antoine Tissandier was accused of being an accomplice to espionage. Hannah, however, faced the most serious charges: treason against the motherland and spying for the enemy during wartime. The case was presided over by three Hungarian military judges. The judicial military advocate was thirty-two-year-old Captain Gyula Simon.*

"Anna Szenes," the president of the tribunal said, "do you plead guilty or not guilty?"

"I plead not guilty. May I have permission to speak?"

"Permission granted."

"No, I don't admit treason against Hungary," Hannah said. "I came here in the service of my *real* homeland, the Land of Israel. Yes, it's true, I was born in Budapest—"

As she went on, she reflected on her early years, born in the aftermath of the Austro-Hungarian defeat in the First World War and the humiliating terms of the Treaty of Trianon, when the Kingdom of Hungary had lost roughly two-thirds of its territory and a third of its population. "The Hungarians were, in the aftermath of the war, a beaten and suffering people. Through my love for them I learned to understand the beaten and the suffering," she said. "My father was a Hungarian author who left an inheritance to me and to others: He taught us to have faith in the inherent decency of humanity."

To be sure, Hungary was her first homeland, and for a long time she had thought that the spiritual Hungary she'd absorbed from great Hungarian authors was the *true* Hungary. "But as I grew up, the streets of the city taught me that as a Jewish woman, I had no place in this country. One by one, Hungarian politicians voted for race discrimination, for deprivation of human rights, for a kind of cruelty straight out of the Middle Ages."

Then one day she had awakened, as if startled from a dream, and realized that she had no homeland there. As far as she was concerned, her citizenship had been revoked by the anti-Jewish laws of 1938 and 1939. Realizing that as a Jew she'd lost her rights in Hungary, she'd gone away to build a new homeland, a Jewish homeland, a homeland of her own. How could she be guilty of committing treason against a nation of which she was no longer a citizen? "Then the war came. And this regime, which misled the people for an entire

*Though the trial transcript was destroyed during the final days of the war, an account was reconstructed from the eyewitness testimonies of Szelecsényi, Tissandier, Fleischmann, and Simon.

generation, brought upon them the worst catastrophe. Unnecessarily, without justification, it dragged Hungary into the war—on the wrong side. You chose to fight on the side of German conquest, on the side of Nazism, on the side of wickedness—"

Angry shouts rang out in the courtroom. The president of the tribunal repeatedly brought down his gavel. "Let her speak," he said.

"You've paid for that choice," Hannah said, "with the lives of thousands—hundreds of thousands of victims."

She spoke of the Hungarian Second Army at the Don River bend; that denouement to the Battle of Stalingrad was already considered a national trauma. In one year as Hitler's allies on the eastern front, the Second Army, originally 190,000 strong—with 17,000 Jewish forced laborers—was decimated: 100,000 dead, 35,000 wounded, and 60,000 sent away to Soviet POW camps. Fewer than 40,000 soldiers of the Second Army had returned to Hungary.

"You joined forces with our enemies—the Germans," she said. "Therefore, you became my enemy. Even *that* was not enough for me to come and fight against you. You also raised your hand against my people—against the Jewish people. And so I returned to Hungary to help them, the persecuted Jews of this nation."

While working on an agricultural settlement in Mandatory Palestine, she testified, she'd enlisted in the Royal Air Force and undergone training in order to parachute into Yugoslavia. From there she'd crossed the border—but only on a voluntary rescue mission. Her aim was to assist British airmen and prisoners of war and to help Hungarian Jews escape into the territory liberated from fascist rule. She'd been trained as a British radio operator in Cairo, but the wireless set had been used only to communicate with her fellow volunteers from British Palestine traveling among the Partisans across the border.

As an active service member in the British armed forces, aircraftwoman second class of the Women's Auxiliary Air Force—equivalent to the rank of honvéd in the Royal Hungarian Air Force—she insisted that she be treated as a prisoner of war and afforded all the protections granted POWs under the Geneva Conventions. "I stand before you as a captured British servicewoman. I'm not guilty of espionage or treason. I'm no traitor to Hungary. The traitors are those among you who brought this calamity upon the Jewish people and upon Hungary itself. Justices, I implore you now—don't add to your crimes. You surely realize that your own day of reckoning is soon coming. Save my people—save the Jews of Hungary—in the short time it remains in your power to do so."

At 11:00 a.m., while the judges retired to deliberate, Katherine was waiting in the empty anteroom. Hannah came out first, followed by her attorney. For a moment, mother and daughter hugged, but they were quickly separated by a courthouse guard, who told them that talking was not allowed until the sentence was passed. Katherine couldn't help but be surprised by Hannah's expression of calm self-confidence. The adrenaline of her defiant courtroom speech was clearly still pumping through her veins. Her cheeks were flushed, and her eyes beamed.

She and her codefendants were called back into the courtroom but returned to the antechamber after only a few minutes. Hannah told her mother that the judges had been unable to reach a decision. "Judgment has been postponed for eight days," Hannah said. "Meaning, next Saturday. November fourth."

The judges, of course, were displeased by Hannah's defiant demeanor, particularly her closing statement about their own culpability in war crimes against the Jews. But the almost daily American air raids and the pounding of the Soviet artillery audible in the city's suburbs had rattled their nerves, no doubt accounting for the weeklong postponement. Was that brazen young Jewish girl right about the nearness of the hour of retribution?

Katherine took the delay as an ominous sign, but Szelecsényi said that it likely had no significance. Such postponements were rare but not unheard of.

"Dr. Szelecsényi has been brilliant, Mother. Please thank him."

Szelecsényi politely excused himself—he had another client to defend—but urged mother and daughter to take advantage of the few minutes they had to talk. Katherine's face couldn't hide her anxiety.

"What difference is a week's delay?" Hannah said. "I'm going to be a prisoner until the war ends—or at least until Budapest is liberated." She studied the yellow star sewn to Katherine's coat. "Mum, how can you be walking around the streets so freely and so frequently under these conditions?" She glanced at the guard nearby and whispered, "Why don't you just disappear? What about all your Gentile friends? Can't they hide you?"

"How can I hide? My only concern is that your case ends well."

"I'll muddle through this somehow, believe me," Hannah said, then gave Katherine another worried look. "But I won't have a moment's peace as long as you're being so reckless."

Accompanying Hannah to and from the jailhouse was the sympathetic young guard who'd once been a waiter at her father's favorite café. He warned them that their time was up but added that now that the trial was over or at least postponed, there was nothing to prevent Katherine from visiting Hannah in the Conti Street prison. She could obtain a visitor's pass without any trouble at the prison office. Katherine thanked him and promised to arrange a visit for the morning of Monday, October 30.

They exited the courthouse. The guard trusted Hannah enough to leave her alone as he dashed ahead, looking up and down the street for the prison transport car. "I'd much rather go by tram," she said, smiling playfully at her mother. "Like in the old days—just to get a glimpse of life again in these city streets."

The guard returned and took Hannah away. Katherine found herself shivering—with both cold and fear—as she watched her daughter slowly disappear into the crowd.

26

October 29, 1944
Bukovec, Slovakia

Near Bukovec in the Carpathian Mountains, Haviva, Rafi, Zvi, and Chaim led the Slovak Resistance team in constructing a makeshift encampment. Their main shelter was a large shack made of logs and covered with a canvas roof. They could withstand the elements there for months if needed.

Their assumption was that in the rocky, forested mountains, at an elevation of more than 3,000 feet, they would encounter only refugees and friendly partisans. The thrust of any Nazi counteroffensive would come in the valleys and smaller hills, where the Wehrmacht Panzers and heavy artillery would be able to advance.

Zvi Ben-Yaakov set a schedule for round-the-clock guard duty. All through the night the embers glowed in the center of the encampment, and from time to time the guards would feed the fire with branches so it would not go out. Once they were settled in, a feeling of accomplishment hung over the camp. The parachutists had successfully extracted the Jewish leaders, both young and old, from the hands of the Nazis and the Slovak fascists.

In the late evening of October 29, a heavy mist blanketed the forest. The flames from the bonfire cast a yellow-orange halo on the fog, and the members of the unit, wrapped up in coats and blankets, sat on logs around the bonfire. Someone began to hum a familiar melody. Members of the Slovakian Zionist youth movements, like members of the Palmach, knew all about the campfire culture of the *chalutzim*, and they began singing along. The parachutists sang

Palmach songs, including one that Zvi Ben-Yaakov had taken from a Slovakian folk tune and translated into Hebrew. It had become a favorite campfire song among the Palmachniks, who knew nothing of its Slovakian origin.

Then the parachutists began to regale the young Zionists with stories of life in Eretz Israel. Haviva got up and talked about the passion of the *chalutzim*, the pioneering spirit, building the kibbutzim and reclaiming the barren earth, the intoxicating scent of ripe fruit in the citrus groves, the breathtaking landscapes of the Sea of Galilee and the Negev desert.

They talked about Yitzhak Sadeh and the formation of the Palmach, their parachute training at Ramat David, and their British training in Cairo. They explained that other Jewish parachutists had been sent on infiltration operations in Hungary, Romania, and Yugoslavia. "They said there was some official British assignment," one young Slovak Zionist later wrote, "but they had come primarily to rescue Jews."

That night, several guards were posted, but most of the group fell into a deep sleep. It was a single but fatal mistake. Under orders from battle-hardened German officers, Ukrainian volunteer units of the 14th Waffen-SS Grenadier Division brilliantly used the element of surprise, attacking from a much higher position on a steep slope, the one section of the camp perimeter that the Jewish partisans had left undefended. At seven o'clock it attacked, using machine guns and grenades. The attack was so sudden and the fog so heavy that the rebels were entirely unprepared.

Sanyo Wollner, Haviva's childhood friend, the artist who'd designed the striking poster Haviva had seen upon arriving in Banská Bystrica, was decapitated by a German grenade. Egon Roth, leaping outside the shack, was instantly killed by machine-gun fire. Soon bodies littered the encampment. Two of the young Zionists swallowed cyanide rather than be taken alive.

During the fighting, Rafi Reiss was hit in his shoulder by a bullet. One of the civilian women managed to remove the bullet with a pocketknife and dress the wound with Rafi's silk scarf, on which there was secretly printed one of MI9's maps.

A unit of the Slovak rebel army, they knew, had a headquarters on Mount Ďumbier, so they headed in that direction. Haviva had escaped the ambush unscathed. She now took the lead. She knew Mount Ďumbier well; for her, it wasn't just a name on the map but a popular resort area where she'd hiked and skied in her youth.

She and Rafi led a group of eight up the slope toward Mount Ďumbier. The group was made up of mostly older civilians, and their climbing was slow. Haviva and Rafi were separated from Zvi Ben-Yaakov and Chaim Hermesh and couldn't signal them, but they assumed that they would head in the same direction.

That had been the plan. "We were a group of six," Ben-Yaakov later wrote. "We quickly took all we could and climbed higher into the mountains. The fog was very thick; we could not see more than fifteen or twenty meters in front of us. We wanted to go eastward along the mountain range of the Low Tatras, and there join the Partisans or what remained of the Slovak army. In the afternoon we heard voices from afar. When we moved closer we realized they were speaking Russian. We went over to them, but that proved a horrible mistake."

The Russian-speaking troops, as it turned out, were Ukrainian volunteers serving in the Waffen-SS. Almost immediately, Ben-Yaakov was disarmed of his Soviet submachine gun and two handguns. "They took us to a place where they were temporarily concentrating all the prisoners, and there I saw, to my great distress, that Rafi and Haviva had been captured as well."

The details of Haviva and Rafi's capture remain unknown. Were they ambushed? Or did they, like Zvi Ben-Yaakov's group, feeling relieved to hear Russian being spoken, walk right into the hands of the Ukrainian Waffen-SS men?

The Waffen-SS unit surrounded them; any exchange of gunfire would have been suicidal. The parachutists knew that the Slovakian Jews with them had excellent forged papers; their false Gentile identities would give them a good chance of survival. Many of the older people managed to convince their captors that they were simply Slovakians who had been wandering in the mountains that morning.

That was obviously not a plausible argument for the three parachutists in British uniform. They spoke to their SS captors only in English, expecting to be treated as prisoners of war and not as Slovakians, who might be regarded as spies.

The descent from the mountain took hours, during which the parachutists whispered to the civilians to say that they had no connection to anyone in a British uniform.

The warm sun pierced the canopy of pine trees and oaks, and as they moved into the valley, Haviva began to see red roofs and church steeples in the villages along the Hron River. By the early afternoon, they reached Brezno, a small town in central Slovakia, where the Gestapo had set up its headquarters.

Among the four parachutists, only Chaim Hermesh had managed to escape, hiding in a ditch along with Putso Goldstein. He then traveled eastward until he managed to join up with a Soviet partisan unit.

The Gestapo interrogated the parachutists, but they refused to speak until a German military doctor saw Rafi Reiss and examined his shoulder wound, which was bleeding heavily. That was another fatal error. When the doctor removed the silk bandage from Rafi's wound and saw that the makeshift bandage was silk, imprinted with a military map of Slovakia, he called for other SS men, who began to interrogate Rafi during treatment.

Rafi, who had studied medicine for several years at the University of Bratislava before emigrating to Palestine, was furious at the doctor—not just for allowing the interrogation but for facilitating it before providing him with medical treatment.

The parachutists were interrogated first separately and then all together. The Gestapo began by asking them political questions and then moved on to the Slovak National Uprising: Where had they really come from? Whom had they met with? Whom had they communicated with while in Slovakia?

Only six months earlier, Haviva, Zvi, and Rafi had listened intently to the lecture given by David Shaltiel at their training course about the Gestapo's methods of interrogation. They had tried to conduct themselves as he'd advised. All of them said that they were British officers. Following the rules of the Geneva Convention, they gave only the required information. Over and over, Haviva repeated, "Ada Robinson. Sergeant. Women's Auxiliary Air Force. Serial number 2992503."

It wasn't long before the interrogators discovered that Rafi Reiss, who identified himself as RAF Sergeant Raphael Stevenson, was Jewish—it's possible that the doctor who examined him noticed that he was circumcised. When confronted, Rafi didn't deny being Jewish. He likely believed that his status as an RAF officer would protect him regardless of his faith.

Haviva also admitted that she was Jewish, for reasons that remain unknown. Her cover name, Ada Robinson, certainly didn't give away any religion. Perhaps it was pride, a desire to show her captors that a female Jewish soldier was contributing to the Allied struggle against Nazi tyranny. In any case, from the moment the Gestapo interrogators found out that the parachutists were Jews, the torture commenced.

Zvi Ben-Yaakov, who was being interrogated separately, saw the brutality with which Haviva and Rafi were treated and made the decision to say that he was not Jewish—his British identity was RAF Second Lieutenant Michael Jamay, and he pretended to speak no language other than English. As a result, "their behavior toward me was entirely different," he wrote in his final letter to his wife. "They did not differentiate between Rafi and Haviva and the Jewish civilians they'd captured. Their treatment of them was horrendous. There are no words for their brutality. They are beasts without emotions."

27

October 30–November 1, 1944
Budapest, Hungary

As the Red Army launched its Budapest offensive, by October 30 and 31, the daytime bombing of the capital by the USAAF was so intense that Katherine couldn't leave the house. She finally managed to take the tram to the Conti Street prison on the first of November. The guard at the gate gestured for her to turn around. "No visiting today," he shouted. "It's All Saints' Day."

When she returned the following morning, the office was open, but she was told that only the military prosecutor, Captain Gyula Simon, could grant permission for visits. His office was in Hadik Barracks. Katherine needed no reminder of how to get to the place. It was where the brute Tamás Rózsa had confronted her with her barely recognizable daughter on the dreadful morning of June 17—so long ago that it seemed like another life.

Hadik Barracks was on Miklós Horthy Street, on the other side of the Danube, and the two-hour window during which Jews were permitted in public was nearly up. The next morning, Katherine took the tram to Hadik Barracks, only to be told by a young military adjutant that Captain Simon had left for business in the country and wouldn't return until the following Tuesday, November 7.

"Isn't there anyone else—a deputy—who might help me?"

"No, only Captain Simon has the authority to grant you a visiting permit."

Meanwhile, Katherine was growing more anxious about the verdict. On

November 5, the eight-day postponement would be up. She contacted Dr. Szelecsényi. The attorney sent her a letter by messenger, reassuring her that there'd been another postponement because the military court had a new chief judge, who needed to study the transcripts. He promised to inform her as soon as he heard any news.

28

November 6, 1944
Mühldorf Concentration Camp

In the first week of November, three Italian slave laborers escaped from the Mühldorf camp, and, as was typical, the Germans imposed a collective penalty on the entire block. Enzo and the other workers were forced to stand outdoors in the cold, without so much as a twitch. In whispers, Enzo passed word between the ranks, encouraging all the men to hold fast and not to give in.

Within forty-eight hours, the three escapees were recaptured and brought back to Mühldorf. Their eyes were blackened, their faces swollen, their bodies broken by torture. They were paraded before their fellow Italians, almost unrecognizable from the beatings. Around their necks hung hand-lettered signs in German:

THREE CHEERS!
WE HAVE RETURNED!

The would-be escapees were stripped, held down by other prisoners over the flogging bench, and forced to count aloud as they were whipped by one of the kapos. At Dachau and its subcamps, the preferred method of execution was pole hanging—an agonizingly slow form of strangulation—as opposed to the instantaneous, neck-snapping death of long-drop hanging.

The other prisoners stood in ranks, forced to silently watch the escapees writhing in the throes of a slow death.

. . .

By now, Enzo had become the spokesman for all the Italians at Mühldorf, serving as interpreter, interlocutor, and newscaster, quick to spread whatever reliable information he learned about what was happening in the world.

After the execution, morale plummeted. The prisoners were cut off from all external contacts and exhausted from carrying the sacks of cement for the underground Messerschmidt factory. The only light, it seemed, was Enzo. As interpreter he had a bit more freedom than the other prisoners; being fluent in German enabled him to overhear conversations among the guards and spread news about Allied advances. "Captain Barda acted as intermediary between us and the Germans," wrote one of the surviving prisoners in his memoirs, "and in this capacity he revealed not only his moral stature but also his tact and intelligence. He helped us in uncounted ways and whenever the tempo of the work allowed it, he would manage to keep us away from the attention of the Germans."

The worst days were when there was a breakdown in the factory—some malfunction in the aircraft production machinery. The kapos would force the prisoners, like Sisyphus in Hades, to unload heavy sacks of cement from the arriving trucks, stagger forward ten or twenty meters, then turn around and reload them onto the trucks while an SS man shouted, *"Schneller! Schneller!"**

*German for "Faster! Faster!"

29

November 6, 1944
Cairo, Egypt

Four months after the meeting with Joel Brand about Eichmann's "Blood for Goods" proposal, Lord Walter Moyne was targeted by the right-wing Zionist militant group Lehi—an acronym of Lohamei Herut Israel (Fighters for the Freedom of Israel)—which the British government derisively referred to as "the Stern Gang." After lengthy detainment in British prisons, Brand became a member of Lehi in early October 1944.

Lehi's leaders had never forgotten Moyne's question "Mr. Brand, where would I possibly put these million Jews?" Brand later testified as a witness against Eichmann in 1961 and repeated under oath his conversation with Moyne. In his autobiography, however, he hedged, maintaining that he'd met a very high-ranking British statesman, but he wrote, "I afterwards heard that the man with whom I spoke was not, in fact, Lord Moyne. Unfortunately, I have no means of verifying this."

In early November 1944, no verification was needed. Moyne embodied the cynicism and indifference of Great Britain's wartime leaders toward the millions of Jews being murdered by the Nazis. Unlike his close friend Winston Churchill, who'd often expressed support for Zionism, Moyne was outspoken against the creation of a Jewish state. In 1942, at the height of the Holocaust, he'd told the House of Lords that when the war ended, the millions of "homeless and stateless Jews" who survived being "uprooted" should not be allowed to enter Mandatory Palestine; instead, he urged, they should be resettled "in Germany, or Poland, or in sparsely populated regions such as Madagascar."

At 1:00 p.m. on November 6, 1944, two young Lehi gunmen, Eliyahu Bet-Zuri and Eliyahu Hakim, were waiting for Lord Moyne in the garden of his home in Cairo. The operation had been ordered by Lehi's top commanders, including Yitzhak Shamir, a future prime minister of Israel. The assassins, ages seventeen and twenty-one, had carefully planned and rehearsed the operation.

When Moyne went home in his limousine for lunch, arriving there at approximately 1:15 p.m., Hakim and Bet-Zuri were spotted by Moyne's driver, Lance Corporal Arthur Fuller. They opened fire with semiautomatic pistols. Fuller was hit in the chest and killed. Moyne was hit by three bullets, in his neck, chest, and abdomen. Critically wounded, he was rushed to the hospital and received multiple blood transfusions but died that evening.

The assassination made front-page news worldwide. Ben-Gurion's Jewish Agency denounced the murder in the strongest terms. It had long advocated cooperation with the British until Nazism was defeated, making the rogue actions of the Stern Gang appear catastrophic for the dreams of an independent Jewish state.

The left-wing daily *Haaretz* wrote that the two assassins "have done more by this single reprehensible crime to demolish the edifice erected by three generations of Jewish pioneers than is imaginable."

Churchill was both grief stricken and furious. On November 17, he told the House of Commons, "If our dreams for Zionism are to end in the smoke of assassins' pistols and our labours for its future to produce only a new set of gangsters worthy of Nazi Germany, many like myself will have to reconsider the position we have maintained so consistently and so long in the past. If there is to be any hope of a peaceful and successful future for Zionism, these wicked activities must cease, and those responsible for them must be destroyed root and branch."

The murder of Lord Moyne would have enormous repercussions for Anglo-Jewish relations, and Great Britain's Middle East policy for years to come.*

*After a long, well-publicized trial, Bet-Zuri and Hakim were convicted of murder and hanged in Cairo. Both stood on the gallows defiantly singing "Hatikvah."

30

November 7, 1944
Budapest, Hungary

On November 7, 1944, Soviet and Romanian troops entered Budapest's eastern suburbs. Once the two pincers of the Soviet offensive joined, the city would be completely encircled, trapping inside nearly thirty-three thousand German and thirty-seven thousand Hungarian soldiers, as well as over eight hundred thousand civilians. Refusing to authorize a withdrawal, Hitler declared Budapest to be a fortress city: Festung Budapest. Just as he'd commanded at Stalingrad, Budapest was to be defended to the last man.

The day was bitterly cold and overcast. Snow was swirling in the streets. Earlier that morning, Hannah had been taken in handcuffs from the military prison on Conti Street to the one in the Margit Körút barracks. The barracks was a massive gray, dismal-looking four-story building. Built to house three hundred prisoners, in November 1944, more than 2,400 men and women were incarcerated there.

Hannah was placed in solitary confinement. She waited in silence until just before 10:00 a.m., when the key turned and Captain Gyula Simon entered her cell. "Anna Szenes, you've been found guilty of treason and sentenced to the supreme penalty."

Hannah stared at him uncomprehendingly. "What do you mean?"

"You heard me. You've been found guilty. You've been sentenced to the supreme penalty. Death by firing squad."

"I want to appeal," Hannah said. "Bring me my lawyer. I want to speak to Dr. Szelecsényi."

"You may not appeal," Simon said. "But, if you wish, you may ask for a pardon."

Hannah didn't flinch. "I was tried before the court of the Commander of the Hungarian Forces, Grade B. I know I am entitled to appeal."

"There is no appeal on a death sentence."

Hannah stared back at Captain Simon defiantly, then at the gray walls of her tiny, freezing cell, Cell 13. She'd overheard some of the longtime inmates calling it "the cell of tears" because it had seen the last hours of so many prisoners awaiting execution. During the last year alone, hundreds of condemned men and women had spent their final moments staring at these same stone walls.

Hannah was certain that she was entitled to an appeal. But what could she do? She had no means of contacting Dr. Szelecsényi or anyone else in the outside world.

"There is no appeal," Simon repeated. "Do you want to ask for a pardon?"

"No," Hannah said. "I won't beg from murderers and hangmen."

"As you wish."

"Captain, I would like to see my mother."

"That won't be possible."

"Let me speak to her."

"There's no time for that. We'll be carrying out the sentence in one hour. You want anything else?"

"Paper and pen."

Simon granted her final request. He left her alone to write two short farewell letters. One was addressed to her comrades Yoel Palgi and Peretz Goldstein, the other to her mother.

Just before 10:00 a.m. Katherine Senesh arrived at the Hadik Barracks, looking for Captain Simon. She found it in chaos. Enlisted men and officers were dashing around, shouting, carrying bags, trunks, typewriters, and bundles of papers, tossing everything into the back of the nearest truck. As soon as one truck was filled, it sped through the gate, heading out of Budapest.

A lone sentry told Katherine that it was pointless for her to go inside. As far as he knew, all the officers had already packed up. Katherine understood. Like rats fleeing a sinking ship, the fascists were racing westward before the Soviets encircled the city. She insisted on at least looking for Captain Simon, and the sentry allowed her to go upstairs.

The halls were nearly deserted, but she found two women in hats and coats frantically packing their things and a young adjutant—the same one who'd told her a week earlier that Captain Simon would be away until November 7. She asked again about obtaining a visitor's pass, and the adjutant told her that Captain Simon had been transferred the previous day to Margit Körút military prison. He gave her an office number there and told her to hurry if she wanted to catch the captain before he left Budapest.

Katherine headed back across the Danube, from Pest to Buda, covering the mile and a half as quickly as she could on foot. Exhausted, she arrived at the prison at half past ten. She raced up one flight of stairs and somehow found the captain's office. It was empty, but she could see a briefcase standing on the desk with a pair of black leather gloves draped over the top. She stood waiting in the corridor until 11:45 a.m., when Captain Simon returned to his office. Katherine followed him inside, introduced herself, and requested a permit to visit her daughter.

"The case no longer has anything to do with me," Captain Simon answered.

"Since when?"

"Since yesterday."

"May I ask who's in charge of the case?"

"I don't know."

"Who's authorized to grant me a visitor's permit?"

"I don't know."

"Should I go to the Conti Street Prison and ask the warden?"

"Sure, you can give that a try."

His cold demeanor and brusque answers released all of Katherine's pent-up frustration. She stood facing him with a stern expression, surprised by her own bravery. "Captain, can you at least have the courtesy to tell me who I need to speak to in order to see my daughter? I can't understand why it's so difficult for me to obtain a simple visitor's pass. I've been granted permission to see my daughter only once—and just for ten minutes."

"Really?" Simon said. "I don't remember allowing that."

"Why hasn't there been a verdict? The eight-day postponement has long passed." When Simon turned away from her, she pressed on. "Captain, *has* there been a verdict?"

"Even if there has," he said, "I'm not authorized to tell you."

"What? How can you legally keep that information from me? I'm the *mother* of the accused." He didn't answer; she asked again, "Has a sentence on my daughter been passed?"

Simon exhaled in annoyance, went behind his desk, then gestured to the empty wooden chair opposite. "Have a seat."

In the long, terrible silence that followed, he focused his glare on Katherine, closely studying her face, looking her up and down. Finally he asked, "Are you a Jew? Or was only your husband a Jew?"

"He was. And I am. Our whole family is Jewish."

"Then why don't I see the yellow star?"

Katherine shifted in her chair, showing him the yellow Star of David stitched to her coat, which she'd been cleverly concealing behind her shoulder bag.

"Are you familiar with your daughter's case?"

"Yes, the lawyer briefed me."

Simon nonetheless gave his prosecutorial summary: "Your daughter claims to have renounced her Hungarian citizenship. She joined the British Armed Forces and trained to be a radio officer and a paratrooper. Last spring she flew from Cairo, via Italy, parachuting into Yugoslavia. She spent a considerable amount of time with the partisans—the Serbian Marxist bandits. Her sole mission—so she claimed—was to rescue Jews and British prisoners of war. No matter. In early June, she made an illegal border crossing into Hungary, bringing with her a British wireless set, and committed very grave crimes against the Kingdom—"

"That's not true," Katherine said. "When we met in the prison yard—briefly in the Gestapo prison—I tried to ask about her mission. She said she couldn't answer me due to military secrecy—but she assured me that she'd done nothing that could *possibly* be considered harmful to Hungary."

"These are not ordinary times," Simon said. "Hungary is under martial law. Your daughter *was* in possession of a British radio transmitter. She admitted as much. The Military Tribunal consequently found her guilty of treason and sentenced her—"

"There *has* been a verdict?"

"—to the supreme penalty."

"Supreme penalty?"

"The sentence has already been carried out."

Katherine's face turned to stone. The entire room went black. Then she remembered Dr. Szelecsényi's letter. Perhaps Simon was merely deriving a kind of sadistic pleasure from torturing her. She finally said, "No, no. That's impossible. This morning, I received a letter from the lawyer stating that the sentence hasn't been passed, that there's been still another postponement, that he'll let me know when the new court date is set. Captain, he's my daughter's defense lawyer. He would certainly have been informed if anything changed."

"Who's the lawyer?" Simon asked.

"Dr. Andor Szelecsényi," Katherine said, fumbling in her handbag. "He represented my daughter in the courtroom at her trial. Look, I brought the letter with me."

Simon took the envelope, glanced quickly at the letter, grabbed a pen, and made a note of Szelecsényi's name and telephone number. "Fine, we'll call him and let him know what's happened."

At that glib remark, Katherine lost all hope. She couldn't speak without stammering. "Is this how things are done? I mean, how—how could this happen? How is it that I—I wasn't allowed to see her, to talk to her?"

"She didn't want to see you." The lie slipped effortlessly from Simon's lips. "She wanted to spare you any further shock." Then he added, as if softening the blow, "She wrote a couple of farewell letters. I believe one was addressed to you. Don't worry, you'll get them."

After another terrible silence, Simon said, "Mrs. Szenes, I must tell you, I was impressed by your daughter's courage and strength of character. She showed great composure until the very last moment. Imagine! She was truly *proud* of being a Jew."

"I don't understand military laws and whether my daughter has broken them, and if she did, whatever the alleged act was—"

"Her crime was very grave."

"—my daughter stands innocent before man and God." Katherine heard her own voice echoing in the office; she couldn't speak of Hannah in the past tense. "My daughter is a gifted, brilliant young woman! She is an exceptional—"

"True, she was an exceptional person," Simon interrupted. "But then, it's always the exceptional people who volunteer for these kinds of assignments. It's a pity she chose the wrong path."

Simon impatiently picked up his black leather gloves, as if to signal the end of the conversation. Katherine didn't move from her seat. "Mrs. Szenes, you'll have to accept what happened," he said. "This war has demanded many sacrifices, claimed many lives. Consider your daughter one of them."

He looked at his wristwatch. "It's after twelve—you're out well past the legal curfew," he said. "The last thing you need is any further trouble. Go straight home. But take this with you—just in case." He picked up his pen again and scribbled a note on military stationery stating that he'd summoned Mrs. Béla Szenes to Margit Körút prison on official business.

As Katherine left his office and walked toward the staircase, she staggered, unseeing, and gripped the banister tight to keep from falling. She suddenly realized, with complete certainty, that Captain Simon had just returned from her daughter's execution.

Katherine's intuition was correct. Less than an hour earlier, Captain Simon had entered Hannah's cell. He had taken her two final handwritten letters, put them into his pocket, and ordered her to follow him.

Eyewitnesses in the prison reported that Hannah had been led out into the courtyard around 11:00 a.m., where she saw the assembled firing squad: three Hungarian soldiers armed with FEG 31M bolt-action rifles. In front of a gray wall at the corner of the small church, a round post stood in sand stained with dried blood.

Hannah's hands were bound behind her back and fastened to the post. She looked straight ahead at the soldiers. Captain Simon approached her with the customary blindfold. She refused—as if daring her executioners to stare directly into her eyes as they shot her.

Captain Simon raised his hand, then barked out the order: "Fire!" The three soldiers squeezed their triggers in unison. They were inept marksmen, unable to strike the heart directly as instructed. Hannah's body slumped to the ground. She was mortally wounded. Death did not come quickly.

31

November 7, 1944
Budapest, Hungary

Dr. Andor Szelecsényi lived in an apartment close to the Margit Körút prison. Moments after Katherine's departure, by sheer coincidence, as he walked past the prison, he saw a black hearse pulling out from the gates. "What's that?" he asked the sentry. "Have there been any executions today?"

"Yes," the sentry replied. "They've just shot the British woman officer."

Dr. Szelecsényi hurried upstairs and found Captain Simon still at his desk. Furious, he accused the military prosecutor of "judicial murder," stating that if his client had been shot, it was an unlawful execution. Where was the final sentence from the military tribunal?

Captain Simon claimed that the tribunal had met in camera and found Hannah guilty of treason. They'd sentenced her to the supreme penalty. He offered no official document to support his claim. In response to Szelecsényi's repeated questions, he described the defendant's final hour. She *had* asked to see her mother, but there had been no time to contact Mrs. Szenes. Jews were, after all, forbidden to own or use telephones.

"And why wasn't I notified?" Szelecsényi asked.

"An oversight, counselor. These are chaotic times."

Szelecsényi concluded that Simon had acted on his own, in gross violation of the law. When the captain mentioned that he'd allowed Hannah to write two farewell letters, the contents of which further proved her guilt, Szelecsényi demanded to see both of them.

"Listen to this," Simon said. He opened a file, unfolded a piece of paper, and began to read aloud from the letter addressed to Hannah's fellow parachutists Yoel Palgi and Peretz Goldstein. "Carry on with our mission," Simon read. "Carry on fighting till the end, until the day of freedom, the day of victory for our people."

Simon refused to give the farewell letters to Szelecsényi, claiming that they were evidentiary documents and thus the property of the state. To this day, neither letter has been found. Captain Simon either destroyed them or took them along when he fled Budapest.

Among the more than 2,400 men and women locked up in Margit Körút prison were Yoel Palgi, Tony Tissandier, and Sándor Fleischmann. On the morning of November 7, they crouched in silence on their folded blankets, leaning against the wall, tightly huddled to preserve the little warmth in their bodies. Suddenly they heard rifle shots coming from the yard.

Another execution? That seemed unlikely. The prisoners by now were well versed in all the details of the execution ceremony: the tramping of the firing squad, the loud reading of the sentence, the Christian prayer, and the bugle call before the fusillade.

One of Palgi's cellmates climbed up to the high window and, looking down, said that he could see a table with a crucifix on it but no sign of an execution. At the same moment they heard voices in the courtyard—an order to rearrange the straw.

Close to noon, another of Palgi's cellmates named Schwartz made an excuse to see the prison doctor. It had been weeks since any of them had managed to leave the cell, and everyone waited anxiously for his return. Thirty minutes later, Schwartz was pale as he slowly removed his hat.

"What happened?" Fleischmann asked.

"The shot we heard was *the* shot," Schwartz said. "They killed Hannah—an hour ago."

"A mistake," Yoel said. It *had* to be a mistake. For a minute he could say nothing else, muttering the words robotically until the volume grew to almost a full-throated shout. "A mistake. *A mistake!*"

Tony pressed his nails into the palm of Yoel's hand. "Calm down. Stop shouting!"

Fleischmann, Hannah's other codefendant, began pounding on the door. The burly Hungarian sergeant took his time unlocking it. "We want to know who was executed an hour ago," he demanded.

"What the hell's that got to do with you?" the sergeant said. "Shut up!"

Before he could turn, Fleischmann changed his demeanor, mimicking the kind of ritualized groveling he'd seen among prisoners who'd been broken under questioning—who'd lost all sense of their former dignity. "Sergeant, sir," he said, his eyes down, "we humbly request, will you please tell us who was executed?"

For the first time the stern guard saw those typically defiant prisoners acting chastened. He saw no harm in answering. "Don't worry," he said. "She wasn't one of yours. Just some young girl. A partisan. An officer. A British parachutist. Who knows? Anyway, they say she was a British spy. But that's surely a lie. Whoever heard of a young girl being a British officer?"

Two days after Hannah's execution, Katherine returned to the Conti Street prison to collect her daughter's few meager belongings. In one of the pockets of her simple dress—evidently unnoticed by the prison staff—Katherine found two small scraps of paper. On one of them was a note, most likely written in the Hadik Barracks in late June, right after Tamás Rózsa had shocked Katherine by confronting her with the sight of her battered daughter:

Dear Mother,

I don't know what to say, just two words:
*A million thanks.**
Forgive me if you can.
You know very well why words are not needed.

With infinite love,
Your daughter

*The two words in the original Hungarian: *Millió köszönet.*

On the other scrap of paper she'd written a poem dated June 20, during the worst days of her torture and solitary confinement. She wrote not in Hebrew but in Hungarian, reverting to her mother tongue in the city of her birth, almost as if closing the circle of life:

One—two—three . . .
eight feet long,
Two strides across, the rest is dark . . .
Life hangs over me like a question mark.

One—two—three . . .
maybe another week,
Or next month may still find me here,
But death, I feel, is very near.

I could have been
twenty-three next July;
I gambled on what mattered most,
The dice were cast. I lost.

20.6.1944

32

November 18, 1944
Dachau Concentration Camp, Germany

On the night of November 18, 1944, two weeks after the three recaptured Italians were taken to Mühldorf for their public execution, an SS man entered the barracks and barked an order: *"Kapitän Barda! Komm her!"*

Enzo knew the drill by now. In the winter months, when you were being taken for interrogation or punishment, it was best to take your most valuable possession: your blanket. The SS man yelled at him, *"Keine Decke."* The meaning of those two words was ominous. No blanket. There was only one possible interpretation. But whatever his fears were, he flashed his usual optimistic smile as he left his fellow prisoners.

The next morning at roll call, it was freezing cold, and the Italian laborers stamped their feet for warmth, looking more demoralized than usual. There was no sign of Enzo. A few hours later, the prison grapevine rang with the news: *Il Capitano è scomparso* (the Captain is dead). Everyone knew that Enzo was never coming back. He had been taken in handcuffs and transferred from Mühldorf back to the main camp at Dachau. The SS clerk in the Dachau office had taken Captain Samuel Barda's index card out of the file and stamped it *Verstorben—18. Nov. 44.**

*Deceased—18 November 1944.

33

November 20, 1944
Brezno, Slovakia

The canvas-covered military trucks left the Gestapo prison on Horna Street and crossed the square named years before after President Tomáš Masaryk, in which the German and Slovakian fascist headquarters were now housed. The convoy continued toward the Hron River. Haviva had only to peer through a gap in the back of the canvas where the armed troops, members of the Hlinka Guard, were sitting to recognize the places they were passing. She knew every stretch of the road along which she had hiked, ridden her bike, and raced on her motorcycle. She saw the church in the village of Kremnička, the house in which Hashomer Hatzair had held its winter meeting before she had left for Palestine; between the trees, some of which were losing their leaves, she could see the white gravestones in the cemetery. The mist began to take on milky shades, but it was still dark outside.

After a short while, around 6:30 a.m., the convoy halted and voices started shouting for the 320 men, women, and children in the trucks to pile out of them. The majority were Jews; the rest were non-Jewish partisans, suspected supporters of the Slovak Uprising, or Romani. Two prisoners were in British uniform: Haviva Reik and Rafi Reiss.

The Hlinka Guards, now joined by SS men, began rushing part of the group along with whips and rifle butts, shouting *"Schnell! Schnell!"* and chasing them in the direction of a deep anti-tank ditch between the edge of the forest and the village houses and fields.

Within minutes the sound of gunfire filled the air. Those who stood shivering, waiting their turn, now began to comprehend what was happening. Panic spread, together with screaming and shoving. Anyone who tried to break for the woods was gunned down. The prisoners were ordered to kneel at the edge of the ditch, facing the corpses—or prisoners who were fatally wounded but still breathing. Villagers later reported having heard many shouts and the piercing screams of children shouting out their last words: "Mama! Mama!"

The most vivid eyewitness testimony comes from Viliam Kratochvíl, a Slovakian soldier who'd escaped from a forced labor camp in Germany and was now hiding in his mother's home in Radvañ, a small town about two and a half miles from Kremnička.

Kratochvíl ran through the woods, following the trucks, and when he reached Kremnička, he hid between the thick trees to observe—to bear witness. "I saw a scene which has haunted me for many years in my dreams, which I will never forget as long as I live," he recalled. "Trucks came to a halt on the road. Members of the Hlinka Guard and Germans dragged people down from the trucks. Children, men, women, and the elderly marched before the hangmen until they reached a gentle slope. The world trembled and everything inside me died. Under a hail of bullets, the people fell as if under a scythe."

The methodical shooting continued until 9:45 a.m. When it was over, the Hlinka Guards covered the bodies with earth and tree branches and left the site before noon. Later analysis upon exhumation determined that some of the victims had not been killed by gunshots; they'd been buried alive and suffocated.

The anti-tank ditch was very long, and part of it was left empty for the next batch of transports. The mass executions continued until February 19, 1945. All told, 747 victims, primarily Jews, were killed in the Kremnička massacre. At Nemecká, seventeen miles to the east, an estimated nine hundred victims were murdered in limestone quarries, though an exact number will never be known since the corpses were burned by the perpetrators. The executions were the largest number of war crimes committed in Slovakia during World War II.

• • •

"Please don't make a national hero out of me," Zvi Ben-Yaakov wrote his wife, Michal, in his final letter, smuggled out of his Gestapo prison cell in Slovakia. "Because this wasn't heroism. Only here did I see how weak we are. No, you can't call it heroism. Anyone would have gone in the same circumstances. And that's how I went: When the hour of need called, I answered. Rafi and Haviva also share my opinion. This is my will."*

Of the Slovakian team, only Ben-Yaakov avoided the grim fate of the mass shooting at the hands of the Einsatzgruppen that took the lives of Haviva Reik and Rafi Reiss. Zvi—always speaking perfect English—was cagey during interrogation; he denied having any connection to Haviva or Rafi and stuck to his story about being a non-Jewish English officer, RAF Second Lieutenant Michael Jamay.

No one knows his exact fate. The evidence suggests that he was transferred to Mauthausen concentration camp and was likely executed in early 1945. There are no traces of his remains.

*More on Zvi Ben-Yaakov's final letter in Appendix II.

34

November 1944–January 1945
Bucharest, Romania, and Cairo, Egypt

In November 1944, the two ships Shaike Dan had helped procure, the *Turos* and the *Saladin*, left the port of Costanţa, Romania, and set sail for Turkey. The *Turos* was overloaded with 958 Jewish refugees, while the *Saladin* carried 547. Both vessels docked and unloaded their passengers safely, and Mossad operatives in Istanbul arranged Turkish exit permits for the Jews, who then traveled by train through Syria and Lebanon into Mandatory Palestine.

Two months later, on January 3, 1945, on the well-worn grass runway of the Pipera airfield near Bucharest, Dan prepared to board the twin-engine RAF Armstrong Whitworth Albemarle on which he was to fly, together with Manu Ben-Ephraim and Baruch Kamin, back to Bari. He paused to take one last look at Bucharest. "Five months ago, we left for a blind drop," he noted as he surveyed the view. "We set out on our mission in June 1944, in British Army uniforms, and in December of that year we are returning, again in the uniforms of His Majesty's army. The missions—to reach the captured pilots and to ignite the flames of *aliya*—were fully accomplished."

The Albemarle disappeared into a bank of clouds and, three hours later, touched down at the Foggia airfield in Italy. Straightaway, the three parachutists boarded a transport ship to Egypt.

Back in Cairo, at the same house they'd left five months before, they quickly fell asleep. In the morning a British Army private brought them three clean, pressed RAF uniforms. They showered and shaved, donned the uniforms, and reported to the office of Colonel Simonds, where they were joined by Reuven Dafni, who'd made it back from Yugoslavia a few days earlier.

The reception by Simonds was spirited and boisterous—"not at all like what we're used to calling British reserve," Dan later wrote. There were hugs, kisses, raucous laughter, then numerous toasts late into the night.

The next morning, in a debriefing in Simonds's office, Dan gave an official report of their work for MI9.

"Yes, I know exactly what you did," Simonds said. Numerous British and American pilots who'd been shot down and held captive as POWs in Romania had told Simonds about the Jewish parachutists' ingenuity and commitment; most of the pilots had returned to their respective air squadrons to fly more bombing missions. "I'll send a detailed memorandum on your activities to both the War Office and Defence Office in London," he continued, adding, in a quieter tone, "You were fair fellows. You could have cheated on me and taken care of only your matters. Thank you for the courage, integrity, and for the work itself."

Until the end of his life, Colonel Simonds felt that the "British Foreign Office did not properly appreciate the work of the volunteer parachutists from Palestine. As for us in the intelligence units, we were well aware of the risk they took, of what they did, and what they achieved. The vital information we received through them on the location of hundreds of our crewmen held captive in Romania was the first light on the road to rescuing them."

35

Fall 1944–Winter 1945
Hungary and Romania

Still in shock at the realization that her daughter had been callously executed, in November 1944, Katherine joined tens of thousands of other Hungarian Jews bound for extermination. The trains from Budapest to Auschwitz had stopped running, but long columns of Hungary's Jews were still being sent on death marches into Austria. The weather was subfreezing, the marchers were often starving, and stragglers and those too weak to continue were summarily shot to death.

One day, during the confusion of an Allied air raid, Katherine and several other women managed to break free of the death march, ripping off their yellow Stars of David and finding shelter in the home of a generous Gentile family. Katherine eventually made her way back to Budapest and linked up with several of the surviving parachutists—first Yoel Palgi, who was organizing a resistance underground of Jewish survivors in Budapest, then Dov Berger, who was still active with the Mossad L'Aliyah Bet in Bucharest.

Without the help of Hannah's comrades, it's unlikely that Katherine would have survived the chaotic winter months in Budapest when the Arrow Crossers were turning the waters of the Danube River into a Jewish cemetery.

Accompanied by Hannah's fellow paratroopers from Budapest to Romania, Katherine needed to live in Bucharest for three months while the preparations for her legal immigration to Mandatory Palestine were finalized. Her concern was almost entirely about her last remaining child. All she could find out was that Gyura was no longer on Kibbutz Maagan; he'd enlisted in the British Army's Jewish Brigade and was serving somewhere in western Europe.

The Jewish Brigade, a unit of the British infantry fighting under the Zionist banner, had been formed in September 1944 and was made up of five thousand Jewish volunteers from Palestine. The brigade briefly saw action against German forces in Italy in the spring of 1945. Gyura enlisted in December 1944, but by the time he'd finished training and was deployed, the war in Europe had ended. Stationed in Austria, he was ultimately transferred to the Netherlands.

Katherine set sail from Constanţa, Romania, aboard the *Transylvania* and arrived in Haifa in October 1945. Not knowing a word of Hebrew, she settled into life on Kibbutz Maagan, a small community where almost everyone could understand her Hungarian. She cared for infants while their parents worked in the fields and taught piano lessons to some of the older children.

Gyura petitioned for a leave from the British Army and arrived at Kibbutz Maagan in December 1945. With tears of joy and grief, mother and son were reunited after more than five years. The thin boy Katherine had last seen was now a well-muscled, mature man. To Gyura's eyes, his mother seemed to have aged two decades.

Gyura remained on active duty but could visit Maagan most weekends. It was enormously difficult for Katherine to discuss everything that had happened to her and Hannah in Budapest. But bit by bit, she unfurled the story for him. By December 1945, Hannah had already entered the realm of Jewish history and had become a national martyr, a symbol of collective loss. By extension, willingly or not, her two surviving family members became the public faces of that loss.

For Katherine and Gyura, of course, it was a loss almost beyond comprehension—profound, personal, deeply private. On Kibbutz Maagan, they needed to spend hours alone together, mourning and remembering, sharing the kind of pain that only they—the two people who'd known the *real* Hannah—could ever understand.

Epilogue

THERE ARE STARS

On February 13, 1945, Soviet military forces captured Budapest, ending the three-month-long siege. Adolf Eichmann had failed to accomplish what would have been the crowning achievement of his SS career: making Hungary *judenrein*. In Budapest in February 1945, more than 119,000 Jews were liberated—over 25,000 of whom had been in hiding, and tens of thousands had been issued protective passports by Swedish diplomat Raoul Wallenberg. Out of the over 800,000 Jews living in Hungary's borders between 1941 and 1944, experts believe that approximately 255,500 survived the Shoah.

Budapest was devastated, with over 80 percent of its buildings destroyed or badly damaged. All seven bridges crossing the Danube had been destroyed by Allied bombs.

In late January 1945, Matilda Glattstein returned to the Catholic convent where she'd left her five-year-old daughter, Tova, in hiding. She was told by the nuns that there was no such girl living in the convent. Now more than eight months pregnant, she found the convent's rear window and pried it open. She spotted Tova, who immediately recognized her. Tova scrambled into Matilda's arms and out the window. They fled together and were reunited with Eliezer Glattstein, Matilda's husband and Tova's father, who'd been moving among dozens of hiding places in the chaotic last few months of the Siege of Budapest.

In the second week of February 1945, as the Glattstein family escaped

Budapest and were en route to their original home in the city of Prešov, Slovakia, Matilda went into labor. On February 12, 1945, in a tiny town in the district of Sárospatak in northeastern Hungary, she gave birth to a son. The infant was healthy, though his body was covered with bruises, the result of the weeks of torture Matilda had endured during her interrogation by the Gestapo early in her pregnancy. Matilda and Eliezar named him Baruch, the Hebrew word for "blessed." The family lived for three years in Karlovy Vary, a popular spa city in northwestern Czechoslovakia. On March 1, 1949, the four members of the Glattstein family made *aliyah* to Israel. For decades they lived a modest life in Ramat Gan, a satellite of Tel Aviv.

Baruch Glattstein went on to have a distinguished career in law enforcement, retiring as a deputy superintendent in the Israel Police's forensics department. After earning a master of science in organic chemistry from the Hebrew University, he published more than forty peer-reviewed articles and, while working full-time in the police department, earned several patents for his innovations. He is best known for inventing the first forensics field kit that can detect explosives, and today many of his practices and products are used by law enforcement agencies around the world.

As the name Hannah Senesh became more and more renowned, the Glattstein family treasured their personal connection to her. Katherine Senesh had met Matilda Glattstein during their brief time together in the Gestapo jail in Budapest. In Israel in the 1950s and 1960s, Matilda and Eliezar visited Katherine twice a year at her small apartment in Haifa. "Mother would tell the story, again and again, to anyone who would listen," Baruch Glattstein said, adding that every year on the Hebrew anniversary of Hannah's execution, the twenty-first day of the month of Cheshvan, he still lights a yahrzeit candle and says the Mourner's Kaddish for the ingenious, brave young woman who'd saved the life of his mother—and himself.

After the end of the war, Katherine Senesh struggled mightily to get some kind of justice for her daughter. Her first effort was to hold Captain Gyula Simon accountable for her unlawful death. She filed affidavits and reported him to the police. Simon was arrested on December 8, 1945, on an accusation of extrajudicial murder—imposing a death sentence on Hannah Senesh that was not lawful. His trial at the People's Court began in 1946 and dragged on into 1947. Because the records of Hannah's military trial could not be found—they'd been lost during the siege—the deliberations focused upon whether the judge had acted by the regulations in force on November 7, 1944. Simon was sentenced to one year in prison and five years of "deprivation of political rights for crimes against the people."

Simon never served a day in prison. He slipped out of Budapest and vanished in the postwar chaos of Eastern Europe. Like Adolf Eichmann and hundreds of other Nazis and their collaborators, he found a haven in South America. He wasn't heard from again until November 1985, when Israeli newspapers carried a report that he was living in Argentina. Dov Shilansky, a member of the Knesset, tracked Simon down and briefly questioned him. As reported by the Israeli evening daily *Maariv*, the seventy-two-year-old Simon claimed that Hannah Senesh had been the only person whom he had sentenced to death during the entire war and that he had no regrets. "If I were to start my life over, I would have chosen again to become a military judge and would have sentenced her to death again," he told Shilansky, adding that Hannah Senesh had "refused to ask for a pardon, and if she had, she might have been spared because the Russians were approaching and the judges were nervous . . . but she made them so angry with her Jewish pride that they decided to sentence her to death."

It was not until July 1993 that a judgment was issued by the Supreme Court of the Hungarian Military annulling the death sentence imposed on Hannah Senesh. She was officially exonerated of all crimes against Hungary, including treason and espionage.

Before he died suddenly of heart failure on June 11, 1945—only a month after the unconditional surrender of Nazi Germany—Eliyahu Golomb, the overall commander of the Haganah and one of the earliest planners of the mission, wrote, "The thirty-two parachutists from Palestine, like flames dropping from the sky, made small pools of illumination in the dark; and by the flickering light they gave, hundreds of thousands of Jews knew that they would not perish alone and that somewhere other Jews had heard their cry and had ventured towards them."

• • •

In spring 1945, one of Hannah's friends at Kibbutz Sdot Yam, Moshe Breslavsky, returned from his service as an infantryman in the Jewish Brigade of the British Army and discovered a simple cloth suitcase under Hannah's former bed. Inside were the four notebook diaries that Hannah had been keeping since she was a thirteen-year-old girl in Budapest. There were also photo albums, letters, and another exercise book in which Hannah had practiced her Hebrew.

Soon Breslavsky connected with Miryam Yitzhak, Hannah's classmate at the Agricultural School for Girls at Nahahal, the only friend she'd made in Eretz Israel. Miryam told him how Hannah had given her something for safekeeping before departing for her MI9 training in Cairo: the lined school exercise book into which she'd neatly copied all her poetry. On the cover she'd printed a Hebrew title, *Lelo Safa* (Without Language), and signed her code name, Hagar.

Hannah's poems and diary entries and a few selected letters were collected, edited by Breslavsky, and appeared in hardcover in 1945 by HaKibbutz HaMeuhad Publishing House. It was a slim book with a simple beige cover and no title—six stark Hebrew letters: the name Hannah Senesh. On the first page of the first edition, Breslavsky added "Journals, Songs, Testimonies."

Within months—two years before the State of Israel came into existence—the book was being hailed as an important contribution to Modern Hebrew literature, establishing Hannah as a new kind of heroine for a soon-to-be-new nation.

As her diary and poems became the publishing sensation of 1945, Hannah's name was in the headlines for a much different reason. Throughout 1945 and 1946, hundreds of thousands of survivors of the Shoah were in displaced persons' camps or roaming through Europe, penniless, their former homes either destroyed or occupied by non-Jewish families who didn't exactly welcome the returning camp survivors back with open arms.

Those hordes of increasingly desperate European refugees became known in Hebrew as *maalpilim*. As they had throughout the Second World War, the British authorities still imposed strict quotas on Jewish immigration, and now the top priority for the Yishuv leadership was to bring the *maalpilim* safely—if illegally—to Palestine on Mossad L'Aliyah Bet ships. The Royal Navy tried to stop the ships—intercepting them in the Mediterranean, boarding them, forcibly removing the Jews, and often returning them to displaced persons' camps in Germany, most famously in the case of more than 4,500 Jewish refugees aboard the *Exodus* in 1947.

Many of the ships were renamed in honor of the towering figures of Zionism: *Max Nordau, Eliyahu Golomb, Berl Katznelson.* In the fall of 1945, the Mossad L'Aliyah Bet purchased an Italian-made 250-ton diesel-powered iron cargo ship named *Andarta* for $40,000 cash. On December 14, 1945, renamed *Hannah Senesh,* she set sail from the port of Savona, Italy, carrying 252 *maalpilim.* (Two later Mossad L'Aliyah Bet ships would be named *Enzo Sereni* and *Haviva Reik.*)

On the night of December 25, *Hannah Senesh* arrived at the Mediterranean shore north of Haifa in stormy seas and very high winds. The date, if not the weather, was fortuitous, since the British patrols were busy celebrating Christmas and not watching the coast carefully. During the storm, *Hannah Senesh* ran aground on the rocky shore of Nahariya, the northernmost city in Mandatory Palestine, only six miles south of the Lebanese border. Gale-force winds caused her to keel over; an elite team of the Palyam—the maritime unit of the Palmach—raced into the waves and saved all the passengers by bringing them ashore using a rope bridge. Swiftly scattered and hidden among the neighboring kibbutzim, every single passenger evaded capture by the British.

Once all the illegal immigrants had left *Hannah Senesh* and been dispersed throughout the communities in the surrounding area, members of the Palmach and Palyam returned to the keeled-over ship. On the rocky beach, next to the black iron hull, they left a massive hand-lettered Hebrew banner. It read, in part:

HANNAH SENESH

THIS SHIP LEFT BEACHED ON THE SHORE OF NAHARIYA IS ONE OF THE TOMBSTONES FOR SIX MILLION OF OUR BROTHERS AND SISTERS. IT IS A SYMBOL OF SHAME FOR THE BRITISH GOVERNMENT.

The repatriation of Hannah's remains was a watershed moment in the early State of Israel. After her execution on November 7, 1944, her defense attorney, Dr. Andor Szelecsényi, arranged to have her corpse buried. She was laid to rest by unknown persons without any ceremony in an unmarked grave in Budapest's Jewish Cemetery, a place where she'd spent much time as a girl, visiting and leaving small stones on her father's headstone.

After long negotiations with the Hungarian government, her remains were exhumed from the plot in the Jewish Cemetery and sent via ship to Haifa in March 1950. The State of Israel, not even two years old, had never seen such a spectacle.

In the early afternoon of March 27, the coffin bearing Hannah's bones was lowered from the ship to the beach, accompanied by the somber strains of the Hapoel Orchestra. The sirens of all the ships were sounded in the port. After a eulogy at Haifa's City Hall, the coffin went on a long state journey, first to Kibbutz Sdot Yam, where it was accompanied by an honor guard; hundreds of people from nearby kibbutzim, former Palmach members, fishermen, and laborers paid tribute. A plane flying over the kibbutz dropped bouquets of flowers by parachute, and three uniformed paratroopers who had landed on the beach of Caesarea took them to the coffin. Several paratroopers and kibbutz members gave eulogies, as did Yitzhak Sadeh, the former commander of the Palmach.

The next morning, the funeral cortege left for Tel Aviv, where all of the businesses along the route were closed out of respect. After speeches by Tel Aviv dignitaries, the journey continued to Jerusalem.

What followed was the grandest military funeral in the history of either the Yishuv or the young State of Israel. All of the Israeli newspapers provided extensive front-page coverage. (Most also carried advertisements for the newly published fourth edition of Hannah's poems and diary.) The final service, with multiple eulogies, was held at the National Complex in Jerusalem, with the Israeli flag flying at half-staff.

Her casket began the slow journey up Mount Herzl. Before Hannah, the only other remains repatriated to the national cemetery had been those of the founder of Zionism himself, the Budapest-born Theodor Herzl. Hannah's casket was accompanied by Katherine and Gyuri Senesh, Yoel Palgi, and several of the *chaverim* from Kibbutz Sdot Yam.

Prime Minister Ben-Gurion and many of his cabinet ministers laid wreaths; a company of paratroopers fired a rifle volley in her honor. Thousands of people who knew Hannah only through her volume of poetry and her now-famous life story lined up to pay their respects. Infantrymen, pilots, sailors, and former parachutists took turns as guards of honor for her flag-draped casket. Ben-Gurion laid the final wreath on Hannah's casket. Moshe Sharett said, "The people living in Zion are filled with pride for our daughter who sanctified its name by her life and death."

The most memorable words were spoken not in Jerusalem but the previous day, at Kibbutz Sdot Yam. With the Palmach disbanded, Yitzak Sadeh—the Old Man—retired from military service, was now a popular playwright, essayist, and short story author.

His tribute to Hannah had appeared in the March 28 edition of the Socialist Zionist daily *Al HaMishmar*, next to a portrait of Hannah in profile taken at age seventeen in Budapest. It was titled simply "Chana Shelanu" (Our Hannah.) Standing next to her casket, Sadeh spoke warmly and poetically of the Hannah he'd known—the enthusiastic young *chalutza* whom all the members of the kibbutz had known. And yet, he asked rhetorically, had they truly known her? "We who knew Hannah didn't see all that was inside her—all her remarkable gifts were hidden from us," he said. "If Hannah had not gone by herself on that singular path of heroism, she would have stayed here, safely, among the *chaverim* at Caesarea."

> Our eyes could not see that which she cloaked so well; our eyes could not see the extraordinary hidden within the ordinary; our eyes could not perceive—our minds could not conceive—the heights to which our Hannah would ascend. The sacrifice that she made demands all of us to follow her, demands all of us to act. Hannah showed us how to remove that outer peel of selfishness we all have—to bury it in the ground—and discover the seed of courage and compassion that's inside us all.

The Hannah of the kibbutz, the Hannah of Caesarea, he concluded, was gone. *Our* Hannah was gone. "But the spirit of Hannah will live on as an example and symbol in one of the most heroic chapters in the book of our people."

With the first publication of Hannah's poems and selected diary entries in 1945 and the repatriation of her remains to Israel, it was as if a collective spiritual transformation had occurred.

Anikó Szenes, the ambitious, brilliant, lonely girl from Budapest, no longer symbolized one of the millions of faceless and powerless Jews slain during the Holocaust. Hannah Senesh, the *chalutza,* the Palmachnik, the paratrooper from Kibbutz Sdot Yam, was now the State of Israel's foundational heroine, a female freedom fighter who'd left the comfort of her cultured upper-middle-class life in Hungary, the safety of her Mediterranean kibbutz as a volunteer, risking her life to save her brothers and sisters in Europe.

Abba Eban, a South African–born Israeli diplomat, politician, and author, wrote in an introduction to a 1972 Schocken Books edition of her diary and poems:

> Hannah became a consecrated image in her people's memory. A whole generation came to see her as the symbol of a vast martyrdom. The personal symbol was necessary precisely because the Jewish bereavement is quite incomprehensible when its dimensions are measured in six million. It comes far more within the scope of perception when it is distilled into a single life and death.
>
> There is a terrible pathos in any torture or death, but the effect is somehow sharpened when the victim has the innocence of youth and the fragile grace of femininity.

For decades, people have asked why Hannah made the choices she did in late 1944. Why did she choose not to escape when she clearly had the means and opportunity to do so? With liberation so near, with the Red Army on the verge of capturing Budapest, why did she refuse to ask for a pardon? Was she intent on martyrdom, as some have speculated? Did she choose to die *al Kiddush Hashem* like the Ten Martyrs killed by the Romans, the sages she'd often thought about while walking through the ruins of Caesarea?

Senator John McCain, in *Why Courage Matters,* came up with a clever theory: "I don't think Hannah wanted to die for the sake of having her memory exalted in history or to prove herself equal to a romantic image she conceived for herself. Her purpose wasn't to die. She died for her life's purpose."

In 1958, to commemorate the tenth anniversary of Israel's founding, the national theater, Habima, held a competition for the best script about

Hannah's life. Habima chose Aharon Megged's play *Hannah Senesh,* which focused mostly on the events of 1944.

A year older than Hannah, Megged—born Aharon Greenberg in Poland in 1920—was well suited to dramatizing her life. He had been a member of Kibbutz Sdot Yam for twelve years and had known Hannah before she had gone on her fateful mission. A poet and novelist as well as a playwright, Megged had been shown some of Hannah's earliest Hebrew poems to critique.*

Megged said he had explicitly modeled his play on George Bernard Shaw's *Saint Joan,* and the parallels only served to heighten Hannah's image as Israel's own Maid of Orléans.

Many of the surviving parachutists vanished from the public spotlight, returning to their kibbutzim to raise families quietly, in pleasant anonymity.

Yoel Palgi wrote a novelistic memoir of his wartime experiences called *Ruach Gedolah Ba'ah* (And Behold, a Great Wind Came), which was an immediate bestseller when it was published in 1946. He served as the commander of Israel's first paratrooper unit in 1948 during the War of Independence; he also cofounded El Al Israel Airlines and was its deputy director from 1949 until 1960.

In 1946, Reuven Dafni traveled to the United States on a covert fundraising mission for the Haganah. Ostensibly, he was trying raise funds for the illegal immigration of the Holocaust survivors. On his tour across America, he met with some of the leading Jewish underworld characters, mobsters such as Benjamin "Bugsy" Siegel and Meyer Lansky in New York and Mickey Cohen in Los Angeles. "I had to find people who know how to get their hands on machine guns," he recalled in 1981. "And, yes, the gangsters helped. I remember Bugsy Siegel closing his eyes, saying 'What do you want from me?' And I said to him, 'We need your help because we are fighting the British.'

"*'Fighting,'* he says to me. 'Fighting,' you mean as in 'killing'?" When Dafni assured him that the Haganah wasn't planning some kind of prizefighting

*Megged was one of Israel's most acclaimed and widely read authors. He was awarded the Bialik Prize, the Brenner Prize, and the Agnon Prize and in 2003 was honored with the Israel Prize for literature.

competition, the mobster enthusiastically agreed. "You've got my total support," he said. Dafni had no illusions about the kind of men he was dealing with. "They were crooks—but they helped. The fact that the Jews were fighting appealed to them. For some of the gangsters, of course, it was a way of cleaning their reputations."

Every week until Dafni left Los Angeles, he received suitcases filled with five- and ten-dollar bills. He estimated that Bugsy Siegel alone had donated about $50,000 to the Haganah. After Siegel was murdered in a 1947 gangland hit in Beverly Hills, mere months after they'd met, he dryly remarked, "Thank God I didn't take a check."

After Israeli independence, Dafni spent the rest of his life as a diplomat: as the first Israeli consul in Los Angeles and, later, consul general in New York City. He also served as Israel's ambassador to India, Kenya, and Thailand and was one of the directors of Yad Vashem.

After World War II, Shaike Dan devoted his life to saving Jews trapped behind the Iron Curtain. As an intelligence agent based in Vienna, working with the Mossad, he led operations to rescue tens of thousands of Jews in the Romanian People's Republic, a regime that as early as the late 1940s was officially denying, in school textbooks, that Romanians had played any role in the Holocaust.

By the 1950s, Romania's Stalinist leadership began persecuting citizens practicing Judaism, arresting Zionists on charges of engaging in "reactionary nationalism" and being "agents of imperialism," and purging Jewish Communist Party members under the old anti-Semitic canard of "rootless cosmopolitanism."

The highest-profile arrest was that of Dr. A. L. Zissu, the Zionist leader with whom Shaike Dan had worked closely to rescue Allied airmen in 1944. Though there's no evidence that Zissu was ever involved in espionage, after months of torture by Romania's secret police, he confessed in March 1952 to being an "inveterate spy" for Israel. Found guilty of high treason in a show trial, he was sentenced to life imprisonment on March 31, 1954. After much diplomatic lobbying, he was granted a reprieve and allowed to emigrate to Israel in July 1956. Broken by the harsh years in prison, he suffered a heart attack and died in Tel Aviv two months later at age sixty-eight.

Though he could do little to help Zissu, Dan, working undercover, disguised as a Romanian businessman, used bribery to influence corrupt Communist officials in Bucharest, who reluctantly allowed small groups of Jews to emigrate. In a long-classified, forty-year-long operation dubbed "the Second Exodus," Dan helped take over a hundred thousand Romanian Jews to Israel.

By the 1980s, the zeitgeist in Israel had dramatically changed. A younger generation of scholars, dubbed the "New Historians," began questioning traditional Zionist narratives long held as sacrosanct. They offered scathing reassessments of the actions of David Ben-Gurion and other Yishuv leaders during the Holocaust.

Regarding the Yishuv parachutists' mission, a consensus emerged: It had been nothing but a cynical political gesture by Ben-Gurion and a failure of strategic planning on the part of the Haganah. Some argued that the operation had been "a fig-leaf to cover the Yishuv leaders' nakedness—their passivity during the Holocaust." The most extreme revisionists posited that the volunteers had been coldly sacrificed by the Jewish Agency as "a last-ditch attempt to cover up its own wartime inadequacies," sent on a suicide mission "to save the Yishuv's honor at the expense of European Jewry," for whom they could offer no means of escape—only exhortations to die with honor, like the fighters of the Warsaw Ghetto Uprising.

In 1981, the Israel Broadcasting Authority—then the nation's only TV network—aired a nineteen-episode documentary series directed by Yigal Losson called *Amud Ha'Esh* (Pillar of Fire), a sprawling history of Zionism from the time of Herzl through the founding of the State of Israel to the present day. In the glossy photo-filled 556-page book that accompanied the series, two pages of images and text are devoted to the Yishuv parachutists.

Like the narration of the documentary, the book makes an astonishing claim: "The parachutists did not succeed in saving even one Jew. Their mission, though of symbolic value only, was an attempt to break through the barrier of hopelessness."

Not surprisingly, that assessment outraged several of the surviving parachutist emissaries, most notably Shaike Dan. In the introduction to his 1992 autobiography, *Blind Jump*, Dan described the day a friend had shown him

Pillar of Fire's "lavish," bestselling photo album. Dan's reaction went from shock to anger. "At first, I didn't believe what I was reading. What is this? 'Did not rescue even *one* Jew?' Looking over the list of the series' consultants and learned professors, I couldn't understand how they came to such a conclusion. I'm too insignificant a person to argue with historians, but I learned, especially in recent years, that there's a vast gap between the writers of history and the *makers* of history."

Dan wrote with biting sarcasm about polite, patronizing historians who wouldn't give credence to the eyewitness accounts of a geriatric war veteran like himself. "Gently they say, 'Well, who knows if you *really* remember?' They have manners, these scholars. But I *do* remember," he wrote. "Not only me. All those who worked with me remember quite well how thousands of Jews were rescued by us during the war. Hundreds of orphans who were about to be sent from Romania back to Soviet Russia, arrived here and they—the rescued and the rescuers—are here in Israel today."

Surika Braverman, the only woman to survive the parachute mission, fought on the front lines during Israel's War of Independence. In 1949, she established the IDF Women's Corps and was instrumental in making Israel the only nation in the world to have compulsory military service for women.

Though often referred to in Hebrew as "the Parachutist Who Did Not Jump," Braverman became known as "the First Lady of the IDF." In 2010, at the age of ninety-two, she lit the torch for the opening of Israel's Independence Day. "We didn't think they would make us heroes," she later recalled. "We never saw ourselves as heroes. We simply wanted to go to the Jews of Europe and extend a hand to say: 'We've come here to help.'"

One trait that all the parachutists possessed was their willingness to die in an attempt to rescue their fellow Jews. "Honestly, I didn't think I would come back," Reuven Dafni said. "I gave it less than fifty-fifty." Reflecting on the mission's aims, he added, "I killed a lot of Nazis—blowing up trains in Yugoslavia. I have no nightmares about that, believe me. None whatsoever."

Interviewed for the acclaimed 2008 documentary *Blessed Is the Match*, directed by Roberta Grossman, Dafni was typically self-effacing. "We parachutists were not supermen nor superwomen," he said. "Supermen exist only on television. We were small, frail, inexperienced romantic people with all the shortcomings of the average person. None of us was unique—except perhaps Hannah. Because of her poetic heritage. She was a spiritual girl guided almost by mysticism. Perhaps one can say she had charisma. She was fearless, dauntless, stubborn. Despite her extraordinary intelligence and prescience, she was a kind of tomboy—a poet-tomboy—which sounds rather odd, I know. A girl who dreamed of being a heroine and who *was* a heroine."

The slip of paper that Hannah had handed Dafni, which he had tossed away in frustration, then fortunately retrieved, entrusting it to Arie Fichman to take to the editors of *Davar*, has assumed a life of its own. The poem continues to resonate in the twenty-first century; virtually every Israeli is taught the verse—often sung to a popular melody—and can recite it by heart.

Throughout the United States and Canada, "Ashrei Hagafrur" (Blessed Is the Match)—has become a piece of modern liturgy, sung regularly in hundreds of synagogues. The poem appears in both Hebrew and English in the most recent edition of *Mishkan T'filah: A Reform Siddur*, the Shabbat prayer book of Reform Judaism, the largest Jewish denomination in North America with nearly 850 congregations and over a million members in the United States and Canada.

For the first few decades after Israel's independence, *Hannah Senesh* was a canonical book; virtually every Israeli household had a copy of it. To date, there have been sixteen Hebrew-language editions of Hannah's diaries, letters, and poems. The most recent English edition, published in 2004, was billed as "The First Complete Edition." Even now, however, Hannah's artistic legacy is scarcely complete; discoveries of previously unseen letters, photos, and poems continue to be made every few years.

But for the average Israeli today, especially the younger generation of Sabras, Hannah's fame rests largely on one short poem she wrote while helping to build Kibbutz Sdot Yam, at age twenty-one, titled "Halicha L'Keisarya" (A Walk to Caesarea).

Set to music in 1945 by David Zehavi, the poem is so universal that nearly eighty years later, Israelis from all segments of society know Hannah's words by heart. Children first hear the song when they're four years old in kindergarten; teenage students study it a part of Hannah's life story when, in high school, they learn about the Shoah.

Considered an unofficial national anthem, the whole country sings it, as a kind of secular prayer on Yom HaShoah (Holocaust Memorial Day):

My God, my God,	אלי, אלי
May it never end—	שלא יגמר לעולם
The sand and the sea,	החול והים
The rush of the water,	רשרוש של המים
The crash of the heavens,	ברק השמים
The prayer of Man	תפילת האדם

The poets leave hell and again behold the stars.

—Dante, *Inferno*

Afterword

Lake Kinneret, the Sea of Galilee, is a popular pilgrimage destination for many Christians, a place of holiness and wonder, the site of many miracles recounted in the four Gospels. But for the surviving members of the Yishuv parachutists' mission and their families, the Sea of Galilee was the site not of a miracle but of an unfathomable catastrophe. The details of the tragedy are so gruesome and bizarre as to strain credulity.

July 29, 1954: a date chosen to commemorate the tenth anniversary of the parachutists' mission. Kibbutz Maagan had been selected to host because three of the parachutists—Yonah Rosen, Yoel Palgi, and Peretz Goldstein—had been founding kibbutz members. The invitation, typed on heavy bond paper, read in Hebrew:

> We are honored to invite you to attend the memorial assembly with the unveiling of the monument in memory of our *chaver,* the parachutist Peretz Goldstein, z"l
>
> The assembly will take place at our kibbutz on Thursday, July 29, 1954, at 6:30 p.m.
>
> Kibbutz Maagan, Jordan Valley
>
> The rally will be accompanied by a military ceremony, including paratrooper units and the IDF orchestra. Attendees are invited to partake in light refreshments at the end of the program.

The rally was attended by over 2,500 people, including Prime Minister Moshe Sharett, cabinet ministers, and dignitaries such as Yigal Allon and Teddy Kollek, as well as members of the Yishuv parachutists' mission who'd returned safely from Europe.

The rally organizer had tried to arrange a military flyover but had been turned down by the Israeli Air Force. Two days before the event, the newly formed private Aero Club of Israel agreed to perform an entertaining flyover with small propellor planes for a fee.

The rally began around 7:00 p.m. with the arrival of Prime Minister Sharett and his wife, who took their places in the first rows of dignitaries. Katherine Senesh sat next to them. An honor guard of the IDF's elite paratrooper unit, in their distinctive red berets, under the command of Lieutenant Simcha Levy, stood at attention near the new monument. A military orchestra played "Hatikvah"; then Dalia Friedland—a young IDF soldier who would later have a successful career in the theater—recited the Yizkor prayer. Yosef Goldstein, Peretz's father, unveiled the memorial plaque for his son, and Peretz's mother and brother laid floral wreaths.

A pair of two-seat Piper planes buzzed in the sky overhead. The plan was for pilot Uri Galin's Piper to soar over the cheering rally, dropping a congratulatory letter from Yitzhak Ben-Zvi, the president of the State of Israel, who was sending his regrets because he had official business in Jerusalem and could unfortunately not attend. The presidential letter, in a cloth envelope, was supposed to float gracefully down under a small parachute.

Galin's Piper arrived from the south and headed toward the crowd, but when he tossed the letter through the side window, the parachute got tangled up in the wing and wheels. Galin handed the controls to Avshalom Stroud, a photographer with no previous flying experience, opened the side door and leaned out. Intent on making the gimmick still work, Galin struggled with the tangled parachute as the plane made several wild turns, gradually losing altitude.

By the time Galin was back at the controls, the Piper's engine was stalling; the plane was losing speed and altitude fast. As the Piper nose-dived, out of control, its propellor struck and killed Lieutenant Levi, the commander of the paratrooper honor guard. Then, skipping over the first three rows, the plane crashed into the stands and burst into flames. Prime Minister Sharett, sitting a few yards from the point of impact, miraculously survived. Katherine Senesh, too, narrowly escaped death.

Panic spread. Over the loudspeakers came a warning to clear the area in case the plane's fuel tank exploded. Thousands of spectators fled, screaming, toward the main kibbutz buildings. The festive scene of moments earlier now resembled a killing field. Severed body parts lay everywhere; the dead, the dying, and the badly wounded lay scattered on the ground. Seventeen spectators were killed. Among them were four of the Yishuv parachutists who'd made it back alive from Europe in 1944 and 1945: Arie Fichman, Lyova Gukowsky, Dov Berger, and Shalom Finchi.

Daniel Sereni, Enzo's only son—who at age thirteen had sent a letter to his dad at the Bari airfield saying "It's okay if you die, Dad, as long as you're brave!"—was killed in the fiery plane crash. So was his pregnant wife, Ofra Sereni. Twenty-five others in the crowd were severely wounded. Pilot Uri Galin and photographer Avshalom Stroud were somehow pulled from the burning Piper without serious injury.

Despite two national inquiries into the errors in planning and the grotesque lack of safety oversight, no one was ever held responsible. Though considered one of the worst civilian tragedies in the first decades of the State of Israel, the Maagan Air Disaster is an episode in the nation's history that I found to be little known today, not taught in Israel's schools or even discussed in public.

I spent much of the summer of 2023 in Israel, retracing the footsteps of Hannah Senesh, Haviva Reik, Enzo Sereni, and the other Yishuv parachutists. One midafternoon in late July, my friend Ilan Benshoshan and I drove up to the gates of Kibbutz Maagan, only to find the place deserted. The gate had been left temporarily unguarded, so we let ourselves in. Walking through the kibbutz grounds, there wasn't a person to be seen.

Deep in the Jordan Valley, with the temperature over 104 degrees Fahrenheit, we'd heard an advisory on our car radio that the poor air quality index made it risky for children and the elderly to go outside. We ignored the warning and followed the curving flagstone path lined by dozens of Israeli flags to the memorial for Peretz Goldstein.

The stunning white granite obelisk overlooking the Sea of Galilee, intended to commemorate only one life—that of twenty-one-year-old Goldstein—now serves also as a memorial to the seventeen men and women killed in the Maagan Air Disaster.

A few hours later, around sunset, I was trying to cool off at the beachfront bar of Yulia, a trendy seafood restaurant near the port of Tel Aviv, sipping a glass of Maccabee lager and thumbing through my hardback copy of *Into the Inferno*, the postwar memoir by Yoel Palgi.

As I glanced to the side, I realized that I was sitting next to Natan Zahavi, the controversial veteran journalist and radio host. He was chain-smoking, drinking Johnnie Walker, and chatting with Ehud Olmert, a former prime minister of Israel, who was dressed in a black T-shirt and well-pressed black slacks. I noticed that Olmert had a few armed plainclothesmen in his security detail discreetly posted, one on the boardwalk and one in the open-air restaurant.

Seeing the black-and-white photo of the young, uniformed Yoel Palgi on the dust jacket, Olmert wheeled away from Zahavi and without so much as a word took the book from my hands, nearly tipping over my glass of beer in the process. "Why are you reading this?"

I explained to the former prime minister that I was an author from the United States in Israel for the summer, researching the Yishuv parachutists' mission. I told him that I'd just returned from a day at Maagan, that I was visiting Sdot Yam, Givat Haviva, Givat Brenner—all the kibbutzim where Hannah Senesh, Haviva Reik, Reuven Dafni, and Enzo Sereni had lived.

Olmert waved his hand dismissively, a typically Israeli gesture that told me I should stop wasting his time by stating the obvious. He read the English subtitle—*The Memoir of a Jewish Paratrooper Behind Nazi Lines*—then scanned the back jacket. He'd seen the book before only in its original Hebrew edition—*Ruach Gedolah Ba'ah*—and was surprised that it was available in English translation and that anyone my age would be interested in reading it.

"You knew him?" I asked.

"Yoel?" he said, nodding, his eyes reflecting a mix of melancholy and respect. "Of course, I knew him well."

With no elaboration, he put the book back into my hands and turned away, resuming his more animated Hebrew conversation with Natan Zahavi about the judicial reform crisis rending Israeli society in two in that overheated summer of 2023.

In today's Israel, the stories of the various parachutists are known only by men and women of Olmert's generation—people in their sixties, seventies, and older. For almost everyone younger, Yitzhak Sadeh is a busy thoroughfare in north Tel Aviv, Haviva Reik a quiet block in the Yad Eliyahu neighborhood. And many cities and towns in Israel have a street named Hannah Senesh.

The younger people I asked—men and women straight out of their IDF service—knew about Hannah, could sing "Eli, Eli," but strained to get the details of her life story right. "Hannah Senesh? She was a great hero. She parachuted into Germany and was tortured to death by the Nazis, no?"

Or: "*Ken, ken.* Hannah Senesh. A very brave woman. She killed herself rather than give up the names of her *chaverim.*"

As I retraced Hannah's steps, clambering through the ruins of the Roman aqueduct in Caesarea, I thought of the Joan of Arc image that had clung to her ever since Aharon Megged's hit play had come out. I thought of what Reuven Dafni had called her late in his life: a "poet-tomboy." Yes, it is an unusual turn of phrase—but to my ears, at least, so much more human and relatable than "holy virgin."

I thought of the poet-tomboy, too, when, at Kibbutz Sdot Yam, I spent a day in Beit Chana, the museum dedicated to her life and mission. Preserved as in a time capsule are her sewing kit, her typewriter, and desk; her German-made Agfa Box 54 camera, and the output of her many years as a photography buff: pictures of her playing tennis in a stylish all-white outfit in Budapest or tanned and sweaty, working with livestock at the Agricultural School for Girls, standing ankle-deep in mud and cow manure.

Looking at some of Hannah's original manuscripts, I noted how remarkably refined her handwriting was, considering that she'd started learning Hebrew only at age seventeen. At nineteen, at Nahalal, she'd fretted about her ability to master the nuances of the language. "Hebrew has become part of me," she noted in her diary on April 4, 1940. "I write it easily now—though incorrectly. But lines that came to mind this morning during my walk in the meadow came in Hungarian. I don't think I shall *ever* be able to write poetry in Hebrew."

A year later, in typical fashion, she'd conquered her self-doubts. In 1941 and 1942, she composed some of the most beloved poems in the Modern Hebrew canon. Yet the nervous charm of the neophyte is ever present on the page. "Look, she did a misspelling—with the word *olam*," Ilan said softly as we stood in the nearly empty museum looking at the original version of "A Walk to Caesarea" that she'd written in her exercise book.

"You're right," I said. "*L'olam*—she's got an aleph instead of an ayin." (Spelled with an aleph, the word refers to a hall—as in a meeting hall.)

In conversational Hebrew, *olam* most commonly means "world." Even many non–Hebrew speakers know the phrase *"tikkun olam"* (repairing the world), a kabbalistic concept now seen as one of the central mitzvot for all Jews, devout believers or not, emphasizing our responsibility to work toward a more equitable, just, and compassionate society. That was something Hannah, in her tumultuous twenty-three years, surely did.

Olam is a complex, flexible word. Used some 430 times in the Bible, it can also describe antiquity, eternity, humanity's continued existence. Many Hebrew prayers include the phrase *"L'olam va'ed,"* best translated as "Everlasting, eternally, forever." That was exactly how Hannah used it:

שלא יגמר לעולם
Shelo yigameir l'olam
I hope that these things never end

Just as in English, it's a word that children typically learn by age six or seven. I suppose that Hannah's typo would be like an American second or third grader spelling *world* as *werld*. I'm certain that Hannah—studious, meticulous, linguistically gifted Hannah—knew the proper spelling. She simply jotted down her Hebrew cursive in haste. Seeing such a basic error in a poem so widely revered was something that I instantly found endearing—and revealing.

In a nation that crafted an image of Hannah that was *impossibly* perfect—the virginal martyr, the woman warrior devoid of fear, the sacrificial lamb whose death had sanctified the people of Zion—such a charming, everyday imperfection made me smile. It made the Hannah of myth come more to life.

• • •

A few days after visiting Kibbutz Sdot Yam, I met David Senesh, one of Hannah's nephews, at Landwer Café in the cultural heart of Tel Aviv, near the Habima Theatre and the Charles Bronfman Auditorium, the home of the Israel Philharmonic Orchestra. David is one of the world's leading psychotherapists specializing in trauma. He lives in nearby Jaffa with his wife, the novelist Ilana Weiser-Senesh.

As we sat outdoors in wicker chairs ordering coffee, fresh fruit, and pastries, I mentioned to David the original handwritten version of "A Walk to Caesarea" in his aunt's notebook and how Hannah had spelled *l'olam* wrong.

"It's true, my aunt didn't have good Hebrew," he said with a laugh. "Because of this, she was a great poet."

It was a clever line—and a perceptive one. As a girl, when writing in Hungarian, Hannah often suffered from the "anxiety of influence," comparing herself to her late father and the esteemed authors in his Budapest literary circle. It surely didn't help her confidence that while she attended the Baár-Madas Református Gimnázium, one of the younger girls in the school's literary society, her friend Ágnes Nemes Nagy, was seen as more talented than she was. Nagy would gain enormous acclaim, not just in Hungary; before her death in 1991, she was hailed as one of Europe's major twentieth-century poets.

Writing in Hebrew, however, Hannah's creativity was unfettered; her minimalism became a strength—the depth of emotion and psychological nuances are profound enough to be studied in university literature courses, the vocabulary simple enough to be understood and memorized by kindergarteners.

In his therapeutic practice, David Senesh specializes in PTSD and the intergenerational transfer of trauma. He knows a thing or two about the subject. In 1973, as an IDF soldier fighting in the Yom Kippur War, he was captured by the Egyptian Army in the Sinai desert. While a POW in Egypt, he was held in solitary confinement and tortured for months. Today, practicing in both Jaffa and Berlin, he works primarily with traumatized clients; not surprisingly, he has particular therapeutic expertise in the treatment of torture victims.

Over our coffee and lunch in Tel Aviv, David—a bearded, joyous-seeming Sabra in sunglasses—downplayed his traumatic experiences of 1973. "Yes," he said, nodding, with a wry smile, "I was a prisoner of war; my father was a prisoner of war. In Budapest, my grandmother was also a prisoner. And of course, my aunt Hannah. I sometimes think it's our destiny—or something in the Senesh family DNA."

Before we said goodbye, David told me candidly, "My aunt wouldn't recognize Israel today. I'm sure she would feel like a total stranger here." Certainly, the nation's politics and culture are a far cry from the values of socialist, spartan sacrifice that Hannah left behind in December 1943.

The transformation of the hundreds of kibbutzim is emblematic. In the 1990s, most kibbutzim began moving toward privatization, becoming hybrids of socialism and capitalism. While the members still live in rather austere shared communities and politically they're the last remaining outposts of secular left-wing Zionists, the most successful kibbutzim are home to booming corporations, many of which are on the cutting edge of the tech sector—giving Israel its twenty-first-century nickname, "Start-up Nation."

Sdot Yam, which no longer functions as a fishery, is the global headquarters of Caesarstone, which was founded as a humble tile factory on the kibbutz in 1987. It is now the world's leader in engineered quartz surfaces (used mainly for kitchen countertops); its stock is traded on Nasdaq, its products are sold in more than fifty countries, and the company had a global revenue of $565 million in 2023.

Givat Brenner, which Enzo Sereni founded and named back in 1928, is today the largest kibbutz in Israel, with some 2,500 members. The fifty fertile acres in whose orange groves and olive orchards Enzo once labored now hold the headquarters of several thriving businesses.

I laughed aloud as I wondered what Enzo would have made of this brave new world—of the fact that among the capitalist ventures based on his old kibbutz is an agricultural tech company that "breeds non-GMO seeds with superior nutrition and crop yields"—sesame, soybeans, chickpeas—and uses its proprietary Manna AI to make breakthroughs in plant genetics "to design top-quality grains . . . central to the booming trend of plant-based meats and protein alternatives."

When I drove forty-five minutes south of Tel Aviv to Givat Brenner, it wasn't to see the wondrous ways AI is changing grain genomes to give us more protein-packed vegan burgers but to visit the remnants of a simpler, more rustic world—a remote past that, as it turned out, wasn't as remote as I'd thought. (When I arrived, I learned that Enzo's granddaughter was still living on the kibbutz.) I was the first visitor in ages to ask one of the administrators to find the key that unlocks Enzo's original house, now a small museum and archive, generally closed during summertime. A simple, blocky building of white concrete, the Hebrew letters over the front door—BEIT SERENI—once painted in bold scarlet are barely visible, faded to a spectral pale pink.

In a national ceremony in 1947 attended by numerous politicians and dignitaries, at which President Chaim Weizmann laid the cornerstone, Enzo's former home was renamed Beit Sereni. Today it serves as a cultural center, with an adjacent theater hall for performances. In addition to being the repository of Enzo's papers, it houses the definitive archival history of Italian Jewry.

I gently held a cloth-bound first edition of Enzo's posthumously published book, *Mekorot ha-Fashizm ha-Italki,* then looked through its Italian version, *Le origini del fascismo*. There has yet to be an English translation of *Sources of Italian Fascism,* even though Enzo's was the first book ever written on the subject. I also studied a collection of articles that Enzo edited (along with R. E. Ashery), published in 1936 with the remarkably prescient title *Jews and Arabs in Palestine: Studies in a National and Colonial Problem.*

"Enzo was like a miracle in my eyes," Prime Minister Golda Meir said at Beit Sereni in November 1969 during a ceremony marking the twenty-fifth anniversary of her friend's murder in Dachau concentration camp. "I cannot remember one discussion with him that was mere small talk. . . . There were always questions unanswered, waiting to be resolved, and Enzo did not let us evade them, especially as far as the Arab problem was concerned. He did not tire of the search for a solution: Maybe there were other ways of living together in Israel."

Reflecting on Enzo's lifelong advocacy for Arab-Jewish coexistence, I drove up north to Givat Haviva, the national education and research center of the Kibbutz Artzi Federation. The wooden sculpture at the front gate welcomes visitors in Hebrew, Arabic, and English. Founded in 1949—the nation's first year of existence—and named in Haviva Reik's memory, the nonprofit institution is the oldest dedicated to reconciliation between Jews and Arabs. The Center for Peace runs year-round seminars that "promote Jewish-Arab equality, mutual recognition, partnership, for the development of a peaceful, just coexistence of Arabs and Jews." (In 2001, Givat Haviva received the UNESCO Prize for Peace Education.)

I strolled through the campus of Younited: Givat Haviva International School, a coed boarding school for students ages fifteen to eighteen, offering an international baccalaureate degree. Younited's ambitious mission is "to transform the Middle East and beyond by developing a powerful network of leaders who will work together for inclusive, democratic societies and a just future for all."*

In addition to its educational programs and seminars, Givat Haviva houses the archives of Hashomer Hatzair. I spent hours in the library, taking notes and staring at the framed artwork on the walls: a 1950s poster for Hashomer Hatzair summer camps in England's Cotswolds; a maritime training poster depicting a pair of strong suntanned hands reeling in a fishing net with the Spanish slogan *"A la conquista del mar!"*; a band of pioneers, arms held high, holding fluttering red flags, announcing a 10:30 a.m. picnic on May Day 1949 with the Hebrew words "The Workers of the World Are United!"

And to me, the most fascinating artifact of all: an election poster, before the founding of the State of Israel, with these rallying cries and party platforms:

ZIONISTS!

VOTE FOR A SOCIALIST POLICY!

- Free Immigration, Settlement, Defence
- Jewish-Arab cooperation
- A binational solution for Palestine
- Alliance with all progressive forces
- Against partition in any form

THE ONLY CHALTUZIC CANDIDATES!

HASHOMER HATZAIR

*Younited's international partners include the US Naval Academy in Annapolis, Maryland, and Fordham University in New York.

Many, though not all, Israelis now regard these ideas as hopelessly naive and outdated. The old-school kibbutzniks, especially those of the far-left variety such as Hashomer Hatzair, are seen as intellectual utopians, fantasists, men and women who spent years drawing up blueprints for a future home that was neither practical nor attainable.

Realistic or not, I thought, scribbling the Hebrew slogans in my notebook, the dream of Jewish-Arab cooperation and peaceful coexistence in the Land was indisputably what Haviva Reik, Hannah Senesh, and Enzo Sereni envisioned for the nation none of them would live to see.

As I wandered over newly mowed lawns, I saw proof of the peaceful coexistence that Haviva dreamt of. It was evident in the faces of Younited's students, teenage Jews and Arabs, sitting together in the shade under trees, studying textbooks, scrolling on iPhones, smirking, laughing with braces glinting on their teeth, showing one another social media posts and memes. It was the afternoon of July 18, eleven weeks before the cataclysm of October 7, 2023.

Before leaving Givat Haviva, I bought a couple of Hebrew books I knew I'd have a hard time finding in America. One was her first full-length biography, published in 2014, *Haviva Reick: A Kibbutz Pioneer's Mission and Fall Behind Nazi Lines*. I skimmed the opening pages, read and reread the Hebrew epigram, a quotation I'd never seen—a passage of intimacy and casual eloquence from the Palmach's commanding warrior-poet.

> I asked myself: "Why have you not written about Haviva?" It may well be that one day there will be a writer who will reveal or perhaps hazard a guess about her illuminating figure. . . . And I—if only I could describe her smile.
>
> Yitzhak Sadeh

Israel is a nation of almost ludicrous extremes; Theodor Herzl picked an inspired title for his 1902 utopian novel *Altneuland*. In the morning you can be in the ruins of Tel Megiddo, the desolate ancient battlefield that the Book of Revelations calls "Armageddon," finding two-thousand-year-old shards of burnt-umber pottery under your feet; and a couple hours later, you're on the Tel Aviv promenade, walking the beachfront past brand-new gleaming high-rise condos—some of the most expensive real estate anywhere in the Mediterranean. Tel Aviv is called "the Nonstop City," and on its beaches every young person seems to be working out, running, doing pull-ups, or playing footvolley, while after sunset the city throbs with partying in its hundreds of restaurants, dance clubs, and artisanal cocktail bars.

For weeks, I sought an escape from the incessant noise of Tel Aviv, looking to immerse myself in an elusive, somber past. I finally succeeded in early August at David Ben-Gurion's house on the broad boulevard that bears his surname, a half block inland from the beach and the Tel Aviv Marina. The house was built in 1931; everything inside is preserved as it was eighty years ago: the austere bedrooms, the piano room, the elegant desk with an oversized clock where Ben-Gurion wrote speeches during his thirteen years as prime minister.

Utterly unchanged is the kitchen where he and his wife, Paula, ate for decades. There's the brown rotary phone on which I imagine he received wartime news; yellowed copies of *Davar* under glass; the white Sunbeam Mixmaster with which Paula made old-country delicacies such as *rugelach* and *mandlebroit*. And a physician's scale with balance beam so Ben-Gurion could watch his weight.

Most impressive of all are the books. In his personal library there are twenty-two thousand volumes; he read voraciously in many languages. Though never a religious Jew, he collected over 150 Bibles, from the Hebrew Tanach to eighteenth-century editions of the King James Version, and numerous Korans.

I walked forty minutes south, taking Allenby Street until I found Beit Eliyahu Golomb at 23 Rothschild Boulevard, now the Museum of the Haganah. Though I couldn't enter through the kitchen side door as Golda Meir had often done during World War II, I did get access to Golomb's home—or at least a good portion of it—preserved as it was on June 11, 1945, when the Haganah's commander died there of a cerebral hemorrhage.

There's the upright piano on which Golomb played his favorite classical pieces; the simple silver samovar—most likely brought from Golomb's birthplace, the town of Vawkavysk in the Russian Empire—with which his wife,

Ada, made tea for every visitor; a large transoceanic shortwave radio, state of the art for the mid-1940s, on which Golomb listened to the BBC and European broadcasts—that was the house Meir described in her autobiography as being the Jewish Agency's secret "nerve center," in which the lights never went off during the entire war and strategic planning took place at all hours of the day and night.

It was stiflingly hot and stuffy in Golomb's home that August afternoon; within minutes my face was dripping as if I'd been running on a treadmill. But for over an hour, no other museumgoers entered. I had a meditative solitude in which to absorb the atmosphere where much of the planning for the Yishuv parachutists' mission had taken place. I could almost see the phantom figures at the long, spare wooden dining table in the winter of 1943—Golomb, Ben-Gurion, Berl Katznelson, Moshe Sharret, Reuven Zaslani, Yitzak Sadeh, and Meir—drinking glasses of hot tea, smoking American cigarettes, debating, shouting, despairing about the fate of the last remaining Jewish communities in Europe—and then strategizing ways to persuade the recalcitrant British authorities to allow them to launch some kind of rescue mission.

"Please don't make a national hero out of me."

I thought about Zvi Ben-Yaakov's final words on a scorching Monday afternoon in Jerusalem as I stood staring at the white marble headstone of that hero who hadn't wanted any memorial. Zvi Ben-Yaakov, absent his remains, is "buried" in the National Military Cemetery on Mount Herzl. A simple white military tombstone, engraved with the silhouette of a parachutist, rests in a verdant V-shaped section, alongside those of the other six parachutists who perished during the mission: Abba Berdichev, Peretz Goldstein, Enzo Sereni, Rafi Reiss, Haviva Reik, and Hannah Senesh.

For an hour or two that July afternoon, I was the only soul visiting the Yishuv Parachutists Plot of the National Military Cemetery. After reading several of Hannah's poems silently, I left a small, jagged white rock on the headstone of each of the murdered paratroopers.

I then paid my respects at the graves of Theodor Herzl, Golda Meir, Shimon Peres, and Yitzhak Rabin and walked the paths of Mount Herzl's sprawling burial grounds, with its distinct sections for Israel's fallen soldiers, those who died fighting in the Haganah, volunteers in the British Army killed in World Wars I and II, and civilian victims of terror attacks.

"Was it needless death after all?" William Butler Yeats asked in "Easter, 1916," recounting the bloody April Rising that had failed, leaving scores of Irishmen dead in the streets, thousands imprisoned, and fifteen Republican leaders executed by firing squads in Dublin. In those verses Yeats grappled with his conflicted feelings about the armed struggle for independence and the double-edged sword of violent patriotism and foresaw that in the wake of the Rising, the people of his yet-to-be-born nation would be "changed, changed utterly: a terrible beauty is born."

The ethos that drove the Yishuv parachutists to take decisive action in 1943 and 1944 reshaped the consciousness of both Israelis and Jews around the world. For two millennia—until the generation of my Polish- and Russian-born grandparents—Jews in the Diaspora survived as intact communities by being nonconfrontational in the face of violent anti-Semitism. We kept our world alive through pragmatism, compliance, appeasement, and flight. Being vastly outnumbered in most of Europe meant that direct resistance to anti-Semitic violence wasn't feasible. Or when it did occur, self-defense was often suicidal.

That all changed between the years 1941 and 1945. It changed with Abba Kovner—like Hannah Senesh, a gifted poet and member of Hashomer Hatzair—who led the Jewish partisans from Vilna during World War II. On New Year's Eve 1941, at an underground meeting of young Zionists in the Vilna ghetto, the twenty-two-year-old Kovner read aloud a manifesto in which he quoted a biblical phrase that quickly spread throughout the other ghettos of eastern Europe, a phrase that has lived on for decades and is still used whenever we speak of the Shoah:

"Jewish youth! Don't trust the deceivers! Hitler aims to destroy all the Jews of Europe. *We will not go like sheep to the slaughter!* It's true, we are weak and defenseless, but the only response to the enemy is resistance! Brothers! It is better to die as free fighters than to live at the mercy of murderers. Resist! To our last breath!"

A terrible beauty was born, too, in the final burst of gunfire that took the life of Mordechai Anielewicz. Another member of Hashomer Hatzair, Anielewicz was the commander of the Jewish Combat Organization during the Warsaw Ghetto Uprising in April and May 1943; he was a charismatic twenty-three-year-old code-named Aniołek (Little Angel) who was able to rally his youthful fighters in their own rebellion—doomed, overmatched, throwing Molotov cocktails at Waffen-SS Panzers, choosing the dignity of a death in resistance over compliant deportation to extermination camps.

Members of Zionist youth groups, especially Hashomer Hatzair, were the vanguard of resistance to the Nazis in almost every ghetto. Kovner's manifesto was essentially a choice between two forms of death: at the mercy of Nazi murderers or with the dignity of Jewish fighters. "I don't want to die," as Hannah told Yoel Palgi in the mountains of Yugoslavia in May 1944. "I want to live. I still expect a lot from life." But she acknowledged that she *was* prepared to give up her life for her ideals. "I need to repurchase my right to life."

For me at least, with the mission of the Yishuv parachutists, with the ultimate sacrifice made by the seven—Abba Berdichev, Peretz Goldstein, Enzo Sereni, Rafi Reiss, Zvi Ben-Yaakov, Haviva Reik, and Hannah Senesh—the Jewish people were changed, changed utterly.

While remaining a uniquely Jewish heroine, Hannah Senesh is becoming more universally known year by year. To date her diary and poems have been translated into more than twenty languages. Would she have been surprised by her fame? Reading her diaries, it's clear that she always knew she was destined to be "chosen" for something higher—if not literary immortality, then a mission that would somehow elevate her from her day-to-day existence.

In July 1940, when she was nineteen, traveling in the far north of Eretz Israel and trying to decide which kibbutz to join after finishing agricultural school, she wrote a diary entry describing the moment: sitting in the shade of a eucalyptus grove near Kfar Giladi, waiting to hitch a ride, watching Miryam carve her name into the trunk of a tree with a small knife. She recounted the previous Saturday morning, when she had hiked to one of the uppermost ridges in the Naftali Mountains between Lebanon and the Galilee: "In the brilliance of the beautiful morning I understood why Moses received the Torah on a mountaintop. Only on the mountains is it possible to receive orders from above, when one sees how small man is. . . . In the mountains one can believe—and must believe. In the mountains one involuntarily hears the question, 'Whom shall I send?' And the answer: 'Send me to serve the beautiful and the good!' Will I succeed? Will I be able to fulfill God's command?"

As I finished writing this book, sitting in the glare of my synagogue's stained-glass windows and flipping through the siddur to the page containing the Mourner's Kaddish, my eyes paused in the section called "Songs and Hymns." In addition to her poems "Blessed Is the Match" and "A Walk to Caesarea," the *Mishkan T'Filah* contains Hannah's "Yesh Kochavim," known in English as "There Are Stars." Printed in both languages, the poem appears alongside selections from the Book of Psalms and the words of Maimonides.

Often sung by choirs at Jewish memorials, "There Are Stars" is now popular with a new generation, non-Jews as well as Jews. I see it frequently online as an inspirational quote, in various translations, set free from the fetters of religion and nationalism.

Hannah most likely found her inspiration when reminiscing about her long-deceased father. But reading it today, reflecting on the terrible brevity and lasting resonance of her life, the poem seems to perfectly capture her own legacy.

There are stars whose radiance is visible on Earth,
though they have long been extinct.
There are people whose brilliance continues to light
the world even though they are no longer among the living.
These lights are particularly bright
when the night is dark.
They light the way for humankind.

ACKNOWLEDGMENTS

At Avid Reader Press, I was extremely fortunate to have worked closely with two brilliant young editors: Carolyn Kelly and Julianna Haubner. Both were attentive and supportive and helped me immeasurably in shaping the narrative and the prose style of this book. Avid Reader's team—"a small band of cheerful literary warriors," as they aptly style themselves—is a remarkable one. I'm grateful for the support of copublishers Jofie Ferrari-Adler and Ben Loehnen, and editor in chief Lauren Wein.

Also at Avid Reader, I'd like to thank the production department's Allison Green, Hana Handzija, Annalea Manalili, Ruth Lee-Mui; the art department's Alison Forner, Clay Smith, Sydney Newman; the publicity department's Dave Kass, Rhina Garcia, Eva Kerins; and the marketing department's Katya Wiegmann.

Simply put, this book wouldn't exist without the vision and guidance of Sloan Harris at CAA. Sloan's been my agent since 1998; he lit a spark in my imagination when I was talking to him in mid-July 2021 about a news story I'd just read: Over one hundred Israeli paratroopers were going to make a jump into the mountains of Slovenia, then retrace Hannah Senesh's route overland to Budapest, where ceremonies would commemorate the centenary of

Hannah's birth, July 17, 1921. The name of the educational mission, I told Sloan, was Crash of the Heavens.

Also in CAA's New York office, I'd like to thank Colin Graham, Taylor Damron, and Saachi Bhandari. And at CAA's London office, thanks to Jake Smith-Bosanquet and Zara Shepherd-Brierley.

In July 2023, my friend Ilan Benshoshan and I flew off to Ben Gurion Airport to test the proposition of whether two very different Jewish men—Ashkenazi and Sephardi—could share a Tel Aviv apartment during an oppressively hot summer without driving each other crazy. (The short answer: no.) Nevertheless, Ilan's expert Sabra guidance was indispensable—driving, translating, interpreting, gesticulating—giving me the freedom to literally walk in the footsteps of Hannah Senesh and the other parachutists of the Yishuv. I stumbled through the Roman concrete ruins of Caesarea where Hannah composed many of her poems; visited numerous kibbutzim from the Negev to the Galilee; spent hours, meditatively, in the magnificent Parachutists' Section of the National Heroes Cemetery on Mount Herzl in Jerusalem.

It was bashert that I should meet, during the summer of 2023, with Hannah's nephew David Senesh and his wife, Ilana Weiser-Senesh, first at a café in Tel Aviv; then we later spent some quality time together in Canada. Several years ago, David and his brother donated all their aunt's diaries, letters, manuscripts, and photos to create the Senesh Family Archive in the National Library of Israel. They've been digitized and proved invaluable in my research. Early on in our friendship David, a world-renowned trauma specialist, told me that he was most curious to know how writing this story would impact *me* personally: "Doug, I am, after all, a psychologist by profession." As of this writing, I have yet to give David a comprehensive answer.

I'm grateful to the staff at Kibbutz Sdot Yam's Anna Szenes House, as well as the administrators at Givat Haviva and Givat Brenner who allowed me so much time in their kibbutz archives.

Thanks to several friends who were early readers, shrewd listeners and occasional fact-checkers: Esther Gilbert, Jake Jennings, Alexander Levinzon, Lila Mydlarski, and Melanie Trossman.

And finally, I'm forever indebted to the two central women in my life: my mother, Marcia Century, and my daughter, Lena Century. Both were willing to listen as I read aloud from fresh passages; both were thoughtful, patient, and unfiltered in their criticism. That's fitting—perhaps the central relationship in this book is that of daughter and mother: Hannah and Katherine. I'd like to think that by processing my raw prose through my own daughter and mother, I gained a better understanding into two brilliant and complex Hungarian Jewish women and—perhaps—even some deeper psychological insight.

Lena's now twenty-two, studying English literature; she's the exact age that Hannah was when she embarked on her fateful mission in the winter of 1943. There were many afternoons when I was sitting cross-legged on the carpet of my mother's small office, reading aloud, and I could see how difficult it was for a parent to process the kind of pain that Katherine must have felt upon meeting her battered daughter in Budapest's Gestapo jail in June 1944. But it also struck me that Katherine surely, on some profound level, took immense pride in having raised a daughter with the kind of talent, conviction, and moral clarity that millions, to this day, associate with the name Hannah Senesh.

APPENDIX I

The following poem was written in Cairo in March 1944 for Hannah's best friend Miryam Yitzhak. In 2012 Miryam's daughter, Hannah Yasur, was sifting through her late mother's belongings at Kibbutz Hatzor when she found it inside a letter.

Hora to an Exiled Daughter

A hora, roaring, tempestuous, blazes around me
With the mystery of rhythm, gladdening and forging
It tugs at my body and heart
The foot marches, the back quivers
The song is ignited, a searing chorus
Dance and song, a wordless prayer,
Hail to the future, hail to creation

But then a figure flutters before my eyes
My arm has escaped my friends' embrace
My heart spurns the tempestuous singing,
Far and near it consumes me whole

Blue eyes
Such a bewildered glance
A sad silence and a stubborn mouth
The stillness grows in me

I remain standing
Alone, in a crowd of a hundred, her and I

Translated from Hebrew by Elie Leshem.

Set to music by composer Nurit Hirsh and sung by Yardena Arazi, one of Israel's most popular singers, the song was released in 2012.

APPENDIX II

Zvi Ben-Yaakov's final letter, written in Hebrew, was smuggled out of the Gestapo jail in Slovakia. To this day no one is certain of his fate; by most accounts he was transferred to Mauthausen concentration camp in Austria in late December 1944.

> *Dear M.! As I'm writing this, my fate is still a mystery. If they don't discover that I'm Jewish, everything will be fine; then I'll probably go to some concentration camp and after a short time I'll return home.*
>
> *But if that's not the case, then my fate is sealed. I'm not afraid of death. I made the calculation a long time ago, and I made my peace with it—even before I took the assignment. If it's my duty to die, I'll go to death quietly; I'm nothing but a brother to the thousands who've preceded me.*
>
> *Please don't make a national hero out of me. Because this wasn't heroism. Only here did I see how weak we are. No, you can't call it heroism. Anyone would have gone in the same circumstances. And that's how I went: When the hour of need called, I answered. Rafi and Haviva also share my opinion. This is my will.*
>
> *Your friend and*
> *father of your child,*
> *Zvi*

Even if his Jewishness was not discovered, if the Nazis continued to believe that he was RAF Second Lieutenant Michael Jamay, his fate was still sealed.

Ben-Yaakov, age twenty-two, was most likely executed in Mauthausen along with seventeen other British officers and American OSS agents captured during the Slovak National Uprising. The torture and murder of these British and American officers is considered one of the worst war crimes committed against Allied POWs during World War II.

In Israeli schools today, Ben-Yaakov's farewell letter to his wife is often part of the curriculum—along with the poetry of Hannah Senesh—when students learn about the Holocaust.

APPENDIX III

In a book of this scope, I couldn't cover every single mission; below are all thirty-seven of the *Tzanchanim HaYishuv*—or the Yishuv parachutists—by destination country.

Hungary

Peretz Goldstein (1923–1945)
Yoel Palgi (1918–1978)
Yonah Rosen (1919–2004)
Hannah Senesh (1921–1944)

Romania

Arie Fichman (1920–1954)†
Dov Berger (1917–1954)†
Lyova Gukowsky (1914–1954)†
Arie Lupescu (1913–1991)
Manu Ben-Ephraim (1914–2006)
Zadok Doron (1918–2002)
Shaike Dan (1909–1994)
Baruch Kamin (1914–1988)
Uriel Kenner (1918–1986)
Yitzhak Shaham (*–1962)

*Exact dates unknown.
†Killed in the Maagan Air Disaster on July 29, 1954.

Abba Berdichev (1920–1945)
Surika Braverman (1919–2013)

Czechoslovakia
Chaim Hermesh (1919–2007)
Zvi Ben-Yaakov (1922–1945)
Rafi Reiss (1914–1944)
Haviva Reik (1914–1944)

Yugoslavia
Nissim Arazi (1917–1980)
Ephraim Dafni (1911–1992)
Reuven Dafni (1913–2005)
Eli Zohar (1917–1989)
Rehavam Amir (1916–2013)
Shalom Finchi (1916–1954)†
Peretz Rosenberg (1919–2008)

Italy
Enzo Sereni (1905–1944)
Yaakov Shapira*

Bulgaria and Greece
Chaim Ben Shoshan (1915–2002)
Jacob Huber*
Pinchas Kleiman*
Aaron Ben Yoseph (1900–1949)
Yosef Varon (1919–2005)
Sasson Pinchas*

Austria
Dan Lener (1922–1988)
Chaim Yaari (1913–1983)

NOTES

PROLOGUE

xvi **Bypassing the building's columned portico:** Golda Meir, *My Life* (G. P. Putnam's Sons, 1975), 175.

xvi **whom they all called Mamochka:** Meir, *My Life*, 175.

xvii **she told him stories:** Shabtai Teveth, *Ben-Gurion and the Holocaust* (Harcourt, Brace and Company, 1996), 74.

xvii **After she finished speaking:** Teveth, *Ben-Gurion and the Holocaust*, 74.

xviii **"appalling horror and brutality":** Anthony Eden, "United Nations Declaration," December 17, 1942, https://api.parliament.uk/historic-hansard/commons/1942/dec/17/united-nations-declaration.

xviii **"the principal Nazi slaughterhouse":** Eden, "United Nations Declaration."

xviii **"bestial policy of cold-blooded extermination":** Eden, "United Nations Declaration."

xix **"We knew that if we could":** Eliyahu Golomb, quoted in Yigal Allon, *Shield of David: The Story of Israel's Armed Forces* (Random House, 1970), 132.

PART ONE: A VOICE CALLED

3 **"In the days of the *chalutzim*":** Rabbi Julian Sinclair, "Jewish Words: Chalutz," *The Jewish Chronicle*, November 4, 2008, https://www.thejc.com/judaism/jewish-words/chalutz-bhhf4x3p.

3 **now she was a self-described:** Hannah Senesh, *Hannah Senesh: Her Life and Diary, The First Complete Edition*, trans. Marta Cohn (Jewish Lights Publishing, 2004), 86.

6 **"A lot of things happened today":** Senesh, *Hannah Senesh*, 43.

6 **"I'm just finishing Daddy's book":** Senesh, *Hannah Senesh*, 43.

7 **"Judapest":** Paul Lendvai, *The Hungarians: A Thousand Years of Victory in Defeat* (Princeton University Press, 2021), 329.

8 **"I have been an anti-Semite":** Admiral Miklós Horthy, quoted in Asher Cohen, Yoav Gelber, and Charlotte Wardi, *Comprehending the Holocaust: Historical and Literary Research* (P. Lang, 1988), 232.

8 **"To my way of thinking":** Senesh, *Hannah Senesh*, 67.

8 **"I don't know whether":** Senesh, *Hannah Senesh,* 67.
8 **"One needs something":** Senesh, *Hannah Senesh,* 67.
9 **"The Maccabees will rise again":** Theodor Herzl, *A Jewish State: An Attempt at a Modern Solution of the Jewish Question* (D. Nutt, 1896).
9 **"When anyone in Hungary":** Senesh, *Hannah Senesh,* 71.
9 **"One of the fundamentals of Zionism":** Senesh, *Hannah Senesh,* 72.
10 **"What will happen to us":** Senesh, *Hannah Senesh,* 65.
10 **"The devil take the Sudeten Germans":** Senesh, *Hannah Senesh,* 65.
11 **"The only thing I'm committed to":** Senesh, *Hannah Senesh,* 74.
12 **Over the next five years:** "British White Paper of 1939," The Avalon Project, Yale Law School, https://avalon.law.yale.edu/21st_century/brwh1939.asp.
12 **"I've got it; I've got it":** Senesh, *Hannah Senesh,* 80.
12 **"Mother, there are already":** Katherine Senesh, "Memories of Hannah's Childhood," in Senesh, *Hannah Senesh,* xxix.
12 **What they'd most feared had finally begun:** Senesh, *Hannah Senesh,* 82.
13 **"I have chosen to work on the soil":** Senesh, *Hannah Senesh,* 81.
16 **"By the rivers of Babylon":** Psalm 137:1 (King James Version), *The Holy Bible: An Exact Reprint Page for Page of the Authorized Version Published in the Year MDCXI* (Oxford University Press, 1833).
16 **the Romans tortured and executed:** The murders of five of the Ten Martyrs are recorded in the Talmud; the others are recorded in Midrash, Zohar, Nachmanides, Rabbeinu Bachye, Yalkut Reuveni. The five references in the Talmud are in Sanhedrin 14a, Avodah Zarah 18a, Berachot 61b, and two in tractate Semachot, chapter 8.
17 **Hannah found the seascape:** Senesh, *Hannah Senesh,* 148.
17 **"with foaming fury":** Senesh, *Hannah Senesh,* 148.
18 **"*Hush, cease all sound*":** "To Caesarea," in Senesh, *Hannah Senesh,* 300.
19 **"Everyone is discussing politics":** Hannah wrote in her diary on April 23, 1941, Senesh, *Hannah Senesh,* 119.
20 **"Greece has fallen":** Senesh, *Hannah Senesh,* 120.
20 **"but no voice comes":** Senesh, *Hannah Senesh,* 119.
20 **"Is it possible to consecrate":** Senesh, *Hannah Senesh,* 120.
20 **"*To die . . . so young to die*":** "To Die?," in Senesh, *Hannah Senesh,* 300.
20 **known in Hebrew as *matayim yamei kharada*:** The phrase was coined by the Israeli journalist Haviv Canaan in *Two Hundred Days of Anxiety: Eretz Israel vs. Rommel's Army* (Mol-Art, 1974), 172–78.
21 **A newly formed SS extermination unit:** Klaus-Michael Mallmann and Martin Cüppers, "'Elimination of the Jewish National Home in Palestine': The Einsatzkommando of the Panzer Army Africa, 1942," *Yad Vashem Studies* 35, no. 1 (2007): 1–31.
22 **"We have victory":** Martin Gilbert, *Winston S. Churchill, Volume VII: Road to Victory, 1941–1945* (RosettaBooks, 2015), chap. 16, ebook.
23 **"just as other underground armies":** Allon, *Shield of David,* 127.
23 **"The War Against the Jews":** From the title of American historian Lucy Dawi-

dowicz's bestselling work *The War Against the Jews: 1933–1945* (Holt, Rinehart and Winston, 1975).

23 **"If international finance":** Hitler's infamous "prophecy" of January 30, 1939, has been translated into English in various ways. See Jeffrey Herf, *The Jewish Enemy: Nazi Propaganda During World War II and the Holocaust* (Harvard University Press, 2006), 71. The original German reads, "Wenn internationale Finanzjuden im und ausserhalb von Europa es fertigbringen sollten, die Völker neuerlich in einen Weltkrieg zu stürzen, so wird das Ergebnis nicht die Bolschevisierung der Erde und damit der Sieg der Juden sein, sondern die Vernichtung der jüdischen Rasse in Europa." For decades, scholars of World War II and the Holocaust have parsed Hitler's diction, particularly his use of *Vernichtung*, translating it as "annihilation," "extermination," and sometimes "destruction."

24 **"Here is a devil":** Winston Churchill, "Mr. Churchill's Broadcast of Aug. 24," *Bulletin of International News* 18, no. 18 (1941): 1132–33.

26 **"Why has there been":** Berl Katznelson, *Davar* newspaper, December 1, 1943.

26 ***"A voice called. I went."*:** "At the Crossroads," in Senesh, *Hannah Senesh*, 304.

27 **"Perhaps I'm not good":** Senesh, *Hannah Senesh*, 156.

28 **"I hate my work":** Senesh, *Hannah Senesh*, 155.

28 **"I feel like an empty vessel":** Senesh, *Hannah Senesh*, 155.

28 **"I'm well, only":** Senesh, *Hannah Senesh*, 153.

29 **"I feel I must be there":** Senesh, *Hannah Senesh*, 155.

30 **"How strangely things work out!":** Senesh, *Hannah Senesh*, 157.

30 **"I see the hand of destiny":** Senesh, *Hannah Senesh*, 157.

31 **"We must support the British Army":** In several 1939 speeches, Ben-Gurion used variations on this famous remark. I've chosen the most common translation. The evolution of these White Paper remarks is recounted by Shabtai Teveth in *Ben Gurion: The Burning Ground, 1886–1948* (Houghton Mifflin, 1988), 717.

32 **saying that the British instructors "knew nothing":** Judith Tydor Baumel-Schwartz, *Perfect Heroes: The World War II Parachutists and the Making of Israeli Collective Memory* (University of Wisconsin Press, 2010), 10.

34 **"It is hard to find":** Tony Simonds, quoted in Amos Ettinger, *Blind Jump: The Story of Shaike Dan* (Cornwall Books, 1992), ebook.

34 **"There's practically not":** Ettinger, *Blind Jump*, 60.

34 **"was always *hopelessly* punctual":** Ettinger, *Blind Jump*, 58.

34 **"There's no such thing as bad beer":** M. R. D. Foot, "Obituary: Lt-Col Tony Simonds," *The Independent*, January 25, 1999, https://www.the-independent.com/arts-entertainment/obituary-ltcol-tony-simonds-1076329.html.

35 **"I was a successful pianist":** Ettinger, *Blind Jump*, 71.

37 **"Nowhere outside Nazi-dominated Europe":** Ettinger, *Blind Jump*, 72.

38 **"I dare say they were not":** Ettinger, *Blind Jump*, 59.

38 **"I have little doubt":** John Bennett, minutes, January 29, 1943, The National Archives, FO 921/58.

39 **"The Jews have been found":** M.O.3 Notes on Interview Between CGS and Zaslani, January 20,1943, TNA, WO 201/2323.

39 **"The scheme would remove":** Moyne wrote, as quoted by Robert O. Freedman in *Present Tense* 7, no. 3 (Spring 1980):59.
39 **"My activities to enlist":** Tony Simonds, quoted in Ettinger, *Blind Jump*, 61.
39 **Simonds calculated that training:** Ettinger, *Blind Jump*, 47.
40 **If even *one* experienced pilot:** Peter Hay, *Ordinary Heroes: Chana Szenes and the Dream of Zion* (G. P. Pubnam, 1986), 140.
40 **"specially trained troops":** Winston Churchill, *The Second World War: Their Finest Hour*, vol. 2 (Houghton Mifflin, 1949), 217.
40 **taken from the Afrikaner units:** Dudley Clarke, "The Birth of the Commandos," *The Listener*, November 25, 1948, 799.
41 **"would provide, select, and coordinate":** Notes on interview between CGS and Zaslani, January 20, 1943, The National Archives TNA, WO 201/2323.
42 **"Together," Simonds later recalled:** Ettinger, *Blind Jump*, 62.
43 **"Such a long silence":** Senesh, *Hannah Senesh*, 158.
43 **"After work—a bit of reading":** Senesh, *Hannah Senesh*, 158.
43 **"I'll soon be twenty-two":** Senesh, *Hannah Senesh*, 158.
44 **"Today he openly stated":** Senesh, *Hannah Senesh*, 163.
44 **"Hannah had expressive":** Miryam (Pergament) Yitzhak, National Library of Israel, trans. by the author from Hebrew.
44 **"She wanted so much":** Miryam (Pergament) Yitzhak, National Library of Israel, trans. by the author from Hebrew.
45 **"define her goals":** Hay, *Ordinary Heroes*, 124.
45 **"You prefer ideas over people":** Joseph Weiss once teased her in a letter. *Sailing a Dream: Love Letters to Hannah Senesh* (Kibbutz Hameuchad Publishing House, 1996).
46 **"We've found a haven":** Yonah Rosen with Yehudit Rotem, *I Was Called and I Will Go* (Kibbutz Dalia, 2002), trans. by the author from Hebrew.
46 **A middle-aged veteran:** Yoel Palgi, *Into the Inferno: The Memoir of a Jewish Paratrooper behind Nazi Lines* (Rutgers University Press, 2002), 5.
46 **he was, in fact, a Jew:** Palgi, *Into the Inferno*, 5.
46 **"My entire being is preoccupied":** Senesh, *Hannah Senesh*, 160.
47 **Operation Typical:** Walter R. Roberts, *Tito, Mihailović, and the Allies, 1941–1945* (Rutgers University Press, 1973), 11.
47 **Churchill dispatched Captain William Deakin:** "Deakin, Sir William, (3 July 1913–22 Jan. 2005), Warden of St Antony's College, Oxford, 1950–68, retired; Hon. Fellow, 1969."
48 **Marshal Tito's forces were well trained:** Teddy Preuss, "Tito and Peretz Rosenberg," *Davar*, July 26, 1977.
48n **"the drafter-in-chief":** Mark Wheeler, "Obituary: Sir William Deakin," *The Guardian*, January 31, 2005, https://www.theguardian.com/news/2005/jan/31/guardianobituaries2.
49 **"I do my daily work":** Hannah wrote in her diary on May 29, 1943, Senesh, *Hannah Senesh*, 159.
49 **"This morning, we visited":** Senesh, *Hannah Senesh*, 3.
51 **Hannah arrived early:** Anthony Masters, *The Summer That Bled: The Biography of Hannah Senesh* (Michael Joseph Ltd., 1972), 125.

51 **The British were represented:** Masters, *The Summer That Bled,* 125.
52 **"You're a very young woman":** For the interview dialogue in the scene at Citrus House, I've relied primarily on the account in Masters, *The Summer That Bled,* 125–26.
54 **"Y. Noded":** Zvika Dror, *The Life and Times of Yitzhak Sadeh* [in Hebrew] (Hakibbuts Hameuchad, 1996).
55 **"I arrived in The Land":** Senesh, *Hannah Senesh,* 160–61.
55 **"But there *is* something":** Senesh, *Hannah Senesh,* 161.
56 **"first poems about the hardships":** Senesh, *Hannah Senesh,* 161.
56 **"the same sort of tristesse":** Senesh, *Hannah Senesh,* 162.
56 **"Would I enlist?":** Senesh, *Hannah Senesh,* 162.
57 **On August 1, five:** Duane P. Schultz, *Into the Fire: Ploesti, the Most Fateful Mission of World War II* (Westholme Publishing, 2007); Steven J. Zaloga, *Ploesti 1943: The Great Raid on Hitler's Romanian Oil Refineries* (Osprey Publishing, 2019).
58 **received the Congressional Medal of Honor:** "Operation Tidalwave: Ploesti, August 1, 1943," National Museum of the United States Air Force, https://www.nationalmuseum.af.mil/Visit/Museum-Exhibits/Fact-Sheets/Display/Article/1519651/operation-tidalwave-ploesti-august-1-1943.
58 **On September 3, the British Eighth Army:** C. J. C. Molony, *History of the Second World War, United Kingdom Military Series: The Mediterranean and Middle East,* vol. 5: *The Campaign in Sicily 1943 and the Campaign in Italy, 3rd September 1943 to 31st March 1944* (HMSO, 1973).
59 **On September 27, 1943:** Molony, *History of the Second World War,* vol. 5.
59 **"It's been about a month":** Senesh, *Hannah Senesh,* 162.
59 **"I bathe in the sea":** Senesh, *Hannah Senesh,* 162.
60 **He liked to think of himself:** Yehuda Ahishar (pen name of Lyova Gukowsky), *To Whom I Was Called* (Am Oved, 1955).
61 **"We have to come to them":** Ahishar (pen name of Lyova Gukowsky), *To Whom I Was Called.*
61 **"Your heart pounds":** Gukowsky, quoted in Baumel-Schwartz, *Perfect Heroes,* 12.
63 **"scoundrels":** Tuvia Friling, "Istanbul 1942–1945: The Kollek-Avriel and Berman-Ofner Networks" in *Secret Intelligence and the Holocaust: Collected Essays from the Colloquium at the City University of New York,* ed. David Bankier (New York: Enigma Books, 2006), 144.
63 **The Dogwood Chain:** Friling, "Istanbul 1942–1945," 121.
63 **He turned out to be:** Friling, "Istanbul 1942–1945," 123.
64 **"reams of intelligence":** Patrick K. O'Donnell, *Operatives, Spies, and Saboteurs* (New York: Free Press, 2004), 75.
66 **"Police Brutality at Kibbutz!":** *Davar,* November 18, 1943.
67 **referred to her as "The Blonde Bombshell":** Baumel-Schwartz, *Perfect Heroes,* 17.
68 **"the girl on the motorcycle":** Tehila Ofer and Zeev Ofer, *Haviva Reik: A Kibbutz Pioneer's Mission and Fall Behind Nazi Lines,* trans. Miriam Talisman (Fawns Publishing, 2014), 59.
69 **"Haviva was ostracized":** Surika Braverman, quoted in Judith Tydor Baumel-

Schwartz, "The 'Parachutists' Mission, from a Gender Perspective," in *Resisting the Holocaust*, ed. Ruby Rohrlich, (Berg, 1998), 95–113.

73 **"he lived it stormily":** Ruth Bondy, *The Emissary: A Life of Enzo Sereni* (Plunkett Lake Press, 2019), introduction, ebook.

74 **"His Majesty's Government":** Balfour Declaration, quoted in Martin Gilbert, *Churchill and the Jews: A Lifelong Friendship* (Henry Holt & Co., 2007), 71.

74 ***"Do not despair. The day will come"*:** Bondy, *The Emissary*, 17.

74 **often carrying a stack of books:** Bondy, *The Emissary*, 104–5.

75 **"seminars on the German spiritual giants":** Bondy, *The Emissary*, 105.

75 **He made regular radio broadcasts:** Meir, *My Life*, 176.

76 **Hannah was reading:** Palgi, *Into the Inferno*, 2.

76 **"bounced around the Western Desert":** Palgi, *Into the Inferno*, 3.

77 **"Excuse me," he said:** Palgi, *Into the Inferno*, 2.

78 **"Oh, I've done my jump training already":** Palgi, *Into the Inferno*, 3.

79 **Out of more than 250 volunteers:** Baumel-Schwartz, *Perfect Heroes*, 10.

80 **So many people said:** Palgi, *Into the Inferno*, 11.

81 **"We, too, did not want":** Ettinger, *Blind Jump*, 62.

81 **"I could not reveal":** Ettinger, *Blind Jump*, 62.

82 **"Either they think I'm very naive":** Senesh, *Hannah Senesh*, 148.

83 **"Here in the Land":** Senesh, *Hannah Senesh*, 148.

83 **"To Miryam Yitzhak":** Senesh, *Hannah Senesh*, 163.

83 **"This week I leave for Egypt":** Senesh, *Hannah Senesh*, 163.

84 **They'd boarded the 10,000-ton ship *Nyassa*:** The scenes of the arrival of Gyuri Senesh, his time in Atlit, and his meeting with Hannah are recounted in detail in Hay, *Ordinary Heroes*, 151–56.

86 **Shaike Dan had been nearby:** Ettinger, *Blind Jump*, 56.

87 **"Eretz Israel is *their* Land":** Ben-Gurion, quoted in Palgi, *Into the Inferno*, 7.

87 **"If no Jews survive this war":** Katznelson, quoted in Palgi, *Into the Inferno*, 7.

87 **"Teach the Jews to fight":** Golomb, quoted in Palgi, *Into the Inferno*, 7.

88 **"Sometimes one writes letters":** Senesh, *Hannah Senesh*, 165.

PART TWO: BETWEEN HEAVEN AND EARTH

91 **Five parachutists in khaki uniforms:** Yoel Palgi, "How She Fell," in Hannah Senesh, *Hannah Senesh: Her Life and Diary, the First Complete Edition* (Jewish Lights Publishing, 2007), 234–35.

92 **each of them would parachute:** Palgi, "How She Fell," 234.

92 **"We were soldiers, arrogant":** Palgi, "How She Fell," 234.

92 **"I want to learn how to drive":** Palgi, "How She Fell," 234.

92 **"Hannah was quite confident":** Palgi, "How She Fell," 235.

93 **"Cairo meant fleshpots or brass hats":** Artemis Cooper, *Cairo in the War, 1939–1945* (Hamish Hamilton, 1989), ebook introduction.

94 **"I'll be drinking champagne":** Blake Stilwell, "'The Suffering Bastard' Is the Cocktail That Beat the Nazis in Egypt," *We Are the Mighty*, July 16, 2022, https://www.wearethemighty.com/popular/suffering-bastard-drink-like-sailor.

94 **"Just wait until Rommel gets to Shepheard's":** William Stadiem, *Too Rich: The High Life and Tragic Death of King Farouk* (Carroll & Graf, 1991), 181.

95 **referring to their headquarters as "The Sandwich":** Ofer and Ofer, *Haviva Reik*, 303.

95 **"I'm now learning to dance":** Ofer and Ofer, *Haviva Reik*, 346.

97 **Brigadier Norman Crockatt:** M. R. D. Foot and J. M. Langley, *MI9: The British Secret Service That Fostered Escape and Evasion 1939–45, and Its American Counterpart* (The Bodley Head, 1979); "M.I.9: The Ingenious Secret Service of the Second World War," Imperial War Museum, https://www.iwm.org.uk/history/mi9-the-ingenious-secret-service-of-the-second-world-war.

97 **A bookish fifty-year-old:** Clayton Hutton, *Official Secret: The Remarkable Story of Escape Aids, Their Invention, Production, and the Sequel* (Max Parrish, 1960); "M.I.9: The Ingenious Secret Service of the Second World War."

98 **Hutton's team managed to smuggle:** Barbara A. Bond, *Great Escapes: The Story of MI9's Second World War Escape and Evasion Maps* (HarperCollins, 2015).

98 **Major Lionel Smiles, an expert:** Ofer and Ofer, *Haviva Reik*, 364.

98 **"But it takes only a minute":** Ofer and Ofer, *Haviva Reik*, 364.

99 **"How come you're walking":** Ettinger, *Blind Jump*, 69.

100 **A young Jewish Londoner:** Leo Marks, *Between Silk and Cyanide: A Codemaker's Story 1941–1945* (HarperCollins, 1998).

100 ***Is de Gaulle's prick*:** Marks, *Between Silk and Cyanide*, 38.

100 ***Le Poète est semblable*:** Charles Baudelaire, "L'Albatros" (1859), in *Les Fleurs du mal* (David R. Godine, 1982), 191.

102 **He read aloud:** This scene and the conversation about cyanide are recounted in Palgi, *Into the Inferno*, 122–23.

103 **Weeks earlier, a Palmach commander:** Ofer and Ofer, *Haviva Reik*, 304.

103 **In blunt terms, he told:** Ofer and Ofer, *Haviva Reik*, 304.

103 **The sadists could break your body [. . .] Where had he gotten his?:** Ofer and Ofer, *Haviva Reik*, 314.

103 **By 1942, the lifespan:** Scott, "Spies & Ciphers."

103 **"the deaths were slow":** Scott, "Spies & Ciphers."

103 **a film that British Intelligence:** Palgi, *Into the Inferno*, 165.

103 **What was the point:** Palgi, *Into the Inferno*, 165.

105 **One by one the Jewish volunteers:** Baumel-Schwartz, *Perfect Heroes*, 10.

105 **"It's the first time":** Interview with Surika Braverman, in *Blessed Is the Match*, directed by Roberta Grossman (Katahdin Productions, 2008).

106 **"In my heart I have two great loves":** Braverman, interview.

106 **"My darling Gyuri":** Senesh, *Hannah Senesh*, 216.

106 **Haviva Reik posed:** Ofer and Ofer, *Haviva Reik*, 350.

107 **Haviva suddenly found herself:** Ofer and Ofer, *Haviva Reik*, 350.

107 **One morning while Shaike Dan was sitting:** Ettinger, *Blind Jump*, 71.

107 **"highly sensitive girl":** Ettinger, *Blind Jump*, 73.

107 **"For many of them":** Ettinger, *Blind Jump*, 73.

108 ***"We gathered flowers"*:** Senesh, *Hannah Senesh*, 305.

108 **One night Enzo Sereni:** Baumel-Schwartz, *Perfect Heroes*, 15.

108 **Hannah had spilled a full bottle:** Baumel-Schwartz, *Perfect Heroes*, 15.

110 **"I'll never forget the discussion":** Reuven Dafni, "The Last Border," in Senesh, *Hannah Senesh*, 224.

111 **"She certainly won't be easy":** Dafni, "The Last Border," 225.

111 **"So what?" Enzo said:** Bondy, *The Emissary*, 221.

111 **His meeting with Marshal Tito:** David Anderson, "Churchill's Son Confers with Tito," *The New York Times*, February 27, 1944.

112 **"There was no replacement":** Bondy, *The Emissary*, 222.

112 **Golda Meir had tried mightily:** Meir, *My Life*, 175.

113 **On March 6, 1944:** Jeffrey Ethel and Alfred Price, *Target Berlin: Mission 250: 6 March 1944* (Greenhill Books, 2006), chap. 3, ebook.

113 **General James Doolittle's Eighth Air Force:** Ethel and Price, *Target Berlin*, chap. 3, ebook.

113 **it was the appearance of the P-51 Mustang:** "North American P-51D Mustang," National Museum of the United States Air Force, April 20, 2015; Jerry Scutts, *Mustang Aces of the Ninth & Fifteenth Air Forces & the RAF* (Bloomsbury, 1995), 47.

114 **"self-indulgent, pleasure-seeking, drug-impregnated":** Ann Tusa and John Tusa, *The Nuremberg Trial* (Skyhorse Publishing, 2010).

114 **"If just one English bomber":** Ian Baxter, *Hermann Göring: The Rise and Fall: Rare Photographs from Wartime Archives* (Pen & Sword Military, 2024), 86.

114 **"When I saw the 'Bluenosed Bastards of Bodney'":** Thomas G. Ivey, *352nd Fighter Group* (Bloomsbury Publishing, 2002), chap. 1, ebook.

114 **"When I saw American fighters":** John Sadler, *Flying Aces* (Rosen Publishing Group, 2018), 126.

114 **"The English press has called":** Josef Goebbels, "Die Schlacht um Berlin," *Das Reich*, February 13, 1944, 1, 3.

116 **The Scottish flight sergeant was gobsmacked:** Reuven Dafni, "The Last Border," in Senesh, *Hannah Senesh*, 225.

116 **"In all these years I've seen":** Dafni, "The Last Border," 225.

116 **When one young American flyer:** Dafni, "The Last Border," 225.

117 ***Dearest Comrades*:** "The Letters," in Senesh, *Hannah Senesh*, 219.

117 **"Remember," he shouted":** Dafni, "The Last Border," 225.

118 **Her smile reminded him:** Dafni, "The Last Border," 225.

118 **"The air seemed lighter":** Dafni, "The Last Border," 225.

120 **Even with the best navigation instruments:** Hay, *Ordinary Heroes*, 161.

123 **"birth of a new type of woman":** Jelena Batinić, "To the People, She Was a Character from Folk Poetry," in *Women and Yugoslav Partisans: A History of World War II Resistance* (Cambridge University Press, 2015).

124 **On February 8, 1943:** Images of the hanging can be seen in Jack Holroyd, *The Second World War Illustrated: The Fourth Year* (Pen & Sword Military, 2022), 75.

124 **"Long live the Communist Party!":** Krste Bjelić and Zdenko Svirčić, *Heroine Jugoslavije* [Heroines of Yugoslavia] (Spektar, 1980).

124 **"I'm not a traitor to my people":** Lepa Svetozara Radić, *Narodni heroji Jugoslavije* [National Heroes of Yugoslavia] (Mladost, 1975).

124 **"Having a woman with us":** "Oral History Interview with Reuven Dafni," United States Holocaust Memorial Museum Collection, June 15, 1981, https://collections.ushmm.org/search/catalog/irn86228.

126 **"We're too late":** Dafni, "The Last Border," 227.

126 **Operation Margarethe, as the Nazis called it:** Deborah Cornelius, *Hungary in World War II: Caught in the Cauldron* (Fordham University Press, 2011), 273; Lambert M. Surhone, Miriam T. Timpledon, and Susan F. Marseken, *Operation Margarethe: World War II, Abwehr, Adolf Hitler, Miklós Horthy, Schloss Klessheim, Salzburg, Hungary During World War II* (Betascript Publishing, 2010).

127 **The most ominous development:** David Cesarani, *Eichmann: His Life and Crimes* (Vintage, 2004), 159–95.

128 **Hungary was divided:** Anthony Masters, *The Summer That Bled: The Biography of Hannah Senesh* (Michael Joseph Ltd., 1972), 125.

129 **Reuven had never seen Hannah cry:** Dafni, "The Last Border," 227.

129 **"It was," he later wrote:** Dafni, "The Last Border," 227.

130 **"All around," Reuven wrote:** Dafni, "The Last Border," 228.

132 **"I'd glance at her":** Dafni, "The Last Border," 228.

131 **members of a *Bandenbekämpfung* unit:** Bob E. Willis Jr., *After the Blitzkrieg: The German Army's Transition to Defeat in the East*, United States Army Command and General Staff College, May 26, 2005, https://apps.dtic.mil/sti/pdfs/ADA436298.pdf.

133 **the Germans had imposed a fine:** Bondy, *The Emissary*, 225.

133 **on October 16, 1943:** Details of the raid can be found in "Jews of Rome Deported to Auschwitz," Yad Vashem, 2020; "1943: The Nazis Deport the Jews from Rome," *Haaretz*, October 18, 2012.

134 **"no Jew openly appears":** Bondy, *The Emissary*, 225.

134 **Yoel watched with fascination:** This scene and the dialogue in Bari are recounted in Palgi, *Into the Inferno*, 13–14.

139 **"I've brought orders":** This scene and dialogue are recounted in Palgi, *Into the Inferno*, 13–14.

140 **"*I don't understand the meaning*":** Bondy, *The Emissary*, 225.

141 **"*Should anything happen to me*":** Bondy, *The Emissary*, 226.

142 **"Despite my age":** Bondy, *The Emissary*, 226.

142 **"Look, I just got a letter":** Palgi, *Into the Inferno*, 15.

143 **"Steely blue, hard and sharp":** Yehuda Bauer, *Jews for Sale? Nazi-Jewish Negotiations, 1933–1945* (Yale University Press, 1994), 92.

144 **"If you could decide":** This scene and conversations have been recounted in numerous books, including Yehuda Bauer, "The Mission of Joel Brand," in *The Nazi Holocaust*, Part 9: *The End of the Holocaust*, ed. Michael R. Marrus (Meckler, 1989), 65–125; Bauer, *Jews for Sale?*; Masters, *The Summer That Bled*; Daniel Brand, *Trapped By Evil and Deceit: The Story of Hansi and Joel Brand* (Academic Studies Press, 2020).

144 **SS Reichsführer Heinrich Himmler had agreed:** Bauer, *Jews for Sale?*.

145 **Waldsee, German for "Forest Lake":** Ernő Munkácsi, *How it Happened: Documenting the Tragedy of Hungarian Jewry* (McGill-Queen's University Press, 2018), 216.

146 **"In Hungary in 1944":** Cesarani, *Eichmann: His Life and Crimes*, 159–95.

148 **Marshal Tito had absorbed:** More detailed biographical information on Moša Pijade can be found in S. Bosiljčić and D. Marković, *Moša Pijade* (Serbian, 1960); Richard West, *Tito: And the Rise and Fall of Yugoslavia* (Carroll & Graf, 1994).

149 **Wherever they went:** Dafni, "The Last Border," 228.

151 **It took a few moments:** Reuven Dafni, "The Last Frontier," in Senesh, *Hannah Senesh*; Dafni, interview. In Dafni's accounts, the woman is unnamed. The nom de guerre "Luca" is a pseudonym.

155 **she had spun around:** Ofer and Ofer, *Haviva Reik*, 321–23.

155 **She'd been handpicked:** Ofer and Ofer, *Haviva Reik*, 321.

155 **Surika remained part:** Ofer and Ofer, *Haviva Reik*, 323.

155 **"The Parachutist Who Didn't Jump":** Braverman, interview.

156 **After the farewell party:** Ofer and Ofer, *Haviva Reik*, 334.

158 **"The partisans were sensitive":** Palgi, *Into the Inferno*, 46.

158 **The crisis came to a head:** This confrontation between Palgi and Major Eden is recounted in Palgi, *Into the Inferno*, 38–39.

159 **Within minutes, he saw:** Palgi, "How She Fell," in Senesh, *Hannah Senesh*, 237.

160 **"For me, this is no longer":** Senesh, *Hannah Senesh*, 238.

160 **He spoke anxiously:** This story, dialogue, and argument and Hannah's eventual acceptance are recounted in "Oral History Interview with Reuven Dafni."

161 **"You Britishers":** Dafni, interview.

162 **As soon as Drapšin and Gromovnik sat down:** Yoel Palgi gave a firsthand account of this meeting with the Partisan saboteur commanders in *Into the Inferno*, 48. For reasons known only to him, he referred to General Drapšin as "Dobszyn" and to General Ivan Hariš-Gromovnik as "Colonel Ilia." For more on General Petar Drapšin, see Roberts, *Tito, Mihailović, and the Allies*; Anna K. Starinov, *Behind Fascist Lines: A Firsthand Account of Guerrilla Warfare During the Spanish Revolution* (Random House, 1995); and Ivan Hariš-Gromovnik, *Diverzantske akcije u Hrvatskoj* (1960).

163 **"Hannah did more for British propaganda":** Palgi, "How She Fell," 249.

164 **Yoel and Hannah watched:** Palgi, "How She Fell," 249.

164 **"If only we had a chance":** This scene and dialogue are recounted in Palgi, *Into the Inferno*, 52–54.

166 **"See you in Budapest!":** Palgi, *Into the Inferno*, 55.

167 **"I can't understand":** Bondy, *The Emissary*, 227.

169 **RC: Roman Catholic:** Brian Leigh Davis, *British Army Uniforms & Insignia of World War Two* (Arms and Armour Press, 1983), 254.

170 **"The average policeman or a gendarme":** Dafni, interview.

170 **"We're committing *moral* suicide":** Dafni, interview.

171 **"She was bubbling with joy":** Dafni, "The Last Border," 230.

172 **"Can you give me one?":** Dafni, "The Last Border," 230; "Oral History Interview with Reuven Dafni."

172 **Now Hannah reached into her pocket:** Hay, *Ordinary Heroes*, 171–72.

172 **he unfolded it and strained to make sense of it:** Dafni, interview.

173 **He searched in vain:** Dafni, interview.

174 **Dan was wearing a belt:** Ettinger, *Blind Jump*, 84–85.
175 ***Sitting with the parachutes*:** Ettinger, *Blind Jump*, 85.
175 **"If only my grandfather could see me now":** Ettinger, *Blind Jump*, 85.
175 **"God bless you!":** Ettinger, *Blind Jump*, 87
175 **"The fourth of June 1944":** Ettinger, *Blind Jump*, 88.
176 **Every movement, every sound:** This scene and dialogue are recounted by Shaike Dan in Ettinger, *Blind Jump*, 88–91.
178 **"In a blind drop":** Ettinger, *Blind Jump*, 91.
178 **"And then," Dan wrote:** Ettinger, *Blind Jump*, 93.
179 **Peter Kallós and Sándor Fleischmann were young members:** Dafni, interview.
179 **The third man, Jacques Antoine Tissandier:** Dafni, interview.
182 **"If we're stopped and questioned":** Hay, *Ordinary Heroes*, 171.
183 **Next to her, Tony Tissandier:** Palgi, *Into the Inferno*, 165.
185 **Fleischmann signaled to Kallós:** This scene and dialogue are recounted in great detail, as Hannah Senesh told it to Yoel Palgi during their time together in a Budapest jail, in Palgi, *Into the Inferno*, 160–71. Further details of the crossing, capture, and torture are supplemented from the postwar testimony of Sandor Fleischmann and Jacques "Tony" Tissandier, who gave a detailed debriefing to MI9.
191 **Suddenly, at a street corner:** Ettinger, *Blind Jump*, 93.
192 **"That Jew didn't know we were parachutists":** Ettinger, *Blind Jump*, 94.
192 **When Dan went to pick up his trousers:** Ettinger, *Blind Jump*, 97.
193 **"Maybe we should report ourselves":** Ettinger, *Blind Jump*, 101.
194 **"You are state property":** Palgi, *Into the Inferno*, 166.
195 **"We found your wireless":** Palgi, *Into the Inferno*, 166.
195 **"When I was first arrested":** Palgi, *Into the Inferno*, 166.
196 **"Szenes," she said:** Palgi, *Into the Inferno*, 167.

PART THREE: BLESSED IS THE MATCH

199 **On June 17, 1944, Katherine Senesh:** Hay, *Ordinary Heroes*, 185.
200 **A close Jewish friend named János:** Hay, *Ordinary Heroes*, 185–87. The Jewish friend in most accounts is unnamed. "János" is a pseudonym I've used solely for narrative fluidity.
200 **Suddenly the bell at the garden gate rang:** Senesh, "Meeting in Budapest," in Senesh, *Hannah Senesh*, 254. The scenes and dialogue that follow are based almost entirely in Katherine's forty-page memoir included in the complete edition of Hannah's life and diaries.
204 **"We communicated only with our eyes":** Palgi, *Into the Inferno*, 167.
210 **"The reward for the momentary delay":** Katherine later wrote, in Senesh, "Meeting in Budapest," 264.
210 **"If I were only a traitorous spy":** Palgi, *Into the Inferno*, 169.
211 **She heard one sentence:** Palgi, *Into the Inferno*, 169.
213 **"I shuddered at the thought":** Senesh, "Meeting in Budapest," 259.
214 **"According to my interpretation":** Senesh, "Meeting in Budapest," 260.
214 **"When I stepped into the corridor":** Senesh, "Meeting in Budapest," 261.
214 **"Using these sort of psychological pressure tactics":** Palgi, *Into the Inferno*, 170.

215 **"We lay among the crates":** Ettinger, *Blind Jump*, 101.
216 **"Clad in our ragged clothes":** Ettinger, *Blind Jump*, 105.
217 **Dan took a trolley:** Ettinger, *Blind Jump*, 106.
218 **During Operation Supercharge:** "Second Lieutenant Theodore Zissu. Service Number: 194232," Royal Tank Regiment, R.A.C. Killed in action, November 3, 1942, Commonwealth War Graves Commission, https://www.cwgc.org/find-records/find-war-dead/casualty-details/2111442/theodore-zissu.
218 **"When I came to their house":** Ettinger, *Blind Jump*, 114.
219 **"I'm at your disposal":** Ettinger, *Blind Jump*, 114.
219 **"The discovery of the exact locations":** Ettinger, *Blind Jump*, 114–15.
220 **"You're lucky not to be branded":** Senesh, "Meeting in Budapest," 270.
221 **"At last, I could hold her close":** Senesh, "Meeting in Budapest," 271.
221 **"We should both be so lucky":** Senesh, "Meeting in Budapest," 271.
226 **Later, as the Partisans became bolder:** Dafni, interview.
226 **Reuven would oversee:** Dafni, interview.
226 **Along with the airmen:** Dafni, interview.
227 **"*The United States demands*":** Jewish Telegraphic Agency, July 16, 1944.
229 **"*Foreign Secretary*":** Winston S. Churchill, *The Second World War, Volume VI: Triumph and Tragedy*. Houghton Mifflin, 1986, 597.
230 **"Mum," she said:** Senesh, "Meeting in Budapest," 275.
233 **"I told [Zissu] to warn them":** Ettinger, *Blind Jump*, 115.
233 **"something that today maybe sounds":** Ettinger, *Blind Jump*, 116.
234 **SS Hauptscharführer Werner Lemke:** *Fórum Társadalomtudományi Szemle*, XVI, évfolyam 2014, 18.
234 **"Take a seat":** The scene and dialogue with Lemke are recounted in Hay, *Ordinary Heroes*, 205–6.
235 **"I knew that Hannah's birthday":** Senesh, "Meeting in Budapest," 272.
236 **"She was soon back in solitary confinement":** Senesh, "Meeting in Budapest," 272.
237 **"Though I have always dreamed":** Senesh, "Meeting in Budapest," 274.
237 **Biedermeier dolls, Rococo dolls:** Masters, *The Summer That Bled*, 245.
237 **"I'm glad my time here":** Senesh, "Meeting in Budapest," 272.
239 **"But Mr. Brand":** Joel Brand and Alexander Weissberg-Cybulski, *Advocate for the Dead: The Story of Joel Brand* (Andre Deutsch, 1958), 192.
239 **"A Monstrous 'Offer'":** "A 'Monstrous Offer": German Blackmail: Bartering Jews for Munitions," *The Times* [London], July 20, 1944.
240 **"A German radio report":** BBC's German-language service, July 21, 1944.
241 **"In that prison it was good":** *Blessed Is the Match*, Grossman.
241 **"*At some period in the future*":** Konstantin Simonov, Krasnaia Zvezda, quoted in Jeremy Hicks, "'Too Gruesome to Be Fully Taken In': Konstantin Simonov's 'The Extermination Camp' as Holocaust Literature," *The Russian Review* 72, no. 2 (2013): 246–47.
242 **"*I have just seen*":** W. H. Lawrence, "Nazi Mass Killing Laid Bare in Camp," *The New York Times*, August 30, 1944.
243 **"*Memories, like paper flowers*":** Hannah's poem, quoted in Masters, *The Summer That Bled*, 252.

244 **Her name, she told Hannah:** Miryam Zakheim, "The Boy Whose Life Was Saved by Hannah Senesh," National Library of Israel, January 22, 2025, https://blog.nli.org.il/en/boy-saved-by-hannah-senesh. In this English translation, the family name is misspelled "Galtstein"; the correct spelling is "Glattstein." Shimon Cohen, "Thanks to Hannah Senesh I Am Alive Today," Channel 7 News (Israel), interview with Baruch Glattstein, July 27, 2021, https://www.inn.co.il/news/500301. Original headline: "בזכות חנה סנש אני חי היום." I've made my own translation from Hebrew. In March 2025, in a series of personal emails, I confirmed the facts of the story with Baruch Glattstein in Jerusalem.

247 **"As far as the Jewish Question is concerned":** *The Goebbels Diaries: 1939–1941*, trans. and ed. by Fred Taylor (G. P. Putnam's Sons, 1983), 252.

248 **"Entering the orphanage":** Ettinger, *Blind Jump*, 124.

249 **he felt he was engaged in rescuing:** Ettinger, *Blind Jump*, 122.

250 **"More than anything else":** Ettinger, *Blind Jump*, 117.

250 **"still hung like a black shadow":** Ettinger, *Blind Jump*, 119.

251 **On August 5:** Timothy P. Maga, "Operation Rescue: The Mefkure Incident and the War Refugee Board," *The American Neptune* 43 (1983), 31–39, https://babel.hathitrust.org/cgi/pt?id=uc1.b4401101&seq=11.

251 **"Manu was my closest friend":** Ettinger, *Blind Jump*, 120.

252 **"the most remarkable and successful":** John Lukacs, *Destinations Past: Traveling Through History with John Lukacs* (University of Missouri Press, 1994), 117.

255 **"the British captain":** Bondy, *The Emissary*, 233–34.

256 **"We frequently quoted verses":** Bondy, *The Emissary*, 234.

257 **"Whoever heard of an educated English lady":** Braverman, interview.

258 **"All of Bucharest":** Ettinger, *Blind Jump*, 127.

258 **"It was a thrilling sight":** Ettinger, *Blind Jump*, 127.

259 **"*A mighty force of hundreds*":** Ettinger, *Blind Jump*, 127.

260 **"We sped up the handling":** Ettinger, *Blind Jump*, 128.

261 **"zaslani also coming on 5 sept":** Ofer and Ofer, *Haviva Reik*, 390.

262 **"And why not me?":** Ofer and Ofer, *Haviva Reik*, 392.

262 **"And what about the men?":** Ofer and Ofer, *Haviva Reik*, 392.

263 **"I'm not some immature child!":** Ofer and Ofer, *Haviva Reik*, 393.

263 **"Those are my orders":** Ofer and Ofer, *Haviva Reik*, 393.

265 **"Where to?" Palgi asked:** Palgi, *Into the Inferno*, 157.

266 **They were led back to their cells:** Palgi, *Into the Inferno*, 160.

268 **One new possible source:** New discoveries in the archives made by Reverend Jovan Čolivrac at The International Institute for Holocaust Research at Yad Vashem in Jerusalem.

268 **The Nazi espionage agent:** Čolivrac, The International Institute for Holocaust Research.

269 **"I'll be seeing you":** Palgi, *Into the Inferno*, 172.

270 **Fichman was one of the first:** Baumel-Schwartz, *Perfect Heroes*, 20, 25.

270 **He handed the slip of paper:** Baumel-Schwartz, *Perfect Heroes*, 25.

271 **"A member who set out":** *Davar Hapoelet*, September 27, 1944.

271 **"Blessed is the match":** Senesh, *Hannah Senesh*, 306, trans. from Hebrew by Marie Syrkin.

272 **Colonel Simonds had left instructions:** Ofer and Ofer, *Haviva Reik*, 395.
272 **"concentrate on finding new task for marta":** Ofer and Ofer, *Haviva Reik*, 397.
272 **"Good news," Taylor said:** Ofer and Ofer, *Haviva Reik*, 398.
273 **She had fond memories:** Ofer and Ofer, *Haviva Reik*, 406.
273 **"Good luck, Marta," he said:** Ofer and Ofer, *Haviva Reik*, 407.
274 **"*My dear friends*":** Ofer and Ofer, *Haviva Reik*, 407.
276 **"for democracy!":** Ofer and Ofer, *Haviva Reik*, 415.
277 **"If you see three young dark-haired men":** Ofer and Ofer, *Haviva Reik*, 446–47.
279 **a "magnet" who "gave us advice":** Ofer and Ofer, *Haviva Reik*, 448.
279 **"viewed Reik as a messenger from God":** Ofer and Ofer, *Haviva Reik*, 428.
281 **Suddenly one of the SS sergeants:** Bondy, *The Emissary*, 236.
281 **Enzo was registered:** Bondy, *The Emissary*, 236.
282 **One night the Italians were awakened:** Bondy, *The Emissary*, 236.
283 **"Today it is obvious":** Liam Athas, *Miklós Horthy: The Hungarian Anti-Hero* (pub. by author, 2023), 223.
284 **"Szálasi came into power":** Senesh, "Meeting in Budapest," 286.
287 **"*Engländer? Italienisch?*":** Bondy, *The Emissary*, 238.
287 **"Who is the Jew":** Bondy, *The Emissary*, 238.
287 **David Srulovitz, a man of about thirty:** Bondy, *The Emissary*, 238–239.
290 **"When I went to visit my home":** Senesh, "Meeting in Budapest," 282.
290 **"Naturally, our conversation":** Senesh, "Meeting in Budapest," 283.
291 **"As an experienced ex-prisoner":** Senesh, "Meeting in Budapest," 283.
292 **"To my everlasting sorrow":** Senesh, "Meeting in Budapest," 285.
293 **Himmler had replaced him:** Ofer and Ofer, *Haviva Reik*, 499.
294 **"We'll go up into the mountains":** Ofer and Ofer, *Haviva Reik*, 500.
294 **"We wanted to establish":** Ofer and Ofer, *Haviva Reik*, 503.
294 **"In those mountains":** Ofer and Ofer, *Haviva Reik*, 502–3.
294 **"Would any of you think":** Ofer and Ofer, *Haviva Reik*, 503.
296 **"Never," she said:** Ofer and Ofer, *Haviva Reik*, 510.
296 **"It's a shame":** Ofer and Ofer, *Haviva Reik*, 516–17.
297 **Matilda Glattstein, the Slovakian Jew:** Zakheim, "The Boy Whose Life Was Saved by Hannah Senesh"; Cohen, "Thanks to Hannah Senesh I am alive today." I've made my own translation from the Hebrew original. In March 2025, in a series of personal emails, I confirmed the facts of the story with Baruch Glattstein in Jerusalem. Senesh, "Meeting in Budapest," 287.
298 **"Whatever the sentence":** Senesh, "Meeting in Budapest," 287.
299 **"I plead not guilty":** The original trial transcripts were destroyed during the Siege of Budapest in 1944–1945, but I have reconstructed the testimony from the detailed accounts in several secondary sources: Masters, *The Summer That Bled*, 286–87; Palgi, *Into the Inferno*, 200–2. In his memoir, Palgi recounted the contemporaneous accounts of Hannah's courtroom testimony as told to him by her codefendants Jacques Tissandier and Sandor Fleischmann. For primary sources, see "Court documents relating to the investigation of the case of Anna Szenes and the sentence of Gyula Simon," in the permanent collection of the United States Holocaust Memorial Museum, https://collections.ushmm.org/search/catalog

/irn503394. These documents were created by the Budapest City Prosecutor's Office and the Budapest City People's Court during the investigation of the case of Anna Szenes and the case of Gyula Simon, president of the military court responsible for the sentencing of Anna Szenes, from 1946 to 1949. Copies of the documents were obtained from the Budapest City Archives by Miles Lerman. Mr. Lerman forwarded the copies to the United States Holocaust Memorial Museum in September 1992.

301 **"What difference is a week's delay?":** Senesh, "Meeting in Budapest," 287–88.

303 **In the late evening of October 29:** Ofer and Ofer, *Haviva Reik*, 523.

304 **Then the parachutists began:** Ofer and Ofer, *Haviva Reik*, 523–24.

305 **"We were a group of six":** Ofer and Ofer, *Haviva Reik*, 528.

306 **Over and over, Haviva repeated:** Ofer and Ofer, *Haviva Reik*, 538–39.

306 **it's possible that the doctor:** Ofer and Ofer, *Haviva Reik*, 539.

307 **"their behavior toward me":** Ofer and Ofer, *Haviva Reik*, 543.

308 **"No visiting today," he shouted:** Senesh, "Meeting in Budapest," 287–88.

308 **"No, only Captain Simon has the authority":** Senesh, "Meeting in Budapest," 288.

311 **"Captain Barda acted as intermediary":** Bondy, *The Emissary*, 240.

312 **"Mr. Brand, where would I possibly":** Brand and Weissberg-Cybulski, *Advocate for the Dead*, 167.

312 **"I afterwards heard":** Brand and Weissberg-Cybulski, *Advocate for the Dead*, 167.

312 **"homeless and stateless Jews":** Lord Moyne, "Recruitment of Jews," UK Parliament. Lords Chamber, vol. 123, June 9, 1942, https://hansard.parliament.uk/Lords/1942-06-09/debates/5eb19cf8-6b05-43d0-b166-86b95b957e36/Lords-Chamber.

313 **"have done more by this single reprehensible crime":** "Comment in Palestine," *The Times of London*. November 9, 1944.

313 **"If our dreams for Zionism":** Winston Churchill, "Palestine (Terrorist Activities)," November 17, 1944, UK Parliament, https://api.parliament.uk/historic-hansard/commons/1944/nov/17/palestine-terrorist-activities.

314 **"Anna Szenes, you've been found guilty":** Captain Simon's sudden sentencing of Hannah has been rendered in various versions. I have tried to create one that is most faithful to those of the most reliable witnesses. See Senesh, "Meeting in Budapest," 292; Palgi, *Into the Inferno*, 206–8; Masters, *The Summer That Bled*, 290.

316 **she could see a briefcase:** Senesh, "Meeting in Budapest," 289.

316 **"The case no longer has":** The conversation with Captain Simon is recounted in detail in Senesh, "Meeting in Budapest," 289–92.

320 **"What's that?":** Senesh, "Meeting in Budapest," 292–93.

321 **"What happened?" Fleischmann asked:** Palgi, *Into the Inferno*, 204–5.

322 ***Dear Mother*:** Senesh, "Meeting in Budapest," 293.

323 ***One—two—three*:** Senesh, *Hannah Senesh*, 306.

324 ***"Kapitän Barda! Komm her!"*:** The account of Enzo Sereni's disappearance comes from Bondy, *The Emissary*, 240–41.

324 ***Verstorben—18. Nov. 44*:** Bondy, *The Emissary*, 241.

326 **"I saw a scene":** Ofer and Ofer, *Haviva Reik*, 557.

326 **All told, 747 victims:** For more details about the massacres at Kremnička and

Nemecká, see Walter S. Zapotoczny Jr., *The Road to Auschwitz: The Deportation of the Slovak Jews by the Hlinka Guard* (Fonthill Media, 2022).

327 **"Please don't make a national hero":** Zvi Ben-Yaakov's final letter to his wife, Michal. See Appendix II.

328 **"Five months ago":** Ettinger, *Blind Jump*, 132.

329 **"not at all like what we're used":** Ettinger, *Blind Jump*, 133.

329 **"British Foreign Office did not properly":** Ettinger, *Blind Jump*, 133.

330 **in November 1944, Katherine joined:** Hay, *Ordinary Heroes*, 225.

331 **The Jewish Brigade:** Morris Beckman, *Jewish Brigade: An Army with Two Masters 1944–45* (Da Capo Press, 1998).

331 **Gyura enlisted in December 1944:** Hay, *Ordinary Heroes*, 248.

331 **Katherine set sail from Constanţa, Romania:** Hay, *Ordinary Heroes*, 244.

331 **The thin boy Katherine had last seen:** Hay, *Ordinary Heroes*, 254.

331 **For Katherine and Gyura, of course:** Hay, *Ordinary Heroes*, 254.

EPILOGUE: THERE ARE STARS

333 **In late January 1945:** Author's interview with Baruch Glattstein in Jerusalem, March 2025.

333 **In the second week of February:** Glattstein, interview.

334 **The family lived for three years:** Glattstein, interview.

334 **Baruch Glattstein went on:** Glattstein, interview.

334 **"Mother would tell the story":** Zakheim, "The Boy Whose Life Was Saved by Hannah Senesh"; Cohen, "Thanks to Hannah Senesh I am alive today."

335 **Simon was sentenced:** Hay, *Ordinary Heroes*, 240.

335 **Israeli newspapers carried a report:** Hay, *Ordinary Heroes*, 240.

335 **"If I were to start my life over":** Hay, *Ordinary Heroes*, 240.

335 **It was not until July 1993:** Hay, *Ordinary Heroes*, 240.

335 **"The thirty-two parachutists from Palestine":** Eliyahu Golomb, quoted in Allon, *Shield of David*, 135.

337 **"HANNAH SENESH":** English translation from a photo of the banner on permanent display in the monument to the Ha'apala (Illegal Immigration) ships, located on the beachfront promenade of London Garden, Tel Aviv.

339 **"The people living in Zion":** *Israel Digest* (United States: Israel Office of Information, 1950), 7.

339 **"We who knew Hannah":** Yitzhak Sadeh, "Chana Shelanu" [Our Hannah], *Al HaMishmar*, March 28, 1950. The issue of *Al HaMishmar* has been scanned by the National Library of Israel. I have made my own translation of Sadeh's article from the original Hebrew.

340 **"Hannah became a consecrated image":** Abba Eban, "Introduction," in Senesh, *Hannah Senesh*, vi–ix.

340 **"I don't think Hannah wanted to die":** John McCain with Mark Salter, *Why Courage Matters: The Way to a Braver Life* (Random House, 2004).

341 **"I had to find people":** The story of the fundraising for the Haganah from Jewish American gangsters such as Benjamin "Bugsy" Siegel is told in Dafni's oral history in the United States Holocaust Memorial Museum.

343 **"a fig-leaf to cover":** Baumel-Schwartz, *Perfect Heroes,* 209.
343 **"A last-ditch attempt":** Baumel-Schwartz, *Perfect Heroes,* 209.
343 **"The parachutists did not succeed":** Yigal Lossin, *Pillar of Fire: The Rebirth of Israel—a Visual History* (Shikmona Publishing Company, 1983).
344 **"At first, I didn't believe":** Ettinger, *Blind Jump,* 14.
344 **"Gently they say":** Ettinger, *Blind Jump,* 14.
344 **"We didn't think":** Braverman, interview.
344 **"Honestly, I didn't think":** Dafni, interview.
344 **"We parachutists were not supermen":** Interview with Reuven Dafni in *Blessed Is the Match.*
345 **"Ashrei Hagafrur" (Blessed Is the Match):** Hannah Senesh, in *Mishkan T'filah: Shabbat, Non-transliterated* (Central Conference of American Rabbis, 2006).
346 ***"My God, my God"*****:** "Halicha L'Keisarya" ("A Walk to Caesarea"), in Senesh, *Hannah Senesh,* 304; *Mishkan T'filah: Shabbat, Non-transliterated,* 367.

BIBLIOGRAPHY

Allon, Yigal. *Shield of David: The Story of Israel's Armed Forces.* Random House, 1970.

Atkinson, Linda. *In Kindling Flame: The Story of Hannah Senesh 1921–1944.* Vallentine Mitchell, 2011.

Bar-Adon, Dorothy and Pesach Bar-Adon. *Seven Who Fell.* Palestine Pioneer Library. Lion the Printer, 1947.

Bauer, Yehuda. *From Diplomacy to Resistance: A History of Jewish Palestine, 1939–1945.* Translated by Alton M. Winters. The Jewish Publication Society of America, 1970.

Baumel-Schwartz, Judith Tydor. *Perfect Heroes: The World War II Parachutists and the Making of Israeli Collective Memory.* University of Wisconsin Press, 2010.

Baumel-Schwartz, Judith Tydor. "Founding Myths and Heroic Icons: Reflections on the Funerals of Theodor Herzl and Hannah Szenes." *Women's Studies International Forum* 25 no. 6 (November–December 2002): 679–95.

Baumel-Schwartz, Judith Tydor. "The Heroism of Hannah Senesz: An Exercise in Creating Collective National Memory in the State of Israel." *Journal of Contemporary History* 31 no. 3 (July 1996): 521–46.

Baumel-Schwartz, Judith Tydor. "'Parachuting to Their People': The Operation of the Parachutist-Emissaries During World War II in Historical Perspective." *Yad Vashem Studies* 25 (1996): 137–80.

Baumel-Schwartz, Judith Tydor. "Parachutists' Mission." In *The Holocaust Encyclopedia,* edited by Walter Laqueur. Yale University Press, 2001.

Baumel-Schwartz, Judith Tydor. "The 'Parachutists' Mission' from a Gender Perspective." In *Resisting the Holocaust,* edited by Ruby Rohrlich. Berg, 1998.

Baumel-Schwartz, Judith Tydor. "Teacher, Tiller, Soldier, Spy? Women's Representations in Israeli Military Memorials." *Journal of Israeli History* 21 no. 1-2 (March/October 2002): 93–117.

Baumel-Schwartz, Judith Tydor. "Re: Parachuting Mission." Personal email. October 31, 2007.

Ben-Yehuda, Nachman. T*he Masada Myth: Collective Memory and Mythmaking in Israel.* The University of Wisconsin Press, 1995.

Bondy, Ruth. *The Emissary: A Life of Enzo Sereni.* Little, Brown and Company, 1977.

Braham, Randolph L. and Scott Miller, eds. *The Nazi's Last Victims: The Holocaust in Hungary.* Wayne State University Press in association with the United States Holocaust Memorial Museum, 1998.

Brand, Daniel. *Trapped by Evil and Deceit: The Story of Hansi and Joel Brand.* Cherry Orchard Books, 2020.

Churchill, Winston. "Fairness to Arab and Jew." In *Zionism: A Basic Reader,* edited by Mordecai S. Chertoff. Herzl Press, 1975.

Dafni, Reuven. "The Last Border." In *Hannah Senesh: Her Life and Diary, the First Complete Edition,* by Hannah Senesh. Jewish Lights Publishing, 2004.

Dear, L. C. B. and M. R. D. Foot, eds. *The Oxford Companion to World War II.* Oxford University Press, 1995.

Ducovny, Amram, ed. *David Ben-Gurion: In His Own Words.* Fleet Press Corporation, 1968.

Elon, Amos. *Understanding Israel.* Behram House, 1976.

Ettinger, Amos. *Blind Jump: The Story of Shaike Dan.* Cronwall Publishing, 1992.

Foot, M. R. D. and J. M. Langley. *MI9: Escape and Evasion, 1939–1945.* Little, Brown and Company, 1980.

Frishman, Elyse D. *Mishkan T'Filah: A Reform Siddur: Weekdays, Shabbat, Festivals, and Other Occasions of Public Worship.* Central Conference of American Rabbis, 2006.

Gelber, Yoav. "Parachutists, Jewish." In *Encyclopedia of the Holocaust,* edited by Gutnam Israel. Macmillan, 1990.

Gilbert, Martin. *Churchill and the Jews.* McClelland and Stewart, 2007.

Gilbert, Martin. *The Holocaust: The Jewish Tragedy.* William Collins Sons, 1986.

Glick, Susan. *History Makers: Heroes of the Holocaust.* Lucent Books, 2002.

Goldberg, David J. *The Divided Self: Israel and the Jewish Psyche Today.* I.B. Tauris, 2006.

Gross, David C. *Pride of Our People: The Stories of One Hundred Outstanding Jewish Men and Women.* Doubleday & Co., 1979.

Grossman, Roberta, director. *Blessed Is the Match: The Life and Death of Hannah Senesh.* Katahdin Productions, 2008. 1 hr., 26 min. https://www.katahdin.org/blessed-is-the-match.html.

Hay, Peter. *Ordinary Heroes: Chana Szenes and the Dream of Zion.* G. P. Putnam's Sons, 1984.

Hecht, Ben. *Perfidy.* J. Messner, 1961.

Herzl, Theodor. *The Jewish State.* Filiquarian Publishing, 2006.

Herzog, Chaim. *Heroes of Israel: Profiles of Jewish Courage.* Little, Brown and Company, 1989.

Lossin, Yigal. *Pillar of Fire: A Television History of Israel's Rebirth,* DVD, Israeli Broadcasting Authority, 2005.

Lossin, Yigal Lossin. *Pillar of Fire: The Rebirth of Israel—a Visual History,* Shikmona Publishing Company, 1983.

Masters, Anthony. *The Summer That Bled: The Biography of Hannah Senesh.* Washington Square Press, 1974.

Meir, Golda. *My Life.* G. P. Putnam's Sons, 1973.

Morris, Eric. *Guerrillas In Uniform: Churchill's Private Armies in the Middle East and the War Against Japan, 1940–1945.* Hutchinson, 1989.

Ofer, Tehila and Zeev Ofer. *Haviva Reik: A Kibbutz Pioneer's Mission and Fall Behind Nazi Lines.* Translated by Miriam Talisman. Fawns Publishing, 2014.

Palgi, Yoel. *Into the Inferno: The Memoir of a Jewish Paratrooper Behind Nazi Lines.* Translated by Reeva Rubin. Rutgers University Press, 2002.

Palgi, Yoel. "How She Fell." In *Hannah Senesh: Her Life and Diary, the First Complete Edition,* by Hannah Senesh. Jewish Lights Publishing, 2004.

Porat, Dina. "Amalek's Accomplices' Blaming Zionism for the Holocaust: Anti-Zionist Ultra-Orthodoxy in Israel During the 1980s." *Journal of Contemporary History* 27, no. 4 (October 1992), 695–729.

Porat, Dina. "Attitudes of the Young State of Israel Toward the Holocaust and Its Survivors: A Debate Over Identity and Values." In *New Perspectives on Israeli History: The Early Years of the State,* edited by Laurence J. Silberstein. New York University Press, 1991.

Porter, Anna. *Kasztner's Train: The True Story of an Unknown Hero of the Holocaust.* Walker & Co., 2008.

Segev, Tom. *One Palestine, Complete: Jews and Arabs Under the British Mandate.* Translated by Haim Watzman. Metropolitan Books, 2000.

Segev, Tom. *The Seventh Million: The Israelis and the Holocaust.* Translated by Haim Watzman. Hill and Wang, 1993.

Senesh, Katherine. "Meeting in Budapest." In *Hannah Senesh: Her Life and Diary, the First Complete Edition,* by Hannah Senesh. Jewish Lights Publishing, 2004.

Senesh, Hannah. *A Voice Called and I Went.* Catalog of the Permanent Exhibition of the Hannah Senesh House, Kibbutz Sdot Yam, Israel. Exhibition Curators: Shonit Gal and Yehuda Wegman; translation from original Hebrew text by Douglas Century. Kibbutz Sdot Yam Publishing, 2020.

Senesh, Hannah. *Hannah Senesh: Her Life and Diary, The First Complete Edition.* Translated by Marta Cohn. Jewish Lights Publishing, 2004.

Senesh, Hannah. *Hannah Senesh: Her Life and Diary*. Schocken Books, 1972.

Syrkin, Marie. *Blessed Is the Match: The Story of Jewish Resistance.* Jewish Publication Society of America, 1947.

Teveth, Shabtai. *Ben-Gurion and the Holocaust.* Harcourt Brace & Co., 1996.

Weiss, Joseph. *Sailing a Dream: Love Letters to Hannah Senesh.* Kibbutz Hameuchad Publishing House, 1996.

Weissberg, Alex. *Desperate Mission: Joel Brand's Story.* Translated by Constantine FitzGibbon and Andrew Foster-Melliar. New York: Criterion Books, 1958.

Weizmann, Chaim. "The Balfour Declaration." In *Zionism: A Basic Reader,* edited by Mordecai S. Chertoff. Herzl Press, 1975.

IMAGE CREDITS

INSERT, IMAGE NUMBER:

1–10, 17, 30, 32, 33

© The Szenes Family Archive in the National Library of Israel, with special thanks to Ori and Mirit Eisen

11, 12, 14, 15, 22, 23

© National Photo Collection of Israel, Photography Department, Government Press Office

13

Grateful acknowledgment to the Simonds Family Archive at www.simondsfamily.me.uk

16, 18–21, 24–26, 28, 29, 31

Courtesy Palmach Archive at the Palmach Museum, Tel Aviv. https://palmach.org.il.

27

© Crown copyright: Imperial War Museums, London, United Kingdom

32

© The Szenes Family Archive in the National Library of Israel, with special thanks to Ori and Mirit Eisen

34

Personal photo taken by the author in July 2023 while researching and writing this book in Israel.

TEXT, PAGE:

271

© The Szenes Family Archive in the National Library of Israel, with special thanks to Ori and Mirit Eisen

INDEX

London
GREAT BRITAIN
HOLLAND
Berlin
BELGIUM
GERMANY
Prague
Bohemia and Mo
Paris
Dachau
Mauthausen
Vienna
Austria
FRANCE
SWITZ.
Szombathely
Bolzano
Dráva
Metlika
Milan
Verona
Zagre
Rijeka
Croa
ITALY
Adriatic Sea
SPAIN
Rome
Ba
Mediterranean Sea
ALGERIA
TUNISIA
0 100 200 miles
0 100 200 300 kilometers
N
W
E
S
British and American airbases and airfields
Jump sites of Yishuv parachutist teams
Tripoli
LIBYA